EMANCIPATORY THINKING

McGILL-QUEEN'S STUDIES IN THE HISTORY OF IDEAS
Series Editor: Philip J. Cercone

1 Problems of Cartesianism
Edited by Thomas M. Lennon, John M. Nicholas, and John W. Davis

2 The Development of the Idea of History in Antiquity
Gerald A. Press

3 Claude Buffier and Thomas Reid: Two Common-Sense Philosophers
Louise Marcil-Lacoste

4 Schiller, Hegel, and Marx: State, Society, and the Aesthetic Ideal of Ancient Greece
Philip J. Kain

5 John Case and Aristotelianism in Renaissance England
Charles B. Schmitt

6 Beyond Liberty and Property: The Process of Self-Recognition in Eighteenth-Century Political Thought
J.A.W. Gunn

7 John Toland: His Methods, Manners, and Mind
Stephen H. Daniel

8 Coleridge and the Inspired Word
Anthony John Harding

9 The Jena System, 1804–5: Logic and Metaphysics
G.W.F. Hegel
Translation edited by John W. Burbidge and George di Giovanni
Introduction and notes by H.S. Harris

10 Consent, Coercion, and Limit: The Medieval Origins of Parliamentary Democracy
Arthur P. Monahan

11 Scottish Common Sense in Germany, 1768–1800: A Contribution to the History of Critical Philosophy
Manfred Kuehn

12 Paine and Cobbett: The Transatlantic Connection
David A. Wilson

13 Descartes and the Enlightenment
Peter A. Schouls

14 Greek Scepticism: Anti-Realist Trends in Ancient Thought
Leo Groarke

15 The Irony of Theology and the Nature of Religious Thought
Donald Wiebe

16 Form and Transformation: A Study in the Philosophy of Plotinus
Frederic M. Schroeder

17 From Personal Duties towards Personal Rights: Late Medieval and Early Modern Political Thought, c. 1300–c. 1650
Arthur P. Monahan

18 The Main Philosophical Writings and the Novel *Allwill*
Friedrich Heinrich Jacobi
Translated and edited by George di Giovanni

19 Kierkegaard as Humanist: Discovering My Self
Arnold B. Come

20 Durkheim, Morals, and Modernity
W. Watts Miller

21 The Career of Toleration: John Locke, Jonas Proast, and After
Richard Vernon

22 Dialectic of Love: Platonism in Schiller's Aesthetics
David Pugh

23 History and Memory in Ancient Greece
Gordon Shrimpton

24 Kierkegaard as Theologian: Recovering My Self
Arnold B. Come

25 Enlightenment and Conservatism in Victorian Scotland: The Career of Sir Archibald Alison
Michael Michie

26 The Road to Egdon Heath: The Aesthetics of the Great in Nature
Richard Bevis

27 Jena Romanticism and Its Appropriation of Jakob Böhme: Theosophy – Hagiography – Literature
Paolo Mayer

28 Enlightenment and Community: Lessing, Abbt, Herder, and the Quest for a German Public
Benjamin W. Redekop

29 Jacob Burckhardt and the Crisis of Modernity
John R. Hinde

30 The Distant Relation: Time and Identity in Spanish-American Fiction
Eoin S. Thomson

31 Mr Simson's Knotty Case: Divinity, Politics, and Due Process in Early Eighteenth-Century Scotland
Anne Skoczylas

32 Orthodoxy and Enlightenment: George Campbell in the Eighteenth Century
Jeffrey M. Suderman

33 Contemplation and Incarnation: The Theology of Marie-Dominique Chenu
Christophe F. Potworowski

34 Democratic Legitimacy: Plural Values and Political Power
F.M. Barnard

35 Herder on Nationality, Humanity, and History
F.M. Barnard

36 Labeling People: French Scholars on Society, Race, and Empire, 1815–1849
Martin S. Staum

37 The Subaltern Appeal to Experience: Self-Identity, Late Modernity, and the Politics of Immediacy
Craig Ireland

38 The Invention of Journalism Ethics: The Path to Objectivity and Beyond, Second Edition
Stephen J.A. Ward

39 The Recovery of Wonder: The New Freedom and the Asceticism of Power
Kenneth L. Schmitz

40 Reason and Self-Enactment in History and Politics: Themes and Voices of Modernity
F.M. Barnard

41 The More Moderate Side of Joseph de Maistre: Views on Political Liberty and Political Economy
Cara Camcastle

42 Democratic Society and Human Needs
Jeff Noonan

43 The Circle of Rights Expands: Modern Political Thought after the Reformation, 1521 (Luther) to 1762 (Rousseau)
Arthur P. Monahan

44 The Canadian Founding: John Locke and Parliament
Janet Ajzenstat

45 Finding Freedom: Hegel's Philosophy and the Emancipation of Women
Sara MacDonald

46 When the French Tried to Be British: Party, Opposition, and the Quest for Civil Disagreement, 1814–1848
J.A.W. Gunn

47 Under Conrad's Eyes: The Novel as Criticism
Michael John DiSanto

48 Media, Memory, and the First World War
David Williams

49 An Aristotelian Account of Induction: Creating Something from Nothing
Louis Groarke

50 Social and Political Bonds: A Mosaic of Contrast and Convergence
F.M. Barnard

51 Archives and the Event of God: The Impact of Michel Foucault on Philosophical Theology
David Galston

52 Between the Queen and the Cabby: Olympe de Gouges's Rights of Women
John R. Cole

53 Nature and Nurture in French Social Sciences, 1859–1914 and Beyond
Martin S. Staum

54 Public Passion: Rethinking the Grounds for Political Justice
Rebecca Kingston

55 Rethinking the Political: The Sacred, Aesthetic Politics, and the Collège de Sociologie
Simonetta Falasca-Zamponi

56 Materialist Ethics and Life-Value
Jeff Noonan

57 Hegel's *Phenomenology*: The Dialectical Justification of Philosophy's First Principles
Ardis B. Collins

58 The Social History of Ideas in Quebec, 1760–1896
Yvan Lamonde
Translated by Phyllis Aronoff and Howard Scott

59 Ideas, Concepts, and Reality
John W. Burbidge

60 The Enigma of Perception
D.L.C. Maclachlan

61 Nietzsche's Justice: Naturalism in Search of an Ethics
Peter R. Sedgwick

62 The Idea of Liberty in Canada during the Age of Atlantic Revolutions, 1776–1838
Michel Ducharme
Translated by Peter Feldstein

63 From White to Yellow: The Japanese in European Racial Thought, 1300–1735
Rotem Kowner

64 The Crisis of Modernity
Augusto Del Noce
Edited and translated by Carlo Lancellotti

65 Imprinting Britain: Newspapers, Sociability, and the Shaping of British North America
Michael Eamon

66 The Form of Politics: Aristotle and Plato on Friendship
John von Heyking

67 War as Paradox: Clausewitz and Hegel on Fighting Doctrines and Ethics
Youri Cormier

68 Network Democracy: Conservative Politics and the Violence of the Liberal Age
Jared Giesbrecht

69 A Singular Case: Debating China's Political Economy in the European Enlightenment
Ashley Eva Millar

70 Not Even a God Can Save Us Now: Reading Machiavelli after Heidegger
Brian Harding

71 Before Copernicus: The Cultures and Contexts of Scientific Learning in the Fifteenth Century
Edited by Rivka Feldhay and F. Jamil Ragep

72 The Culturalist Challenge to Liberal Republicanism
Michael Lusztig

73 God and Government: Martin Luther's Political Thought
Jarrett A. Carty

74 The Age of Secularization
Augusto Del Noce
Edited and Translated by Carlo Lancellotti

75 Emancipatory Thinking: Simone de Beauvoir and Contemporary Political Thought
Elaine Stavro

EMANCIPATORY THINKING

Simone de Beauvoir and Contemporary Political Thought

Elaine Stavro

McGill-Queen's University Press
Montreal & Kingston • London • Chicago

ISBN 978-0-7735-5354-5 (cloth)
ISBN 978-0-7735-5355-2 (paper)
ISBN 978-0-7735-5391-0 (ePDF)
ISBN 978-0-7735-5392-7 (ePUB)

Legal deposit second quarter 2018
Bibliothèque nationale du Québec

Printed in Canada on acid-free paper that is 100% ancient forest free (100% post-consumer recycled), processed chlorine free

This book has been published with the help of a grant from the Canadian Federation for the Humanities and Social Sciences, through the Awards to Scholarly Publications Program, using funds provided by the Social Sciences and Humanities Research Council of Canada.

Funded by the Government of Canada | Financé par le gouvernement du Canada | Canada

Canada Council for the Arts | Conseil des arts du Canada

We acknowledge the support of the Canada Council for the Arts, which last year invested $153 million to bring the arts to Canadians throughout the country.

Nous remercions le Conseil des arts du Canada de son soutien. L'an dernier, le Conseil a investi 153 millions de dollars pour mettre de l'art dans la vie des Canadiennes et des Canadiens de tout le pays.

Library and Archives Canada Cataloguing in Publication

Stavro, Elaine, 1952–, author
Emancipatory thinking: Simone de Beauvoir and contemporary political thought / Elaine Stavro.

(McGill-Queen's studies in the history of ideas; 75)
Includes bibliographical references and index.
Issued in print and electronic formats.
ISBN 978-0-7735-5354-5 (cloth). – ISBN 978-0-7735-5355-2 (paper). – ISBN 978-0-7735-5391-0 (ePDF). – ISBN 978-0-7735-5392-7 (ePUB)

1. Beauvoir, Simone de, 1908–1986. 2. Political science – Philosophy. I. Title. II. Series: McGill-Queen's studies in the history of ideas; 75

B2430.B344S73 2018 320.092 C2017-907848-8
C2017-907849-6

This book was typeset by Marquis Interscript in 10/12 New Baskerville.

This book is dedicated to my parents, Sally and Steve (in memoriam).
While they were unfamiliar with continental philosophy,
they instilled the values of hard work and a belief in passionate
engagement that made this book possible.

Contents

Acknowledgments

I want to thank dear friends, colleagues, and students at Trent University who supported and stimulated me over the lifetime of this project: Charmaine Eddy, Winnie Lem, Nadine Changfoot, Colleen O'Manique, Veronica Hollinger, Jo Ann Colson, Joan Sangster, Feyzi Baban, Constantin Boundas, Norm Slater, Carolyn Kay, Jeremy Leipart, Hasmet Uluorta, Jonathan Greene, Philip Guirlando, Devin Penner, David Holdsworth, James Dexter, Doug Torgerson, and Betsy Struthers. Without the sabbatical leaves that Trent University granted me, this project would not have been accomplished. I also appreciate the efforts of the McGill-Queen's group who guided this manuscript to publication, especially Mark Abley and Kathryn Simpson, as well as the three anonymous readers, who agreed on little, but offered constructive comments.

I want to express my sincere gratitude for the stimulating conversations I have had over the years with local and international colleagues: Diana Coole, Davide Panagia, Frank Pearce, Patricia Dailey, Sonia Kruks, Emilia Angelova, Nick Rogers, Susan Ehrlich, and Ian Balfour.

In addition, I would like to acknowledge my dear friends in Toronto and London who provided support and lively distractions: Catherine Doran, Penny Woolley, Beatrice Hyams, Gareth Humphries, Carol Pardu, Rundi Phelan, Bonnie Alter, Michal Bodemann, Cathy Clark, Peter Fitting, John Gilbert, Barbara Lambert, Kari Lie, Bonnie MacTavish, Annedale MacTavish, Andrea Margles, Robin Ostow, Andrew Ranachan, Richard Rose, Gavin Smith, Cathy Saunders, Elizabeth Taylor Jones, Maxine Molyneux, Norm Slater, and especially Alexander Tarnopolsky.

I want to thank my sons Rory and Blake, who have been a continual source of joy and irritation, and my recent daughter-in-law Stephanie. And finally I thank my sisters: Connie, Deborah, and Stephanie, as well as my uncle Chris (in memoriam) and the entire Stavro clan who have been a source of pleasurable diversions.

This book has been published with the help of a grant from the Federation for the Humanities and Social Sciences, through the Awards to Scholarly Publications Program, using funds provided by the Social Sciences and Humanities Research Council of Canada.

EMANCIPATORY THINKING

Introduction

IN RECUPERATING BEAUVOIR, we witness the struggles of a philosopher trying to make a political difference. Beauvoir goes beyond narrow academic circles, where all too often theorists stay within well-charted pathways, taking their stand on the most recent theoretical turn. Beauvoir was writing as significant paradigm shifts emerged, she was not preoccupied by tedious theoretical debates – or only insofar as they furthered her political projects and existing revolutionary forces.

However, as I will show, Beauvoir's existentialism and philosophic problematic of embodied and situated subjectivity informed her political activism and offered a compelling way of navigating political dilemmas of her time. In this book, I bring together Beauvoir's philosophy and her political interventions, respecting the diversity of her resources (novels, essays, autobiography, philosophic texts) to produce complex thinking on emancipation.

Although Beauvoir's political thinking (apart from her feminism) is for the most part ignored, I will recuperate her ideas and explore how they underpinned her political activism and helped her navigate the dilemmas that post-war revolutionary thinking faced. In addition to looking at the theoretical and political debates she confronted, I will employ her existential insights and philosophic problematic of embodied and situated subjectivity to approach theoretical debates that have defined more recent times.

For Beauvoir, freedom is a movement that requires both personal and collective transformation. It is not guaranteed by world historical systems, material structures, wilful action, or discursive practices, but requires engaged subjects who are able to take creative risks as well as synchronize with existing forces to work towards collective change. Beauvoir resisted the trend of anti-humanism that has dominated French thinking since the 1960s, yet she also managed to avoid the pitfalls of voluntarism and individualism that afflict many humanist thinkers. In fact, I argue that she appreciated the effects of material, socio-economic, and institutional forces without forgoing the capacity to initiate. While she is critical of the dualisms of mind/body, self/other, transcendence/immanence, she neither endorses a monism – like many Deleuzeans who believe in the generativity of the immanence of the world – nor does she believe we are constituted by discursive practices. She does not forgo the power of the individual to act nor the collective subjects to mobilize and "transcend" existing relations. While she saw herself as a Marxist, her attention to multiple agents of change as well as the power she attributed to the subject troubled many Marxists of her day. Humans are neither determined by external forces nor defined by pre-existing discourses, but nor does Beauvoir believe that their effects could be ignored. Beauvoir believes in the human capacity to creatively navigate their specific situation. Beauvoir does not rely upon the transcendental capacity of will and free choice, but presumes that in creatively synchronizing with the concrete situation we can contribute to broader social and political forces. Working on several fronts simultaneously, she acknowledges the importance of tackling personal impediments to living a freer and more engaged life, as well as recognizing that changes in the economy, political institutions, and cultural and political strategies require collective action. One is differentially enmeshed in the world and with others, with differing capacities to act; nevertheless, one is never a simple effect of one's situation.

In acknowledging the significance of the micropolitical as well as the macropolitical and movements between them, Beauvoir knits together domains of the political that often remain separate. In contrast to the post-'68 French thinkers, who focus upon micropolitical forces to unsettle capitalism, and liberal democrats and Marxists, who focus upon macropolitical determining the personal, Beauvoir appreciates the need to work on both levels to further human emancipation.

Rejecting strong essentialism and urging the unsettling of identities and sedimented patterns and structures, Beauvoir has some affinity to poststructuralist and postmodernist thinking; nevertheless her ontology in service of political and social goals and her prompting actors to take their bearings in history and act to enhance collective freedom aligns her with modernist/enlightenment thinking. This ambiguity between the modern and the postmodern, the real and the constructed, is distinctive.

In fact, her formulation of the concept of ambiguity to capture paradoxical aspects of human existence is noteworthy. It underpins her belief that we share the world, yet we approach the world from our distinctive situations. Her problematic of embodied subjectivity "*en situation*" accommodates difference without getting trapped in the singular; believing in our irreducible distinctness, yet also our capacity to communicate and collaborate across difference. While Beauvoir understands the ubiquity of power like Michel Foucault, she does not forgo the possibility of collective freedom or the goals of leading a freer or less oppressed life. While the concepts of freedom, oppression, and autonomy have been rejected as naive – relics of Eurocentric thinking – Beauvoir's notion of embodied and situated subjectivity revives them, without presuming an abstract universalism. For this reason, it is useful to revisit her thinking and political activism: her efforts to respect difference are tackled in theory and practice. Beginning with one's specific situation "we must affirm the concrete and particular thickness of the world and the individual reality of our projects and ourselves" (*EA*, 106). Beauvoir believes this is the basis for building bridges between subjects who can successfully collaborate and work towards the freedom of all.

THE POLITICAL FIELD TODAY

In order to understand and appreciate Simone de Beauvoir today, it is not enough to establish a more or less coherent position that she held throughout her life, as if her work provided timeless truths that could be applied to any situation. That would do little justice to her philosophic problematic of situated and embodied subjectivity. Since we are embodied and situated in time and place, our historical, social, and cultural coordinates are as indispensable to our ideas as are our political and ethical probings. Her work reflects her attention to the needs of her times and her attempt to accommodate the plurality of political postures that she encountered. And yet, very much because of this mattering of context and her (related) refusal of essentialism, Beauvoir's theoretical problematic of embodied and situated subjectivity speaks to contemporary readers and her ideas are relevant to the questions we ask today.

While our historical context is very different from post-war Europe, we share a sense that existing orders of capitalism and traditional forms of political governance are no longer viable or trustworthy. When Beauvoir was writing in the post-war years, there was a spirit of optimism about revolutionary change and the prospect of democratic socialism in Europe. In fact, Beauvoir believed that capitalism would be defeated. Such optimism regarding socialism is still shared by some South and Latin American countries but is not popular in most Western liberal democracies. Yet, as the crisis in capitalist economies persists (if not grows) and as existing forms of democracy are being blamed for failing to protect their citizens or regulate economies, radical political solutions like democratic socialism may enjoy renewed interest. The recent support for Bernie Sanders's democratic socialist program in the American Democratic primaries and Jeremy Corbyn's popularity in the United Kingdom are cases in point.

The rise of populism in recent elections in Western and Eastern Europe also reflects an awareness of the failures of traditional forms of liberal democracy; so far, the turn to extreme right-wing solutions to counter the problems of late capitalism seems more characteristic than a turn to the left. In France, the run off between presidential candidates Marine Le Pen (of the far-right Front National) and Emmanuel Macron (who formed his own party, En Marche!) was a contest between two outsiders. Both in different ways capitalized upon anti–big government sentiments and a desire for change. In Britain, the British National Party has grown in popularity; UKIP (United Kingdom Independence Party), the upstart anti-EU/anti-immigration party, has come just two points below Britain's conservative party (20 May 2013). UKIP was a force in the recent success of the leave campaign. Brexit in the UK, the triumph of Trump in the USA, and the non-confidence vote of Matteo Renzi, the prime minister of Italy (5 December 2016), all signal the success of the right, but also a concern about the failures of existing liberal democracy to tackle unemployment and ever-increasing inequalities. The *Guardian* (18 January 2016) noted that the richest sixty-two people in the world are as wealthy as half the global population combined. One per cent of the people own more wealth than the other 99 per cent combined. These political developments show a taste for strong populist leadership, and the crisis of capitalism is blamed on immigration and refugees. Anti-immigration movements have taken hold in France, the Netherlands, Hungary, Russia, and Germany; the Tea Party movement in the United States signals a similar movement to the right.

At the same time, there are growing critiques of traditional liberal democratic politics from the left. In France, the emergence of the Nouveau Parti Anticapitaliste (NPA) attests to this. In Greece, the Coalition of the Radical Left (Syriza) (inspired by democratic socialism, anti-capitalism) has been more popular than the traditional Socialist Party (PASOK), which still relies upon state-centred solutions and social democracy at the time of this writing. The rise of anti-globalization, apparent at meetings of the World Trade Organization (WTO), the G7, and the G20, combined with protests against the wars in Iraq and Afghanistan and environmental activism, signal a strong opposition to politics as usual. The Occupy movement (starting in 2011) and the student strike in Quebec (2012) are evidence of struggles against institutionalized liberal democracy. The growing Black Lives Matter movement (2013) has drawn our attention to the violence and systemic injustice the Black community faces and the failures of liberal democracy to assuage them. Most recently, in 2016 Dakota protestors (a coalition of environmentalists, activists, and Native Americans) were successful in blocking the building of the oil pipeline alongside Native land.

The crisis in capitalism has prompted serious rethinking of the neoliberal strategy of privatizing public services and the practice of giving autonomy to financial institutions. US president Barack Obama's interventions in the economy (in the wake of the economic crisis of 2008) and spending programs challenge some of the core ideas of the New Right: that government intervention is evil, that individual initiative and resilience is hijacked by regulations, and that the market works best and in the best interest of the many if unfettered. Nevertheless the recent Trans-Pacific Partnership (TPP) that Obama signed onto marked a return to free market ideals, albeit state orchestrated. Bernie Sanders's support for Hillary Clinton was premised upon his insistence that the Democratic Party repeal the TPP. The introduction of new regulatory strategies with their newly embedded and attached identities is not an impediment but a facilitator of democracy. So, the ideas of radical change, and the spirit of popular democratic engagement, are becoming more relevant to the mood of our times. However in light of the recent successes of the Brexit campaign and the election of Donald Trump, it is difficult to be optimistic. The promise of job creation and infrastructure spending appealed to those left behind by globalization and neoliberalism, so while this too is symptomatic of the problems of existing capitalism, their proposed solutions and undemocratic processes of change mark a serious threat to democratic negotiation.

While emancipatory movements and right-wing populist challenges seem to be enjoying a rebirth, it is unclear whether feminist politics are. Beauvoir's *The Second Sex*, published in 1949, was written during an era of hopefulness about radical possibilities and was central to the surge of second-wave feminism in the late 1960s in European and Anglo-American countries. Unlike the first wave of feminism, which occurred up to and during the first decades of the twentieth century and which focused on women's struggles for the vote and the right to work, the second wave was concerned with more personal issues: reproductive freedoms, sexual abuse, and cultural and social forces that kept women in a demeaned and subordinate role. This shift involved a turn away from the political and socio-economic in order to acknowledge cultural, legal, and social considerations. Beauvoir is particularly interesting in this context since she addresses historical and socio-economic concerns as well as cultural or aesthetic impediments to women's liberation, theoretically underpinned by the move from more humanist assumptions to postmodern and poststructuralist ones. There was a turn against the second wave for falsely unifying women, thereby ignoring women's differences in terms of class, race, sexuality, and ethnicity. This political challenge ended in undoing the focus on feminist perspectives and shifted study to intersectional forces and minority struggles, differentiating experiences of oppression or subordination. Attending to how the general category Woman excluded marginalized women, the third wave celebrated difference and complexity. Theoretically this shift was inspired by feminists like Luce Irigaray, Hélène Cixous, and Julia Kristeva in France, and bell hooks, Patricia Collins, and Judith Butler in the USA. Anti-humanism was the rallying call of this generation proclaiming "the death of Man," the end of universal thinking, and the culmination of the pursuit of emancipation (Braidotti 2013, 23–5). They distanced themselves from the hubris of European philosophy that believed knowledge would guarantee human progress and the amelioration of the human condition. In focusing upon those who have been excluded, these theorists approached politics by a turn to the specific and singular. Though they most often scorn identity politics and celebrate difference, they haven't theorized how differences can be woven together, how they can be made to collaborate to work towards common goals. For example, Judith Butler calls for strategic essentialism and pragmatic politics and promotes collaborative work, but she doesn't have a philosophy that furthers collaboration; Beauvoir's ontology and situated subjectivity offers this.

Poststructuralist thinking, often associated with the post–May '68 generation, challenged the unified and universalist perspective associated with liberal feminism and the politics of socialist feminism. But these anti-humanists don't appreciate the complexity of Beauvoir's radical humanism (*EA*, 41), which presumed neither universal sisterhood, sovereign rational subjects, nor a future resolution of history through economic change alone.

We generally attribute this theoretical shift from general abstract subjects to specific embodied ones to third-wave feminism, which rightly identified the problems that the universal voice of the second wave encountered – presuming a common gender experience, with which all women could identify, excluded and marginalized minority women. However, it is important to remember that in the post-war years the left remained unconcerned/uninterested in (distinguishing/articulating) women's needs. This is the context in which second-wave feminism arose, pushing for progressive social and political policies that served all women (decriminalizing abortion, granting the right to contraception, identifying sexual harassment and violence). These movements, which took various forms depending upon the country, contributed to improving Western women's participation in the public sphere as well as respect for their social standing. So while they may not have attended to the specificity of different women's needs/identities, this "homogenizing" movement had progressive political effects. Today there is a growing sentiment, especially in the liberal democratic countries of Western Europe, North America, and Oceania, that women are no longer oppressed; it is assumed that we live in a *post*-feminist[1] world. An entire generation of girls born in the last three decades of the twentieth century have been brought up and educated in a world where the shortcomings of sexist practices were continually identified and challenged. Yet sexism in our economic and cultural practices is far from eradicated. Battles that were won on the issues of abortion, sexual harassment, and cultural representations of women are no longer secure. Access to abortion is now under threat in the United States, as the Republican majority in the house and Senate are poised to introduce legislation that would deny abortion rights to many. Representations of women as objectified sex objects seem to persist in popular culture: for example, critiques by women of the feminine avatars and heavily masculine culture of gaming are common. Austerity programs in the UK and US differentially affect women; gender remains relevant in public policy. Most recently in light of the shift to the extreme right in the USA with the election of the Donald Trump and the selection of his advisors, new energy has been injected into anti-feminist and pro-family and pro-life forces. With the election of Trump, and the possible overturning of Roe versus Wade (1973) threats to abortion legislation, endorsement of sexual harassment and sexual abuse, universal gendered considerations may again be potent sources of political mobilization.

While there have been economic successes over the last forty years, getting women employed in occupations and in positions of power from which they were formerly barred, the majority of women suffer in the present economic climate. Moreover, since many of the jobs that have been created are part-time or involve casual work, and since women are disproportionately represented in these jobs, the livelihood of the working middle-class and poor families in the North has declined. It is at least

1 My use of the term "postfeminist" refers not to the field of feminism influenced by poststructuralist theories of subjectivity and politics, but to the more popular socio-political conjuncture that presumes that feminist demands have been achieved and hence feminism is no longer necessary. For discussions of postfeminism across media, popular culture, and feminist studies, see Stéphanie Genz and Benjamin Brabon (2009).

true in Canada that single-parent families headed up by women are the poorest of the poor (Townson 2009, 6). Since women are often highly represented in the public economy, as the neoliberal state cuts back on public workers, women workers' jobs are under threat (Chelliah 2014). Given the erosion of public and welfare provisions in liberal democratic countries more generally, women's livelihood is at risk.

Such sweeping generalizations are also true in the South where economies are dependent upon producing goods (e.g., small electrical goods, clothing, flowers) for Western consumers. To keep wages low, women have often been brought into the waged economy; this is as true today as it was in earlier times. With the loss of waged work, unwaged work takes prominence; such work usually falls to women whose lives have been acutely affected as they struggle to keep their families from starving. The growth of sex-trafficking and increase of domestic violence against women in these times of economic woe are noteworthy (Chelliah 2014; Phillips 2013). I suspect a new wave of feminist activism may emerge in response to the present forms of exploitation and prejudice that women around the world are presently experiencing, but let us be reminded that economic and institutional changes on their own are not sufficient to liberate women from their oppression. Beauvoir was prescient in approaching the sexual and social impediments to agency through literature and philosophy: tracing how prejudices and demeaning images and attitudes are promulgated and perpetuated.

In addition to tackling social structural forces, Beauvoir believes individuals must be engaged in the process of renouncing their old identities and reconfiguring themselves. Thus, Beauvoir's thinking is less out of sync than might be assumed both with our present historical reality and with current theoretical positions. Beauvoir's non-foundational approach to philosophy, her use of multiple theoretical frameworks to understand the subordination of women, the aged, and racial and aboriginal minorities, is far from passé. In fact there is much to gain from Beauvoir's ability to accommodate difference while not forgoing the goal of emancipation.

For half a century, notions of collective agency have been challenged: concepts of class, gender, community, oppression, etc. have been problematized in the name of difference. The focus on who and what is excluded in emancipatory projects, and a distaste for consensus as totalitarian, have stymied thinking about common action and common goals. The discursive approach dominates literary and cultural studies, and the focus upon agency or subject-centred thinking and strategy is a narrow approach to the political. As Fredric Jameson points out and Ian Buchanan and Kristen Ross echo, "by repudiating the Same and the collective, under the utterly misconceived banner of 'anti-totalization,' cultural studies has for all intents and practical purposes divested itself of two of the most basic prerequisites of politics, namely the potential for common action and a common goal ... and has led inexorably to political paralysis" (Jameson 1994, in Buchanan 2008, 19).

The situation is beginning to change: crises in the capitalist economy, growing precarity, loss of confidence in liberal democratic systems of governance, divisive international politics, and fundamentalist politics all call for new ways of thinking. Global events and an awareness of big problems call for the renewal of general theorizing and collective action. Edward Said identified the need for a critical humanism that is cognizant of its double movements. That is to say, although universalism has been used to exclude and demean minority populations, it also serves to acknowledge distinctively human aspects of being that can challenge orientalism and divisive politics in our bellicose world. Thus Said distinguishes Eurocentric universalism from a universalism that fosters mutual respect of all humans. Sharing Said's concern, Judith Butler draws attention to the notion of loss and shared vulnerability that ties humans together in their struggles against torture, suffering, and oppression.[2] As Sonia Kruks points out, since the events of 11 September 2001 and the torture of inmates at Guantanamo, Butler has shed her anti-humanist stance and "cautiously affirmed the power of 'the human' and 'humanism' as necessary to the repertoire of a critical politics" (Kruks 2012, 31). Butler, like Said, sees the human as an "ideal norm" that is constantly doubled, and used in coercive and exclusionary ways, but it also has some traction in drawing attention to those who are treated inhumanely, whose suffering and death do not seem to count (Butler 2004b, 91). More recently Bonnie Honig (2013) has challenged this turn to mortality and fragility as common essential traits.[3] In turning to Antigone and her political decision to transgress the political order in burying her brother, Honig wants to validate those who take risks, protest, and derive joy and pleasure in political activities. She is concerned about the lack of affirmation at play in a politics of precarity. However, one need not go back to Antigone to find a woman who speaks out against political forces

2 Although Butler (*Gender Trouble*) is renowned for drawing attention to how previous normative theorists produce normalizing practices that reassert rather than challenge norms, her more recent work (*Precarious Life*) provides a minimal ontological assumption about human existence as shared vulnerability that goes against the grain of her previous anti-essentialist position.

3 Honig's approach to political agency is distinguished from Beauvoir's in her tactical disposition to democratic politics and her interest in asking (the Foucauldian question): what is the politics at stake in this recent turn to vulnerability?

that silence her, or speaks up for those who resist the state; Beauvoir, in thought and deed, provides an existential ontology that privileges human participation and celebrates the joyfulness of political activism. Conceiving freedom as situated and embodied, both personal and collective, she urges us to will our own freedom and work towards the freedom of all.[4] In spite of changed historical and political circumstances that make parallels between the post-war and early twenty-first century difficult, I think Beauvoir's radical humanism has much to offer in rethinking radical political agency – a materially, historically sensitive theory of embodied agency that allows for collective and individual human agency.

Since Beauvoir was not an academic and her primary interest was in fostering forces of radical change, she was less inclined to devote time to esoteric academic debates. Yet as an engaged novelist, critical intellectual, and committed existentialist, she was nevertheless implicated in those debates. Beauvoir's work challenges top-down and centralized forces of change, as well as emancipatory politics that rely upon historical materialism or systemic theories alone. She believes that focusing on existing struggles, trying to appreciate the full breadth and specificity of their democratic potential, will move political intervention towards democratic socialism. Her existentialist thinking inserts normative and subjective considerations into politics without strong essentialism or metaphysics.[5] As such, her work has some affinity to the poststructuralists and the spirit of non-foundationalism; however, she was more hopeful than most poststructuralists about the possibility of freedom and working collectively towards a revolutionary goal. Challenging the authoritarian politics of the communist party and extending agency beyond the proletariat as the universal agents of change, she has much in common with the philosophers of May '68. Of course, her turn to the personal as political (or what is more recently theorized as the micropolitical) was prescient, as were her critiques of objective neutral knowledge, but rarely is her prescience appreciated. Given that changes in one's conduct/habits as well as the existing institutions and economic relations are necessary to emancipation, her focus on consciousness (interior processes of intentionality usually associated with phenomenology) is often exaggerated. So there have

4 Although Beauvoir herself is culpable of Eurocentrism in her reflections on Muslim women, her theoretical problematic of embodiment and situatedness can appreciate difference and thereby avoid abstract universalism and Eurocentrism.

5 Beauvoir is critical of a metaphysics that transcends this empirical world, and subscribes to deep structures; nevertheless, she does describe her literature as metaphysical insofar as it explores human existence (see ch. 7).

been many glib readings of Beauvoir that I hope to tackle. Her focus on situated and specific action, a mingling of the inside and outside in embodied synchronicity and participation, brings her closer to contemporary performative theories of agency that spurn reflective agency.

Most theorists focus on *The Second Sex*, hence highlighting Beauvoir's attention to gender and ignoring or glossing over the more universalist claims found in her earlier work. In *The Ethics of Ambiguity*, she sketches an ontology of freedom that involves the appreciation of ambiguity, contingency, and embeddedness in history. She also offers critiques of Hegelian linear thinking and Marxism's deterministic assumptions. In returning to the subject, an encumbered and concrete one, Beauvoir offers an alternative to the anti-humanist thinking of her day, without lapsing into abstract universalism. Her embodied and situated phenomenological approach appreciates the potential of lived experience and the distinctiveness of various social worlds in contrast with the Hegelian/Marxist dialectic of the "negation of the negation" that presumes the oppressed are immiserated and destitute class subjects. In addition Beauvoir brings ethics to bear upon her revolutionary thinking. She urges us to "will our freedom" and in doing so she believes one "wills the freedom of all" (EA, 13). Prompting humans to accept their ambiguity and contingency and will their personal and collective freedom, she provides support for a radical critical humanism. Her theory of universality is different from the abstract universality with which she is usually confused.[6]

Since Beauvoir believes we are situated and embodied subjects, she respects our differential situations and doesn't imagine that we are all fundamentally the same, as liberal or abstract humanists do. Yet she urges us all to engage in action that will loosen forces of oppression and restriction. She does not endorse socialist humanism's ideal of the individual being fully realized in community; in fact, she boldly states that "in democratic socialism ... class would be abolished but not individuals" (SS, 67). So our individuality or situatedness will not be surmounted in democratic socialism, but democratic socialist forces can and must be engaged to live a freer and more equal life. Moreover she does not believe that one's personal freedom and collective freedom are at odds, for living a less constrained (more autonomous) life involves being enriched by others.

6 As we will see, Susan Hekman, Iris Young, Julia Kristeva, and Tina Chanter make the case that Beauvoir's universal humanism presumes that women should emulate men to be liberated: act rationally and assertively and engage in dangerous life-risking activities. Such readings of Beauvoir will be contested in the course of this book.

In *The Second Sex*, Beauvoir refuses to see women from an essentialist (universal) lens as if all women were the same, but she equally spurns those who situate women "beyond their sex" (SS, 4). Beauvoir traces diverse sedimented social patterns sketching the generality of women's gendered existence. Through multiple voices and genres, she traces how women have been marginalized in the economy, denied full participation in social and political life, and symbolically rendered inferior. Her fictional and non-fictional work, she believes, will facilitate the recognition of social inequality (whether it be based upon gender, class, race, ethnicity, and even age) and promote a commitment to change. Without being a humanist in the sense of assuming a sovereign rational male subject and idea of history as "complete" (EA, 41), nonetheless she endorses a minimal ontology privileging equality and freedom.

Beauvoir borrows philosophic concepts from the nineteenth and twentieth centuries and insights from many disciplines (anthropology, biology, and literature, as well as their diverse discourses in psychoanalysis, historical materialism, and race theory). In doing so, she admits the power of the discourses in informing the terrain of subjectivity and politics. However, unlike discursive theorists, for whom agency is read off specific discursive analyses, Beauvoir turns to experience and historical engagement to understand subjectivity. She is not stymied by difference nor overwhelmed by complex subjectivity, but believes class, gender, and other social forces, like age, factor into one's situation and hence one's agency. Her criticism of the French communist party for imposing strategies top-down, her challenges to prevailing Marxist theories for their determinism, and her distance from the universalism of liberalism demark the space in which she operates. She is intent on forging more flexible, subject-centred notions of concrete freedom that will contribute to larger emancipatory forces. Her responses – to psychoanalysts, her poststructuralist feminist opponents, and the artistic avant-garde – are part of this larger project that accommodates the personal and cultural within emancipatory discourses.

ENGAGING THEORETICAL INTERLOCUTORS – ANTI-HUMANISTS AND RATIONALISTS

In this book, in addition to exploring some of her theoretical interlocutors, I try to construct debates that she, herself, did not explicitly address (i.e., debates on the body, psychoanalytic debates upon desire, Foucault's anti-humanism [1984], Deleuze and Guattari's affect theory [1987, 1994], and insights on neuroscience that occurred after her death). In bringing Beauvoir's thoughts to bear on debates that she did not have, I provide a more or less coherent lens through which we can explore the current theoretical landscape, staging conversations between different approaches that did not often take place. Also exploring different theories of agency, and speculating as to how Beauvoir might have responded to their concerns, we see there is more room for communication and collaboration than might have previously been thought. Bringing Beauvoir into conversation with our present has been pursued by Nancy Bauer (2001), Sonia Kruks (1990, 2001, 2012), Lori Marso (2012a, 2012b), Ursula Tidd (1999), and Penelope Deutscher (2008); however, for the most part, contemporary scholars have focused on Beauvoir's philosophy rather than her political thinking.

Beauvoir's concern with embodied agency facilitates the staging of a conversation between the past and present, since concerns about the micropolitical and the body are central to contemporary debates. Without searching for the "real world," or a transcendental subject, or devising universal normative criteria to guide people's action, Beauvoir begins with the embodied and situated self (the place from which the world and others unfold) to explore human efforts to live a freer and more ethical existence. Without presuming foundational knowledge or transcendental subjectivity, she subscribes to a minimal ontology, or weak ontology,[7] that privileges free and ambiguous forms of subjectivity. In doing so, she operates differently than the Marxist humanists who assume the subject is complete and history is resolvable (EA, 47) and instead reveals an affinity with the current materialists of indeterminacy and the non-rational. While she does not attend to the indeterminacy of the subatomic world of contemporary science, nor does she subscribe to their anti-humanism, she privileges the dynamic flow of energies, albeit attending to the persistent human need to articulate and instantiate oneself. Beauvoir's phenomenology focuses on the generative capacity of embodied experiences: the body is the place of exchange between interior and exterior forces. In contrast to both new and old materialists and discursive theorists who focus on the "outside" structuring the inside, whether it be in determinate lively matter, social structures, or discursive practices, her approach is also distinct from the phenomenologists who

7 Steven White (2000) uses the term "weak ontology" to highlight the work of those who refuse theories of human nature, and therefore essentialism, and yet avoid the shortcomings of skepticism and relativism. By privileging certain forms of human life, weak ontologists avoid the normative deficit that afflicts poststructuralist thinkers. Although White does not explore the existentialists in detail, their insights do fit his thesis – the irrepressible vitality manifest in human existence, and the importance of attunement, fit his notion of weak ontology.

privilege the "inside" (consciousness or experience) "without regard to their possible 'outside' constitutive sources"[8] (Kruks 2010, 259). Beauvoir's existential phenomenology begins not with the "inside" but with the threshold experience of the in-between, where embodied subjects finesse existing forces and discourses – producing freer and more engaged action. Hence she distances herself from the liberal thinkers who believe freedom is autonomous – "freedom from" social forces and the will of others – as well as materialists who see freedom as structurally or discursively determined. The conversations that will ensue in the course of this book do not provide a meta-narrative – a coherent picture within which these different approaches to subjectivity, oppression, violence, and justice will fit – for this presumes a sense of the whole that is not possible. The book does however suggest that there is more overlap of concern amongst these theorists than is usually appreciated, for they all challenge the modern masterful subject and theorize agency as embedded and requiring synchronicity with others and the world. However Beauvoir's humanism appreciates the capacity to act, to initiate, to intend – capacities that have been dismissed by anti-humanists.

In employing Beauvoir's embodied subject, I believe one is able to navigate different theories of subjectivity and different theories of politics. Like Beauvoir, I will emulate writing as *bricolage*, piecing together concerns, concepts, and frameworks that speak and work towards the furthering of conversations about freedom and creative human engagement.[9]

To appreciate Beauvoir's radical humanism, I will have to address those critics who have dismissed her as an abstract humanist and rationalist (amongst them are Rosi Braidotti, Elizabeth Spelman, Iris Young, Susan Hekman, Julia Kristeva, Hélène Cixous, Luce Irigaray). In doing so, I will draw upon her theory of embodiment and ambiguity. Although she speaks of "will" and "choice," these always occur in situations one has not entirely willed or chosen. For Beauvoir, we are free and yet constrained, our actions are structured by historical/material and cultural forces, yet in assuming them in our distinctive way, individual and collective actions are engaged. Here she takes her distance from liberal

8 Sonia Kruks makes a strong case for distinguishing phenomenologists who privilege consciousness and inner experience from Beauvoir's existential phenomenology. "Existential versions of phenomenology also considers how we may theorize human freedom in the face of facticity (the apparently 'outside' or 'objective' aspect) of both bodily and socially structured dimensions of experience" (2012, 259).

9 However, unlike the postmodern *bricoleurs*, Beauvoir's embodied subject struggles towards sense, towards coherence, presuming belongingness and weaving together the personal performances and symbolic gestures with revolutionary politics.

humanists who assume freedom is freedom from the wills of others, as well cautioning against the certainty and predictiveness assumed in existing Marxist humanist thinking. Unlike contemporary deconstructionists and new materialists, she pays more attention to the effects of history and socio-economic relations on agency. Herein lies Beauvoir's distinctive humanism. Her living body's engagement with other bodies can potentially have positive effects, materially instantiating freedom. Consequently, she attends to physiology as well as the importance of socio-historical and cultural factors. Unlike the historical materialists who believe that change is historically determined, Beauvoir insists upon contingency and the open-endedness of human action; while action is affected by existing social structures and sedimented patterns, it is not determined. In doing so she avoids liberal voluntarism that overestimates the power of the individual and the power of ideas, as well as the Marxists and new materialists who severely restrict human agency in the name of socio-economic structures or non-human matter. Struggles for greater human freedom are encouraged, aligning with others and the world, but there is always the risk of failure. Beauvoir does not despair, nor is she bothered by human failures; she says that even the most optimistic ethics have all started by underlining the element of failure included in "man's condition: without failures, no ethics" (*POL*, 291). This acknowledgement contributes to an affirmative radical politics that materially instantiates freedom not in one fell swoop, but continuously. Violence, conflict, and the objectification of others will not be eliminated from history and human relations (as Marxist revolutionaries assumed) but they can be significantly diminished through collaborative action.

One of my aims in this book is to show how active engagement in historical events informs shifts in theory. Problems with Marxist political praxis (i.e., the failure of proletarian agency, the institutionalization of violent and hierarchical party practices, and the priority of the economy) prompted rethinking theories of historical materialism in the post-war years and beyond. The Algerian War, the rise of decolonizing and social movements (specifically the women's movements), and the events of May '68 all intensified the need to respect local concerns and diverse struggles and confirmed problems with existing party practices. These movements were not always connected to the labour movement or economic issues, and the shortcomings of left-wing parties prompted decentred and uncoordinated agents of change. Here I contest Braidotti, who traces the emergence of social and political movements (the women's movement, anti-colonial struggles, environmentalism) to anti-humanism and poststructuralism (Braidotti 2013, 16, 17). As we will see, there were critical voices of the socialist left in France (prior to May '68) that did not speak in a universal rational voice, nor support communist party practices, nor presume the linear development of history. Beauvoir is one: she was neither Hegelian nor socialist humanist, in the strict sense of believing in the resolution of history through consciousness raising; rather, she believed that embodied agency and uncoordinated movements could enrich radical forces and further human emancipation.

As I will show, Beauvoir's radical humanism endorses diverse struggles against injustice and inequality. She goes some way to counter hierarchal authorities by accommodating the diverse and decentred agents and struggles she confronted. So pluralism is not simply associated with anti-humanism or poststructuralism, as Braidotti claims. Beauvoir's practical pluralism[10] was complemented by a theoretical pluralism – working within and expanding allegedly monistic theories like Marxism, Freudianism, and biology, rather than dismissing them. Challenging their totalizing and systemic tendencies by employing them like a bricoleur, she moves away from tracing structural forces and discursive practices that define agency and acknowledges how living body subjects as openings are influenced by these social structural and discursive forces, and yet able to singularly finesse these forces. In doing so, she acknowledges a non-identical self, but a subject that coheres over time and space. One's personal style and specific social and political engagements with the world attest to that.

Beauvoir's phenomenological treatment of the body works towards appreciating a more vital and specific approach to revolutionary agency without losing sense of the sedimented fields in which we act. In doing so, Beauvoir works at both the micro- and macropolitical levels (accommodating the actor and structure, culture and the economy, the local and general) producing emancipatory strategies. "To capture the complexities of human life and account for the phenomena of social oppression," Sonia Kruks argues, "Beauvoir works in and across the interstices between phenomenology and a Marxist-inflected and also a culturally oriented structuralist materialism" (Kruks 2010, 260).

The project of this book (the recuperation of Beauvoir) goes beyond narrow academic circles, where all too often theorists stay within well-charted pathways, academics taking their stand on the most recent theoretical turn. I hope to break with this practice, by revealing affinities between many of these turns, and Beauvoir's capacity to navigate their

10 I don't want to overstate this position, since in the 1950s Beauvoir strongly supported revolutionary options and vigorously attacked anti-communist thinkers in "Right-Wing Thought Today" (*POL*, 103–94). Sonia Kruks is correct to point out how this approached the position of dogmatic faith, which she had been clear to challenge in *The Ethics of Ambiguity*.

specificity in the name of freedom. I hope to influence thinkers to similarly go beyond the present paths of political theory, which often get defined in terms of a modern and postmodern disposition – according to their identification with Habermasians or the poststructuralists (Deleuzeans, Foucauldians, and Derrideans). In the spirit of Beauvoir, I respect the ambiguity of these theoretical oppositions; I side with the deliberative theorists in my belief in the possibility of shared conversation and collective meanings, yet, by theorizing the significance of affect, bodily gestures, and non-rational communication, I lean towards the postmodern.

The poststructuralist critique of deliberation has led to profound skepticism about the capacity to communicate across difference. While these theoretical interventions have been important and timely, far too often they have sabotaged shared meanings and problematized collective action. However tenuous and presumptive the belief in transcultural and transhistorical communication of embodied (living and speaking) subjects may be, it should not be ruled out of court pre-emptively, given how important it is today to struggle towards cross-cultural understanding and collective action. In urging us to be responsive to the sensory/sensible world and affective registers of experience as well as the linguistic and socio-economic aspects of material experience, Beauvoir is well positioned to take up the mantle of critical humanist, something presumed in this book's staging of dialogues with different interlocutors. Beauvoir's notion of embodied and situated subjectivity and our practical engagement with the world helps make ourselves and the world mappable. However difficult it is today – given that the postmodern world we live in has challenged boundaries between the natural and social, the technological and cultural[11] – it is still desirable to look for acts of sense-making, enacting/materializing one's freedom within contexts/environments not of one's choosing, rather than endorse skeptical or relativist attitudes. Sense-making presumes a purposive relation of bodies to the world – linguistic as well as spatial meanings, cognitive as well as sensory ones – and thereby extends agency beyond rational argument to struggle for shared understandings. Beauvoir does not hold an absolutist position that gets rid of bad theories of subjectivity or disproves false theories of the world, but rather encourages communication between contending interpretations and encourages their conversion into

11 This is particularly true of "posthuman theories that identify thinking as 'informational patterns' rather than 'material instantiation' so that embodiment in a biological substrate is seen as an accident of history rather than an inevitability of life" (Hayles 1999, 2).

more effective action. She respects various ways of approaching the world we live in and encourages efforts to make sense of the world and to live in it more fully.

BROADENING THE POLITICAL

Since the '70s, there have been several theoretical turns. First there was the linguistic or discursive turn against the materialists (historical materialist and phenomenological thinkers). Assuming the subjects and the real were discursively constituted marked a break with humanist theories and ontologies that favoured stable subjects and praxis following from consciousness (internal mental states of disembodied knowing subjects as the point of departure). More recently there have been concerns regarding this discursive constructivism of poststructuralism, and a return to sensory experience (affect) and an appreciation of aesthetics as informing political agency. These theorists, sometimes called affect theorists or new materialists or vital materialists, believe that matter is not inert, nor given meaning or form by an external agency; "its proponents describe an immanent ontology of becoming in which matter is not a state of being but a dynamic process of materialisation" (Coole 2013). Without endorsing naturalism, affect theorists equally eschew social and cultural constructionism. Borrowing from Deleuze, as well as Bruno Latour, they focus upon non-humans as social actants: things have social effects that cannot be ignored, though they are not agents in the full sense. Yet their own lively energies can impede or enhance human agency. Further, their effects are not reducible to the human agents who employ them. This theoretical move is seen as particularly important in environmental politics; in challenging humans as exceptional beings, affect theorists engage recent theoretical moves that rethink boundaries between humans and animals, the organic and inorganic life, which have been driven by the most recent scientific research. However in doing so they eschew the importance of human reason and intention, as well as the capacity to creatively initiate projects. Beauvoir manages to appreciate the role of affect and emotion in mobilizing political commitment, but does not lose sight of the role of reason, the power of ideas, or the making of arguments. In this sense, she attends to the emotive and affective factors, particularly in her literary works, but she departs from Deleuzeans who focus upon non-human, material sources of vitality. For them, affect is separate from emotion: affect is self-generating and should be plugged into the system; it should destabilize identities. Deleuze does not encourage us to make sense of it, for meaning-making tames revolutionary potential.

Concerns about the effects of the social constructivist turn of the '80s have led to a turn back to the material world. Unlike older forms of historical materialism that focused on sedimented human patterns and history that blocked human agency, the new materialists welcome the indeterminacy and the subatomic non-human world. Unlike the new materialists who appreciate the agentic capacity of matter – the power of things to affect humans – Beauvoir is interested in intra-human or intersubjective action and the effect of power relations. While Beauvoir had little to say about the power of things driving action, she was aware of the limitations of rational and interest-driven human agency. Indebted to Marxism that respects the structuring powers of capital and liberal democracy to produce institutional life correspondent to its needs, she still believes in the power of humans to transgress them.

While Beauvoir does not anticipate the insights of new materialism, its subatomic and indeterminate realities, she does capture the insights of the older materialism that recognizes how the historical/social world is structured – yet avoids its reductionist and teleological tendencies. Granted classical science is obsolete and so some of the assumptions that find their way into human thinking are problematic, however the excessive distribution of agency to non-human actants and non-human assemblages that exceed the human leave little space to explore human plans and designs, nor to address pressing power-related problems of current social/political realities. While the new materialist rightly identified the hubris of humanist thinking, and while their post-humanist or non-human thinking may have some insights, it is not clear how these forces can be harnessed to human agents and political projects. Focusing on the power of affects, things, matter energy flows, and assemblages to trigger political movements has not been particularly useful in understanding how affects can further persistence, attachment, or the development of these democratic movements.

Just because the subatomic world of matter proves to be creative, self-organizing, indeterminate, Sonia Kruks (2015) has argued we can't assume the human material/social world is as well. In fact there is much evidence to suggest the contrary; it tends to be more stable. Global capital and its neoliberal market-driven logic of deregulation favours the maximization of profit. As workers and refugees migrate around the world in search of work and security, this increasingly cosmopolitan citizenry is not open and welcoming of difference, but rather retreats in fear that foreigners will take from them. Culling insights from historical materialism, as well as thinking through the potential for change, from ethical, cultural, or democratic practices, is one way to proceed. Hegemonic powers are more stable than presumed. While there may be energy flows and indeterminate matter, social relations are not always so flexible. The agentic capacity of humans becomes blocked through institutions that prioritize socio-economic inequalities and undemocratic practices. Affects, bodily sensations, and things may shake up the system and catalyze new forces of change, yet it is not clear how democratic moments get transferred into democratic practices. While I agree that dialogue and argument are insufficient to understand political mobilization, there is little talk amongst new materialists as to how commitment is fostered or resilience cultivated. Persistence is urged, but having erased the subject and having glossed over the importance of emotion and commitment there are few resources to sustain democratic movements. Democratic projects should accommodate affective receptivity, bodily communication, and deliberative as well as democratic practices.

Poststructuralists and affect theorists do not believe historical context is important. The former feel history is incorporated in discursive events and the latter feel that the vital materiality of living matter ought to be pursued. Though one might argue that the context is comprised of various discourses, to recognize the power of some over others, the contexts in which they arise and how they are used remains important. So, unlike Foucault who believes that the past is constituted by discursive practices, or Latour who believes that human and non-human assemblages comprise agency, through lived experience Beauvoir's embodied agent accommodates the effects of physiological facts, psychological history, and social structures. Toril Moi aptly describes Beauvoir's notion of the situation "not as an 'external' structure that imposes itself on the individual subject, but rather an irreducible amalgam of the freedom (projects) of that subject and the conditions in which freedom finds itself. The body as a situation is the concrete body experienced as meaningful, and socially and historically situated" (Moi 1999, 74). Our lived experience encompasses bodily sexual difference, "but is built up by many other things and experiences" (78). Thus the historical and socio-economic context and power relations in which discourses arise are significant. Throughout this book, I place Beauvoir's ideas in historical context, which helps highlight her efforts to respond to political events of her time. While it is possible to comprehend her without appeal to historical context, such context certainly enhances our understanding of her ideas.

Without seeing political agency simply in terms of conversations or structures, constitutions imposed from the outside, Beauvoir tries to acknowledge the personal face of power as well as the macroinstitutional and socio-historical forms that must be engaged in acting. While she accommodates the role of affect and emotion in political mobilizing (hence her political fictions are important), she has not been fully apprised of the significance of space, image, or non-human actants in political change. While I make the case that Beauvoir's problematic of embodied agency and her radical humanism are worth recuperating, specifically in our anti-humanist times, Beauvoir herself does not understand the complexity of the non-human world nor does she fully appreciate non-rational forms of life. I'm not proposing that Beauvoir's thinking is able to resolve the problems of our times, but rather that her thoughts on social engagement and freedom are worth thinking about. As we emerge from an era in which political theory was oriented towards language's role in defining problems, bodies, and goals rather than towards the intentional action of subjects, Beauvoir represents an alternative to social constructivism as well as neurologically and naturalistically informed politics and psychological theories. Beauvoir's humanism does not involve the kind of humanism criticized by poststructuralists and structuralist Marxists, centred on a sovereign subject and comprehensive vision of history, nor does it involve the voluntarism and individualism associated with liberalism. Yet her radical humanism or critical humanism endorses the distinctive powers of the human subject, to initiate, commit, and act collectively and responsibly. The anti-humanist move is not up to the challenge. One cannot just expand non-human agencies without tackling the intransigent social hierarchies and institutions that have been humanly organized and that will involve human initiatives.

Exploring the shifts from humanism to anti-humanism within Marxism, the developments within psychoanalytic theory from Freudian, to Lacanian, to object relations theory, and finally the turn from historical materialism to postmodernism, poststructuralism, and new materialism[12] will introduce some students of politics – and younger academics – to theories of which they often have a scant knowledge. Their presentist attitude leads to a creeping myopia and contempt for the past that often poorly equips students to understand fully the references and parameters of contemporary debates. Postmodern readings of texts suggest that bygone meanings are irretrievable – or discussion of them is

12 Admittedly these terms lack the specificity that one requires to think about the present. There are many differences between Foucault, Lacan, Irigaray, and Deleuze that warrant more precise explication; nevertheless, when I use the terms postmodern and poststructuralist, I refer to theories that assume that subjects are constituted discursively, through the language they use, the things said, without reference to their historical context. This is a break with the more human-centred thinking of Beauvoir, who assumes that subjects are influenced by discourses but also rooted in a socio-historical reality. While she respects that discourses are woven into the fabric of social relations and contribute to agency, for her they are not constitutive of agency in the way that poststructuralists assume.

minimized, since there is fear of essentializing or homogenizing the past. Historians would think otherwise. Furthermore, the technical language and neologisms that are used in shifts in contemporary theory often obfuscate rather than facilitate understanding. For this reason I will try to avoid them as much as possible.

This taste for the new and the immediate amongst young scholars is in part a function of the role of the performative in theory, and symptomatic of the hegemony of the postmodern. There are no longer bodies of knowledge and a historical past that should be retrieved and understood to enhance understanding and direct one's action; all too often they are dismissed as Eurocentric, and gendered. The past must be revisited so that we can fully appreciate the effects of the colonized and gendered past on the present; indeed, such investigations provide insights well worth retrieving. Further, the ready accessibility of information on the Internet and the Internet's effect of making individuals less patient and less able to linger and puzzle through difficult ideas (Carr 2010) may also have a role to play.

Many are less interested in understanding the history of ideas and are ill disposed towards studying them in great depth, believing that their performative politics need not engage the past, nor need be based upon an analysis of the present. The radical skepticism arising from the postmodern turn has meant theory has been supplanted by theorizing. It is no longer necessary to provide a heuristic framework to make sense of the past/present and to orient our actions, nor is historical analysis useful towards this end – hence wild gestures are encouraged. While I am not contesting the import of the unexpected, nor the more creative approach to philosophy, in the work of the surrealists, psychoanalysts, and Deleuzeans, I am concerned that the thinkers' role in facilitating analysis and understanding of events and phenomena, however tentative, ought not be dismissed. Nor would I jettison the role of acquiring an understanding of the past. Enlarging one's perspective is possible, and I believe will also contribute to meaningful and more effective action.

The creative role of theory production, espoused by Deleuze and Guattari (1991), and an aleatory understanding of change that emphasizes contingency and chance events inspired by Althusser (2006) contribute to a failure to analyze historical precedents. Further, Foucault's genealogical approach to history spurns the return to origin as not only impossible but also masking the complexity of other subjugated knowledges. Insofar as historians and theorists are devoted to the pursuit of truth/certainty and employ precise scientific methods, Foucault argues, they homogenize and unify history and thus contrary readings are denied. Postmodernists have disrupted the work of trying to piece together or make sense of texts – for their approach to reading, which heralded the reader instead of the author, strove to disrupt rather than render more coherent a text. One could argue that poststructuralists, in their insistence upon going beyond structuralism, do implicitly acknowledge alleged foundations of knowledge – if only in order to repudiate them. "Assuming that history exists and that cultural forms are produced according to knowable logics – postmodernism has a history and can be grasped theoretically" (Short 2014, 1). Nevertheless its analysis is not possible within the parameters of postmodernism. Jameson argues that an analysis of postmodernism "is inconsistent with the spirit of the postmodern" (Jameson 1991, 37–8).

The insights of Fredric Jameson are worth considering – sympathetic to poststructuralism, he remained thoroughly Marxist and Hegelian. Taking his distance from Jean-François Lyotard's statement that denounced the end of metanarratives, he insisted that that claim itself presumed a metanarrative (1991, 3). While he too felt it was impossible to endorse state socialism and the modernist ideals of German Idealism, he does not give up connecting cultural and political phenomena to history and the economy. Unlike Habermas, who remained committed to modernist values, Jameson believes postmodernism is not a methodology that can be refused, for it is a concept used to describe the phenomena of the cultural revolution associated with late capitalism. Granted postmodernism fails to provide a foundation, values, or an orientation from which to access culture and politics – yet those absences, Jameson believes, cannot be willed away. Nevertheless he "attempts to think the present historically in an age that has forgotten how to think historically" (Jameson 1991, ix), arguing that "all isolated and discrete cultural analysis involves a repressed or buried theory of historical periodization" (3). His theory of historical immanence and his emphasis upon a lived experience of culture avoid teleologies and totalistic logic that plagued more traditional dialectical theory. The significance that Jameson attributes to history in its non-teleological form and concrete culture resonates with Beauvoir's interest in history. She too relies upon Hegelian and Marxist thinking, devoid of teleologies and determinism; nevertheless, Beauvoir is more appreciative of the power of the individual. In urging one to take one's bearing in history and act, she appreciates the potential of the individual as well as collective subjects in the process of change.

TIMELINE

Beauvoir's oeuvre is often partitioned into her early ethical phase and her later political phase. This characterization of her work is glib. While she focused more upon ethics and philosophy in the '40s and became more politically engaged in the '50s, this is more like a transition than a radical break. Her ethics reaches into the political; in willing oneself free, she insists one pursue the freedom of all. Further we have to take a stand against oppression and injustice and this presumes political solidarity. Beauvoir's turn to activism and fiction, in the '50s, is not a turn from philosophy and ethics to politics, but a way of concretely engaging philosophy to think through political dilemmas and movements of the day. In her later fictional and non-fictional works ('60s and '70s) she explores the impediments to human freedom and recounts how she practically engages and supports specific struggles to mitigate oppression. Beginning with the singular concrete situation, she strives to approach the universal. This is also a concern of her early and later essays, *The Second Sex*, and her fiction. I resist the temptation to classify Beauvoir's work as either belonging to ethical/philosophical or to political phases, for I believe she always tried to incorporate the ethical/philosophical concerns in her later work, be it her fiction or her political activism.

Beauvoir was herself irritated by her early moral period, for being abstract and idealistic.[13] In fact, she admonishes herself and Jean-Paul Sartre for still clinging to the idea of radical freedom and to their bourgeois identities. I think her auto-critique is harsh. As early as *Pyrrhus et Cinéas*, she began to realize the role of others and the context in which freedom is achieved – hence her ontology of freedom is neither as abstract nor as individualistic as she presumes. Her irritation with the *Ethics*, twenty-five years after it was written, is an effect of her having lived through the Cold War and having supported the emancipatory struggles of the '60s (i.e. anti-colonialism, feminism, revolutionary socialism) both in France and elsewhere. So her sentiment that the book was ethical and abstract – not sufficiently grounded in history – is understandable.

Nevertheless I argue that *The Ethics of Ambiguity* is important in Beauvoir's political project, and more important than most Beauvoirian scholars assume. For example, Nancy Bauer and Michelle Le Doeuff believe it is a transitional text supplanted by *The Second Sex*; they believe Beauvoir's early essays and the *Ethics* are compromised by her efforts to vindicate Sartre. While I would agree that Beauvoir does try to vindicate Sartre, she did so from her distinctive philosophic position, even though

13 Twenty-five years later Beauvoir reflects negatively on her *Ethics of Ambiguity* as "the book that most irritates me" (*FC*, 67). She condemns her work as abstract; noting Hegel's influence, she complains her descriptions "are even more abstract and arbitrary than his" (67). She also complains that she "inaccurately presents a problem and offers a solution quite as hollow as the Kantian maxims" (67).

she often spoke as if she was a disciple of Sartre. While I agree with Le Doeuff and Bauer that *The Second Sex* is a more accomplished work, *The Ethics of Ambiguity* is not a transitional text. They are different kinds of work: *The Ethics of Ambiguity* is more an abstract philosophic text, while *The Second Sex* is a philosophically informed concrete study of women's social existence. Both are equally important aspects of Beauvoir's thinking. Beauvoir does not leave *The Ethics of Ambiguity* behind, I argue, for it frames her later concerns. In order to appreciate Beauvoir's political thinking beyond the pervasiveness of gender and towards a general emancipatory theory, *The Ethics of Ambiguity* is an important resource. Here Beauvoir lays the groundwork for democratic socialism, furthering emancipatory forces that are not limited by proletarian nor gender politics. Her recognition of human ambiguity and contingency, her critique of Hegelian philosophy, her recognition of the tentativeness of theory and potential failures, are all well established here. Nonetheless her critique of communist practice, and her appreciation of Marx, is underexplored.[14] These ideas provide the conceptual framework of her distinctive radical democratic approach to revolutionary politics, and, as I will show, underpin her existential supplement to Marxism. In returning to the historical context of post-war France and the lively debates amongst the existentialists in *Les Temps modernes*, as well as their political support for the non-communist left, Beauvoir's democratic socialist project is evident.

CHAPTER SUMMARIES

In chapter 1, I stage a conversation between Beauvoir and feminist epistemologists. While she never explicitly addressed the issue of epistemology, she was quite aware of how philosophy, science, and social sciences marginalized and demeaned women as objects and authors of research. Like the feminist standpoint theorists, who believed that knowledge was affected by the social material circumstances of the author, she recognizes how gendered and capitalist macrostructures circumscribe thinking and action. Yet she also appreciates the need to unsettle the general and approaches the specific, like postmodern feminists. While she is suspicious of objective truths and unsituated knowing, truth-seeking and model-building, as a feminist activist she nevertheless believes common understandings can be approached that would further her political work.

14 Revealing the significance of ethics in Beauvoir's existentialism and her attempts to reconcile politics and philosophy, Vintges wrongly claims that there are "no explicit references to Marxism in *The Ethics of Ambiguity*" (1996, 70).

In chapter 2, I place Beauvoir in the context of the most significant debates in feminism in the twentieth century, the sex/gender distinction. Understanding the context, the need to challenge biology, and the importance attributed to women's role in reproduction, second-wave feminists introduced gender or the social construction of femininity. Beauvoir never subscribed to this sex/gender dichotomy, though, nor did she reduce biology to a socially constructed category as Judith Butler did. Beauvoir differentiates the physiological living body from the social circumstances in which women's bodies were configured; in doing so she avoids the reduction of the living body to social/cultural constructs, and yet appreciates that the social and cultural practices can be reconfigured to alleviate women's domination.

In chapter 3, Beauvoir confronts psychoanalysis. Again this discourse has had a huge effect on feminism and cultural and literary studies, though it is generally not appreciated amongst political theorists, given their rationalist predisposition; nevertheless, since it has altered the parameters of emancipatory thinking it is worth including. In the previous chapters, I apply Beauvoir's insights to these debates; however, in this case, I rely more heavily on Beauvoir's own comments, since she actually engaged the psychoanalytic thinkers of her day. She never endorsed the unconscious, and believed engagement in social life could undo the repetitive conduct that psychoanalysts argued trapped humans. In spite of her reservations, I show how Beauvoir found psychoanalysis useful to think about gender identities. As I will show, her thinking has more affinity to object relations theory and Lacanian philosophy than to Freudian thinking, though she was never acquainted with the former and only minimally connected to the latter. Wary of treating the social as epiphenomenal to the psychic, which she believes psychoanalysis was guilty of, she differentiates one's psychic disposition and social circumstances. In doing so she appreciates the capacity of women to change their social roles and circumstances and thereby facilitate their freedom, without undergoing analysis.

In chapter 4, I look at Beauvoir's engagement with Marxism in theory and practice. To understand her position fully, I place her thinking in the context of communist and non-communist left politics of her day. I place Beauvoir in the context of critiques of the base/superstructure as well as the humanist and anti-humanist debates. As an activist she was not involved in theoretically defending herself from the charge of humanism, but there is much theoretical evidence that she subscribed to neither teleologies nor the idea that individuals were fulfilled and fully reconciled with the community. In this chapter, we appreciate how she differed from Sartre.

Beauvoir's existentialism acted as a supplement to Marxism, allowing her to address the problems of ethics and democracy. In *The Ethics of Ambiguity* she challenges historical materialism for not acknowledging the importance of commitment, and not fostering reciprocity and democratic practices. In *The Second Sex*, I will explore her critique of Engels and other Marxists for failing to adequately think about the significance of gender oppression. In approaching the micropolitical in *Must We Burn Sade*, and in novels like *The Blood of Others*, she explores the interface between the specific and general, authentic choices and socio-historic forces, challenging both Kantian abstract universalism and Marxist functionalism. Again Beauvoir believes in the synchronization of individual and collective forces to further projects of freedom, but acknowledges the importance of contingency and failures. While Jean and de Sade are framed by their class position, through passionate commitment and action consistent with existing forces, they are more and less successful in transcending the narrowness of their class and living an authentic if not politically effective life.

In chapter 5, Beauvoir's activism provides the context in which her philosophy is played out. Her efforts to broaden revolutionary agents beyond the proletariat is evidenced in her work with unwed mothers, students, and postcolonials. Her strong commitment to counter-hegemonic movements involves publicizing these struggles, mobilizing them, and thereby enriching radical politics. Criticizing top-down party politics and encouraging local grassroots and social movements, she believed, would further democratic socialism. Her support was not unqualified or uncritical, as we shall see. Committed to providing a rich public sphere to politicize minorities rather than simply extend public opinion, Beauvoir invites comparisons with Hannah Arendt and Jürgen Habermas. She supported liberal feminism, but not radical separatist feminism, because she felt the former had a greater potential of contributing to the freedom of all. Situating her in debates that transpired in the Anglo-American world, where radical feminists and post-socialists call for both redistributive and recognitional claims, we see a similar move in Beauvoir. Beauvoir's freedom as enrichment through attachment, rather than as simply negation, recognizes the ethical and aesthetic register of experience as well as the importance of political institutions and socio-economic structures.

In chapter 6, I stage debates between Beauvoir and the French post-structuralists Foucault and Lyotard, as well as Indian and American feminists Gayatri Spivak and Linda Alcoff, pertaining to the role of the critical intellectual. Tarred with the brush of the universal intellectual, Foucault claims the Marxist intellectual, Beauvoir included, presumes to know "the just-and-true-for-all" (Foucault 1984, 68). I will show that Foucault's charge does not fit. Beauvoir and a Tunisian lawyer, Gisèle Halimi, defended Djamila Boupacha, a member of the FLN who had been raped by French soldiers. They shared neither identities, nor political allegiances, but rather worked towards a specific common end – the defence of Boupacha and the liberation of Algeria. Their collaborative work had more affinity to a specific intellectual goal than to a universal one that assumed an objective perspective. Although Beauvoir was aware of her privilege, and would have preferred that Boupacha tell her own story, she also knew that Boupacha was not in a position to do so. Beauvoir did not retreat, letting the oppressed speak for themselves, but rather facilitated Algerian independence, particularly by trying to foster international empathy and support for the cause. Her journalistic efforts were not always praised – in fact they were often condemned as highly emotional and self-serving. While Beauvoir believed it was important to use argument to persuade, she also recognized the importance of affect and emotion in mobilizing support. Debates around the use of emotion, affect, and reason to further agency will be explored.

In the final chapter, I will address those who argue for the significance of literature in thinking politically. Debates about the capacity and worthiness of fiction to supplement or supplant political theory have played out in debates between Judith Butler (1999) and Martha Nussbaum (1999). These debates also provided a context to rethink humanism. Martha Nussbaum's *Cultivating Humanity* calls for a liberal education to cultivate world citizenship; this approach is in sharp contrast with Butler, who felt that humanist approaches valorized Eurocentric values and politics. More recently, affect theorists inspired by Deleuze (Panagia) have entered the fray, jettisoning distinctions between fiction and non-fiction, as well as focusing on the effects of sensation and diminishing the significance of narration entirely. Like Butler, Beauvoir navigates a position that avoids Eurocentric conclusions – nevertheless she believes that literature and its exemplary characters can contribute to self-development and emancipatory projects. Hence she distances herself from Judith Butler's position that rejects literature as having any *specific* usefulness. Beauvoir believes that literature has a metaphysical role in trying to express the inexpressible, the joys and mishaps of life, and contributes to thinking through the micropolitical, narrating personal obstructions to freedom, and exploring how macroprocesses of power affect the individual. For Nussbaum, literature helps unsettle prejudice, but for Beauvoir this is not enough – she has revolutionary goals, believing power differentials must be tackled if freedom of all is to be possible.

1

Feminism and Epistemology: Debunking Male Epistemic Privilege

WHILE SIMONE DE BEAUVOIR WAS WRITING *The Ethics of Ambiguity* and *The Second Sex*, there was a dearth of feminist activism and little appreciation of how one's gendered identity might affect the production of knowledge. Feminist critiques of epistemology were not to emerge until the late 1960s and 1970s, coinciding with the explosion of second-wave feminism. Second-wave feminists challenged the purportedly universal voice of philosophy as well as the ostensibly objective stance of social scientific research. Critics of modernity tackled the idea of a self-certain subject who is able to take an objective stance and produce apodictic certainty. In stressing embodied action and sensory experiences as ingredients of subjectivity, Beauvoir already aligns herself with critics of modernity.

In *The Ethics of Ambiguity* she is critical of those who assume an impartial perspective, but she does not appreciate a gendered lens until *The Second Sex*. Far from elaborating the basic truths of human nature and the principles by which all knowledge claims are judged, she recognizes that science and the human sciences are affected by power relations. In *The Second Sex* – by looking at how women have been represented in scientific and social scientific theories as well as in novels – she traces women's epistemological marginality and exclusion.

GENDERED KNOWLEDGE: INDEBTEDNESS TO PHENOMENOLOGY AND EXISTENTIALISM

Most scholars acknowledge the role that G.W.F. Hegel and Sartre played in Beauvoir's philosophical development. Nonetheless, there is some disagreement as to the nature of that debt. Nancy Bauer sees Beauvoir's encounter with Hegel as central to her intellectual development (by allowing her to distance herself from Sartre and come into her own in *The*

Second Sex), yet I think this position risks overplaying Hegel and underplaying the significance of Søren Kierkegaard in her thinking. Inspired by Kierkegaard, Beauvoir refuses to compromise the specificity of lived experience to the philosophic system, as Hegel does (Heinämaa). Echoing his enthusiasm for literature, she believes it makes space for paradoxes and the opacity of experience and thereby modifies traditional philosophy (*FC*, 282). Beauvoir pointedly remarks that she leaves philosophy as system building to Hegel and Sartre (Simons 1999, 9).

Beauvoir was clearly indebted to Alexandre Kojève's interpretation of Hegel's master/slave struggle for recognition. This was evident in her first novel, *She Came to Stay* (published in France in 1943 and in the United States in 1954), as well as being present in the introductory chapter in *The Second Sex*. Nonetheless her reformulation of Hegel's and Kojève's thinking is not always understood. She admits that women have never been treated with mutual respect and as equal combatants in struggle, as men have, but envisions women as moving towards that end. Eva Lundgren-Gothlin (1996, 2003) fails to appreciate this. She argues that Beauvoir's application of the Hegelian model to the relation between men and women is inappropriate, as the Hegelian master/slave dynamic presumes a fundamental reciprocity between subjects that is absent in historical relations between men and women. Since woman does not demand recognition from man, Lundgren-Gothlin holds, woman is stable and approaches the undialectical condition of "absolute Other" – hence departing from the Hegelian model of the slave. In acknowledging the ambiguity of human existence, as Beauvoir does, then the relations between "Man" and "Woman" are not permanent. While women, historically, have not pursued recognition as slaves or Jews have, this doesn't mean that they are not in pursuit of recognition and the status of full citizenship. As Kruks says, although men try to deny or to drastically curtail women's ambiguous embodied freedom, they cannot actually succeed in doing so (Kruks 2012, 59n). Beauvoir's ontology of being-in-the-world and being-with-others, borrowed from Heidegger, does not fit with the zero-sum logic of Hegel's master and slave relation or Gothlin's interpretation of women as the absolute Other. Beauvoir's attention to embodiment and ambiguity requires a theory of subjectivity that respects connectedness, as well as solidarity – finitude-defying pure states and final solutions are at odds with her thinking. Freedom is not the radical negation of the past that brings forth a new positivity, but rather the act of synchronizing with the actions of others in order to enhance collective and personal freedom. Humans cannot escape negativity, lack, and ambiguity. Beauvoir insists that "we must affirm the concrete and particular thickness of the world and the individual reality of our projects and ourselves" (*EA*, 106).

This brings us to Beauvoir's specific use/alteration of Hegel's dialectic: she rejects the idea of the dialectic as transcending all opposition and eliminating human conflict from history (*EA*, 163). Kruks (2012, 43), Vintges (1996), and Deutscher (2008) confirm this reading; however, Bauer does not. In fact, Bauer glosses over Beauvoir's criticisms of Hegel in *The Ethics of Ambiguity*. Since she interprets this text as a transitional/immature work, she is untroubled by its "un-Hegelian feature" (Bauer 2001, 185). When Beauvoir writes, "This is why the life of the human being is never plenitude and rest: it is lack and movement; it is struggle," Bauer notes that this statement is hard to square with Hegel's *Phenomenology*. "The idea of ceaseless struggle is not a part of the *Phenomenology*, in which the master slave dialectic is only a stage in the journey of Geist" (Bauer 2001, 185). Admittedly Beauvoir is not consistent with Hegel, but this is entirely consistent with her reworking of Hegel's dialectic in *The Ethics of Ambiguity*, where the individual and concrete sensible thickness of the world is valued and conflict is never presumed to be fully eliminated. Vintges expresses it thus: "Hegel considered incorrectly that the negativity which our life as individuals comprises is a phase that can be overcome; man can recognize himself in his humanity and thus rise above his individuality. In contrast Beauvoir argued that the individual exists at all times, and as a result, negativity, the human lack, continues to exist as does man's desire to escape it" (Vintges 1996, 57).

Again, Beauvoir's use of the term "conversion" (*EA*, 13) rather than *Aufgehoben* is significant; instead of sublating all that is positive from the past and shedding the negative, the dialectic must respect the negative and that which cannot be sublated – the concrete thickness of existence. Instead of the resolution of dualisms into a higher synthesis, Beauvoir assumes "the conquest of freedom is never finished" (157). Beauvoir uses the theoretical trope (master/slave) to reflect upon the structured power relations between man and woman, without presuming her usage to be analytically precise. This is entirely consistent with Beauvoir's eclectic approach to philosophy.

USING SARTRE'S CATEGORIES TRANSGRESSIVELY

Beauvoirian scholars are more preoccupied with Beauvoir's indebtedness to Sartre and Maurice Merleau-Ponty than to Hegel. Debra Bergoffen (1997) has shown that Beauvoir has two voices in her work: the dominant voice of liberation and project that follows from Sartre, and the muted voice of phenomenology that struggles against Sartre's dualism, instead highlighting the intersubjective and embodied aspect of existence. This minority voice takes its cues from Merleau-Ponty and Edmund Husserl. Debra Bergoffen makes this case, but by representing Beauvoir as spoken by a majority and muted voice, I fear, Bergoffen does not respect Beauvoir's intent to move existentialism from a subjectivist philosophy and a theory of absolute freedom towards an intersubjective and materially informed theory of freedom. I believe Bergoffen exaggerates Beauvoir's affinity to Sartre's *Being and Nothingness* by identifying it as the dominant voice. Even in her early philosophic essays Beauvoir challenges his assumptions of ontological dualism and absolute freedom. Furthermore, Bergoffen's trope of a dominant and muted voice leaves the impression that her thinking is derivative of these two men. I argue her existentialism triangulated the thinking of Sartre and Merleau-Ponty, producing a unique philosophy. Very early on Beauvoir appreciated human ambiguity (*EA*) and the role of the situation (*SS*) – thereby challenging Sartre's absolute theory of freedom. Beauvoir's interest in concrete and engaged philosophy preceded Sartre's. Nevertheless since she expressed her indebtedness and loyalty to Sartre's philosophy her philosophic independence is underappreciated. While her body subject was influenced by Merleau-Ponty, her attention to gender and emancipatory politics differentiated her from his thinking.

For Sartre, those who will their nothingness through free creative activity live authentically. Conversely, those who deny their free will and allow themselves to be determined by social forces live inauthentically. They turn their life into a determinate thing – dead matter. Humans who emulate things are inert, weighty and immanent rather than free and transcendent; they deny the creativity of the negative, the realm of the "for-itself," and try to provide fixity or stability to their self. Sartre describes inauthentic humans as living out prescribed social roles rather than transforming them, living in "bad faith" rather than assuming one's freedom. Sartre is adamant that people struggle for an impossible synthesis of being-in-itself and being-for-itself (*EA*, 10, *PW*, 291). Since only God is capable of such a synthesis, humans feel useless in the face of their finitude and incompleteness (*EA*, 10, *PW*, 291). They are neither immortal nor omniscient, and thus suffer from their fate. Such a portrayal of ambiguity as a radical split – leading one to cleave to one side or the other, involving a desire to eliminate ambiguity – is a sentiment shared by Sartre but also by Immanuel Kant. Beauvoir is insistent that ambiguity must be assumed, not eliminated. Sartre's pessimism, reflected in his assessment that "man is a useless passion" (*EA*, 10, *PW*, 291), is based upon the assumption of man's overwhelming wish to be omniscient and eliminate ambiguity. This feeling in part explains Sartre's failure to produce an ethics.[1]

Beauvoir has the following, rather different, attitude to the ambiguity of existence: I am at once consciousness and body, thoughts and fleshy materiality, both free and yet also constrained. I experience the emptiness of lack; I am neither a god, nor do I wish to be God. My ambiguity need not be a source of despair. Instead of trying to flee one's facticity one accepts one's thrownness (what is given) and tries to make one's mark on this world. Given the existence of human ambiguity and human finitude there are no guarantees that freedom is immanent in history, hence Beauvoir urges humans to will their freedom, while realizing it will never be a pure or uncorrupted act.

In *Pyrrhus and Cinéas* Beauvoir tackles not only the solipsism of existence but also Sartre's conflictual ontology as captured in the refrain "Hell is other people." Like Sartre, Beauvoir understands human relations as potentially "dangerous" and "foreign" (PC, 128), but she also recognizes the positive role the "Other" may play in my life. The Other does not simply threaten my projects, but facilitates my acts of transcendence: "I need them [the others] because once I have gone beyond my own goals, my action will fall back upon them inert and useless, and if they are not carried by new projects towards a new Future ... through other men my transcendence is always being extended further than the project I am now forming" (PC, 135). The Other asks nothing of me, yet each of my acts in falling in the world creates for him a new situation. I must assume these acts (PC, 90). In doing so, I am responsive to the Other, instead of the Other being an objectifying glare that makes me feel insufficient – a persistent theme to be found in Sartre – his being is a condition of my subjectivity. My actions do not try to freeze or objectify the Other but are appeals, calls for others to respond. So the Other may offer a beneficent glance as it helps me extend myself beyond the present.

For Beauvoir, humans are not self-sufficient or solipsistic beings, but are interdependent and co-implicated in the world. Although we might try to cut ourselves off from others, we cannot successfully do so, because we are *being-for-others*. For Sartre the "look" robs me of my security, threatens my sense of well-being, while Beauvoir conceives of it as potentially facilitating. The "look" from another constitutes recognition and facilitates my being able to take risks and act in the world. I must overcome

1 Nancy Bauer is careful to delineate differences in Beauvoir's position vis-à-vis Sartre's thinking in *Pyrrhus and Cinéas* and *The Ethics of Ambiguity*. While she argues that Beauvoir doesn't come to her own until *The Second Sex*, she demonstrates how Beauvoir acknowledges that Sartre's existentialist premises do not lend themselves to producing an ethical theory.

my initial hatred, fear, and conflict with others to allow them to participate in and facilitate my project. Contrary to Sartre, who feels that the gaze of the Other steals the world from me, Beauvoir insists that others are the condition of my subjectivity and bear witness to my achievements.

The radical ontological dualisms of freedom and bad faith, mind and body, are evident in Sartre's early work. He scorns the idea that the situation may affect one's freedom; the prisoner in solitary confinement is as free as anyone else since freedom is absolute and ontological. Beauvoir emulates this statement. She writes: "You can throw a man in prison, leave him there, cut off his arms, lend him wings; but his liberty remains infinite in every case. The automobile and the airplane do not change anything with regard to our liberty, and neither do the chains of the slave" (*PC*, 124).

The prison in itself does not impede the prisoner; only if imprisonment is lived as an obstacle does it become one. Nor does the car or plane enhance one's powers, unless the subject allows them to. The ethical subject is able to creatively define what constitutes a limit to one's project in order to realize one's goals; in this sense, one is autonomous and self-determining. Sartre is aware that historical situations affect one's actions and projects, but by focusing on the extent to which their meaning is a consequence of prior free choices, the socio-historical context is bracketed and does not have any effect – unless the individual so wills it.

Departing from Sartre's theory of absolute freedom, and his "practical solipsism" (Vintges 1996, 61) Beauvoir moves towards recognizing the constitutive role of Others and how one's own ontological freedom is circumscribed by the situation. While in 1975 Beauvoir was critical of the abstract tone of her ethical insights, she did acknowledge that historical and cultural contexts matter in *The Ethics of Ambiguity*. She provides the example of the Islamic woman and Black slave who are so oppressed they lack the capacity to reflect on or emotionally critique their situation. Yet Beauvoir adds a caveat in the next line that even though their behaviour can be judged within this given situation, it is possible that in this situation, which is limited like every human situation, they nevertheless realize a perfect assertion of their freedom (*EA*, 38). This notion lends credence to Bauer's position that *The Ethics of Ambiguity* is a transitional text, for Beauvoir appears to be still tied to Sartre's theory of absolute freedom – in spite of the material/cultural oppression, these humans can still be free. This supports Bauer's interpretation that it is not until *The Second Sex* that Beauvoir comes into her own and realizes that freedom is definitively mediated by one's situation. Nonetheless I read this differently: although Beauvoir recognizes that freedom is materially and historically mediated, in *The Second Sex* there is always the possibility, however limited, of reconfiguring oneself and loosening the ties of one's situation. Beauvoir avoids Sartre's insight about free choice and the Marxist insight that agency is determined by the socio-economic system. She refuses Sartre's voluntarist assumptions that the individual will is the source of one's actions. In addition, she denies the functional implications of Marxists and some feminists who see women as a victim of their role in the economy, or their sexuality. Following Heidegger, she sees that humans are thrown into a world, a world not of their own choosing, yet they must make something of themselves. Echoing Marx, she acknowledges that social structural power affects one's situation, yet she gives more power to the subject in living that situation differently. Woman as a human being has the potential for freedom – yet her day-to-day life, defined as it is by patriarchal and capitalist practices, is restricted. Although her situation compels her to submit to forces that subordinate her, she is not simply a cipher:

> Every time transcendence falls back into immanence, stagnation, there is a degradation of existence into the "en-soi" – of freedom into facticity; this fall is a moral fault if the subject consents to it; if this fall is inflicted on the subject, it takes the form of frustration and oppression; in both cases it is an absolute evil. Every individual concerned with justifying his existence experiences his existence as an indefinite need to transcend himself. But what singularly defines the situation of women is that being, like all humans, an autonomous freedom, she discovers and chooses herself in a world where men force her to assume herself as Other: an attempt is made to freeze her as an object and doom her to transcendence, since her transcendence will be forever transcended by an essential and sovereign consciousness. (SS, 17)

In this passage we see how Beauvoir employs Sartre's binary categories of transcendence and immanence, or freedom (authenticity) and stagnation (bad faith), in a transgressive way. Beauvoir describes men instantiating freedom and women revelling in the world of things. Many feminists have read this gendered characterization of men and women as essential and universal, whereas I believe Beauvoir's statements are socially and historically specific. She explicitly says so in the introduction to Book II (in the Parshley translation): "When I use the words *woman* or *feminine* I evidently refer to no archetype, no changeless essence whatever; the reader must understand the phrase 'in the present state of education and custom' after most of my statements. It is not our concern here to proclaim eternal verities, but rather to describe the common basis that underlies every individual feminine existence" (SS 1974, 279). Consistent with Heinämaa's and Vintges's interpretations of Beauvoir, transcendence is not escaping the body, or rising above others, but assuming "the contingent facticity of existence" (EA, 156). "He must assume his freedom and not flee it; he assumes it by a constructive movement: one does not exist without doing something; and also a negative movement which rejects oppression for oneself and others" (156). Since humans are embodied subjects, transcendence is embedded and is never pure negativity, actions must take into account facticity, social existence, and one's personal history. Free action does not arise *de novo*, nor is it a pure negation, but presumes engaging what is given (existing relations) and willing a project on the basis of facticity. Since action is situated, women think and act from within the context they find themselves, respecting the social, cultural, and historical specificity of their life. In this way, Beauvoir not only eschews the universal voice of thinking that treats humans abstractly, but she equally denies essentialist conceptualizations of woman and man. "I was right to reject essentialism, I knew already what abuses could follow in the train of abstract concepts such as the Slav soul, the Jewish character, primitive mentality, or *Das ewige Weib*, the eternal feminine. But the universalist notions to which I turned bore me equally far from reality. What I lacked was the idea of the 'situation,' which alone allows one to make concrete definition of human groups without enslaving them to a timeless and deterministic pattern. But there was no one outside the framework of class struggle, who would give me what I needed" (PL, 165–6).

Beauvoir makes an effort to break down the sexually coded binary oppositions of the free man who acts in the world and the oppressed woman who stays home and is relegated to uncreative labour. Since he is the producer, it is he who goes beyond the family interest to the interest of society, and who opens a future to her by cooperating in the construction of the collective future: it is he who embodies transcendence.[2] "Woman is destined to maintain the species and care for the home, which is to say, to immanence. In truth all human existence is transcendence and immanence at the same time; to go beyond itself, it must maintain itself; to thrust itself toward the future; it must integrate the past into itself; and while relating to others, it must confirm itself in itself" (SS, 443).

Beauvoir does not urge women to emulate existing forms of male transcendence and escape traditional female activities of caring; rather, she calls for the integration of these spheres in a single existence. This involves the integration of mind and body, not an escape from the body or

2 This thesis is found in Saint Paul, the Church Fathers, Rousseau, Proudhon, Comte, and D.H. Lawrence amongst others.

a relegation of women to activities of care. Each existence to expand into the future must integrate its past; for each existence to transcend itself, it must maintain itself.

OVERCOMING DUALISM WITH THE ASSISTANCE OF MERLEAU-PONTY'S LIVING BODY

By focusing on concrete freedom – freedom as arising in situations and experienced from the perspective of a relational embodied subject – Beauvoir distances herself from Sartre's theory of radical ontological freedom and draws closer to their friend and contemporary, Maurice Merleau-Ponty (1908–1961). In her efforts to make existentialism more materially sensitive and to consider gender as a factor in freedom, Beauvoir draws upon Merleau-Ponty's formative work, *The Phenomenology of Perception* (1962).

Beauvoir wrote a positive review of *The Phenomenology of Perception* in 1945 for *Les Temps modernes*, distinguishing Merleau-Ponty's theory of situated or incarnate freedom from Sartre's theory of absolute freedom. Without explicitly criticizing Sartre, she draws attention to the problems of ontological dualism and its voluntaristic assumptions by endorsing Merleau-Ponty's notion of consciousness:

> While Sartre in *Being and Nothingness* emphasizes above all the opposition of for-itself and in-itself, the nihilating power of consciousness in the face of being and its absolute freedom, Merleau-Ponty on the contrary applies himself to describing the concrete character of the subject who is never, according to him, a pure for-itself ... for Merleau-Ponty my history is incarnated in a body which possesses a certain generality, a relation to the world anterior to myself, and that is why this body is opaque to reflection, and why my consciousness discovers itself to be "engorged with the sensible." It is not a pure for-itself, or, to use Hegel's phrase which Sartre has taken up, a hole in being: but rather a hollow, a fold, which has been made and which can be unmade. (Beauvoir 1945, 366–7)

In the passage quoted above, Beauvoir is candid in showing her preference for Merleau-Ponty over Sartre. This is unusual; most often she glosses over her differences from Sartre by stressing their likeness or actively moving to correct his shortcomings. In this way, as we found in *The Ethics of Ambiguity*, she seems to allow contradictions to persist in her text. These are not signs of confused thinking, but rather part of her larger project to carry forward Sartre's existentialism and transform it as need be. Further, given her loyalty and affection for Sartre, she could hardly acknowledge her intellectual debt to Merleau-Ponty or could do so only in passing. We saw this strategy of correcting or supplementing Sartre's thinking in her ethical work, where she transformed his ontology and its assumption of conflictual human relations to appreciate responsive and enriching relations.

Merleau-Ponty is critical of Sartre's philosophic dualisms. He believes that Sartre did not pursue Husserl's reduction sufficiently: being-in-itself and being-for-itself are objectivist abstractions, not descriptions of preconceptual experience. Merleau-Ponty sees no absolute distinction between intentional behaviour of the mind and the realm of body, the cognitive and the sensible/visible; rather, these worlds are connected via the body. Merleau-Ponty explores this further: "in abolishing the opposition of subject and object, it is impossible to define an object apart from the subject by whom and for whom it is the object; the subject reveals itself only in relation to the objects that it is engaged with" (Merleau-Ponty 1962, 363).

Clearly Beauvoir is at odds with Sartre's dichotomies of the "for-itself" as pure nothingness, translucent, and without weight and the "in-itself" as an inertial force that weighs down the spontaneous upsurge. The creative capacity of the "for-itself" is always *of* the world and entwined with others and things of the world. Therefore, my freedom presumes bodily contact and resonance with others and the world. "Engaging in the world" (EA, 78) is an encumbered concrete movement. Although Beauvoir insists upon willing, one's choices and actions emerge from the situation. "It is not a mysterious essence that compels men and women to act in good or in bad faith, it is their situation that disposes them more to seek the truth to a greater or lesser extent" (SS, 15).

Although she attributes her theory of the body "as situation" to Heidegger, Sartre, and Merleau-Ponty (46), Beauvoir proceeds to draw upon Merleau-Ponty's specific ideas of embodiment. Quoting Merleau-Ponty she says: I am thus my body, as least inasmuch as I have my experience, and reciprocally my body is like a natural subject, like a tentative draft of my total being" (41f). "Merleau-Ponty worked through the idea of a structure or "preliminary sketch" without determinism that Beauvoir finds useful: In the *Phenomenology of Perception* "Merleau-Ponty points out that human existence calls for revision of the notions of necessity and contingency. 'Existence has no fortuitous qualities, no content which does not contribute towards giving it its form; it does not give admittance to any pure fact because it is the process by which facts are drawn up'" (24). She continues: "It is also true that there are conditions without which the very fact of existence itself would seem impossible." Beauvoir explores some preconditions of human existence – we must accept the conditions of our earthly existence, "a consciousness without a body or an immortal being is rigorously inconceivable, she says, "whereas a society can be imagined that reproduces itself by parthenogenesis or is composed of hermaphrodites" (24). So while humans are differentiated by their reproductive role and their sexuality, Beauvoir insists, this is less definitive of their experience than their bodily existence. Embodied consciousness and mortality have a permanence that gender does not. Akin to Merleau-Ponty, Beauvoir manages to appreciate the concrete and singular aspects of subjectivity (one's distinctive style or "casting oneself into the world," EA, 41) as well as the general experiences of the embodied subject.

Carrying further the ideas of Husserl, Merleau-Ponty appreciates the powers of the lived body: "Consciousness is in the first place not a matter of 'I think' but of an embodied 'I can'" (Merleau-Ponty 1962, 137). The lived body is "an expressive unity" (206), involving our participation in the anonymous, pre-reflective realm as well as our conduct. "Who one is," how one moves, gestures, speaks, is a bodily act, hence one's body is one's "focal point of living meanings" (151). Again Beauvoir subscribes to a living expressive body, appreciating Merleau-Ponty's elaboration of the pre-reflective, anonymous, pre-linguistic communication that transpires between a body subject and the world. Beauvoir urges us to assume a responsive relation to our anonymous pre-reflective experiences. "I would like to be the landscape that I contemplate; I would like the sky and this calm water to think themselves in me, that it might be I whom they express in flesh and blood, and that I remain at a distance … I delight in this very effort toward an impossible possession. I experience it as a triumph, not as a defeat" (PW, 292). While Beauvoir recognizes the impossibility of the sky and calm water actually thinking itself in me, I cannot possess them; she writes that they are "foreign" and "I remain at a distance" (EA, 12). Yet this "original attachment to the world," "wanting to disclose being," is encouraged. This relation to the world is a sensory and affective one – the responsiveness is seen to be the basis of our more intentional relations.

Beauvoir displaces an instrumental relation to the world recognizing our bodily being as having an aesthetic, affective, as well as cognitive modality. By stressing that consciousness is always embodied and situated, and those features have effects upon our knowing, the body is not a tool of the mind or consciousness, but has an embodied style. Where our eyes focus and where our hands are placed, how we grasp objects with our hands, influence our sensible appreciation of the world. She insists that the world is bound to seem a very different thing when apprehended in one manner rather than another. If we try to close our eyes and ears, try to remove ourselves from the sensory world, we lose out. She describes this deficient situation as that of a sub-man. "They have eyes and ears, but from their childhood on they make themselves blind and deaf, without love and without desire ... they reject the 'passion' which is the human condition" (EA, 42). The sensory and affective life of the human body have a role to play in human existence. Their importance has been ignored or dismissed by rationalist thinkers, though Merleau-Ponty and Beauvoir acknowledge its significance in human action.

Beauvoir relies upon Merleau-Ponty's theory of the body to ground her understanding of freedom, but in attending to the gender specificity of the body, she goes beyond him. Merleau-Ponty's abstract treatments of bodily action and its breakdowns (i.e. aphasia, a phantom limb) reveal that in spite of physical disablement, such as an amputation, the body feels its lost leg and acts as if it has not been severed. This phenomenon reveals the operative intentionality of the body: how the body is an upsurge of vitality, directed towards the world in spite of loss. Beauvoir relies upon this idea of a living body to see how women, whose bodies are construed within gendered relations, interact with other gendered bodies. "Woman, like man, is her body; but her body is something other than herself" (SS, 33). While she identifies an existential fact, a human tendency towards alienation (57), in a patriarchal society woman's body is experienced as particularly "alien." Her sexuality, for the most part, ties her to reproductive functions hence is in the service of the "species" (44) rather than her own desires for sexual pleasure (43). "Woman experiences an even stronger alienation in gestation" (42). "Contrary to an optimistic theory that is so obviously socially useful, gestation is tiring work ... and demands serious sacrifices" (42). In a patriarchal and capitalist order, her body is symbolically and socially primed to do repetitive and uncreative work. While men too experience their body as alien, it is not alien as women's bodily experiences are. Men are more likely to experience their bodies as enhancing their agency: their sexuality and the species interest complement each other (38). Women are more likely to experience their body as an obstacle to their creativity.

Following Merleau-Ponty, she is a critic of naturalism. The living body is not biologically/physiologically determined, but influenced by cultural and social meanings. Beauvoir relies upon Merleau-Ponty's insight that one is "a being who is not fixed, who makes himself what he is" and further that "man is not a natural species: but an historical idea" (45). Again, by making Merleau-Ponty's abstract and general philosophical statement speak to the particular historical context of women's oppression, Beauvoir historicizes what appears to be woman's destiny (363, 754). Critical of the contemporary tendency to compare man and woman "to reduce her to what she has been," Beauvoir stresses that "woman is not a fixed reality, but rather a becoming; she has to be compared with man in her becoming: that is her possibilities have to be defined: what skews the issues so much is that she is being reduced to what she was, to what she is today, while the questions concerns her capacities" (45). But since "capacities manifest themselves clearly only when they have been realized" so "it is never possible to close the books" (46). While the past ties woman to a subordinate status, she should be seen in terms of her present, which is open to the future and capable of being rewritten.

Merleau-Ponty himself did not pay attention to gender, but his theory of embodiment has been useful to feminists.[3] It helps overcome the radically dualist and solipsistic ontology of Sartre that is often identified as masculinist. One can't call Merleau-Ponty's theory of subjectivity "feminine," for his approach is universalist and rarely attends to women specifically or acknowledges their sexual differences. Nevertheless, his attention to embodiment and the importance he places on perception, sexuality, and sensuality in selfhood decentres Descartes's rational *cogito* and respects figural images as well as ideas. Merleau-Ponty moves beyond phallic or goal-directed behaviour that does not involve others towards more relational, erotic, and responsive behaviour. Beneath intentionality – that is, willed, goal-directed, conscious behaviour – Merleau-Ponty posits operative intentionality, which is an involuntary bodily movement towards the world and others. In fact, he grounds cognitive activity in pre-reflective (involuntary and habitual) bodily action, thereby avoiding rationalism. Moreover, his concept of reversibility presumes movement of affect and sensation between embodied subjects without will or conscious intention. Tracing this intersubjective bodily communication is one way of critiquing the enlightenment project and moving beyond rationalist humanism (see Bergoffen 1997 and Coole 2007). Not that action or projects don't involve a decision or will at some level, but there is a level of anonymity, of pre-reflective exploration or affective communication between bodies called reversibility that underpins decisions.

Rejecting this dualistic or split approach, Beauvoir never advocates a simple monism or fusion. While Beauvoir acknowledges the plurality of concrete beings, she would not endorse the Deleuzean formula that pluralism = monism. Here she is different from Deleuze and Deleuzeans who reject will and transcendence altogether and find generativity in immanence. Merleau-Ponty and Beauvoir endorse entwined existences

3 Iris Young (1989), Judith Butler (2004a), and Elizabeth Grosz (1994) have all employed Merleau-Ponty to think beyond the rationalist assumptions of much modernist philosophy.

that encourage communicating with others, enriching human and non-human exchanges through action.

Again their approaches to philosophy are different. Merleau-Ponty believes Hegel is a resource. "The attempt to express the immediate experience is not to betray reason, but to work for its aggrandizement." Referring to Hegel, in his early years, Merleau-Ponty says, "it is he who started to explore the irrational and integrate to an expanded reason which remains the task of the century" (Merleau-Ponty 1964a, 63). Likewise, Beauvoir does not reject reason, or our reflective capacity, but seeks to enlarge it by recognizing our pre-reflective anonymous relations as well as our affective attachments to others and the world. Insofar as human experience is bodily, the for-itself's activities must be supplemented to account for these pre-reflective anonymous experiences. These experiences cannot be fully revealed or understood discursively. She agrees with Merleau-Ponty that "the most important lesson that the phenomenological reduction teaches us is the impossibility of a complete reduction" (Merleau-Ponty 1962, xiv). Nonetheless she does not give up on philosophy or our reflective activity, but strives to augment them.

GENDERED KNOWLEDGE: INDEBTED TO CRITIQUES OF OBJECTIVITY AND IMPARTIALITY

In *The Second Sex,* Beauvoir shows awareness that philosophy and science are gendered, although this was not her major concern. She was more concerned with exploring the experiences of women's Otherness: how the young girl *becomes* woman, how she assumes a subordinate social identity. Of course, discourses of science and social sciences have a significant role in the Othering of women, so they become a resource for her. In contrast to subsequent generations of second-wave feminists, Beauvoir recognizes that knowledge was gendered; however, she does not dismiss the insights of male thinkers as gender blind; instead, she refits them. In fact, she believed that in reworking the categories of phenomenology she could bring to visibility the oppression of women. Insofar as the phenomenological tradition failed to attend to gendered experiences, she departs from her predecessors – although she eclectically uses their theoretical frameworks and concepts for feminist ends.

Beauvoir expresses her dependence on Husserl's *epoché* or bracketing in her own way: "Let man put his will to be in parentheses and he will be brought to the consciousness of his true condition" (EA, 14). Abandoning the scientific pursuit of transcendental subjectivity,[4] Beauvoir is interested in bringing to light the truth of the human condition: our ambiguity, our sensibility, and our contingency. Again her interest appears to be more ontological than epistemological. Yet in the process of exposing the masculinist assumptions of existing epistemologies, she makes suggestions for improved epistemological insights.

Again Beauvoir does not pursue a transcendental subjectivity, nor a universal voice that could surmount subjective perspectives. Neither does she search for abstract knowledge outside of history. We begin from the givenness of the situation to enlarge our perspective by approaching the interpretations of others; she believes this will deepen our understanding. This does not produce certainty; on the contrary, it involves recognizing the limits of our knowledge claims. But Beauvoir is optimistic that an enlarged understanding and common ground will loosen our ties to our specific social location and enable us to be more responsive to the knowledge and experiences of others. Improving our understanding, she believes, will allow us to enrich our lives as well as act more effectively. Since understanding presumes bodily and sensory experiences as well as rational conversations, Beauvoir's notion of enlarged thinking differs from those of Arendt and Habermas. Her approach to understanding, I believe, locates her ambiguously between a modernist and postmodernist disposition.

Beauvoir begins with references to Kant and Hegel. Kant assumed that a more universal standpoint was possible if a researcher put themself imaginatively in the position of others. Overcoming the partiality of one's own perspective and pursuing a broadened perspective made a more universal approach to political practices and ethics both possible and desirable. In his *Critique of Judgment,* Kant speculates that "if he overrides the private subjective conditions of his judgment, in which so many others are locked into as it were, and reflects on his own judgment from a universal standpoint (which he can determine only by transferring himself to the standpoint of others)" (Kant 2007, para. 40), the researcher can overcome the privateness of his own perspective. Judgment does not invoke the ideal of transcendental reason, but tries to approach universality, by seeing one's own judgment from the perspective of others. This does not presume a single objective standard or neutral truth,

4 However, there are some scholars (i.e., Eleanore Holveck, 2002) who believe that Beauvoir employs Husserl's project of bracketing in *The Second Sex* and *The Ethics of Ambiguity.* Insofar as Beauvoir struggled to uncover the presuppositions of various theories, she employed the *epoché* or bracketing, but again in a looser, less systematic way.

but rather encourages multiple experiences, allowing one to get a feel for what resonates with the many. "The existence of multiple perspectives does not undermine universality, for the test of broadness implies [that] the capacity to make judgments [is] universally communicable" (161). Does this not allude to transversal experiences, experiences that are confirmed by others' perspectives? It does take us beyond the subjective and objective to the intersubjective realm, where our diverse experiences are communicated, thus broadening our perspectives.

Hegel challenged the abstractness and formalism of Kantian thinking. For him the universal standpoint could be found in the culmination of the dialectical development of history. Just as the slave, in the master/slave dialectic, has privileged access to understanding, so too, by implication, does the proletariat. History presumes human conflict; the struggle to the death and its resolution are essential to subject formation as well as collective emancipation. Hegelian Marxists assumed the oppressed and slaves had full knowledge of the system and were willing to risk their lives to change it. In post-war years, Hegelian Marxists attributed this privileged position to the proletariat by virtue of their structural position. As the most alienated and exploited, the proletariat understood the system's operation like no others. Their knowledge and negative experiences of the system made them a candidate for revolutionary agency – they had nothing to lose but their chains. By articulating their excluded perspective, which remained invisible in the present worldview, they thereby corrected the false universality of the master's viewpoint and contributed to their empowerment.

Beauvoir was wary of Hegel's dialectical synthesis that subordinates the individual to the community and supplants the individual by the universal. She did not share Hegel's belief that history was resolvable without remainders. She distanced her thinking from the Hegelian *Aufhebung*, "for in Hegel the surpassed terms are preserved" but "only as abstract moments, whereas we consider that existence still remains negative in the positive affirmation of itself." So Beauvoir contests the Hegelian "negation of negation by which the positive is reestablished" (*EA*, 13). In fact, she sees the dialectic as a conversion; its movement does not wholly transcend the past but assumes lack and negativity (13). For Beauvoir the existence of lack or negation does not deny the possibility of positive projects of change, but it does mean that the individual will never be fully realized in them and that there will be remainders. Lack and conflict will persist as part of the human condition; however, as one lives a freer existence, these experiences will be allayed. In addition, as we shall see, she does not believe the individual should be sacrificed to the social good. Nor does she believe that the most oppressed are best suited to know and articulate the system.

Beauvoir's *Second Sex* challenges previous universal perspectives. In posing the question "What is woman?" and asking whether she is destined to subordination, Beauvoir traces various theoretical and fictional responses. She begins by surveying biological, psychological, and historical materialist discourses. Each of these discursive fields has very different explanations of why Woman is "Other" or, in other words, why she is inferior. Beauvoir does not choose any one theory as more adequate than another. In fact, she deconstructs them, pointing to their un-reflected assumptions. They fail to admit that their truths are historically contingent and their methods are partial. Furthermore, they make sexist claims.

Beauvoir's phenomenological approach is not interested in explaining the causes of women's sexual subordination, but rather explores the concrete manifestations of gender. The anatomists, Beauvoir cites, presume women have inferior bodies and brains (SS, 44–5). She contests some of their gendered facts and assumptions. She also approaches the inadequacy of psychoanalysis and historical materialism, where women's distinctive desire or labour patterns were not sufficiently explored. Beauvoir recognized that science, social science, and philosophy are not impartial and objective. Their results, she says, are underpinned by a specific "ethical background and interest" (16). In fact, she claims, men "profit" from this androcentric knowledge for it helps preserve their social and political privilege. Yet she doesn't presume that all research produced is reducible to male values or interests.

Like Arendt or Habermas, Beauvoir prods women and men to enlarge their perspectives. But unlike them, she doesn't believe that a universal perspective is possible, nor does she believe that one's embodied existence can or should be bracketed or kept out of conversations. Neither Arendt nor Habermas are feminists, hence their suggestions do not attend to gendered differences in the way Beauvoir's do. She brings to visibility women's alterity and helps women articulate their discontent with their situation of inequality.

Beauvoir does not believe truth will be the outcome of her analysis; nevertheless she is optimistic that we can enlarge our understanding by appreciating a plurality of perspectives. Much in the spirit of Hannah Arendt, Beauvoir believes that our understanding will be deepened in seeing the world through another's eyes (FC, 369). Arendt does not believe one ought to engage in actual conversations with others: one should try to imagine what others might wish, desire. "Political thought is representative. I form an opinion by considering a given issue from different viewpoints, by making present to my mind the standpoint of those who are absent; that is, I represent them" (Arendt 1993, 241). This imaginative exercise would broaden one's understanding and improve the capacity to judge astutely and act effectively. Beauvoir too, supports enlarged thinking, but unlike Arendt stressed the significance of embodiment and the effects of one's historical social situation on one's knowledge. Instead of just imagining what others might experience, Beauvoir engaged in actual conversations with minorities (in chapter 5 we will see how she communicated their claims thereby facilitating the struggles of silenced *colonized* women). Again Beauvoir did not believe we could fully understand the situation of another, challenging the notion of an all-surveilling (*pensée de survol*) objective or god's eye perspective. But recognizing our understanding may be limited by our situation (our gender, class, and ethnicity) she still believed enlarged thought was possible.

BEAUVOIR'S PLACE IN FEMINIST EPISTEMOLOGICAL DEBATES

Feminist Standpoint Theory

In the 1970s and 1980s, feminists struggled to rectify gender blindness in the humanities and social sciences. Existing social scientific techniques, methods, and philosophic procedures (all identifiable as modernist) had to be reconceived to include women as researchers and women as subjects of research. Knowledge shaped by men and with men as objects of research, feminists claimed, produced categories, findings, and hypotheses that were male-centred and treated women as deficient men. Women as researchers and subjects of study were sorely absent, and their absence was reflected in the knowledge they produced. It was agreed that the "add women and stir"[5] approach would not work. Simply adding women as subjects of research into pre-existing universal categories would perpetuate an androcentric bias. Neither existing qualitative nor quantitative research methods were able to acknowledge gender as a factor in thinking, for they believed their methods were impartial. Believing that women had a privileged location from which not only to better understand the world but also to better address the omission of women from research, Dorothy Smith (1987, 1990), Nancy Hartsock (1986), Sandra Harding (1986), Allison Jagger (1978, 1983), and Rosemary Hennessy

5 This approach is advanced by J. Evans (1986, 1–6) and much criticized by Jones and Jónasdóttir (1988, 1–10).

(1995) forged a feminist standpoint theory that they believed would overcome androcentric thinking and make women's oppression visible.

Articulating women's experiences/knowledge, feminist-standpoint feminists challenged the narrowness of the male perspective, the presumed universal. In fact, they argue, universal knowledge helps sustain women's subordinate status. Nancy Hartsock, one of the original standpoint theorists, saw her work as an "attempt to develop, on the methodological base provided by Marxian theory, an important epistemological tool for understanding and opposing all forms of domination. Marxism was useful to feminism in that it understands the social ensemble of economic, political, and ideological arrangements" (Hartsock 1986, 28). Rosemary Hennessy (1995) confirms this perception. She reiterates Hartsock's comment that the Marxist theory of class domination is easily transferable to the oppression of women – which, amongst other things, is based on gender biases. She acknowledges that despite criticisms of Marxian theory for its lack of attention to gender, it is nonetheless important because Marx's distinction between appearance and essence, ideology and truth, is valid to understand women's experience and position in the mode of production. Following Marx, who believed knowledge was produced by the ruling class to serve their class interest, socialist feminists added that powerful men produced knowledge that also kept women in a subordinate position. The exclusion of women from public spaces, their sexual objectification, and their role in reproducing labour power and providing unpaid domestic labour, all contributed to the accumulation of capital and the power of men over women. Beauvoir explores the knowledge that legitimated their social and sexual subordination and calls for a different approach to knowledge.

Standpoint theorists were inspired by Marxism but had to refit Marxist language and concerns to attend to the experience of women. His category of wage labourer did not accommodate women's work, which was unwaged. Standpoint theorists not only adapted Marxism but provided a critique of the putatively neutral terms of traditional sociology, which, Dorothy Smith believed, made women's experience invisible. Carol Pateman (1988) draws a similar conclusion in studying liberal democratic theory: categories and modes of analysis purportedly applied to all citizens, but, in fact, women were often excluded from citizenry by virtue of their presumed lack of rationality.[6] The categories of wage labourer and housewife, citizen and private individual, are cases in point. Male

6 In a renowned article Pateman (1988) shows how women were deemed sufficiently rational to sign marriage contracts, however insufficiently rational in the seventeenth and eighteenth centuries to be granted the vote.

breadwinners and male participants in the public sphere are their points of reference. Consequently, women who care for their children and are embroiled in domestic life were often excluded from public life and omitted from research. There is a tension amongst standpoint theorists: those who approach women's experience from a macro (historical materialist) perspective versus those who begin with women's lived experience (phenomenological perspective). The former approach, illustrated by Nancy Hartsock, presumes a coherence of women's experience and assumes that the contradictions in the system would bring forth the revolution. These theorists have an affinity to Hegelian Marxism; by negating their present negative existence, these dialecticians believe the oppressed become subjects. Since women have nothing to lose but their chains, they must be active participants in the revolution that negates their present negative existence to bring forth positive existence. The Husserlian phenomenological tradition valorizes the living body's everyday experiences – women speaking and acting from immediacy and involvement in their everyday life have been excluded but are not immiserated. Dorothy Smith is a representative of this group. Women were not simply effects of capitalism and patriarchy: given their different situations they exhibit differential agentic capacities. Although they are economically exploited and sexually objectified by capitalist patriarchal relations, in the late 1960s they were beginning to agitate, catalyzing changes in public institutions, hiring practices, and educational opportunities. The phenomenological thinkers begin with women's specific embodied situation, but recognize that the macrostructural forces affect it.

Problematically, early standpoint theory (Nancy Hartsock) provided a coherent account of women's Otherness: seeing women's experiences from a macroperspective allows for generalization. Hartsock presumes that one could talk of woman's experience rather than women's experiences. This led to problems of essentialism and the marginalization of minority women's experiences. It also created difficulties linking up a feminist standpoint with women's standpoints, and also linking up woman's subordinate experiences to "knowledge" of their oppression. Poststructuralist feminist Joan Scott challenged the importance of experience in the production of knowledge (Scott 1992, 24). Experience cannot provide incontestable evidence of one's oppression. The oppressed are not best suited to understand or explain how or why that oppression transpired. Standpoint theorists not only assumed that the oppressed carried the "truth" of the system within their lived experience; they also believed that the oppressed had the authority to articulate their experience and challenge the representation of other more privileged women lacking these experiences. This reflection upon their experience created a direct link between theory and practice, which, postmodern feminists argue, is naive. Scott argues that experience is shaped by a discursive system, so that must be understood, to come to terms with the state women are in.

Standpoint theory also came under attack for assuming there was something identifiable as woman's experience and thereby not appreciating local and specific differences. Standpoint theorists were charged with essentialism, ignoring the diverse experiences of minority women, and elitism, assuming that white feminists could matter-of-factly represent all women.

However inadequate standpoint theory was, it was a preliminary move in drawing attention to the gendered assumptions in epistemology. Sandra Harding (1986) tried to accommodate her critics by thoroughly historicizing the subjects (women) and challenging the criticism of essentialism. So, too, did bell hooks (1984, 1994). In her early work, hooks recognizes the importance of acknowledging a "black identity" to help black women become agents in their own right. This general identity and these essentializing strategies helped include minority women; and as these movements got more established, hooks argues, black women would be able to manage their differences without this kind of general identity.

Beauvoir's Affinity to Standpoint Theory

Since feminist standpoint theory had not been formulated when Beauvoir was writing *The Second Sex*, one can only speculate as to her position. She was aware of the tension between a Hegelian dialectical perspective that saw women moving towards their liberation (negating their present existence) versus the phenomenological experience of embodied women that appreciates the capacity of women to navigate change from within their present concrete existence. As we have seen, Beauvoir challenges some of the assumptions of the Hegelian dialectical position that presumes the reconciliation of self and others in a final synthesis – a transcendence of the present. Her phenomenological position helps her do so, without denying the potential of collective projects to radically improve their situation. Conflict, ambiguity, lack, and failure will persist (*POL*, 291), hence there will be no absolute freedom or resolution of history; however, those limits did not undermine the possibility of emancipatory projects. In fact, she consciously recognizes the need for refusing the present system, while at the same time constructing an affirmative project from within (*EA*, 156).

Debra Bergoffen identifies this tension in Beauvoir as an effort to mediate the struggles between Sartre and Merleau-Ponty, or the revolutionary versus the phenomenological approach to change. This interpretation, however, does not appreciate Beauvoir's distinctive philosophic or political motives, to appreciate both the macro and micro processes of life. One begins from one's situation; nevertheless that situation has been formed by macro structures, as well as one's personal response to them. In *Volume I,* she focuses upon macrotheories and discourses that have constituted femininity (as it were from the outside). In *Volume II,* she focuses upon the lived experiences of women, which include Formative Years (Childhood, the Young Girl, etc.) and the Situation (the married woman, the mother, social life of prostitutes and hetairas, etc.). Here she explores the specific and diverse ways women live: how they take up exogenous forces. These exceed her own experience, but help her understand the general condition of women. To understand the general condition, she spurns "a priori doctrines" and "dubious theories," but looks "at the concrete manifestations of sexuality" (EA, 26) through phenomenological descriptions. Some thinkers believe these experiences are exemplary: they exceed the specific without proposing abstractions. I tend to agree, since her autobiographies as well as novels, which she calls philosophic, help appreciate the impediments women confront in becoming more engaged – how concrete women navigate their situation or fail to do so.

Taking "the given as a start," Beauvoir encourages individuals "to reconquer their freedom upon the contingent facticity of existence" (156). In doing so one must both reject the oppression of oneself and others, as well as construct new relations. She must refuse alterity, her identity as Woman, refuse her sexual subordination, but also create more reciprocal and responsive relations to others. These personal concrete beginnings, Beauvoir believes, will further political struggles for women's liberation.

Thus Beauvoir identifies women "as beginning to take part in the world," though they are still "heavily handicapped" (SS, 9). Since the eighteenth century, democrats and socialists have seen women as human beings and liberals have recognized their "rights." But these political thinkers have produced abstract thought not respecting the complexity of the situations women find themselves in; Beauvoir writes "longstanding habits keep them from being concretely manifested in customs" (9). Hence, changes in one's habits are required. And what is most important is that these positive changes are shifting attitudes and behaviour: "women are beginning to share in the making of the world" (10). So women are beginning to challenge their position as absolute Other – as Woman. Actually existing concrete women are not immiserated, nor reduced to slavery as the Hegelian Marxists presumed. In assuming their situation and refusing their complicity with the existing male order, they are struggling *towards* their independence.

Navigating between Standpoint Theory and Postmodernism

Beauvoir's approach to gendered knowledge and action is worth pursuing. She manages to navigate a position between feminist standpoint theory and postmodern feminism. Like the standpoint theorists, Beauvoir recognizes that women's oppressed experiences must be made visible, which will inform action; like the postmodern feminists she proceeds to destabilize existing identities, while acknowledging that disclosing women's oppression does not in itself produce change. Women have to locate themselves in relations of power and commit to change them. As we have seen, Beauvoir did not believe there is a totality, nor does she believe in objective knowledge. Human sciences cannot be objective in the positivist sense of not bearing a trace of human subjects that produced them; however, she still believes in philosophic and literary efforts to disclose, unveil, and clarify the world (27–8). Philosophy and literature do not simply reflect or record the real; they employ the imagination. Literature is not about recording the real, "but establishing communication with others by starting from the singularity of [their] own experiences and going beyond it" (*ASD*, 130). So, again, one's writing bears the mark of one's singularity.

Since we are situated subjects, our knowledge is going to be affected by our socially located embodied experiences; however, the acknowledgement of our unique situations does not itself lead to relativism for Beauvoir. She urges us to act authentically, accepting the parameters of the human condition and our embodied experiences while struggling towards freedom.

Emily Zakin and Karen Vintges believe that Beauvoir's project of deconstructing discourses, reorienting the universal through the particular (Zakin 2006, 48) and the disappearance of universal moral theories (Vintges 1996, 5) puts her in the postmodern camp. One might add Beauvoir's concern with the limits of knowing: her rejections of foundations based upon Truth or God (5), and her attitude towards contingency, failure, and ambiguity, bring her into the postmodern camp. While there is some basis for interpreting Beauvoir in that way, her commitment to dialogue between multiple perspectives, and the possibility of research leading to an understanding, sits badly with postmodernism. Like Habermas, she believes conversations or communicative action will further understanding and collective projects, though she is less concerned with arriving at consensus and more concerned with collaboration. As finite beings, uniquely situated, our thoughts and adventures are "all open to the infinity of the future and thereby imply each other without destroying each other" (EA, 122). She continues: "Without raising the question of historical comprehension and causality it is enough to recognize the presence of intelligible sequences within temporal forms so that forecasts and actions are possible" (122). Beauvoir does not seek apodictic certainty, nor does she presume we come to an agreement about our interpretations, but, assuming a "practical attitude" (123), she believes we can decide upon the opportuneness of an act and attempt to measure its effectiveness without knowing all the factors that are present (123). She believes that dialogue between oppositional positions can lead to good political strategies. Yet she has a more modest approach to knowledge and action than do the feminist standpoint theorists. Given "lack" at the heart of being, and the singularity of existences, Beauvoir believes consensus is unlikely – without ruling out of court communication, or collaboration based upon that communication.

However, Zakin rightly identifies the problem with Kristeva's and Young's portrayal of Beauvoir as a universal humanist. They believe her egalitarian thinking is masculinist, that Beauvoir tries to insert woman into a time of project and linear history. Kristeva's claim ignores Beauvoir's problematic of embodied subjectivity, which involves being both subject and object, both transcendence and immanence (SS, 443.) As well, they gloss over her critique of Hegel and Kant, and their assumptions of an abstract universal man. In the conclusion to *The Second Sex*, Beauvoir confronts those who believe women's freedom will produce uniformity, calling for differences in equality: "Differences between man and women will always exist: her eroticism, and thus her sexual world, possessing a singular form, cannot fail to engender in her a sensuality, a singular sensitivity; her relation to her body, to the male body, and to the child will never be the same as those man has with his body, with the female body, and with the child" (765).

Young identifies Beauvoir as a humanist feminist who presumes the abstract category hu(man) as the norm and goal of politics, claiming "Humanist Feminism consists in a revolt against femininity" (Young 1985, 173). In endorsing the existential distinction between immanence (bodily existence) and transcendence (free consciousness), Young argues that Beauvoir sees "gender difference as accidental to humanity" (174) and identifies the human with man (175); hence, for woman to be equal she must become manlike. To accomplish this Young ignores how Beauvoir challenges the common use of man: how it falsely represents an absolute human essence. Beauvoir does not endorse disembodied and reflective masculine activities and spurn feminine ones, but rather encourages women to refuse traditional forms of femininity that are foisted upon them, inviting women to reconfigure their lives. In addition, she urges men to integrate caring activities with action. Furthermore, Young wrongly reads Beauvoir's treatment of women's bodies as essential: an impediment to freedom.

Zakin also contests Singer's interpretation of Beauvoir as a gynocentric thinker. Beauvoir's relational subject (a being-for-others) provides a foundation, or ground, for freedom, but Zakin disagrees: not only does freedom not have a ground, it cannot have a ground; it is nothing more than this lack of fixity (Zakin 2006, 38). While Zakin is right to point to the lack of fixity in human subjectivity, she seems to ignore Beauvoir's weak ontology, which prioritizes individual and collective freedom. Hence Zakin does not appreciate how Beauvoir straddles the enlightenment/postmodern divide.

Beauvoir believes our preflective anonymous existence and bodily being facilitate communication and conversations where we come to agreement on a course of action. She believes knowledge/understanding should inform/assist our "practical attitude" (*EA*, 123); she sides with enlightenment assumptions while avoiding rationalism. Here she parts ways with the postmodern skepticism regarding the link of theory and practice. Postmodern theorists criticize standpoint theory for precisely this assumption: that a "knowledge project that correctly produces knowledge will lead to the adoption of the best political strategies" (Andermahr et al. 1997).

As I have said, Beauvoir was not intent upon producing a new epistemology nor striving for correct knowledge that included women and minorities; rather her expectations were more modest. By exploring the concrete manifestations of sexuality through phenomenological descriptions, she felt she could understand herself better and approach an understanding about women's gendered existence. The standpoint theorists believed they could capture the truth of the system by including women's experiences and explaining their oppression. Beauvoir seeks understanding without establishing causality.

In her introduction to *The Second Sex*, she raises epistemological concerns. In posing the question "What is a woman?" she addresses women's exclusion from philosophy. Beauvoir briefly illustrates how women are differently positioned: "If I want to define myself, I first have to say I am a woman and all other assertions arise from this basic truth" (*SS*, 5). Yet "a man never begins by positing himself as an individual of a certain sex" (5). Herein lies a demonstration of man's universality: his subject position is not in question, he does not have to authorize his work, his subject location is not a concern. Yet it is for women thinkers. While "the categories male and female appear symmetrical in formal documents" Beauvoir believes their relation is asymmetrical in practice: "men represent both the positive and neutral pole" (5).

Both Nancy Bauer and Toril Moi explore in some detail Beauvoir's intentions in this passage. Beauvoir employs philosophic categories and engages in philosophic debates that legitimate her work as a philosopher, and in doing so she brings woman into philosophy. Philosophy has for the most part been the work of men on man. Nancy Bauer convincingly argues that by creatively appropriating philosophers in her way, Beauvoir redefines what constitutes philosophy. By returning to the arguments of Descartes in the *Càrtesian Meditations* and the other canonical fathers of philosophy, she validates her feminist project, which challenges the boundaries of philosophy in philosophic terms. But Beauvoir's relationship to philosophy is not unproblematic. Philosophy has knowingly or unknowingly excluded women as distinctive subjects of research, and when women are explicitly addressed, they are seen to be inferior to men. So she takes her distance from conventional philosophers by raising the issue of philosophers' exclusion of women, as both subjects of study and as thinkers capable of executing the study. Not only does Beauvoir prove herself to be a philosopher, mastering the "tools" of philosophy, but she also challenges philosophy's gender blindness and offers philosophy a gendered lens. However, unlike many feminist philosophers she does not wholly dismiss previous thinkers' insights as masculinist. Beauvoir also is aware of other shortcomings of philosophy: it does not sufficiently appreciate the uniqueness of the situation of choice (436); hence, she turns to fiction.

In posing the question "What is woman?" with attention to one's embodied and situated location, she confronts male bias. "He grasps his body as a direct and normal link with the world that he believes he apprehends in all objectivity, whereas he considers woman's body as an obstacle, a prison, burdened by everything that particularizes it" (5). While a man's anatomy does not seem to figure in or interfere with his thinking, women's "ovaries and a uterus … lock her into her subjectivity" (5). "Some even say she thinks with her hormones" (5). Having rejected objective truths and what Merleau-Ponty calls *pensée de survol* or "high altitude thinking" (Merleau-Ponty 1968, xxviii), she endorses an embodied and situated approach. Rejecting the universal approach of an anatomist that defines agency in physiological terms, she thinks from the experience of the living body: "It is not as a body but as a body subjected to taboos and laws that the subject accomplishes himself" (*SS*, 47). Beauvoir says "it is no doubt impossible to approach any human problem without partiality: even the asking of questions, of adopting perspectives, presupposes hierarchies of interests." Every objective description "is set against an ethical background" (16). If this is so, she asks, who is in the position to explore the question "What is woman?" (5). In jest, she considers several options: "Perhaps an angel, though difficult to find, or an hermaphrodite, but neither would understand all the givens of the problem" (16).

So one's living embodied experiences may facilitate one's understanding, but this is not sufficient to deliver an objective or unbiased position. Beauvoir writes: "Men are party and judge; so are women though that doesn't put them on equal footing … Men profit in many ways from women's alterity" (13), so they are unlikely candidates. In the end, she supports women who "know the feminine more intimately than men" because "they have their roots in it." "We grasp more immediately what the fact of being female means for a human being" (13) and are more invested in such knowledge. Hence they are likely to pursue this question with passion. Like the standpoint theorists, Beauvoir recognizes that experience is an important ingredient in knowledge, and while one's values and interests are embedded in this knowledge those alone do not disqualify it as partial. However, unlike the standpoint theorists she does not believe the most oppressed women will be able to articulate "the truth" of the system. Beauvoir is not only wary of pursuing certainty, but she is unconvinced that the most oppressed would have had requisite social, educational, and political opportunities necessary to be able to pursue such a study. In the end, she claims those "women today fortunate to have had all the privileges of the human restored to them can afford the luxury of impartiality"[7] (15). Women like herself, who have been educated and are beginning to participate in public life, are more likely to be able to approach an understanding. While rootedness in the situation is important, in the next breath she values detachment. She says women "who have never felt their femaleness as an obstacle" are likely to be more detached and hence she hopes "their attitude will be objective" (15). Having some experience of oppression as well as some privileges, so one is not crippled by one's oppression, seems to be the key. Beauvoir also believes that one must be sufficiently motivated to do

7 Beauvoir's use of the term impartiality is interesting. Elsewhere she challenges notions of absolute truth – disembodied and unsituated knowledge – so how is impartiality possible? My suspicion is that she believes through communication and debate one goes beyond the specificity of one's situated perspective towards an intersubjective one, and this is as impartial as can be expected. Since she is not concerned with absolute truth, but rather furthering a practical attitude (*EA*) that helps her act more effectively, the goal of impartiality is less demanding.

the research necessary to counter the gender-blind perspectives and disclose women's otherness. Hence a feminist commitment is warranted.

Here Beauvoir appears to provide an argument that empowers engaged intellectual women; while they too have been oppressed by the patriarchal system, they are less oppressed by patriarchal relations and hence have the potential to be more active and creative. As we will see in chapter 6, this does not authorize any female intellectual to speak for minority women. Rather, it means Beauvoir moves away from seeing all women as victims and all women as equally oppressed by their absolute otherness. Also even the most oppressed women have the potential for freedom.

THE SITUATION: SITUATED KNOWING AND THE POSSIBILITY OF COMMUNICATION

Beauvoir navigates between modernist and postmodern assumptions: we share the world and yet we approach it from our singular situations. Beauvoir does not believe the individual reflective subject can know the world, however she presumes that each singular situation envelops the entire world (*LIT*, 198). "This does not mean that one knows it, but that one reflects it, typifies it, or expresses the world" (199). Hence, "there is a world that is the same for us all, but on the other hand, we are all in a situation in relation to it. This situation involves our past, our class, our condition, our projects, basically the entire world ensemble of what makes up our individuality" (198–9). "The singularity of our situation is an irreducible fact ... but at the same time there is communication in this very separation" (199). "This world exists for us all and ... allows us to agree upon what is green and what is red for example" (199). Beginning with our specific (complex social) situation, Beauvoir believes we can loosen our ties to our specific situation through communication and collective action. In this way she acknowledges that we are situated and affected by our embodied situation, however we also have the potential to enlarge our perspective and challenge existing knowledges that define women.

Knowledge can be sexist; she demonstrates as much in the first part of *The Second Sex*: biologists and physiologists have privileged male bodies while psychoanalysts and historical materialists have privileged male minds and male action. Drawing attention to their ideological assumptions, she believes, proves useful to promote feminist consciousness. Having acknowledged how male domination has been supported by gendered knowledge practices, she acknowledges the cultural forms that oppression takes. However, she does not conclude, as Foucault does, that power/knowledge is constitutive of women's subjectivity. Her ontological speculations about the human condition – freedom, finitude, contingency, and ambiguity – distinguish her from the postmodernists who refuse ontology. Furthermore, she believes that dialogical exchanges between contesting truth claims can be helpful in approaching an understanding and guiding action (EA, 122). She does not jettison philosophy or the pursuit of knowledge, but reconfigures what one can expect from the pursuit. She does not provide a model of theory/practice to be followed; however, in unmasking sexist knowledge and unsettling its assumptions, she hopes to mobilize women. Here, again, her position on truth seems to be paradoxical. Believing that knowledge as understanding is possible, and furthermore that it can enrich one's political practice, puts her into a feminist standpoint camp. Respecting the limits of knowledge, and not proposing directions for change, aligns her to the postmodern.

In deconstructing theoretical discourses, revealing their gender biases, challenging strong distinctions between knowledge and ideology, and finally endorsing the role of literature, Beauvoir is linked to postmodern thinking. However, in contrast to the postmodernists, literature, for Beauvoir, elucidates pre-reflective communication as well as concrete ethical and political dilemmas that go beyond the specific. As a consequence, she calls these works "philosophic literature," or "metaphysical novel[s]" (PW, 269–77). Hence, for Beauvoir this is not a turn away from philosophy, for fiction helps philosophy proceed. Literature is ideally suited to deal with ethical and political choices at the level of concrete human existence: thereby disclosing the subjective truth of human existence. As we see in the final chapter, she shares some affinity with Martha Nussbaum, who acknowledges how the specific can exceed itself and can be exemplary; this attitude draws her back into the enlightenment camp.

Since scientists, psychoanalysts, and social scientists have used males or masculinity as the basis of their research, Beauvoir appeals to fiction in order to understand women's existence. Her recognition that knowledge and culture are gendered has been almost completely ignored by her French poststructuralist critics (in particular Irigaray, Kristeva, and Cixous) who have blamed her for covering up sexual differences or producing phallic universalist knowledge. Since they believe she is indebted to knowledge that privileges masculinity (i.e. robust individualism) and males, they accuse her phenomenological perspective of articulating a male point of view. As I have shown, this reading is inaccurate. Embodied and situated subjects are not robust individuals, but relational subjects whose powers are imbricated in the situation.

However, Beauvoir is continually vilified as an abstract humanist and essentialist because of her use of phenomenological/philosophic categories, which are believed to be phallogocentric and rationalist. In such readings, Beauvoir's attention to the situation and embodied subjectivity that begins with the contingent facticity of sexed, affective, situated bodies is glossed over, as is the importance she attributes to fiction in exploring women's existence.

In the post-war years, Beauvoir was not sufficiently conscious of the implications that followed from women's exclusion from philosophy or the social sciences. There were very few women in the academy in the 1930s and '40s, and even fewer feminist philosophers or social theorists thinking about such things. Critiques of gendered knowledge were not circulating at the time she was writing her major philosophic works. Thus her efforts to come to terms with the effects of sex and gender on epistemology should not be summarily dismissed.

Moreover, it can be argued that Beauvoir "engendered" phenomenology. She used phenomenological ideas that were reputed to be gender blind, or masculinist (by radical cultural feminists and poststructuralists), to capture women's gendered experience. Her phenomenological descriptions were not oriented towards establishing a new gender-free epistemology, but directed to further political change. In assuming one's past (the existing social hierarchies of one's particular situation), in the process of change women have the possibility of loosening its effects on the present.

In *The Second Sex* Beauvoir reveals the parallels between women and minority men (Jews, Blacks, and aboriginals): they are all oppressed by their situations, and deemed inferior. Although they are oppressed – that is, structurally disadvantaged and dominated in their personal relations – Beauvoir believes there is the possibility of transgressing those relations because their situation is not determining.

Far from being passé, her embodied and situated approach to subjectivity is timely and not culpable of universal phallicism, as Kristeva (2008) assumes. Without dismissing philosophy or the social sciences as phallogocentric and intrinsically masculinist, as radical cultural feminists have, Beauvoir allows a rethinking of embodied subjectivity that takes into account a historicized sexual existence. Another asset to her theorization of gender is that she assumes that gender is not the central determinant of human social behaviour. One does not become a subject by taking up positions around the phallus (à la Lacan) nor is one's sexual identity primary, for one's class, race, ethnicity, and age comprise one's social circumstances (*SS*, 122) and inform one's knowledge. But unlike anatomists, psychoanalytic thinkers, and historical materialists who narrowly define the social, Beauvoir distinguishes its various aspects, treating physiological facts, psychological history, and social circumstances separately (436). Furthermore, although she doesn't fill out the effects of racialized oppression, she does allude to it.

FEMINIST CRITIQUE OF EXISTING RESEARCH AND PHILOSOPHY

In the early 1970s, feminists began to ask how one should approach traditional research methods, social theory, and philosophy, which all excluded women. Feminist standpoint theorists called for the rejection of all existing philosophy, human sciences, and literature that was not produced by women or not self-consciously feminist. The French feminists of difference called for the rejection of the master's tools – research tools, existing language, and logical thinking that were deemed masculinist. Still others were involved in rereading and reinterpreting existing gender-blind philosophy and social scientific research from a feminist or women's perspective. Beauvoir's approach has much affinity to this final course of action. Radical feminists relegated gender-blind theories and privileged male thinkers to the dustbin of history. Included amongst them were thinkers like Hegel, Marx, Husserl, Heidegger, Sartre, and Merleau-Ponty. The philosophic canon of phenomenology was deemed to be the product of dead white males and their ideas were treated as unthinkable for feminist purposes. As we have seen, this approach to existing gender-blind philosophy was not one that Beauvoir adopted.

The significance of the counter-tradition in the history of philosophy (which implicitly tackles rationalism and works to include the non-rational) has been huge. Its contribution to social and political theory and the problematic of autonomy and freedom, in spite of its gender blindness, has been significant. Existentialism and phenomenology provided insights and categories (freedom, facticity, situation, the Other, transcendence and immanence, being-in-itself and being-for-itself, ambiguity, contingency) that helped Beauvoir appreciate that we are relational and embodied.[8] We are not sovereign beings who ought to try to escape or negate the present. Instead, she imagines, women will foster their creativity and self-transformation by enriching our relations with others, by embedding ourselves in history and participating within existing struggles. However, this position is complex. The masculinist discourses of biology, psychoanalysis, and Marxism help us understand the "exogenous forces" within which women are presently constituted, but Beauvoir also relies upon women's own experiences of their oppression to further our understanding.

8 Deutscher (2008). Deutscher seems to understand Beauvoir's appropriation of other thinkers' ideas in terms of conversion. While it is true that Beauvoir uses the term conversion to replace the notion of progress of the dialectic, I would describe her use of other thinkers less as conversion of their ideas into her own and more as her eclectic use of their ideas insofar as they support her own theoretical project of freedom for all.

Beauvoir spurns abstract thinking, so she doesn't assume one can read women's experiences from the categories of these various theoretical discourses. Her study of woman is historical; she reminds the reader that her usage of terms like "woman" or "feminine" should be qualified by the statement "in the present state of education and custom" (SS 1974, 1). Looking at the concrete manifestations of women's sexuality (EA, 26), she provides a patchwork of insights that help elucidate the process by which women have been Othered, without establishing causal relations or presuming comprehensive theories. However, to understand the specific, the particular, Beauvoir believes one must not only elucidate the singular but have an understanding of exogenous (general) forces within which woman is inscribed.

In a 1976 interview, Susan Brison asked Beauvoir about her feminist methods. She confirmed the approach she took in *The Second Sex*, which was to make sense of women's experience. When asked "Should women completely reject the masculine universe or should they find themselves a place in it? Should they steal their tools or change them?," Beauvoir responded, "We are not going to recreate language from one day to the next … but must remain aware that language bears the mark of men, nothing prevents you from changing it at the same time." The point is not for women to take power out of men's hands since that wouldn't change anything about the world: "It's a question of precisely destroying that notion of power" (Brison 2003, 190). Beauvoir encouraged feminists both to make use of and yet also transform existing language and theory.

Beauvoir's approach to philosophy differs from her French poststructuralist critics (Cixous, Kristeva, and Irigaray) who see language and discourse as constitutive of experience,[9] and existing logical and analytic thinking as phallogocentric; hence, they turn away from philosophy to embrace poetry. Irigaray and Cixous both espoused *écriture féminine* – non-phallic writing of poetry and literature. While Beauvoir admitted women's multiple differences from men – "they don't have the flaws attributed to the possession of power" (Brison, 202) – she rejected the idea that women had positive differences worth promoting. In contrast, she believed that language was sufficiently malleable to reflect any psychological or social changes that might transpire. Instead of language constituting identities that must be resisted or resignified, Beauvoir believes collective projects will transform identities and language. Furthermore, she says Cixous's writing is incomprehensible and

9 As I have argued above, history is important for Beauvoir and not subsumed within general abstract categories or discursively given.

severs relations with others; Beauvoir encourages women to use common language to facilitate communication, and warns against tackling symbolic forms of women's oppression alone without making legal and political reforms.

Beauvoir did not conceive of existing language as phallogocentric and constitutive of experience. Since language is a social practice that both bears the marks of male power and yet is also able to critically capture patriarchal experiences, it is more flexible than is sometimes presumed. Language can equally be used for emancipatory purposes or to shore up existing power relations. Beauvoir did not turn away from philosophy or logical thinking, as her critics did, for she believed both had contributions to make. However, she also thought that philosophy must be reconceived to deal with the non-rational aspects of human life, taking into account the sensory, emotional, and rational registers of action. Refusing system building and a search for certainty, phenomenology allows for the exploration of lived experience; fiction and autobiography are important resources to further this end. Hence, philosophy is not rejected but reconceived.

Beauvoir avoided the strong alternatives posed by her interviewer, that language is either a tool of the master that must be rejected or a neutral tool that can be used to disclose power relations. She also rejected a stark opposition between feminists either shunning this masculine world or finding a place within it. Again capturing ambiguity, a space between these two extremes, she presumes language can both be a tool of its master as well as an instrument of liberation. Her writing, she believed, would facilitate women's understanding as well as contribute to forces of change; hence language can be transformative. Beauvoir says that if "the oppression of women were completely eliminated … society would be shaken to its foundation … the point is not for women simply to take power out of men's hands … it's a question precisely of destroying that notion of power … I'm certain, in fact, that this idea of domination is one of the features of the masculine universe that must be totally destroyed, that we must look for reciprocity, collaboration, etc." (Brison 1976, 189–91). For Beauvoir, women's engagement in this world is not simply about women taking a place in a man's world or, on the other hand, simply refusing this world altogether. Admittedly women are "heavily handicapped" (*SS*, 8) in this masculine world, but she sees institutions and practices beginning to shift. Change requires active women to be engaged in projects of freedom, which will disrupt the logic of domination.

Many American radical cultural feminists have not understood this, and have argued that Beauvoir is a "male-stream" theorist employing "the stir and mix approach" (Jones 1986, 1–16), stirring women into categories conceived by men and with men in mind. The French feminists of difference had a variation on this critique, characterizing Beauvoir as a universal humanist. In using pre-existing philosophic categories, from Sartre, Husserl, Heidegger, and Merleau-Ponty, she sees women through a universal masculine or phallic lens, thereby eliding "the feminine."

Beauvoir employs categories created by male thinkers but in a way that is responsive to historical context and social differences, particularly in *The Second Sex* and *Old Age.* In attending to specific complex situations, defined by gender, race, and class relations, she avoids the universalist and abstract tone of much existentialist and phenomenological thinking. Furthermore her situated and embodied problematic also avoids phenomenology's focus upon consciousness. Beginning with a uniquely situated subject, she uses descriptions of sexuality's concrete manifestations (EA, 26) to understand women's gendered existence.

Not being a self-conscious feminist at the time she was writing *The Second Sex,* Beauvoir's goal was not explicitly to bring gender to bear on existential phenomenology, though she did some significant work towards this end. With the flourishing of the feminist movement in France in the late 1960s and 1970s and her participation in the women's movement, Beauvoir declared herself a feminist. This involved a shift in her political position. At the time of writing *The Second Sex* she was optimistic that socialism would deliver women's liberation, but by the early '70s she was no longer confident, and prioritized feminist organizing and separatist feminist struggles. This change in position was more strategic than theoretical. Beauvoir's insistence on praxis – that theory be useful – informed her work. As I have shown, her philosophy accommodates pluralism and she espouses the importance of democratic societies (EA, 106). However, in order to realize these values, she believes authentically socialist societies are necessary (SS, 721, 161). Nonetheless her commitment to socialism exceeded proletarian agency. Even when she was committed to socialism in 1949, she focused on gender oppression and acknowledged the equally significant oppression of Jews and Blacks. Again, when she espouses her strong support for feminist movements, at the outset of second-wave feminism, her commitment to plural struggles of emancipation were evident: her manuscript *Old Age* focused on men and the effects of ageism.

CHALLENGING GENDER AS A UNITARY AND SINGULAR CONCEPT: THE IMPORTANCE OF HISTORY

When Beauvoir describes women's subordination, she often speaks in general philosophic terms, and consequently is believed to be indifferent to difference. Spelman (1988) believes that Beauvoir's exploration of women's experience is limited; she claims that Beauvoir fails to explore the lives of women who are subject to racism, classism, and imperialism, and is thus oblivious to her privilege (1988, 71).[10] True, Beauvoir did not include the stories of non-European women and hence their distinctive experiences are absent. This had more to do with the scant anthropological work done of non-European women at the time, rather than being a symptom of her privileged stance. Furthermore, although her novels or philosophic essays seem to focus upon European women, she did significant activist work with non-European women: Algerian, Japanese, Chinese, and African women. Also, her theoretical approach, which begins with the concrete thickness of the world and singular situations, is able to accommodate the diversity of women's experiences – even if she does not herself do so.

Spelman claims that Beauvoir's failure to explore how her theoretical perspective colluded with the exclusion of minority women is a sign of her privilege. This I am not convinced of. It is a convenient trope used by postmodernists to dismiss enlightenment/humanist thinking as necessarily universalist, elitist, and Eurocentric (Braidotti 2013, 20). It also contributes to their skepticism regarding communication: language is so culturally specific that shared meaning is impossible. It is not surprising that literary and cultural theorists play this card and historians or social/political researchers, who believe they are able to disclose a world, and are committed to producing an understanding, do not. Again, Spelman and Braidotti (2013, 20), like other postmodern feminists, believe that Beauvoir is a universal humanist, and in doing so they ignore Beauvoir's attention to embodied subjectivity, a problematic able to accommodate difference. Beauvoir's project is not simply a deconstructive one, focusing upon exclusion, but also one engaged in disclosing women's differently lived situations, albeit tentatively, in the service of enlarging those who are included. Nevertheless, Beauvoir does admit that one cannot but exclude some constituents. Far from simply tolerating others, Beauvoir's commitment "to authentically democratic societies that Marx heralded, [presumes] there is no place for the Other" (*SS*, 161). So, while she may not have attended to the Eurocentrism of her thinking, she did make some efforts to theoretically and politically tackle the exclusion of non-Europeans.

Beauvoir's lack of attention spent elaborating the lives of racial and indigenous minority women has to be seen in the context in which she was writing. Given that she wasn't an anthropologist (when even

10 Sonia Kruks points this out (2012, 49).

anthropologists of the day were circumscribed by their Western perspective), it isn't surprising that she made orientalist statements.[11] Her awareness of the power of the micropolitical to destabilize the logic of oppression and her awareness of universalist thinking's exclusions, as we have seen above, were prescient. Just as women were Othered by male epistemological privilege, so were Blacks and Jews. Edward Said's *Orientalism* and Gayatri Spivak's "Can the Subaltern Speak" were yet to come, but there are some interesting overlaps between their works and Beauvoir's.

Insofar as Beauvoir uses universal philosophic categories to explore concrete historical situations, she is believed to gloss over differences. However, this criticism is glibly assumed, rather than substantiated. While I have talked about Beauvoir's appreciation of difference, I must now establish it. Beginning with the binary oppositions of male/female corresponding to Subject/Object, active/passive, reason/emotion, Beauvoir sets out to trouble and unsettle them. Further evidence of her appreciation of difference comes with historicizing universal philosophic categories. The gendered binaries of transcendence and immanence, active and passive that map on to men and women are more complicated when one looks at Beauvoir's concrete historical examples. Beauvoir looks at women in very different social locations distinguished as much by their class, race, and nation as by their gender. While she didn't attend sufficiently to non-Western women, and that is definitely a shortcoming, her historically sensitive embodied problematic has the capacity to explore diversity and difference. Although Beauvoir acknowledges that women have been traditionally represented as Other, situated as passive and docile objects in masculine culture, she believes that in their concrete existence they exceed this characterization.

Looking at France before the Revolution, Beauvoir notes that working-class women had more financial independence from their husbands, and were more active participants in their communities, than women of the middle and upper classes. Women who were financially dependent upon their husbands were for the most part relegated to the private sphere and excluded from public spaces. During the Revolution, middle-class women took up the cause of liberty and equality for women. In 1789 Olympe de Gouges proposed the Declaration of the Rights of Women as equivalent to the Declaration of the Rights of Man, calling for elimination of male privilege. However, there was no great sympathy for

11 However, given her claim that the situation is not entirely determining, she cannot be totally forgiven for her shortsightedness.

her amongst the revolutionaries, and in the end she was imprisoned and hung (*SS*, 123). Beauvoir does not use this example to underline the revolutionaries' sexism or define women as passive, but rather draws attention to the important work of women revolutionaries. While revolutionary forces were not "feminist-friendly," they introduced legal changes that loosened the middle-class family unit. In 1792, the exclusive right of inheritance of the firstborn male was abolished, and a law was introduced to establish divorce. The revolutionaries did not intend to give more freedom to women, but the effects of their actions/projects did in fact do so. However, while Napoleonic law abolished divorce from 1826–84, women could be killed for acts of adultery and husbands could be excused for killing adulterous wives. From this exploration of women's position in pre- and post-revolutionary France, it is clear that gender is not a unitary phenomenon: its historical specificity must be appreciated. Furthermore, the extent of women's oppression is influenced by their complex positions in the economic, legal, and political institutions and practices of the day.

Beauvoir's treatment of gender does not presume that there is a shared women's experience, as early feminist standpoint theorists did, for one's gendered experience is affected by various factors, including class, race, and sexual orientation: "When economic power falls into the hands of the workers, then it will become possible for working women to win rights and privileges that parasitic women (of the nobility or middle class) never obtained" (*SS*, 123). She does not present a uniform picture of gendered work experiences, recognizing that if one's life is dominated by domestic labour, then it is very different from the life of those women who are wage earners (123).

In dealing with abortion, Beauvoir attends to how this experience depends upon various factors in one's situation. Privileged women are aware of contraception and can afford therapeutic abortions: working women are less likely to aware of modern contraceptive techniques and cannot afford a visit to Switzerland where abortion is legal and safe (528). So the context in which women choose affects their ability to choose as well as the consequences of their choice. In addition to the class inequalities, Beauvoir recognizes cultural differences: intolerance of unmarried mothers can drive women "to commit suicide or infanticide" (528). The shame associated with intolerance of a child born out of wedlock as well as the pain associated with infertility are not class-based experiences. In addition, individual women's desires for children vary: while abortion may be a heinous option to some, it is a relief to others. She recognizes how one's emotive/affective life has a role to play in one's experience. However, unlike many liberal theorists who presume this means that people are free to experience their lives as either oppressive or free, Beauvoir believes that social circumstances affect the prospects of freedom.

Religion also factors into gender experiences. Beauvoir draws attention to the power and significance of the church and speculates on the role that religion had on women's sexual lives in France. Since the Catholic church saw sex outside of reproduction as a sin, it hardly cultivated attitudes of enjoyment.

The specificity of gender experience is illustrated in the novels of Honoré de Balzac (1799–1850). In spite of the progressive ideals of many of his cohort, he reiterated anti-feminist bourgeois attitudes. He writes: "woman is a possession acquired by contract: she is personal property and the possession of her is as good as a security" (129). He saw marriage as a loveless institution, so he encouraged men "to rein in wives to total subjugation" (129), denying them education and culture, so as to ensure that they were not adulterous. At the same time, most socialists were allying themselves to feminist ideals, for reciprocal relations between men were carried over into reciprocal relations between men and women. However, some were hostile to women's increased entrance into the paid economy; serving as a reserve army of labour, women workers drove down the wages of working classes. Beauvoir cites the anarchist Pierre-Joseph Proudhon (1809–1865) whose anti-feminist comments exceeded an economic rationale. She quotes Proudhon: "Woman should be dependent upon man; man alone counts as a social individual … Woman is inferior to man first because her physical force is only two-thirds that of the male, then because she is intellectually and morally inferior to the same degree … she is worth 8/27 of the stronger sex" (131). While most socialists supported feminism: Proudhon "broke the alliance of socialism and feminism" (131). Thus, for Beauvoir, attitudes to feminism can't simply be read off one's social location.

Also these passages reflect how class, political, religious, cultural, and even generational differences all factor into woman's specific experience of gender. There is no common experience of abortion, sexual maturity, infertility, or marriage. As Toril Moi rightly points out, an overly sexualized approach to experience fails to appreciate differences in social location. Moi writes that "pervasive sex saturates not only the person but everything the person touches. The modern world is a world steeped in *sex*: *every habit*, *gesture*, and *activity* is *sexualized* and *categorized* as male or *female*, *masculine* or *feminine*" (1999, 12). Like Toril Moi, Beauvoir was wary of treating women's agency in a primarily sexualized register. She did not assume a shared experience of one's gendered existence, nor the conceptual priority and singularity of gender. In fact, given her attention to a plethora of social differences, she conceives of women and men as defined in terms of the specifics of their situations. Beauvoir begins with the specific "every concrete human being is uniquely situated"; however, she insists "no woman can claim without bad faith to be situated beyond her sex" (*SS*, 4). She also draws attention to the complexity of oppressions; it is not just women who experience this, but also aboriginal peoples, Jews, Blacks, and proletarians as well. Though their experiences are very different, they are located in structurally similar situations. These people are positioned as subordinate in various ways (economically, culturally, and socially). Beauvoir's attention to these other subordinate groups, in almost the same breath as she first talks of gender oppression, is telling. She matter-of-factly challenges the assumption of gender as a primary axis of power.

Beauvoir was amongst the first to understand the effects of gendered cultural practices and sexist knowledge on women. Furthermore, her intersectional approach to power avoids some of the serious problems that second-wave feminists and standpoint theorists encountered – namely, the failure to account for difference and specificity. Beauvoir's way of accommodating macro forces of power – speaking in terms of class, race, gender – while also acknowledging that these forces are singularly configured in one's specific situation allows her to avoid essentialism. She believes "the world is the same for all of us"; however, she admits we approach the world from our specific situations. "The singularity of our situation is an irreducible fact ... but at the same time there is communication in this very separation" (*LIT*, 199). We are not trapped in our singular and specific existence, since we are of the world; while there may be miscommunication, misunderstanding, or worlds lost in translation, communication is possible. Unlike postmodernists who focus upon excluded identities and the failures of communication, Beauvoir provides the basis for communication – without ignoring its pitfalls.

2

Rethinking the Sex/Gender Distinction

THE SEX/GENDER DISTINCTION is the hallmark of second-wave feminism. It was first employed as a strategy to tackle the biologism that underpinned woman's exclusion from public life, her marginality in the economy, and popular attitudes regarding her ostensible anatomical inferiority. Second-wave feminists distinguished sex from gender; our immutable body was bracketed and feminists focused upon social relations and cultural processes that were largely responsible for women's inequality. Beauvoir's famous statement "One is not born but becomes a woman" (*SS*, 283) initiated social constructionism. By focusing upon the latter, feminists hoped to liberate women from their subordination to biology. This distinction is often attributed to Beauvoir, but as we will see in the course of the chapter, this attribution is false.

The sex/gender distinction has been the subject of much debate. Poststructuralist and postmodernist critics claim it is bankrupt because it falsely stabilizes the sexed body (Fuss 1989 and Spelman 1988). In particular, Judith Butler is renowned for challenging this distinction since it treats sex as the immutable ground of gender and thereby normalizes heterosexual relations and fails to tackle biologism (the idea that anatomy determines social relations). This distinction was also taken to task for essentializing and prioritizing gender relations and thereby underestimating the effects of race, class, ethnicity, and sexuality on gender identities. The Coombe collective drew attention to this, as did socialist feminists. More recently, new materialists (Bennett 2010; Coole 2010; Connolly 2002; Frost 2010) and neuroscientists have criticized the discursive turn that produced a socially constructed body while ignoring the effects of subatomic matter. The body is comprised of lively material (disclosed through physiology as well as brain-networking) that should be respected when it comes to exploring agency.

In the course of this chapter, I will look in more detail at the assaults and corrections that the sex/gender distinction has faced. But more importantly, we will return to Beauvoir's non-essentialist historically sensitive sexed body that appreciates anatomical differences as well as cultural and social ones. While Beauvoir did not uphold the sex-gender distinction, her notion of the body lent itself to this distinction. Beauvoir did not bracket or occlude biology, in fact she recognizes the effects of physiological facts, but sees these as socially and culturally meaningful. I concur with Toril Moi, who says "no feminist has produced a better theory of embodied, sexually different human beings than Beauvoir in *The Second Sex*" (1999, 7). Moi heralds the importance of Beauvoir's philosophy that "finds a third way for feminist theory, one that steers a course between the Scylla of traditionalism essentialism and biologism and the Charybdis of idealist obsession with 'discourse' and 'construction'" (vii). However, I part ways with Moi when she rejects the sex/gender distinction altogether (7), for I believe the distinction is philosophically important and strategically useful.

As critiques of social construction flourish, Beauvoir provides an alternative to the neurologically and materially informed theories of the body that have emerged. Instead of focusing upon sexed bodies, Beauvoir distinguishes – rightly, I would argue – between "physiological facts, psychological history and social circumstances," thereby avoiding the pervasiveness of the sexual (Moi 1999, 78) that is associated with the French feminists of difference. However, acknowledging the "conditions of existence of the experiencing body" (*SS*, 24) does not dictate what one does with one's body. One's conduct is influenced by biological facts, cultural factors, and social norms. While Beauvoir does not support the classic sex/gender distinction, her distinction between "physiological facts, psychological history and social circumstances" (436) does appreciate both bodily materiality as well as social historical materiality, thereby respecting various forms of social inequality.

APPROACHING THE FEMININE: FRENCH FEMINISTS OF DIFFERENCE VERSUS BEAUVOIR

In continental countries, feminists did not rely upon the sex/gender distinction to ground feminism. This had much to do with the linguistic structure of the romance languages. In French, the word "gender" translates as *genre*, meaning kind or species, and therefore is not appropriate to signal anything related to sex. This is also true of other romance languages where gender has no allusion to sex but is a part of speech.

Although there is no equivalent word in these languages for this term, nevertheless feminist strategies did reflect similar concerns. Historical materialists, for example, approached the specifically social and political aspects of sexed differences, ignoring the anatomical and psychoanalytic discourses. The psychoanalysts, psychologists, and cultural theorists considered the sexed (psychobiological or psychosocial) as well as cultural differences between men and women; however, Beauvoir charges these thinkers with "determinism" and "essentialism" (*SS*, 49–61).

Debates within feminism in continental countries revolved around different strategies, but, as in Anglo-American countries, they are summed up by the terms "equality" versus "difference." In the late 1960s in France, the crucial divide was between the egalitarians, theoretically framed by historical materialist analysis, and those wedded to difference, who pursued cultural analyses. The former thinkers were inspired by socialist and Marxist ideas and concerned with the material conditions of women's lives calling for equality of condition. The latter were indebted to Lacanian and post-Lacanian psychoanalysis and focused on the power of the discursive or symbolic order to create meaning. Whereas the former feminists focused upon historical analysis and engaged in political and legal struggles, the latter group were concerned with shifting prevailing cultural forms – their primary concern was with the "phallus in our [women's] heads" (Ringart, 1977).

The Mouvement de libération des femmes (MLF)[1] grew out of the disillusionment with the radical left politics of May 1968, when women recognized that men dominated political action and speech and that, even though they claimed to be anti-hierarchal, they were not. Four currents emerged (each with its distinctive approach to women's oppression; there was no coherent theory or project, though they did pragmatically act together on occasion) (Duchen 1986). The *tendance luttes des classes* (class struggle group) saw feminism as an integral part of the struggle for communism. *Féministes révolutionnaires*, a group of radical cultural feminists, gave priority to sex over class. The *Questions féministes* collective (QFM), under Beauvoir's tutelage, worked within historical and cultural analyses of women's oppression, informed by socialist feminism, more broadly defined (Duchen 1987, 56). And, finally, adherents of

1 For a fuller treatment of the history of women's movements in France, see Duchen (1986 and 1987). For a more extensive coverage of their diverse ideas see *New French Feminisms: An Anthology*, eds Elaine Marks and Isabelle de Courtivron; and *French Feminist Thought: A Reader*, ed. Toril Moi.

Psychanalyse et Politique (Psych and Po)[2] (47–54) used psychoanalysis to recover the repressed femininity or woman-ness from the unconscious; they thought that power, abstract theory, and existing language were male, and called for "women-only" policies and new feminine speech and writing; and they rejected phallocentric language and sexist political practices. Existing formal procedures of debate, lists of speakers, appointment of a chair were masculine practices that had to be jettisoned, to recuperate repressed femininity. They encouraged women to speak up and talk about their own experiences and called for separatist politics.[3]

The philosophic and political thinkers who influenced Psych and Po were the French feminists of difference (i.e., Cixous, Irigaray, and Kristeva). They were also theoretically informed by the poststructuralist thinkers Roland Barthes, Michel Foucault, Jacques Derrida, and Jacques Lacan. As such, Psych and Po reproduced the latter's mission to escape the logocentric system that dominated Western thought by abandoning universalist theories and efforts to find an all-encompassing explanation of the world. In doing so, they too, criticized Marxism as a totalizing philosophy and often assumed anarchist attitudes.

By way of example, Luce Irigaray's (1993) examination of the central texts of Western philosophy shows how "the feminine" has been excluded and the phallus has dominated philosophy. Lacan says very little about Woman; Kristeva reiterates "Lacan's scandalous sentence 'there is no such thing as Woman'" (1986, 205). Woman does not exist and cannot exist because of the symbolic significance of the phallus. Irigaray recognizes the limitations of conceptualizing the feminine in this way and attempts to define Woman provisionally; she goes beyond the phallic libidinal economy to feminine *jouissance* (feminine pleasure). This experience, she believes, is foreclosed with the resolution of the Oedipal drama and women's exclusion from the symbolic order, yet she believes it can be recuperated. Cixous and Irigaray (and Psych and Po more

2 Antoinette Fouque was one of the founders of Psychanalyse et Politique, created on the heels of May '68. Alongside Monique Wittig and Josiane Chanel, Fouque was intent upon lifting the censorship of the body that had been put in place by the masters of contemporary thought. Fouque defines the women's movement as having two orientations – the struggle for equality or integration and the struggle for identity. By this she means the recognition of "the uniqueness of the other, not the sameness" (1991, 10).

3 In 1975 Beauvoir supported separatist organizations for women, however she never affiliated herself with the psychoanalytically inclined feminists or Monique Wittig. Psych and Po, in a stealthy move that shocked other feminist groups, copyrighted the label MLF (Mouvement de libération des femmes) as their own; this was hardly consistent with their theoretical critique.

generally) hold a similar position and attempt to draw out the feminine through women's writing, écriture féminine.

As previously mentioned, sexual difference is co-extensive with language; there is no possibility of taking a position in language outside of differentiating moves. Thus the distinction of masculine and feminine is within a symbolic register that precedes social relations. This means that sexed differences are linguistically produced; language produces the social rather than simply mediating it. Hence language is constitutive of male/female identities. Lacan doesn't allow for the latitude of social relations to structure the symbolic (Lacan 2002, 69). He ignores the role of the social outside the symbolic; since the symbolic is paired with masculine and feminine, it has difficulty dealing with sexual variety. Feminists who were directly or tangentially associated with Lacan, as well as those who spurned Lacan for being masculinist, nevertheless assumed that the subject was psychically constituted: to become a speaking subject, one must relinquish one's relations to the maternal and accept the law of the father. In doing so one assumes the role of the phallus and the exclusion of the feminine.

The Psych and Po collective wanted to go beyond the power of the phallus, to invent new forms of speech and culture around feminine sexuality. They did so by giving significance to the maternal. They called for women-only venues and specifically feminine writing that involved writing the body, since masculine thinking focused on reason and refused the body. Antoinette Fouque founded a women's press devoted to publishing women's work. This group of separatist feminists had no sympathy with the *Questions féministes* collective, under the leadership of historical materialists such as Beauvoir and Christine Delphy.

The historical materialist/socialist feminists (the QFM) saw the source of women's oppression differently: they focused on social relations that were inscribed in institutions, not the socio-symbolic world of the psyche; in fact, they believed that the social produced the psychic. Woman's role in the social division of labour and in reproducing labour power, and her relegation to domestic life, were all symptoms of her subordinate role in the patriarchal capitalist economy. Her cultural marginality was also an effect of masculinist hegemony. While Beauvoir was one of the leaders of this group of socialist feminists, offering a supplement to Marxism, her attention to the effects that submissive social and political roles have on one's psyche was not always in line with their historical materialist work. Nevertheless, there were historical materialists who also attended to the psychological. In fact, the *Questions féministes* collective split over the question of lesbianism and heterosexuality. Two articles published in the same volume triggered this split. Those inspired by Monique Wittig's article "Straight Thinking" "denounced the heterosexual logic which is oppressive for all women," while E. de Lessep's piece "Heterosexuality and Feminism" argued that you can be both a feminist and a heterosexual (Duchen 1987, 85). Lessep furthermore claimed lesbians didn't choose their sexuality, hence their lifestyle was not the result of political commitment. This claim was particularly provocative; many lesbians argued to the contrary. In fact emphasizing their political commitment was more radical than homosexual or heterosexual feminists, who having slept with men "collaborated with their oppressors" (87). Battle ensued; lines of struggle were drawn, the journal collapsed. The lesbians saw themselves as "fighting the mechanisms of hetero-patriarchal society which objectifies, oppresses and kills women … rather than carving out a space for themselves within it" (89). The *Nouvelles Questions féministes* launched by Christine Delphy with the support of Beauvoir condemned the position of Wittig "that excluded heterosexual women from the class of women" (Tidd 2004, 81). *NQF* refocused the debates on the more explicitly political interventions: how could feminists become involved in "general struggles" given the current repressive conditions in "Afghanistan, Law and Order Bills and the Third World War" (Duchen 1987)? The lesbian and homosexual contingents were furious with these male-identified feminists for appropriating the journal's name, and for turning away from the more radical struggles around sexuality.

Even before the divide in QFM, Beauvoir and the historical materialist/socialist feminists were at odds with the Psych and Po collective. Unlike the Psych and Po collective, who refused to cooperate with other feminists, the QFM strategically allied with liberal feminists, radical feminists, and other reformers who campaigned for women's rights to contraception and abortion (i.e., the Le Choisir group). Psych and Po opposed most of these feminists for being egalitarians, believing they papered over differences between men and women in their feminist struggle. For this reason, the Psych and Po refused the label "feminist" and preferred to call themselves members of the women's movement. Beauvoir and the QFM – the phallic feminists, as they were called – were their prime targets. Psych and Po charged Beauvoir with squeezing women into categories conceived by men with men in mind (i.e., of endorsing existing forms of male culture and male institutions). Irigaray and Kristeva argued that Beauvoir denied women's social and cultural differences and their creative relations to other women by presuming that women should emulate independent men. Insofar as Beauvoir appeals to male-centred philosophy, they argued, she is trapped by logocentrism and the symbol of the phallus. As we have seen in chapter 1, Beauvoir was optimistic that language was more permeable to change: one didn't have to invent a new language to liberate women from their previous identities, since she was not a semiologist nor did she support the idea that speaking involved a sexual positioning. Elizabeth Fallaize's comment is astute: "Although the emphasis on the signifier as the sign of the unconscious has relegated the signified, and with it the notion that language translates experience, to an ancillary position … Beauvoir remains one of the few major figures on the contemporary French intellectual scene to explore the signified and its representations" (Fallaize 1998, 145).

Since Beauvoir begins with the specific and explores the singular situations of multiple embodied women, equality may be a goal but it is not a uniform strategy imposed from above, for it must respect differently situated women. The goal of equality is not to ensure the same (equal) treatment of all, but to allow women to equally enjoy a meaningful life. Zakin contests the charge of the French feminists of difference, who believe equality denies difference. She points out that "equality is a call for a situation of equal possibilities, for a politics in which each subject's pursuit of her own identity can be unimpaired by political restrictions that impose a pregiven status upon bodily configurations" (2006, 48).

To portray exchanges between Beauvoir and the French feminists of difference as debates is a misnomer; positions were taken, accusations were hurled at each other, but there was little actual debate. Without carefully reading their works, Beauvoir dismissed the French feminists' use of psychoanalytic theory as culturalist and essentialist (a charge that does not quite stick, since feminists of difference do not presume natural/essential bodily meanings). Both sides were guilty of glib readings of their opponents. Psych and Po accused Beauvoir of universal humanism and masculinism without carefully exploring her ideas. Kristeva's essay "Women's Time" (1986) came closest to a succinct argument against Beauvoir. She charges Beauvoir's socialist/humanist feminism with masculinism. "In the egalitarian and universalistic spirit of Enlightenment Humanism, the idea of a necessary identification between the two sexes as the only and unique means for liberating 'the second sex'" (Kristeva 1986, 195). Apart from assuming there is only one sex – the male sex that purportedly underpins Beauvoir's philosophy – her socialist ideas portend the total eradication of femininity inspired by a sadomasochistic logic. Instead of the transcendence of the master/slave relation, the logic of domination will be reiterated by Beauvoir's liberated women. So far from freeing women, Beauvoir's feminist strategy, Kristeva believed, will trap her in relations of domination. Women will dominate men, reversing the master/slave relationship rather than breaking out of it. However, a less glib reading shows that Beauvoir believed the master/slave relationship could be transformed, so that reciprocity was possible.

Interestingly Beauvoir and Kristeva had more in common[4] than they then realized; no doubt they were affected by the position taking that defined the MLF at the time.

Given the vociferous battles both within the QFM collective and between them and the Psych and Po grouping, Beauvoir's aversion to psychoanalytic or sexual approaches to feminism were overdetermined. Perhaps this explains in part why Beauvoir's theoretical problematic of embodied subjectivity in *The Second Sex* has been glossed over. It is all too easy to read her in terms of the gender-blind consciousness of phenomenology or Sartrean humanism, but this ignores the extent to which Beauvoir respects various women's points of view and recognizes woman's body as different. The French feminists of difference almost completely ignore Beauvoir's notion of embodiment and have failed to understand the roles one's situation and the historical/social fields play in choice. They also concentrate on her reliance on universal theories (i.e., phenomenology, existentialism, and Marxism) without acknowledging how she tailors them for her own purposes. Irigaray and Cixous believe she treats the woman as the Same. Kristeva also believe Beauvoir "globalizes the problems of women of different milieux, ages, civilizations or simply varying psychic structures, under the label 'Universal Woman'" (Kristeva 1986, 194). Although Beauvoir used the term Woman, she did not homogenize and demean women as charged. Nor is her demand for equality grounded in an abstract universal. Rather Beauvoir's "finite 'we' can be understood as a demassification of the universal, difference, and the feminine" (Zakin 2006, 49).

Beauvoir is also criticized for disparaging women's bodies and failing to recognize the value in the activities of childbearing and rearing. While these charges are true, they again require contextualization. Since, for Beauvoir, a woman's body and her sexuality are constructed in a "man-made" world, where the male body is the norm, it is not surprising that women are alienated from these constructions and representations. When *The Second Sex* was written in the late 1940s, women had just been given the vote in France and were denied the employment and educational opportunities afforded men. It was necessary to oppose those who identified women as biologically and psychologically suited only to mothering, for it was precisely these sorts of arguments that plagued women who were striving to participate in the economy and public/political life. Beauvoir challenged the notion of anatomy as destiny and the idea of

4 Kristeva was a key sponsor of the conference to celebrate the fiftieth anniversary of the publication of *The Second Sex* in Paris (1999), and readily acknowledged Beauvoir's philosophic significance.

the "eternal feminine" (*SS*, 4). She stresses that woman is a "becoming," a process, a movement from the position of gender oppression towards a world that would allow more freedom. Beauvoir's critique of maternity and childcare must be understood in this context. When abortion and birth control were criminalized, and maternity was not a choice but socially and legally enforced, it would hardly have been liberating to celebrate maternity, for it was precisely the naturalization of mothering and the romanticization of mother/child relations that preserved traditional gender roles and kept women from participating in the public world. Beauvoir does not condemn maternity in itself, only when it is not freely chosen – as was the case in the post-war years. Beauvoir's approach to social phenomena like motherhood and abortion would have been very different if women were able to "choose" motherhood rather than being forced into it.[5]

French feminists of difference drew attention to the body, treating it under the rubric of sexual difference. However, seeing the biological, physiological, socio-economic, and political in terms of women's sexed difference is reductionist, for it assumes the primacy of sexuality in social relations and institutional life. Where the sex/gender distinction allows for the appreciation of different sorts of experience, the conflation of various registers of experience under the term sexed difference does not. This ahistorical and discursive approach to the social makes it difficult to think through the processes of oppression and to propose policies and strategies for change.

NORTH AMERICAN CRITIQUE OF SECOND-WAVE FEMINISM – BEAUVOIR ANTICIPATING INTERSECTIONALITY

In response to biologism, many second-wave and some third-wave (postmodern/poststructuralist) feminists upheld a socially constructivist theory of subjectivity. If sex is gendered, as Butler so powerfully argues in *Gender Trouble*, why sustain these dualistic categories? If sex is the product of discourses and discursive practices, then its anatomical and physiological life are open to be performed in an infinite number of ways. This position, which I will call hyper-constructivism, is not without its

5 Today in most liberal democratic societies women enjoy the "right" to choose maternity; however, as I write this book several American states are making access to abortion difficult, if not impossible, in practice. Beauvoir is correct in attending to the importance of social context. Battles that were fought and won now have to be restaged to ensure that maternity is a choice.

problems – discussed by several contemporary poststructuralists including Elizabeth Grosz and Rosi Braidotti. Grosz has identified "a strange decorporealization" and "neutralization of the body" by those feminists who insist upon the discursivization of bodies. She goes on to say that "analyses of the representation of bodies abound, but bodies in their material variety still wait to be thought" (Grosz 1995, 31). Aware of the problems that essentialism and historicism can create for biological, physiological accounts on the body, Grosz calls for social cultural conceptions of the body that are non-biologistic and non-deductive. She wants to invert the priority or centrality of the mind (consciousness), the psyche, the interior, by giving primacy to the corporeal body by seeking a non-reductionist, non-dualist, and non-physicalist materialism. In a similar vein, Deleuzean feminist Rosi Braidotti has argued that in spite of the postmodern turn towards the body, it has been subject to both overexposure and erasure (Braidotti 1991, 1994, 2002). She calls for conceiving the body as a nature/culture continuum (Braidotti 2013, 3). Rejecting the dualism of nature/culture, given and socially constructed, she sees the body as lively material, always as self-organizing (3). Judith Butler herself was concerned about an overly discursivized body. Addressing critics of *Gender Trouble* (1990) who believe she saw the body as a linguistic effect, Butler wrote *Bodies That Matter* (1993), where she insists the body is produced by power relations that are materialized or inscribed on the body. Hence, the body is not simply a linguistic effect, but a materialization of norms, within a coercive heterosexual regime.

Throughout the 1990s there was a continuous assault on the idea of gender as a singular and primary category. This loosely defines the concerns of third-wave feminists, but also captures Beauvoir's historical treatment of gender as discussed in the previous chapter. A general theory of gender was spurned for its insensitivity to difference. Feminists who endorsed a politics of identity (whether it be Black, Asian, Latino, etc.) insisted on their distinctive experiences of gender, thereby challenging the commonality of gendered experiences. Identity politics generated an intense reaction from many feminists. In particular, third-wave feminists (i.e., poststructuralists) saw subjectivity in terms of complex social locations and the effects of diverse discourses, thereby denying both the stability of identity and the possibility of shared experiences. Butler in particular argued that identities presume exclusions, hence are not the best basis for organizing for change (Butler 1990, 1–6, 142–9). The idea that one has to have a stable identity before political interests are to be elaborated and political action taken (142) is false. Also given Beauvoir's existential ontology, which acknowledges "lack" at the heart of being and the uniqueness of one's situation, shared experiences are impossible.

Unlike third-wave feminists, who resist the concept woman as essentialist for privileging women's reproductive roles, Beauvoir uses the term woman, while representing women's experiences as complex and different. As we have previously seen, Beauvoir identifies woman as absolute Other in the socio-symbolic level; however, she believed women worked to disrupt its meaning. Beauvoir did not presume that feminist work depended on a unitary gender identity – thereby, in fact, unwittingly anticipating the concept of intersectionality. Women's experiences were diverse and complex and could not be reflected in any single social group identity; this didn't prevent her from representing Boupacha, an Algerian women raped by French soldiers, nor did it stop her speaking on behalf of unwed mothers or battered wives (*ASD*, 472). She did not believe she had to share their identities, social locations, or experiences to help them represent themselves. Recognizing the singularity (*LIT*, 199) of women's experiences, she eschewed identity strategies. She knew she was differently situated – privileged – but that didn't stop her from collaborating with minority women and when necessary representing their claims. Unlike contemporary feminists who feel their privilege stops them from doing so Beauvoir was not stymied. Nor did these differences stop her from using the term Woman.

The model of intersectionality constructs women "in a variety of political contexts that often exist simultaneously and overlaid on top of one another" (Mohanty 1991, 65). The social body is inscribed with race, ethnic, class, sex, and gender differences. Gender is not a unitary concept, nor the origin of all women's struggles, but rather one social axis of power amongst many. But when gender oppression is linked to other sources of oppression, women are severely disadvantaged. Beauvoir, like Mohanty, did not presume the pre-discursive (sexed body) as the grounds for action, nor does she dispense with gender and sexed identities. Both admit that new identities are an important factor in catalyzing forces of change. Feminist movements require critiques of existing sexist practices, symbols, and identifications, and must foster new practices, identifications, and symbols to mobilize against existing ones that tie women to their position of subordination.

BUTLER'S CRITIQUE OF THE SEX/GENDER DISTINCTION

Focusing on women's reproductive functions in society, according to Butler, second-wave feminists produced a form of feminism that was essentialist and exclusionary: it essentializes who and what women do and then excludes women who aren't engaged in these activities. The focus on reproduction as a woman's issue means that women who decide not to have children or decide never to care for children are excluded. Many women do not engage in childbirth or childcare, because they are too old, too young, or physically incapable, or because they choose not to. Butler asks ironically whether they should not be considered women.

Since the second-wavers were trying to unify women politically, they focused on the social processes that unified women and kept them out of the labour force. Hence, they focused on social hierarchies: the division of labour, institution of marriage, the nuclear family, and maternity. Women's role in reproducing labour power perpetuates her subordinate role: she is kept at home, out of the labour force, or as a part-time worker. Or, if she is a poor, working-class woman, she may find herself caring for other children. Institutions, social roles, and attitudes that normalize motherhood have a negative effect on the prospect of women participating in public and economic life; their subordinate positions encourage dismissive attitudes about their capacities as citizens. Butler is unconvinced by this reading of women's condition and has challenged it, arguing that if feminism focuses on women's common experience as mothers, it thereby excludes many women. In defence of the second wave, Beauvoir draws attention to the significance of the role of mother and caretaker of not only the young, but also the elderly. She attempts to unify women without ever implying that all women had to share these experiences. Just because women are not mothers does not mean that they are unaffected by the societal forces that treat them as natural caretakers and in the process subordinate them. To simply treat reproductive and caring roles as contingent, as Butler does, is foolhardy.

This problematic is even clearer in the discrepancy between Butler's and Beauvoir's conceptualizations of reproductive functions and the perpetuation of the society (as composed of physical bodies). Beauvoir notes that sexual reproduction does not require two sexes, however she doesn't underestimate the power of this belief. By contrast, in seeing reproduction as contingent rather than as a sedimented social practice Butler risks ignoring the power of men, and the masculine, in our culture. Furthermore she glosses over how women's role in reproduction, as unpaid labour, has contributed to women's social inequality.

Butler targets the sex/gender distinction for leading to a form of social determinism. By bracketing sex, the second-wavers presumed that sex was stable, immutable, the ground for gender norms. The patriarchal system produces gender roles and gendered behaviour that women assimilate in the process of their development. Since second-wave feminists believed gender and the body were socially produced, they felt women could be resocialized, reprogrammed, to accept new more liberating gender roles. Butler's exploration of the process of gender identification is subtle and avoids the determinism of many second-wavers. Since sexual and biological discourses are not stable, but socially and culturally variable, sex, which is socially constructed, is gendered and likewise variable. She refuses the idea of sex/gender as a fixed structure or system and the idea that one is socialized to accept norms and gendered identities. Butler insists that one must *perform* one's gender, relying upon existing norms and identities or boldly refusing existing restrictive identities. Body identity is constituted through the reiteration of discursive practices, thus stabilizing them. The law, disciplinary mechanisms, and morality train humans to perform socially sanctioned acts and to refuse subversive or transgressive identities. This means that heterosexuality, women's desire for men as sexual partners, and their desire to have children are supported by the law, social institutions, and morality. Since identity is actualized as it is performed, it must be continually repeated, since there is no social model or authentic original to copy; because the repetitions are never the same, Butler introduces an element of chance and change. Given the disjunction between the anatomical body and gender identity performance, she believes that everyday performances can be disruptive. This theory, which emphasizes singular body performances and ultimately the indeterminateness of these performed acts, assumes an overly open theory of identity. Since change occurs through the reiteration and resignifying of discourses, in the process of performing one's identity, one can also undo it. While performing one's gender identity may be variable over time, this doesn't mean that it is resignified or radically altered. Butler produces a novel way of approaching agency, but it is limited. Even if norms and practices can be lived differently through their resignification, however, conceiving change as the resignification of norms is narrow.

In focusing upon how heterosexuality is performed, through the reiteration of heterosexual norms, in a coercive regime, she seeks to destabilize heterosexual normativity, she discusses the "materialization" of "sexed" bodies almost entirely in terms of norms – but with no sense of where these norms come from or why they reproduce gender divisions or heterosexual hegemony (Hennessy 1998). The social is thus reduced to the normative and what is normative goes unexplained. Furthermore, there is no consideration of how norms relate to social practices and social hierarchies.

Butler traces how heterosexual norms, regulatory regimes, and the law constrain gay, queer, intersexed, transgendered, transsexed people. But she doesn't explicitly attend to the institutions and hierarchies that secure these norms. More recently, in *Undoing Gender* (2004b), she provides a philosophic ontology, departing from the Foucauldian position of *Gender Trouble* that disparages ontological formulations. Affirming the Hegelian tradition that "links desire with recognition," she says, "it is only through recognition that one is constituted as a socially viable being" (Butler 2004b, 2). However she also attends to the problem with the Hegelian model that "conferred humanness on some beings and others were excluded as less than human" (2). Existing norms do not accommodate diversity – hence recognition is withheld because of one's gender (sexual preference). "The 'I' that I am finds itself at once constituted by norms and dependent on them but also endeavors to live in ways that maintain a critical and transformative relation to them. This is not easy, because the 'I' becomes, to a certain extent unknowable, threatened with unviability" (3).

In order to lead a less oppressive life, in order to become socially viable and persist, sexual minorities must undo existing gender norms and "seek recognition of their sexual preferences" (4). Seeking recognition is difficult and Butler is aware of the legal and institutional changes necessary to provide safe space for those who do so. Butler not only acknowledges that gender discrimination works "against women" (8); she also recognizes that "gender discrimination" (8) does not "take into account the differential ways in which women suffer from poverty and illiteracy, from unemployment " (8).

While Butler understands the need to recognize other forms of suffering and oppression that women experience, whether it is an effect of class or race, she has not been particularly helpful in exploring them. In fact I'm not sure she provides the basis for theorizing them.[6] Insofar as Butler is interested in tracing queer identities that transgress conventional heterosexual norms and practices, she leaves aside all those women whose gender performances ambivalently reiterate conventional gender assumptions. In coming to terms with how one can live a less oppressive life, understanding the significance of reproduction within state policy, of women's role in the labour force, and of unpaid labour in the

6 Saba Mahmood, another poststructuralist, makes this point in her book *The Politics of Piety* (2005). Studying the women's mosque movement in Egypt, she shows the insufficiency of Butler and Foucault who see agency in terms of simply resignifying norms and discourses. In fact, she also frames her feminism in terms of refusing a simple reading of Western feminists, who presume a negative theory of freedom, freedom from, or absolute transcendence of, existing relations. Whether Mahmood is thinking of liberal or Hegelian theories of freedom, she does not acknowledge Beauvoir's notion of freedom as embodied and situated, needing not only to negate oppression, but also configure a positive project.

family are all important. However Butler doesn't sufficiently attend to these macro socio-economic forces.

PERFORMATIVITY: BEAUVOIR ALONGSIDE BUTLER

As we will see, Beauvoir too has a theory of gender performativity, thereby avoiding static essences. However, for her, a relation to the past and others is important and consequently distinct. For Beauvoir "woman is a becoming" (*SS*, 37), a process neither biologically nor socially determined. In acting, speaking, and narrating themselves, women perform and realize themselves amongst others – their embodied subjectivity is an intersubjective accomplishment. Unlike Butler, who calls for the refusal of existing identities and norms and sees this occurring between the singular body and the law, Beauvoir also allows for a more creative identity to emerge. One struggles to alter one's past relationship to oneself and others in the process. This is no mean feat. Most importantly it is a social and political achievement. Butler pays insufficient attention to how one's performances involve others, in an intersubjective (social) world, not merely a relation of a singular body and the law. Beauvoir assumes that in performing one's gender, one takes up past/present patterns of sexist behaviour, images, and symbols to reconfigure new relations. To become a subject one must creatively engage existing language, symbols, and patterned behaviour attributed in social structures and policy. Beauvoir recognizes how significant changes in public policy can have positive effects on women's social existence, and facilitate less oppressive gender norms. For Beauvoir this involves a commitment to socio-political movements.

Beauvoir has some thoughts about how creative embodied change occurs. All human functions (sexuality, perception, motility) are integrated in our bodily and temporal syntheses; transcendence as conversion involves taking up these syntheses. How we take them up has to do with our own gestures and personal style (*LIT*, 200). Our experience is always organized, and our body plays a role in organizing experience, but not the sole role – the body is a condition of possibility of organizing experience. One must assume sedimented patterns, which are social, cultural, and political in nature, but Beauvoir also refers to physiological facts that delimit what is possible. Hence, the relations between anatomy, performance, and acts are not as contingent, as they are for Butler. "Physiological facts, one's psychological history, and social circumstances" (*SS*, 436) have roles to play in women's becoming. Hence, it is not singular acts of performance but acts that work on existing social relations, that may even have biological underpinnings. As one performs one's gender to enhance one's openness and engagement, one shifts one's past relation to oneself and others. There are general social processes at work, but also physiological facts that contribute to women being is defined as Other. While the body is socially constructed, it is not wholly so, and given the persistent patriarchal relations and persistence of sexual reproduction, transgressing conventional gender is also more difficult than Butler presumes. Beauvoir's notion of "body as situation" (46) takes on board the historical context, as well as the need to co-ordinate with political movements that are most effective. Hence Beauvoir believes that collective projects struggling against oppression will challenge women's position as Other and enhance women's freedom and autonomy.

This approach is at odds with the presentism of much contemporary poststructuralist theory, in which past cultural or socio-economic conditions are not considered. The historical context is presumed to be incorporated into the discourse and therefore not in need of further explication, or only in passing as conditions of performance-performativity (Butler 1990).

Beauvoir gives more space tracing the impediments to reconfiguring one's past gendered relations. By recognizing the historical context, social structures, public policies, and attitudes that keep restrictive gender practices in place she goes some way toward understanding resistances to change. Focusing upon the transgression of existing discursive practices and norms through performance, as Butler does, is not enough.

Beauvoir does not assume that an ungendered future is in store, but holds out the possibility of altering our present gendered relations. Clearly, she believes that in a world where women are active in cultural and social life, the phallus will not play the same role as it does in the present. In fact, she imagines that woman's bodily relationships to her sexuality and the symbolic order will change, but she will still have a woman's body. So again, Beauvoir contests those French feminists of difference who assume that the symbolic is prior to or separate from the social. Further, she does not believe that women will be free from their body or gender processes if emancipated, but rather recognizes that there will be other, more reciprocal ways of being a woman. She talks about how there will be symbols expressing female power in a world where women are free. For Butler, informed by psychoanalysis, the possibility of reconfiguring one's desire is more difficult. For Beauvoir, the subject becomes an agent in social relations so that new social and political movements can have a positive effect on one's present gender relations and hopefully spawn change in one's desire. Whereas for Butler and for the Lacanians, the subject becomes one by accepting the law of the father or through a painful separation from a significant (M)other. Without going through these intrapsychic processes, "freer" and more mature relations are implausible. Butler's attention to the longing for love and yet the submission to parental power (in *The Psychic Life of Power*) as well as the irretrievable vulnerability experienced in the face of the powerful Others – (Mother and Father) structures the psyche. Future relations are predisposed by these psychic structures, one's capacity to empathize or feel fear/hate in the face of others. While Beauvoir appreciates psychic limitations on one's ability to be more autonomous, she is more optimistic about the possibilities that new social and economic roles and political institutions have on the psyche. Feminism may have essentialized women by stressing the significance of their reproductive functions, but to treat these aspects of women's experience as contingent, as Butler does, is shortsighted. All societies have to reproduce themselves (supplying the next generation of workers, citizens, caretakers), and sexual reproduction and female caretaking are still the most common forms these reproductive functions take. Beauvoir was prescient in challenging traditional reproductive relations between men and women without denying their connections to sexually differentiated bodies. While many philosophers believe for "union to occur, there has to be the differentiation of the two sexes," Beauvoir finds this "demonstration unconvincing" (*SS*, 23). She insists that reproduction doesn't require two sexes: she explores various examples of parthenogenic reproduction in non-human life (22, 26, 30). From "the discoveries of parthenogenesis, she claims, some scientists have reduced the role of the male to a simple physicochemical agent (26). Finally, she writes that consciousness without a body or an immortal human being is rigorously inconceivable, whereas society can be imagined that reproduces itself by parthenogenesis or is composed of hermaphrodites (24). But having said that, she still sees the world divided between men and women, so for women to ignore their sex is naive, bad faith (4). Fifty years later the argument that diminishes the power of the male is even stronger, for synthetic sperm and perfected techniques of artificial insemination make possible asexual reproduction. However, even today conventional sexual relations and gendered caring practices are the norm. The nuclear family is no longer the majority-favoured unit. Still women are doing the majority of the caretaking roles. Women increasingly work as well as have children and couples refuse the institution of marriage. LGBTQ couples are increasingly having and rearing children in family structures, in married relations or not.

To deny the significance of hegemonic patterns of conception and heterosexuality in an effort to avoid heterosexism – Butler's tactic – is problematic. Her critique of compulsory heterosexuality, Rosi Braidotti insists (1991), does not appreciate the significance of the phallus in our largely heterosexual population. Irigaray, Grosz, and Braidotti are also concerned about the strong social constructivism impulse in Butler's work. While it may unsettle hegemonic heterosexuality, Braidotti thinks Butler's thesis doesn't attend to the phallic underpinnings of the dominant culture (1991). Moira Gatens (1993) also critiques Butler for not attending to the morphology of the body or biological facts and how those play into one's gendered identity.

Thus, Butler sees sex as gendered and scorns the reiteration of dualistic sexed differences as essentialist and politically regressive, but by stressing physiological or biological registers of sexed experience, one becomes overly concerned with reproductive functions. Furthermore, her theory of gender performance, which emphasizes that the body is singular and relations between anatomical sex, gender identity, and gender performance are contingent, loses sight of the persistence of reproductive and biological discourses in our society and the significance of these relations in transforming one's identity.

Moi successfully argues, I believe, that Butler wrongly presumes the sex/gender distinction leads to biologism. One can identify primary sexed differences, Moi argues, without assuming a biological essentialism. While there are difficult cases, where primary sexed differences are not present in individuals, most women have ovaries, whether they function or whether they are used to produce children or not (Moi 1999). The recognition of women's anatomy, the existence of ovaries, does not mean that all women are assumed to be mothers. Moi argues that Butler assumes biological determinism where there is none.

I believe it is necessary to resist the temptation to reject the sex/gender distinction altogether. Butler argues that sex is as socially constructed as gender: that sexual practices are as variable as customs. However, as I have argued, the significance of reproduction in most societies, past and present, makes sexual reproduction an enduring relation. As such, Butler's strategy tends to render it contingent – which is admirable, but also naive. She concludes that by using the terms man and woman, a fixity is achieved that must be avoided. I concur with Toril Moi and Ludwig Wittgenstein who believe "that the meaning of the word is its use in the language" (Moi 1999, 7). Hence it is necessary to use the term "woman" to grasp women's specific oppression. I concur with Moi that there is a tendency amongst feminist theorists "to make the word woman slim down to nothing" (7), which is particularly unhelpful for (a remembering that is necessary to) feminist politics. Interestingly Spivak considers the strategic use of essentialism and implores women "to take a risk"

(Spivak 1988, 3–4) in using the term. Moi surmises that "not all essentialisms are equally politically harmful" (Moi 1999, 37).

Toril Moi, rightly I believe, attributes some of Judith Butler's problems to her dependence upon the sex/gender distinction. This distinction was formulated by Anglo-American feminists and has been politically and socially useful; nevertheless it reiterates a biological foundationalism that is not helpful. Sex is turned into a disembodied ahistorical entity (7). Both Toril Moi and Sara Heinämaa believe Butler misreads Beauvoir by attributing to her a sex/gender distinction. As I have shown and will show, Beauvoir does not assume a factic body (sex) and a socially constructed realm of femininity (gender). Moi argues that many European feminists – be they French, Italian, or Scandinavian – refuse the term gender and yet accommodate a non-essential subject with a historically sensitive sexed body; so, she asks, why should we retain this distinction? I think it is important to resist the temptation to see the living body as simply a social cultural construction. One might argue the recent return to neuroscience is a response to the hyper-social constructivist thesis of Butler. Yet it too has its problems, often lapsing into another form of biologism. While new theories of human behaviour ought to be explored, the problem of biological determinism looms. For the neuroscientists and affect theorists see brain networking or physiology determining what is possible – an underdeveloped cortex, an over-performing amygdala make it difficult to regulate emotion – and sideline the significance of environmental factors. Furthermore there are neuroscientists who believe the brain is more adaptable, malleable (Doidge), so to assume the "finite window" thesis, as some neuroscientists do, rules out the possibility of remapping the brain to allow for positive emotional development. Moreover neuroscience functions as foundational, trumping social or historical factors in exploring human agency.

Beauvoir proceeds rather differently than all of the above. In exploring the lived body, she explores various dimensions of bodily being. Not all bodily capacities or processes are reducible to sexed differences, so Beauvoir challenges "sexual pervasiveness"[7] (Moi 1999, 11, 78). She doesn't go as far as Grosz or Braidotti in privileging bodily agency, for she still retains a role for reason, choice, and emotion (animating intentions of will) in a way that Grosz, Braidotti, and Butler do not.

Beauvoir does not assume there is a pre-discursive or natural body. Nor does she uphold the alternative position that treats the body as

7 Moi references Thomas Laqueur's discussion of a twentieth-century scientist, who produced a two-sex model of subjectivity, where biological sex seeps out from the ovaries and testicles into every cell of the body until it has saturated the whole person (Moi 1999, 11).

social cultural construct. Her theory of embodied subjectivity attends to the complexity of bodily experiences, encompassing differing levels of experience: whether they be physiological, psychological, or social (*SS*, 436). These diverse registers can be differentiated, but they are not wholly distinct. Beauvoir urges woman to "perform" her body (although she does not use that term), that is, to assume the various discourses and sedimented patterns that influence her bodily being in a creative way.

Thus, Beauvoir's use of the term woman does not presume a unified subject that serves as the foundation or base upon which feminist struggles ensue, nor does she endorse nominalism, believing women are free to define themselves as they wish. As I have shown, gendered experience is socially diverse and historically complex, but the term woman can accommodate that complexity and difference. In *The Second Sex*, she states that in order to understand herself she must understand her gendered existence. The effects of myths and cultural stereotypes cannot be ignored, but nor are they immutable. Furthermore, anti-feminists, or nominalists, who feel that women are free to choose their life and identities ignore the effects of gender on women's social lives. Unlike many feminists in the second wave with whom she is compared, Beauvoir does not believe gender is a primary or unitary category of analysis, but instead sees gender as inflected by various other social and cultural experiences.

RETHINKING THE SEX/GENDER DISTINCTION: LESSONS FROM SIMONE DE BEAUVOIR – ADDRESSING HER ANGLO-AMERICAN CRITICS

Beauvoir has been seen as the mother of the second wave of feminism in the 1960s, and her statement "One is not born, but rather becomes, woman" (*SS*, 301) inspired the sex/gender distinction. "Becoming a woman," she insists, is a social/cultural and material process. That it was not tied to anatomy was a great relief to those who feared that biology was destiny. However inspirational Beauvoir was, it is a mistake to see her as an exemplar of the sex/gender distinction, for she has a very different reading of the sexed body and a different approach to the gendering process. She did not bracket the body nor see it as neutral or irrelevant to the process of becoming a woman; she did not see the biological body as natural, or the stable base for female identity, nor did she see the body as simply a social/cultural construct. For Beauvoir, the body is our point of contact or our "grasp on the world and the outline of our projects" (*SS*, 46). The body is not factic, defined by static biological facts, that feminists should bracket – nor is it simply invented, a medium for expressing existing cultural/social/political discourses. Nevertheless biology and physiology are relevant as cultural and socio-economic factors in shaping a gendered bodily being. The living body is not produced by brute facts (*EA*, 7); it is the site of physiological givens (i.e., biological sex characteristics), facticities rooted in one's social class and past historical events. Hence, the living body entwines nature and culture, biology and society, the symbolic and the material, and the cultural and socio-institutional. This treatment of embodied subjectivity avoids the equally unsatisfactory alternatives of naturalism, which assumes that there is a stable body whose facts are knowable through science, and its stark alternative, social constructivism, which assumes these facts are socially and culturally constructed. The former interpretation – that the body can be known through objective scientific truths and that historical cultural aspects of the body do not figure in the biological/physiological body – is shortsighted. Social constructivism, on the other hand, makes short shrift of biology, neurophysiology, transcultural structures of experience, and ontological/existential speculations, which is likewise problematic.

Feminists have misunderstood Beauvoir's treatment of the body. She has been read as a universal rationalist by American feminists Susan Heckman and Iris Young as well as the French feminists of difference. Hence the significance of embodiment is denied. More recently, Linda Zerilli and Emily Zakin see her work as unsettling stable meanings and hence identify her with third-wave feminists. However, as I have said, Beauvoir's ontology problematizes her place amongst postmodern feminists.

Social constructivism, which follows the sex/gender distinction in seeing the body as a social and cultural artifact, tends to conflate physiological and biochemical bodily processes with cultural ones. Although Beauvoir respects the body as a cultural social artifact, she speaks of physiological facts. She also goes some way to appreciate transcultural features of embodiment in a way similar to Merleau-Ponty. In *The Phenomenology of Perception* (1962) Merleau-Ponty points to anatomical features: one's hands move towards a maximal grasp on things; one adjusts one's distance to see and hear clearly. Hence, the living body strives towards life and the enhancement of sensation. It equally avoids death. These bodily features are transcultural.

Beauvoir talks about the importance of structures of existence: the bodily motility, bodily intentionality, and figure/ground schema. Since the embodied subject is always historically and socially situated, the embodied self as figure is dependent upon ground as situation. Our praxiological body may move in particular ways, which is in part a result of our physiology, but equally important are their social and cultural meanings.

If the body is produced by social and cultural discursive practices, then it is assumed it can be rewritten by shifting cultural meanings. Beauvoir acknowledges that the body is culturally and socially constructed, yet she also distinguishes physiology, psychology, and social circumstances. In doing so, she refuses to see the body as constructed tout court. Specifically, in her book *Old Age* she traces the body's physiological decline – yet this is not an external structure that uniformly imposes itself on the subject, but rather facts that are variously lived.

As we saw above, poststructuralist feminists challenge the sex/gender distinction of second-wave feminists by destabilizing the assumption of a "natural sexed body" as distinct from social gendering processes. Beauvoir has been a common target for their critiques. Judith Butler is more appreciative of Beauvoir than are most poststructuralists, although she wrongly believes that Beauvoir upholds the classic sex/gender distinction: for Butler, the Beauvoirian body is conceived of as "a passive surface or site" of "natural" facts (sex) upon which social norms and practices (gender) are played out (Butler 1993, 4). It is treated as a stable foundation or residual facticity outside or prior to the social. Beauvoir does not assume that there is a pre-social or pre-cultural body, but that doesn't mean bodily experience is reducible to the social register. Many poststructuralists charge Beauvoir with somatophobia, a visceral disgust and fear of the body, particularly woman's body, and with thinking that reflects the male's point of view. Moreover, they frequently dismiss Beauvoir's feminism as humanist – universalist, rationalist, and "indifferent to difference." Poststructuralist feminists have pointed to Beauvoir's visceral disgust with woman's body as symptomatic of a philosophic humanism that disparages bodiliness and celebrates rationality. In employing universal philosophic categories of being-in-itself and being-for-itself, they believe she fails to respect how sexual difference affects one's agency. In fact, they insist that Beauvoir wants liberated women to emulate men, because their sexuality and their bodies are impediments to their freedom. Irigaray decries that Beauvoir's "wish to get rid of sexual difference is to call for a genocide more radical than any form of destruction there has ever been in History" (Irigaray 1992, 12). This extreme indictment of Beauvoir contrasts with Chanter's more modest claim that "Beauvoir's final message is that sexual differences should be eradicated and women must become more like men" (Chanter 1995, 76). Elizabeth Grosz, too, believes that Beauvoir flees the female body since it inherently limits "women's capacity for equality ... Insofar as woman adopts the role of mother, her access to the public, social sphere is made difficult if not impossible, and the equalization of the roles of the two sexes becomes nonsensical" (Grosz 1994, 15). Hekman (1990) identifies the contradictions in Beauvoir's position that women's body and her reproductive function are the source of her subordination and yet that she is able to assume a social constructivist position.

Although Beauvoir was guilty of some negative statements around the female body – she describes the vagina as a hole and her desiring body as slime, a bog, akin to plant life – she does so in the context of describing women's alienated experiences of their body within a masculinist culture. In particular Hélène, the main protagonist in her novel *The Blood of Others*, experiences her body in this way – but also has serious psychological problems. She is unable to enjoy sexual or erotic experiences or even sustain friendships at the outset of the novel. It is a mistake to identify the body Beauvoir comprehends as essentially male-identified or phallic. In fact, she clearly distinguishes the male libidinal economy from female desire (*SS*, 389–90). Whereas male desire is goal driven, female desire radiates throughout the body and is more diffuse.

Characterizing Beauvoir as an existential modernist who celebrates the capacity of individuals (men in particular) to wilfully transcend their bodies and their situations, misses the mark of feminist desire. So too does the assumption that woman's body – closer to nature and further from culture – is an impediment to her liberation and therefore inferior to the disembodied male subject. These conventional readings of Beauvoir ignore her theoretical problematic of embodied subjectivity, the "body as situation" (*SS*, 46), as well as the historically nuanced treatment of the body and the philosophic categories of transcendence and immanence, that is, being-for-itself and being-in-itself (Stavro 2000).

Beauvoir attributes her theory of embodied subjectivity to Heidegger, Sartre, and Merleau-Ponty: "the body is not as a thing, it is a situation, as viewed in the perspective I am adopting – that of Heidegger, Sartre, and Merleau-Ponty; it is our grasp (*point d'appui*) on the world, and an outline of our projects" (*SS*, 46). Translating *point d'appui* as instrument, rather than grasp, avoids the intimate connection between body and world by presuming an instrumental relation to the world, a relation that occludes the interconnectedness, attunement, and mutual permeability of both. When translated as point of contact with the world, it sees the body as a threshold onto the world and the subject as more responsive to the world and less purposive in its relations. The body is not ontologically opposed to the world; it doesn't share the same substance, but it is of the world. It is both a medium of expression as well as a site upon which transcultural physiological structures, biological facts, cultural forms, and social and economic relations are inscribed. As a medium of our expression, the body is neither a mirror nor a blank slate upon which the social/linguistic is inscribed, for there are biological and anatomical facts and social circumstances that delimit what is possible. These have a role to play in action, but are fully historical and social in nature. Quoting Merleau-Ponty, Beauvoir insists that one must understand "the conditions without which the very fact of existence would seem impossible" (24). He theorizes that transcultural bodily processes underpin conduct, yet she insists that structured experience is utterly social and cultural in character. Appreciating the physiological, or the co-mingling of the natural and cultural, the ontological and social, Beauvoir avoids the ahistorical and naturalist body that is often attributed to phenomenology.

Another glib label that is attached to Beauvoir's feminism is "egalitarian" (Grosz 1994). Granted, Beauvoir is concerned with equality, with providing opportunities for women to participate in public life and the economic world as equal participants. These measures, however, are not equalizing in the sense of making women the same as men or the same as each other, given that she acknowledges that women are differently situated. However, she does recognize that changes in institutions and social roles, as well as attitudes, are necessary to provide more opportunities for women. So micro and macro politics are on the agenda. Since we begin from our specific social situation, change must start from the specificity of the situation, so there can be no general solutions to the problems of hierarchies and inequality. When Beauvoir's critics (Irigaray, Cixous) read her through the lens of phallogocentrism (a socio-cultural linguistic privileging of the phallus) they gloss over all the differences that Beauvoir attends to and all too readily assume she endorsed the detached masculine subject of modernity. As we have seen, this is not so.

AVOIDING SEXUAL PERVASIVENESS – RECONFIGURING THE SEX/GENDER DISTINCTION

Clearing away the parodied readings of Beauvoir allows us to appreciate her in a new way. Her novel treatment of bodily being as having biological as well as cultural and social registers of experience is worth rethinking in light of the contemporary critiques of the sex/gender distinction (Rahman and Witz 2002). She respects the interpenetration of psyche and soma, but larger socio-economic and political forces are also articulated in what she calls "social circumstances" (*SS*, 436). Where the physiologists are often culpable of biologism, and psychoanalytically inclined theorists see the socio-economic and political as epiphenomenal to the psychic (436) or within the frame of phallogocentrism, Beauvoir avoids this reductionism by insisting upon distinguishing physiological facts, personal psychic history, as well as social circumstances (436). She notes that the UN is demanding women's equality (15) and women are more likely to participate in making the world today; however, these "objective" gains don't necessarily get translated into attitudinal ones. She notes that "some have never felt their femaleness an obstacle" (15), yet others refuse to give up the benefits they derive from their position as Other. Feminists must struggle on all fronts (personal and political) for emancipation to be possible.

In identifying sex as gendered and gender as sexed, the Foucauldian feminists (e.g., Judith Butler and Joan Scott) see the body as a target of bio-power. Poststructuralists reject the sex/gender distinction altogether, preferring the term sexual difference instead. For Judith Butler the sexed body is conceived of "not as a fact nor a static condition" but is produced through the forcible reiteration of norms, "a process whereby regulatory norms materialize sex" (Butler 1993, 2). Consequently, sex is always influenced by gender: the prevailing social norms of our liberal democratic capitalist society cultivate sexual relations that are system enhancing: for example, maximizing childbirth and producing stable social relations of marriage and fidelity. Heterosexuality is just that sort of sexual relation. Butler believes that "the distinction between sex and gender turns out to be no distinction at all" (Butler 1990, 7); however, her own example of gender performance requires such a differentiation. The male drag queen subverts sexual stereotypes but relies on the contrast between male bodies (sex) and feminine behaviour and women's clothes (gender) to do so (see Moi 2000, 53). Thus gender performance relies upon the connection between sex, bodies, and gender. This attests to the need to distinguish between sexualized and gendered experiences, rather than conflating them.

Judith Butler and Joan Scott, drawing upon the research of Anne Fausto-Sterling, insist that the scientific recognition of multiple sexes (some say five) challenges the heterosexual binary of two sexes. This, they argue, will have a progressive political effect. Moi claims by contrast that there is no reason to believe that being stuck with five gender norms would be less oppressive than two (Moi 1999, 38). I too am unconvinced that the mere admission of this scientific fact and the circulation of various new categories will translate into a more tolerant or liberated society. Such a position assumes that biological or sexual facts would irrevocably change social norms and practices. This I am not convinced of. Any scientific facts that are revealed, even those that challenge heterosexism, can be used in an intolerant way. This underlines the need to distinguish sexualized and gendered processes:[8] sexual identities don't necessarily translate into gendered realities.

In rejecting the sex/gender distinction, the psychoanalytically inclined feminists prefer to see the body as an effect of sexual difference. By eschewing the category gender as distinct though related to sex, such feminists are prone to ignore other aspects of life beyond the sexual that factor into their domination. There are the more-than-fleshy-aspects of women's lives, i.e., women's domestic labour, their religious practices, that contribute to their oppression; this is not sufficiently considered in this theory. Since the subject becomes one by taking up a linguistic position in a phallogocentric libidinal economy, the social is reduced to the socio-psychic order. In order to alter this situation, the subject is urged to reconfigure its relation to desire and lack. However, this doesn't sufficiently acknowledge the importance of differences in race, ethnicity, and age on one's sexual existence or the role of social roles, economic and social participation, or political organizations within which one acts. Moi rightly points out: "If sex is not pervasive, sexual difference does not saturate a woman through and through. Rather, our lived experience encompasses bodily sexual difference, but it is also built up by many other things that per se have nothing to do with sexual difference" (Moi 1999, 78).

It is suggestive to assume that a masterful and domineering stance towards others would involve the scapegoating of others and the treatment of others as abject, but this doesn't sufficiently attend to institutional mechanisms of racism and classism that sediment these values and practices. Beauvoir's concept of otherness captures different forms of marginalized and demeaned existences without sexualizing these experiences. One sees how she anticipates the intersectional theories that would arise in response to identity politics and their Black feminist and critical race theory critics.[9]

One of the criticisms launched by the poststructuralists is that the categories of sex and gender are treated as bi-morphic, presupposing

8 Anne Witz astutely describes the problem of these new philosophies of the body that "lose distinctive grip on the complex more-than-fleshy sociality that the concept gender gives a purchase on" (Rahman and Witz 2002, 6–7).

9 The Combahee River Collective (1977) felt that Marx had identified the significance of socio-economic factors in their oppression but his ideas had to be supplemented to deal with the specific oppression of Black women. Critical race theorists and theorists of intersectionality refined and elaborated the complex intersections of race, class, and gender.

simple distinctions between sex and gender, male and female, nature and culture. Beauvoir does more to challenge these simple dualities than has been assumed. She denies strong distinctions between the male and female sexes and (as already mentioned) draws our attention to asexual reproduction amongst lower species and the presence of intersexuality and hermaphrodites in animals and humans. "The perpetuation of the species does not necessitate sexual differentiation. True enough, this differentiation is characteristic of existence to such an extent that it belongs in any realistic definition of existence. But it nevertheless remains true that both a mind without a body and an immortal man are strictly inconceivable, whereas we can imagine a parthenogenetic or hermaphroditic society" (*SS*, 8).

The "body as situation" allows Beauvoir to various registers biological, cultural, social, and historical markers of gendered experience. She uses both social myths and scientific findings to make her case regarding the role of the two sexes in reproduction. In primitive matriarchal societies, the father was believed to play no part in conception; ancestral spirits with living germs inseminated women. Up to the seventeenth century, scientists thought of female genitals as "feminine testicles" and when the ovary was identified and named it was "regarded as a homologue of the male gland" (25). Scientists imagined that "woman merely fattened a living and active, and perfectly constituted, principle" (25), as illustrated by Hartsaker, a Dutchman who drew a picture of a "homunculus" hidden in the spermatozoon in 1694. The masculinist idea of the sperm as being the positive and creative force persisted long after scientists had challenged these ideas (25). Contemporary science discovers both gametes fusing in the fertilized egg; both are suppressed in becoming a new whole, so both are active and reactive (28). However, popular science still identifies the egg as quiescent and the sperm as vital.

Beauvoir uses experiments in parthenogenesis and asexual multiplication to challenge the androcentric version of reproduction. In many cases, the male seems radically useless (22): Drawing from science, she sees the sperm "as simply a physiochemical agent" (26), like "an acid or mechanical stimulation" that initiates the cleavage of the egg, and the development of the embryo and from that it was assumed that the male gamete was not necessary for generation (26). She goes to boldly suggest that "one day male's cooperation in procreation would become useless" (26).

Since sexual and asexual reproduction appear and there are no grounds to assume that the former is basic or more fundamental or favoured, Beauvoir resists treating bi-morphic sexual reproduction as universal. Rejecting any a priori doctrine or implausible hypothesis and resisting physiologists and biologists who use a more finalistic language, Beauvoir concludes, "we can affirm that any living fact indicates transcendence, and that a project is in the making in every function" (26). In doing so, she is not putting forward a new science of life, but hopes to grasp the significance of sexuality by studying it in its concrete manifestations and thereby overcome the masculinist bias. In doing so, she believes "the content of the word 'female' will come to light" (26).

Looking at the "concrete manifestations" of sex, as Beauvoir does, the sex/gender distinction does not hold up. This is also true when she looks at social processes and institutions, where the notion of the "feminine woman" or the "eternal feminine" is unsettled. "The chief misunderstanding," she says, "is that it is natural for the female human being to make herself a feminine woman: it is not enough to be a heterosexual, even a mother, to realize this ideal"; "the true woman" is an "artificial product that civilization makes, as eunuchs were produced in the past. These supposed 'instincts' for coquetry, docility, are inculcated in her just as phallic pride is for man" (421). "Man as a matter of fact, does not always accept this virile vocation; and woman has good reason for accepting with even less docility the one assigned to her" (421). Femininity is socially produced, and its particular forms correspond to larger socio-economic forces. There is some expectation that woman will emulate this ideal of femininity, but there are good reasons for her to refuse the ideal of the "true woman." Beauvoir recognizes the role of the individual in making this choice: some women try to embody this ideal, whereas others do not (421). These socially produced norms and practices cannot simply be ignored, but Beauvoir sees women taking up, refusing, and reconfiguring their cultural ideals in varying degrees. In fact, she sees lesbianism, in part, as a choice some women make when confronted with the norms of docility imposed by heterosexuality.

Beauvoir describes gender as an identity in process, consisting of norms and roles that are taken up and lived. At the same time, she admits that these gender roles connect up with larger socio-economic and political forces. Because the system requires women to pursue their reproductive roles, they produce maternal, docile, and domestic identities. The self is not the source of these latter norms and practices; instead, they are produced at the macropolitical/social level to legitimate and sustain patriarchal capitalism. Butler rightly identifies Beauvoir as her forebearer to the extent that they both realize that sexed and gendered identities require performance, a subject to take up these cultural representations. She points to her affinity to French existentialism, since they believe our acts do indeed define us, we are what we do (Butler 1999, 112). Women are not simply externally coerced or socialized to carry out their gender roles, as naive sociologists assume. In the context of Beauvoir's notion that woman is not born, but becomes, Butler attributes to her the sex/gender distinction, she assumes a factic body and "gender is that aspect of identity that is acquired" (Butler 1986, 35). However this is a mistake given Beauvoir's notion of the body as situation. Butler dismantles the relationship between sex, gender, and sexuality (35–49). "If a pure body cannot be found, if what can be found is the situated body, locus of cultural interpretations, then Beauvoir's theory seems implicitly to ask whether sex was not gender all along" (46).

Although Beauvoir did not use the term performative, she might well have, since she believes that at some level women "choose" their gender identity amongst the norms and representations offered. Their choices are also limited by their body – not just their ovaries, but indeed their everyday use of their body. The term "choice" has to be used with caution, since Beauvoir emphasizes pre-reflective bodily orientations, habits that inform choices. Despite their differences, both Butler and Beauvoir are anti-essentialists, however insofar as Beauvoir's lived body appreciates diverse social experiences, Butler is more concerned with gendered differences. Moi astutely summarizes this: "In Beauvoir's reminder that a child explores the world through the whole body, not just the sexual parts alone, we find another echo of her refusal to consider a woman a giant ovum or a monstrous vagina. If sex is not pervasive, sexual difference does not saturate a woman through and through. Rather, our lived experience encompasses bodily sexual difference, but it is also built up by many other things that per se have nothing to do with sexual difference" (Moi 1999, 79).

While Butler acknowledges that gender is not static, but "involves an ongoing interpretation and stylization" (Butler 1999, 33), for Beauvoir "freedom" involves experiences other than one's gender. She is distinct from Butler in that she seems to give more space to the subject to creatively craft a new identity, rather than simply refuse pre-existing ones. Also Beauvoir's existential/Marxist disposition not only privileges creative action and engagement in the world but also recognizes that these conventional acts/norms contribute to patriarchal capitalism. It is not simply enough for an individual woman to undo her gender challenging a "highly rigid regulatory framework" (Butler 1999, 33), but Beauvoir believes one can reconfigure one's identity by engaging in action and in collective projects. Encouraging women to engage in behaviour that destabilizes conventional norms and attitudes, she recognizes the importance of macropolitical action and collective projects and patriarchal capitalist forces that impede women's struggles. Beauvoir and Butler refuse essentialism and biologism, yet Butler configures women's struggles differently: rejecting notions of patriarchal capitalist power and emancipation, she supports transgressive practices. In reiterating conventional norms, the embodied subject never simply reproduces them; in struggling against the law, a shift is possible. Butler's understanding of action, however insightful, has a limited conception of the process of change; focusing upon the transgression of discourses, she fails to theorize how socio-economic forces and political institutions support those norms and thereby impede change.[10]

Since Butler was involved in queering gender, she spends much time showing how heterosexism's dimorphism has restricted multiple gender identities and charting transgressive gender practices, and in my opinion insufficient time in exploring persistent sexist and patriarchal practices that shore up women's reproductive roles in society. As Moi remarks: "For Beauvoir women exist, for Butler they have to be deconstructed" (Moi 1999, 76). Tidd speculates that Beauvoir would have rejected Butler's "early anti-materialist position and her focus on the reification of gender identities; for Beauvoir as for Delphy and Wittig, the category of 'woman' is a social and material reality" (Tidd 2004, 123). However differently women experience their lives, they are subject to structural inequalities in patriarchal societies (Jackson 1996, 137–8). For Beauvoir, changes in the structures and institutions can trigger change in sexed or gendered practices. Allowing women into paid employment, professional life, and the academy would have significant positive effects. However these material changes are insufficient. Still some women will strive to emulate the "truly feminine," whereas others will struggle against the norms of docility for a profession or a career. Interestingly, Beauvoir talks about another impediment to change, a psychological one. "The 'feminine' woman tries to entrap man, by becoming a passive prey, tries to reduce the male to carnal passivity, by the desire she arouses" (754). She must refuse this behaviour. "The 'emancipated' woman wants to be active, a taker, and refuses the passivity man means to impose upon her. The 'modern' woman accepts masculine values; she prides herself on thinking, taking action, working, creating on the same basis as males" (754). Instead of trying to drag men into immanence or belittle them, she declares herself their equal (755). Beauvoir believes women are beginning to break out of the prison that has entrapped them. They must

10 Nancy Fraser makes a similar point when she claims that discourses and culture are not free-floating, but sedimented in institutions (2000).

not only refuse the laws and practices that decreed them inferior, but insist upon being treated equally, with reciprocity. Men will find the loss in status as absolute superior, sovereign subject difficult, so conflict will ensue. Hence the process of emancipation is difficult: overcoming years of having denied one's desires and living a life of bourgeois housewife and mother will involve personal as well as institutional changes. Such was the world of Beauvoir's mother that she narrated in the *Memoirs of a Dutiful Daughter*. Of course, difficulties of class and racial positions complicate this further.

Beauvoir identifies another impediment to women's freedom: "maternity is still almost impossible to undertake in complete freedom" (735). She seems to frame this bodily activity as a natural impediment; however, she then proceeds to acknowledge how social/political factors can lighten the burden of maternity. She writes: "In England and in America women can refuse it at will, thanks to the practice of birth control … In France she is compelled to costly and painful abortions" (735). Choice is limited not only by public policy but also by social attitudes. Illegitimate birth makes procreation without a spouse and marriage a stain on the child (735). Given the lack of well-organized day care and kindergartens, even one child is enough to paralyze a woman's activity (735). "She can continue to work only by abandoning the child to her parents, friends, or servants" (736). Thus woman is forced to make a difficult choice between sterility, often experienced as a painful frustration, and burdens hardly compatible with a career (736). "The independent woman of today is torn between her professional interests and the concerns of her sexual vocation. It is difficult for her to strike a balance between the two; if she does, it is at the price of concessions, sacrifices, acrobats that keep her to be in a constant state of tension" (775). This constant state of tension must be explored. Beauvoir confirms that she believes it is more psychological than physical. She writes: "It is clear that menstrual pain does have organic causes, and I have seen the most energetic women spend 24 hours in bed every month in the throes of pitiless tortures; but their enterprises were never hindered by them" (736). So, although working women embrace the "masculine" values of paid labour, this doesn't automatically translate into their sexual liberation. For their relation to their body must be reconfigured. Beauvoir describes this as manifest in a "moral tension": living actively and practicing freedom conflicts with the norms of femininity, which requires subservience to male sexual pleasures and viewing their body as a burden. She distinguishes psychological and physical tensions from social and political bulwarks. Some very responsible and competent women submit to masochism – "they enjoy annihilating themselves for the benefit of the masterful will" (769).

Others, like Madame de Staël,[11] had resounding victories on both fronts. Beauvoir believes that men find it particularly difficult to accept sexually liberated women. They accept equality in the workplace more readily than in their emotional lives. Beauvoir holds out the possibility of reciprocal relations in one's sexual as well as work relations, while still recognizing how rare it is in present circumstances.

Even if women are formally granted opportunities in the work place (as occurred in socialist societies), their independence is not secure. Even those ambitious women who pursue their careers single-mindedly, Beauvoir complains, "remain dominated by the male universe" and lack "the taste for adventure, gratuitous experience, or disinterested curiosity" (740). The professional woman "builds a career the way others build a happy life … she lacks the audacity to break through the ceiling … she does not lose herself in her projects. She has a tendency to attach too much importance to minor failures and modest successes" (740). She either gets discouraged or swells with vanity (740). Beauvoir believes that "they can have honorable careers with such methods, but will not accomplish great things" (740). What we see in Beauvoir's descriptions is a myriad of ways that women emotionally respond to the situations in which they find themselves, and how they will approach their struggle for equality. Some act more resolutely while others more readily are affected by the impressions of others. Even as women take up more responsible roles and enter professional life, there is no simple liberation, a transformation of character; women will have to struggle with men to achieve mutual respect and struggle against themselves to become emotionally autonomous. In addition they will have to confront institutions that reproduce women as submissive and passive.

Beauvoir provides a complex reading of the sexed body: it is neither a simple product of biological facts (anatomy or hormones), psychological history, nor social and economic factors. Sexual choices are influenced by physiology and by both socially validated identities as well as new identities that emerge. Vaginal and clitoral pleasure are different from each other and different from male erection and orgasm; these have to do with anatomical differences as well as socio-cultural ones. The coition culminates in ejaculation, whereas women can be impregnated without orgasm. "The normal sex act effectively makes woman dependent upon the male and the species" (385). "She can be taken at any time by man, while he can take her only when he is in a state of erection" (385).

11 Madame de Staël (1766–1817), a French writer, famous for her novels and letters, was a proto-feminist who was exiled from Napoleon's France.

"Coitus cannot take place without male consent, and male satisfaction is its natural end" (385). "Woman is penetrated and fecundated by way of the vagina, which becomes an erotic centre only through the intervention of the male, and this constitutes a kind of violation" (416). Dependence and violence characterize the present erotic life of a woman. An act of violence changes a girl to a woman, hence "taking" a girl's virginity and "defloration" are the terms employed. "Man reaches out to his partner, but he himself remains at the centre of this activity … he projects towards the other without losing his independence … he gains access to the qualities he desires, as with any object" (415). Beauvoir insists that biological facts are not freestanding but are given meaning from within their particular society. She approaches women's sex/eroticism as very complex processes, not subscribing to either a theory that focuses on drives or one that focuses on social identities.

The category woman is in process and can be influenced by multiple anatomical, social, and cultural fields; however, it is a sufficiently coherent phenomenon to warrant the use of the term.

LESBIANISM AS AN ILLUSTRATION OF A COMPLEX SOCIAL BODY

Beauvoir's treatment of lesbianism helps us understand how the Beauvoirian body mediates and expresses various diverse registers of experience without collapsing them into each other.[12] She rejects biological determination and the drive theory of psychoanalysis: "Anatomy and hormones never define anything but a situation and do not posit the object towards which the situation will be transcended" (418). Consequently, physiological factors are a factor, but so are one's psychological disposition and social circumstances. So anatomy may frame what is possible, but one's desire towards certain objects and not others is influenced by social and cultural factors. Thus anatomy, sociality, and culture play into one's sexuality. One may be physiologically disposed towards a lesbian identity, but one's desire is not determined by physiological processes alone. It is produced in social contexts. Men with perfectly masculine physiques may be homosexual, while women with virile characteristics may desire women (418). But women might also "assume virile qualities" out of feelings of social inferiority. So, in addition to physiology influencing one's homosexuality, the construction of one's

12 Boldy Beauvoir wrote a chapter on lesbianism in *The Second Sex*; her treatment is more philosophic than sociological in nature.

sexual desire is an effect of social and cultural factors as well: "A person with a vigorous, aggressive, and exuberant vitality wishes to exert himself actively and usually rejects passivity; an unattractive and malformed woman might try to compensate for her inferiority by assuming virile qualities" (418).[13]

To understand relations and movements between the anatomical, the psychological, and the social I will employ the metaphor of the Möbius strip. Beauvoir would have been familiar with Merleau-Ponty's description of the reversible movement between the kinaesthetic, tactile, psychological, and social body, although she never used the metaphor of the Möbius strip herself.[14] Through a torsion or drift, the inside (the genetic or psychological) moves out and the outer (the social, cultural) moves in, rendering the distinction between the inside and outside volatile. The biological and genetic drifts into the psychological and social, and vice versa. These fields flow into one another, yet they are still distinguishable. In this way Beauvoir challenges ontological binaries and philosophical dualisms and helps us understand how sex is gendered and gender is sexed. She does not, however, draw Butler's conclusion that there is no distinction between these two spheres – these registers are distinguishable though interdependent.

Sexual personhood for Beauvoir integrates multiple physiological, psychological, and social factors. She does not prioritize one over the other but assumes they all play a role in the determination of subjectivity: "Childhood eroticism is clitoral; whether it remains fixed at this stage or is transformed has nothing to do with anatomical facts; nor is it true, as has often been maintained, that infant masturbation explains the ulterior primacy of the clitoral system ... The development of feminine eroticism is ... a psychological situation in which physiological factors are included, but which depends on the subject's overall attitude to existence" (418). Clitoral pleasure is underpinned by anatomy – the presence of erotic zones and the pleasure of rubbing associated with them – but social and psychological forces also factor into this pleasure

13 Interestingly enough Beauvoir does not reiterate the psychoanalytic theory of sexual identification in terms of desire/identity with one's parents, but rather employs a more open theory of sexual identification.

14 In *Volatile Bodies* Elizabeth Grosz uses the term Möbius strip as a model for the subject. However, she attributes the term to Lacan rather than Merleau-Ponty (1994, xii). It allows the rethinking of the relation of mind and body that shows the inflection of mind into body and body into mind as, through a kind of twisting, one side becomes another. It also rethinks the relation between the psychical interior and corporeal exterior, not as reducible to each other, but as distinct, as through the torsion or inversion the inside moves outside and the outside moves in.

or its denial. Given societies' investment in reproducing the species, Beauvoir believes there is a push to move women away from clitoral gratification and on to vaginal orgasm, for the former does not lead as necessarily to reproductive sex as does the latter.

As Beauvoir points out, although lesbianism is more pervasive in societies where women are dominated (341) and existing forms of femininity involve passivity, it is not exclusive to these societies. So far, female sexuality has been produced where masculine desire and the needs of reproduction have dominated, and, consequently, a distinctively female sexuality has been marginalized if not eliminated. Women's failure to experience socially useful pleasures that contribute to reproduction have been pathologized by modern psychiatrists. Consequently, the inability to displace clitoral pleasure with vaginal orgasm is seen as a sign of an underdeveloped or immature sexuality. Beauvoir understands the profession's sexism as following logically from the male-dominated society, where phallic pleasure both is the norm and is believed to embody the positive expression of the libido. Thus, women are not the object of research, and their pathologies are seen as a consequence of their failure to adapt to their social roles of wife and mother. Beauvoir references Wilhelm Stekel, a more recent psychoanalytic thinker. He sees female homosexuality as a sign of immaturity or personal pathology (defining it as frigidity). Although Stekel did not subscribe to all the tenets of Freudian psychoanalysis, he too assumed "it is natural for the human female to make a feminine woman of herself" and believes the lesbian is "making an inauthentic choice" (420). Beauvoir clearly rejects this interpretation. She socializes "the psychological problems" that women encounter: women's alienation is a response to their social reality of oppression.

Lesbianism arises in part due to the stark and unsatisfactory choices imposed upon woman by the androcentric culture of which she is part. Because she is not satisfied by the passive and submissive role, lesbian identity becomes an expression of her effort to support a more positive, engaged, and affirmative mode of being embodied. In particular, Beauvoir talks of women who "claim their freedom and refuse to abdicate in favour of another human being" (422–3); she recognizes herself in her acts, not in her immanent present. They scorn the servile position and the soft flesh of the ideal female body: "Many woman athletes reject this ideal of the passive flesh of a body … it does not inspire caresses, but is a means for dealing with the world" (423). Artistic women may also, Beauvoir claims, prefer not to play the role of the weak, needy woman: "Even if she has a good figure and is pretty," she does not want "male desire reducing her to the limits of her body" (422–3).

She sees lesbianism as a choice – not as a rational decision, but as a way in which woman solves the problems posed by her condition: "Woman's homosexuality is one attempt amongst others to reconcile her autonomy with the passivity of the flesh" (419). "It is an attitude that is *chosen in situation*; it is both motivated and freely adopted" (436). None of the factors "physiological facts, psychological history or social circumstances – are determining, but they all contribute to explaining it" (436).

Beauvoir's chapter "The Lesbian" in *The Second Sex* follows her analysis of sexual initiation and precedes the section on marriage. This graphically illustrates her treatment of lesbianism as a transitional and transitory phase of development. Such a reading in fact fails to appreciate the complexity of sexual identities. Elizabeth Fallaize argues Beauvoir's definition of a lesbian has more to do with her own circumstance (where she saw herself as heterosexual, in spite of her relations with women). "According to Beauvoir, lesbians do not simply enjoy sexual relations with women; the decisive point is that is *all* they enjoy ... Lesbians are women who never consider men potential objects of pleasure, on this definition ... she herself is heterosexual" (Fallaize 1998, 77). In her letters to Sartre during the phony war (the period before the Second World War when Sartre was at the front) she exposed her relations with young women, yet she insisted throughout her life that she was not a lesbian. She saw this time as a period of experimentation, which is precisely how she treated it in her work. One might also wonder whether she felt a relationship with men was harsh and violent and therefore withdrew into the safety of women's relations to women: "The homosexual affair represents a stage, an apprenticeship, and a girl who engages in it most ardently may well become tomorrow the most ardent of wives, mistresses or mothers" (455). She also claims that every adolescent female fears penetration and masculine domination, and she feels a certain repulsion for the male body; the female body is for her, as for the male, an object of desire (*SS*, 454). She describes woman's longing for contact with the soft smooth flesh of the young boy, a woman, flowers, fur, a child (436). The lesbian experience is a temporary phase for some: she describes women wounded by male lovers temporarily escaping the roughness of male domination. These forms of lesbian identity may not be necessary in a world of equality; however, they are necessary in the present.

If the equality of the sexes were actually brought about, the obstacle of male roughness would disappear. While certain social causes of lesbianism would thus be removed, it nevertheless would persist as a phenomenon, for it is not simply an effect of women's social oppression. Beauvoir distinguishes transitional or temporary lesbianism from those defined identities when it is manifested "with unusual strength." She also traces it to the desire for the female/mother's body that is never wholly expunged for women. For this reason she says "one can say that all women are naturally homosexual" (359). Insofar as Beauvoir assesses lesbian relations in terms of broader human relations, Claudia Card complains (2003) that she fails to understand specifically lesbian identities and practices.

Beauvoir's work on lesbian sexuality is clearly deficient; nevertheless it was one of the first candid treatments of lesbianism. However inadequate it is, one must remember it was written in 1949, hence transgressive for its times. She challenged "the reigning determinist discourse of psychoanalysis" (Fallaize 1998, 145). In addition, her recognition of the significance of social constructionism, without reducing biology or anatomy to social construction, is insightful. While hormones and physiology may have a role to play in lesbian identity, she refuses a causal connection. Beauvoir recognizes the individual's role in her "self-making" and performing of her identities, but it must be underlined that she sees this emerging from the situation; it is not a wilful choice, but more an embodied (habit) practice. Consistent with her existentialism, "one is neither irrevocably heterosexual or homosexual ... one continually choses one's sexuality" (Tidd 2004, 67). However forward-looking Beauvoir was, she did not explore the restrictions that lesbian women were subject to in conventional patriarchal societies (Ferguson 1990, 285). Hence her focus on choice as well as exploring it as "an individual experience," in particular as a transitional or an adaptive practice as separate from any political or community considerations is overall a serious shortcoming (Fallaize 1998, 145).

RETHINKING BODILY STRUCTURES BEYOND NATURALISM AND SOCIAL CONSTRUCTIVISM

Feminist debates seem to have fallen prey to simplistic thinking: either the body is natural and ahistorical, raising all the fears of scientism, socio-biology, and biologism (that is, that biological weakness dictates social relations),[15] or woman's body is presumed to be socially or

15 The recognition that nature has a history, that it is not simply outside the social, has been a worthwhile contribution of phenomenological and poststructuralist theorists. The rethinking of "nature as a set of dynamic interrelations" (Butler 1993, 4) is found in the work of Gilles Deleuze and contemporary Deleuzeans such as Rosi Braidotti (1991, 1994, 2002) and Jane Bennett (2001). Merleau-Ponty and Beauvoir's theorization of the body as the co-implication of the natural and the cultural are alternative approaches to rethinking the "natural" body.

culturally constructed and so she is able to escape her inferior status.[16] In the past, biology lent credibility to a stable material body; women were identified in terms of their reproductive functions and the processes associated with them, thus intensifying bi-morphic identities. Bodily processes were marked as immutable and sexed. However, as we have seen, this is changing.

Contemporary science has challenged simple dualist (gendered) theories of reproduction, as well as the idea of the material body as stable and immutable. Due to the proliferation of scientific techniques (genetic engineering, cosmetic surgery, nanotechnology), the material restructuring of the body is possible: nature is no longer conceived of as static and inert (see Bennett 2001, 2010; Wilson 1998). In this light, biology as a "natural" source of women's subordination is less of a worry today than it was fifty years ago. In fact, the new materialists focus upon the agentic capacities of things and vibrancy of the material world (Coole and Frost 2010). While in the past biology and physiology tended to be a worry for feminists, today this is less the case – especially amongst those who think of the material/nature as lively and vibrant, active rather than inert. However, the anti-humanism implicit in these theorists sits poorly with feminism, since their focus upon non-human agency has eclipsed thinking about human agency in general and differential women's agency.

In the past, the sex/gender distinction alluded to the power of the cultural to transform masculinist relations; today that seems to be less the case. Culture and society seem to endlessly reproduce gender inequality in their representations, practices, and institutions, there is little reason to be optimistic that in labelling phenomena as socially constructed one furthers women's liberation. In spite of feminist gains over the last fifty years, since second wave feminism drew attention to the cultural and social effects of patriarchy, the nuclear family, "the stay-at-home mum," and the romantic narratives around marriage and maternity persist, as do beliefs in the evils of single-parent families.

Beauvoir permits a rethinking of the nature/culture distinction that avoids the unpalatable opposition of naturalism and social constructivism. She neither calls for a return to naturalism – the belief in biological and physiological facts that can be apprehended by objective scientific

16 Myra J. Hird (2002) believes that momentous shifts in natural science emphasize an openness and play with living and non-living matter, which warrants a rethinking of the relationship between the physical and cultural world. This has ramifications for the sex/gender distinction and discussions of the body. She encourages theorists to go "beyond a reaction against dualism."

method – nor does she reduce biology to its political effects as illustrated by Foucault's theory of bio-power, which involves a genealogical and discursive analysis of the social sciences. Admittedly the nature/culture distinction itself is a cultural or political artifact, and linguistically or discursively articulated, but that doesn't mean all bodily experience is socially and/or discursively constructed.[17] Reliant on the work of Merleau-Ponty, who presumes the existence of innate structures of experience, transcultural bodily experiences, the gestalt, and ontology (see White 1999),[18] Beauvoir acknowledges cross-cultural experiences without denying that they are socially and culturally mediated. In her work we find the natural and cultural deeply entangled and deeply co-implicated.[19]

Beauvoir appeals to Merleau-Ponty who explores the structures that are fundamental to human experience. Merleau-Ponty identifies a pre-cognitive body-organizing schema. Bodily habituation is an open structure that influences how cognitive processes and external factors are synthesized. This does not pre-determine behaviour, but it does have effects. This allows a more complex relation between the biological and the social. The bodily organizing schema structures what is possible but does not determine it. He also avoids seeing the body subject as an effect of, or as subordinate to, cognitive processes or external social forces like bio-power: "The way a child structures his social environment is not unrelated to hereditary or constitutional dispositions of his nervous system … internal characteristics of the subject intervene in his way of

17 Butler (1993, 6) distinguishes her theory from radical or linguistic constructivism (the belief that everything is discursively constructed). She believes that such a theory denies that gender construction "operates through exclusionary means … through a set of foreclosures or radical erasures" (1993, 8) and refuses the possibility of cultural articulation. However clever this response, it is not convincing, for most discursive theorists recognize that the boundaries of the discourse are constitutive of behaviour, even if normalization is refused. Interestingly enough, Butler provides no evidence of a theorist who exemplifies linguistic monism (determinism) or radical constructionism. Even if, as she claims, they simply read off subjectivity or social agency from discourses, many attend to how discourse also inversely creates those who are excluded/refused. Even if Butler is not a discursive determinist, the attention she places on language and efforts of identity formation, like Lacan, do not adequately attend to the affects of the social fields in which performativity takes place.

18 White's distinction between weak and strong ontology is useful in this regard; we could make use of the adjective weak to describe Beauvoir's ontology.

19 While Beauvoir decentres the subject she does not endorse the anti-humanism of the new materialism. Her attention to human agency and the significance of choice, albeit delimited by the situation, is more human-centred than the new materialist would accept.

establishing his relations to what is outside him ... it is never simply the outside that molds him; it is he himself who takes a position in the face of external conditions" (Merleau-Ponty 1964a, 108). The body is not simply molded by exterior social or material forces, nor by inner psychic forces, for the body is a unique conduit or threshold between these endogenous and exogenous factors. Attending to the structures of body experience (innate and acquired), or the organizing schemas of the body, allows Beauvoir to explore the "how" of knowing and perceiving, not the "what." The body subject is not a natural or fixed entity, for how these structures are assumed is specific. One's style is utterly social and variable. However, these structures are not socially constructed; such a construction would lose sight of their cross-cultural and innate character. To dismiss these insights under the rubric of essentialism ignores the fact that Merleau-Ponty's structures accommodate a high degree of complexity and difference; they neither substantivize human behaviour nor tie women to traditional gender roles. They consequently are not essentialist in the negative sense. Beauvoir commends Merleau-Ponty for recognizing the capacity of the body to integrate various structures, social patterns, and events into human existence without producing a determinist or causal theory: "Merleau-Ponty notes ... that human existence requires us to revise our ideas of necessity and contingence. 'Existence,' he says, 'has no causal, fortuitous qualities, no content that does not contribute to the formation of its aspect; it does not admit the notion of sheer fact, for it is only through existence that the facts are manifested.' But it is also true that there are conditions without which the very fact of existence itself would seem impossible. To be present in the world implies strictly that there exists a body, which is at once a material thing in the world and a point of view toward this world" (*ss*, 7).

Challenging previous theories of causality and contingency and traditional notions of inside and outside permits a rethinking of determination without determinism. Beauvoir respects patterns and structures (that are bodily and socio-historical in nature) and yet nevertheless allows for fluidity and openness for change. Seeing the subject as a "fold which has been made and can be unmade" (Beauvoir 1945, 366), an interface of the pre-personal and personal, the social and the specific, Beauvoir allows change within structures.

Without supporting a strong ontology that substantivizes human nature and presumes that humans have identifiable positive attributes that distinguish them from non-human life, Beauvoir subscribes to a weak ontology that tentatively theorizes distinctive human qualities. Women, like men, she says, aspire to freedom. This, though, is not freedom as licence (doing what you want), but freedom as creative engagement and attunement with others in the world. Beauvoir departs from a theory of negative freedom, which assumes women must simply negate and thereby transcend the past. Although woman's agency is presently thwarted by persistent social and cultural patterns of patriarchy, Beauvoir believes that creative engagement in the world is ontologically privileged. Her ontological and historical insights highlight the experiences and social preconditions of women's agency and can accommodate a high degree of complexity and difference. To dismiss her as "universalist, Eurocentric and heterosexist" (Braidotti 2013, 20) or essentialist is glib.

Beauvoir does not encourage women to master their situations nor does she endorse wilful choice, for concrete freedom presumes embodied subjects intertwined in their situations and yet able to creatively express them by virtue of that very entwinement. Woman is able to make herself out of what the world has made of her. Herein lies Beauvoir's appreciation of a new way of approaching materialism that allows for human creativity without voluntarism or determinism. Woman is not the source nor effect of her situation, for the body subject is a hinge onto the world and must therefore have the requisite "subjective" preconditions as well as "objective" factors if concrete freedom or agency is to be realized (Moi 1998, 78).

Women are thwarted on socio-psychological and socio-economic levels of their existence. Socio-psychological forms of passivity and other-directedness associated with conventional femininity militate against women's expression of their desires for freedom and active engagement in the world. New post-patriarchal identities and narratives are required to further such action. On a socio-economic level, Beauvoir identifies a lack of participation in the economy and public life as a barrier. However "work is a thankless task for many, the chore is not offset by a concrete conquest of her social dignity, economic autonomy … it is understandable that many women workers see no more than obligation in the right to work, and choose marriage to deliver them" (*ss*, 156).

If women are to be active agents, existing domestic practices (154) and institutions must be transformed. Democratic socialism (or equitable economic structures of labour and democratic processes) must replace capitalism (with its power differentials and hierarchies). Political institutions that exclude women as participants must be made more inclusive. However, even in the absence of revolutionary changes, Beauvoir suggests that purposeful engagement in the world, despite being more limited, is nevertheless possible. The pursuit of one's projects and desires is restricted when one is oppressed, but authentic and engaged behaviour is not ruled out of court.

RETHINKING BIOLOGY BEYOND NATURALISM AND SOCIAL CONSTRUCTIVISM

While second-wave feminists were prone to naturalism or social constructivism as evidenced in their support for the classic sex/gender distinction, third-wave feminists almost exclusively endorsed social constructivism. Yet, towards the end of the millennium, there was a turn to a new materialism implicit in the works of Deleuze and Deleuzeans, such as Braidotti (2002), William Connolly (2002), Jane Bennett (2001), Coole and Frost (2010), as well as new social scientific theorists such as Bruno Latour (2005). Both Elizabeth Grosz, with her theory of non-physical materialism (1994, 1995), and Elizabeth Wilson, with her rich theory of affect and connectivist theory of cognition (1998), also promote a new materialism. Critical of hypersocial constructivism, social and political theorists have waded in, with the help of neuroscience and new scientific findings, to focus on the agentic capacities of things. In doing so, they have challenged the centrality of cognitive functions (rational and emotional) driving human agency. By focusing on non-cognitive functions – subliminal non-human affects (the entrainment of pheromones or apperception of sensorial bodily experiences) – the roles of rational decision-making, choice, and emotions are usurped. Focusing upon humans being party to non-human assemblages, connecting to things, one partakes in their non-human power. Deleuzean thinkers are anti-humanist. They challenge human exceptionalism and consequently challenge the distinctiveness of humans to initiate projects, creatively and reflectively plan, or be responsive to norms. Another source of this rethinking comes from reconstructing the post-phenomenological theories of embodiment derived from Merleau-Ponty: consider Diana Coole (2007), Sonia Kruks (2010, 2016), and Dorothea Olkowski (see Hass and Olkowski 2000, 13); these theorists decentre cognitive human functions, but do not wholly embrace an anti-humanist trajectory. In the *New Materialism* volume (Coole and Frost) Sonia Kruks attempts to retrieve previous historical materialist theories of agency that have been glossed over in this new turn to non-human agency. While she admits the flow of energies at the subatomic level of life may be in constant motion, she perceptively notes life at the level of social and political tend to be more resistant to movement and change. She tries to accommodate historical materialism, and subscribes to a modest human exceptionalism, which challenges these new vital materialists.

Neuroscience has altered discussions of human agency: there is evidence that brain networks (established in early life) structure the capacity of humans to relegate their emotions and think. The social-constructivist thesis – that assumes one's psyche and embodied self are discursively constructed and hence can be changed through resisting and reconfiguring these discourses – has been challenged. Neuroscientists have found that a brain template has been formed in an infant by the age of three years old; this determines the ability of the future self to manage feelings and anxiety, and ultimately determines one's sociability (Sue Gerhardt-Brunner, 2004). Since the pre-frontal cortex develops in the first few years of life with touch and attentive care, those babies whose needs for care are not met have an almost blank pre-frontal cortex, in striking contrast to those babies who have been attended to. Neglected orphans in Romanian orphanages in the 1980s provided material for research (89). Their deficient care was written on their brains: they had undefined pre-frontal lobes and under-developed amygdalas. Too much cortisol as a consequence of lack of attention, in early years, will produce a smaller brain (less pre-frontal cortex) (85). Physiological and affective deficiencies make the management of emotions and the capacity to focus upon an activity very difficult. These findings do not deny the significance of social factors, but suggest that insufficient and unreliable care (environment) in the first three years of life has significant physiological and psychological effects. A deficient brain will be produced that is significantly less capable of regulating emotions, focusing on tasks, and being responsive. In fact, they argue lack of care leads to dysfunctional and criminal conduct. While these theories are not biologically determinist, they are often being used in a determinist fashion that lays the responsibility for child development upon mothers. This ignores the role of environmental factors in possibly correcting or mitigating early neglect. So all those social reformers who believe that deprived children can be reformed through social welfare programs are misguided, for damage has been done to the brain, and the capacity to alter their brain is very limited. Neuroscientists who believe in "this finite window thesis" are culpable of a biologism and determinism that Beauvoir would be wary of.

Beauvoir manages to avoid the dualism of naturalism (which assumes the body is a brute fact, pre-discursive, and ungendered) as well as social constructivism (which assumes the body is a psychic or social effect of discourses and textual practices). While she is not a new materialist, she does admit the significance of the body, not as lively matter, but rather as bio-social fact. Biological and physiological facts will have effects, but how they are lived depends upon the society, personal history. Through the lived body, as shown in her treatment of lesbianism, she identifies the co-mingling of nature and culture, the personal and the social, sex and gender. Through performative engagement, she believes a rewriting (though she does not use this term) of the body subject is possible. This permits Beauvoir to think beyond binary oppositions and provide an interesting alternative that accommodates both the social construction of the body, and physiological, biological facts. The impact of biology on human agency becomes clearer in Beauvoir's book *Old Age*, where she admits the biological decline of the body. The weakening of muscles, the wrinkling of skin, the losing of teeth, and general losing of energy happens in old age. These facts, she says, can be lived differently, but they cannot be ignored as though the body did not decline.

Unlike many second-wave feminists, who bracketed biology for fear of biologism, Beauvoir has little difficulty acknowledging women's physiological facts, and in many cases women's physical disadvantages, but she insists that these do not produce "anatomical destiny" (*SS*, 417) nor necessitate subordinate social relations. This is an advance over second-wave feminists who generally assume that women's bodies are the same as men's, or same enough that the body doesn't matter. Alternatively, some second wavers treat the body as a "coat hanger" – an empty signifier – whose meaning is socially determined. Germaine Greer's book *The Female Eunuch*, 1970, is a prime example of this disposition. She argues that women have been cut off from their desire: they have been castrated and rendered passive by patriarchy. To liberate themselves they must bracket their body and its reproductive capacities.

For Beauvoir, the biological body is not outside the social, nor is it sufficient to understand bodily being in terms of social processes alone. She takes on biological facts,[20] and what she calls bodily "structures of existence," without assuming they are brute, unchangeable, or dictate specific social relations. In doing so, she treats them also as social facts, thereby avoiding the determinism of biologism and the problems associated with abstract ontological theories. This illustrates the importance of retaining a distinction between biological, sexualized, and gendered identities.

As a phenomenologist, Beauvoir starts with women's lived experience.[21] To ground women's equality claims on biological sameness or on

20 She uses the word *faits*, which carries the meaning of facts or events when translated.

21 Feminists have criticized Beauvoir's phenomenological approach that focuses on lived experience, one's specific inherence in the world as being overly Eurocentric. It would be hard to defend Beauvoir from this charge. Given she did her research in the Bibliothèque Nationale at the end of the Second World War, where new anthropological studies were in short supply, it is not surprising that she does not turn her attention to the lived experiences of women in non-Western countries. However I would argue, her problematic of situated and embodied subjectivity could be used to explore the lived experiences of women in non-European societies.

an indifference to biological difference (a strategy of second-wave feminists) proved a weak strategy. Phenomenological descriptions that look at the concrete experiences of women's living bodies cannot avoid looking at biological or sexed differences in their differing historical and social contexts. Bodily experiences, however, are not treated as universal or immutable in character, nor as predetermining social relations,[22] for one explored them from one's particular grasp or point of contact with the world, from one's specific experience. Though both men and women use their bodies as the means of casting themselves into the world, women more frequently experience their bodies as an impediment to the will, as lacking instrumentality, as having an alien vitality. In menstruation, pregnancy, and lactation the female body undergoes physiological changes that cannot be changed at will; however, again, these processes are not brute facts, for they are affected by the society within which these processes take place. In masculinist societies, female bodily processes are deemed to hamper rationality and encumber the will – but any bodily condition could also be seen to be a impediment on the will.

Unlike many of her feminist followers, Beauvoir had little problem recognizing the physical discomfort, pain, and intrusiveness of women's bodily processes. Unlike most second-wave theorists, Beauvoir spilled much ink describing woman's biological disadvantages: "Woman is weaker than man; she has less muscular strength, fewer red blood cells ... she runs less quickly, lifts less heavy weights, there is practically no sport in which she can compete with him ... her grasp on the world is thus more restricted; she has less firmness and perseverance in projects that she is less able to carry out, less steadiness available for projects. This means her individual life is not as rich as man's" (*ss*, 46). These sorts of statements have caused much concern amongst feminists, for they describe women's bodies as negative and inferior to men's.

Since Beauvoir sees the body as our point of contact with the world, and describes the body as "our grasp on the world" (38), presumably having "a less firm grasp on the world" and "less steadiness available for

22 Given Beauvoir's attention to biology in part 1 of *The Second Sex*, it is hard to explain the claim made by Chanter, Irigaray, and Grosz that she denies sexual difference. Although there is some textual support for reading her treatment of women's bodies as inferior to men's bodies, if these statements are read as historically specific rather than universal, the charge of androcentrism cannot be supported. These critics ignore Beauvoir's insistence that the meaning of biological facts are not given in themselves but in social contexts. Hence, biological inferiority does not dictate social inferiority. Further, for Beauvoir, biological inferiority is not an essential condition of woman but a historically specific one, characteristic of women in patriarchal society; as such, she welcomes its reconfiguration and social transformation.

projects" would mean that woman's body was a less competent body. Yet, in spite of her attention to these biological "facts" (46), Beauvoir resists biologism: "Certainly these facts cannot be denied – but they do not carry their meaning in themselves. As soon as we accept a human perspective, defining the body starting from existence, biology becomes an abstract science; when the physiological given (muscular inferiority) takes on meaning, this meaning immediately becomes dependent on the whole context; weakness is weakness only in the light of the aims man sets for himself, the instruments at his disposal, and the law he imposes" (46).

Since we no longer live in a society that requires muscular strength, Beauvoir believes that woman's general muscular inferiority is no longer a liability. This illustrates how the natural and social are entangled in the living body. Strength or bodily competence are not determined objectively but depend on social and political contexts. Having admitted the significance of biological facts, and given the significance of the body in human projects, Beauvoir insists that "these facts cannot be denied, but they do not carry their meaning in themselves" (46). She is adamant that women's social subordination does not follow from these biological facts, for it is "the whole society" that gives them their meaning (38). She is able to acknowledge biological differences without assuming that subordinate relations follow.

In describing the physical effects of sexed bodies, Beauvoir does not naturalize the sexed body, but nor does she assume ontological or biological facts are contingent. How we move in the world, and our physiological facts, do not determine women's projects, but they structure what is possible. Beauvoir tells us "Most women – more than 85% show more or less distressing symptoms during this [menstrual] period … there are frequent cases of fever, the abdomen is painful … glandular instability weakens the nervous system … women are more emotional and irritable than usual" (41). It is not surprising that it has come to be known as the curse. Women experience an even stronger alienation in gestation (42). Beauvoir describes pregnancy as "not harmful to the mother if normal circumstances of health and nutrition prevail; [but] with loss of appetite and vomiting … loss of phosphorus, calcium and iron" (41). All that one can hope for is to recoup her losses without too much trouble, but often serious disorders occur during pregnancy and afterwards. Further, she claims that childbirth can be "dangerous and painful" (42). Given the array of female bodily crises, it is not surprising that woman feels her body is an alienated, opaque thing (41). Woman's body does not always meet the needs of either the species or the individual (42).

On the other hand, Beauvoir describes man's development as comparatively simple. The male's sex life is normally integrated into his individual existence in terms of desire and coitus, fulfilling his desire does not tie him to collective needs of society, the reproduction of the species, as it does for women. Not only does sex involve different risks for men and women, but there are differences between masculine and feminine pleasure. Feminine pleasure is valued for being less goal-driven and more responsive and reciprocal. In *The Second Sex*, she celebrates distinctive feminine jouissance that radiates through the whole body and is not focused upon genitals (409). "Coitus for man has a precise biological end: ejaculation … certainly many other very complex intentions are involved in aiming at this end; but once obtained, it is seen as an achievement … On the other hand, the aim for women at the beginning is more psychic than physiological, she desires arousal and sexual pleasure in general, but her body does not project any clear conclusion" (409). "Feminine pleasure radiates through the whole body: it is not always centred in the genital system; vaginal contractions even more than a true orgasm constitute a system of undulations that rhythmically arise, subside, reform, reach for some instants of paroxysm, then blur and dissolve without ever completely dying. Because no fixed goal is assigned to it, pleasure aims at infinity: cardiac fatigue or psychic satiety often limits the women's erotic possibilities, rather than precise satisfaction" (409, 410).

On the one hand, she celebrates feminine pleasure as exemplary of positive human relations, while also describing restrictive aspects of women's bodily being. While Beauvoir admits that the correlation of biological facts with their physical and emotional effects may be historically or culturally variable, she also identifies cross-cultural patterns of gendered experience that are routinely painful, disruptive, and restrictive. Attention to these facts and patterned meanings avoids the implicit voluntarism that follows from a hyper-constructivist position that assumes that bodies can be infinitely resignified or transfigured – that the sexed body and gendered existence do not matter. The disruptiveness or alienation that women experience in their bodily processes is worth noting, but Beauvoir does not believe these processes condemn women to inferiority. Nor do they dictate social norms or social roles. But neither are these persistent patterns and meanings arbitrary.

From all this talk of "biological data" one might infer that Beauvoir lapses into naturalism, insisting upon ungendered, ahistorical, scientific facts. This, however, is not the case. Beauvoir reports that some biologists and psychoanalysts have produced androcentric interpretations of the female body. Far from producing neutral, objective knowledge, these scientists often replicate the values of patriarchal culture and have been instrumental in women's subordination. Beauvoir reveals the bankruptcy of "certain materialist savants … who have engaged in trifling discussions regarding the absolute and relative weight of the brain in man and woman – with inconclusive results" (37). She rejects these efforts to scientifically and "objectively" prove that women's bodies are more infantile, less advanced than men's. She draws attention to science as gendered, but she does not dismiss scientific study as useless.

Indebted to Husserl's distinction between *Körper* (the body as an object described by science) and *Leib* (the lived and experienced body), Beauvoir attends to the living body as the basis for research. The living body is both an opening upon a field of sensations and history, a relatively stable locus of understanding our direction, distance, and movement, as well "as the outline for our projects" (46). In addition to thinking about the organizing features of the body, Beauvoir regards the living body as pro-active and pro-social. This avoids the postmodern drift into skepticism as well as the Deleuzean body without organs, where neither up or down, in or out, near or far can be determined.

Scientific facts often give meaning to the living body, and so they cannot be dispensed with (e.g. when one finds out one has cancer one begins to live one's body differently), but it is also the case that some scientific facts cannot be experienced; thus to appeal to experience as the basis of knowledge is insufficient. Although science presents itself as producing abstract and universal truths, this is not so, since they are historically and culturally inflected. Beneath the bio-scientific paradigm, which claims objectivity, Beauvoir finds humans valorizing this attitude, so it is not impartial or free of bias. Scientific theories are produced within societies and are not immune to underlying social inequalities or political agendas. As scientific theories are popularized, they ultimately inform women's experience of their bodies. But it is equally possible that women's bodily experience reflects cultural norms.

Beauvoir says that biological facts are keys to studying women, but denies that they establish a fixed and inevitable destiny; they are insufficient for setting up a hierarchy of the sexes (36). "Examining them in the light of ontological, economic, social and psychological contexts," she says, the body is an essential element, but alone cannot answer the question why woman is Other (48). She gives weight to the physiological or organic foundations of bodily being without falling into naturalism (biologism) and equally avoids lapsing into a simple social constructivism. The way my eyes and hands are placed has effects on how I encounter the world. My bodily being is my point of contact with the world and further orients me towards things in the world. She insists upon the exploration of biological facts or structures of bodily being yet, like the social constructivists, Beauvoir acknowledges that bodily processes are socially and culturally variable. However, some anatomical sexual differences have a semi-permanence about them: she contrasts the sexual pleasure in ejaculation from female sexual pleasures which are less goal oriented. However, these pleasures are not fixed, but can be remade due to social forces. Yet, Beauvoir's theoretical approach, which appreciates some anatomical and bio-physical differences, while equally recognizing that these are gendered, is timely; it avoids the inadequate theories of the body as natural, a passive surface, or alternately the site of social processes. The body is a co-mingling of nature and culture, sex and gender, and, further, the place where bio-physical, sexual, psychological, and socio-economic fields are entwined. Such an understanding avoids the constructionism of the overly discursivized bodies and overly sexualized treatments of the phallogocentric logic of the feminists of difference. In theorizing multiple contexts (ontological, economic, social, and psychological), Beauvoir appreciates the situations within which discourses arise, rather than simply assuming these discourses are constitutive of reality. My attention to historical and theoretical contexts – both Beauvoir's and contemporary ones – furthers her approach.

In reflecting on woman's bodily and reproductive processes, and describing the pain and difficulties encountered therein, Beauvoir's feminist critics essentialize her comments. This led Tina Chanter (1995) and Elizabeth Grosz (1994) to conclude that, for Beauvoir, women's bodies are an impediment to their freedom, the male body being more fitted to transcendence. This reading of Beauvoir comes at least in part from treating her pejorative statements as universal or essential statements, rather than historically specific ones. If women's biological inferiority is to be understood in economic, social, and historical contexts (48), as Beauvoir assumes it must be, then its negativity has to do with the existing patriarchal patterns and meanings attached to it. The body is never unmediated, but it has so far been mediated exclusively within a man-made world. Far from being male-identified and culpable of somatophobia, Beauvoir's phenomenological descriptions of bodily processes are a feminist strategy.[23] Since philosophers, with their aversion to the body and their inclination to prioritize reason, will, and intention, have for the most part ignored female bodily processes, Beauvoir's attention to this affective domain is worthy of consideration. Calling attention to woman's "messy" and unmanageable body in exploring her particular history, Beauvoir inverts modernist priorities, making the body the very stuff of subjectivity.

23 In defence of Beauvoir's disparaging statements about maternity, Linda Zerilli argues that Beauvoir does not re-articulate the subject of modernity, for "it is a sophisticated and underappreciated feminist discursive strategy of defamiliarization" (1992, 112).

Feminist critics point to Beauvoir's fiction, where she describes the vagina as a hole and the desiring women as animal and plant-like, as a symptom of her phallicism. She describes Hélène as "enveloped in a pale and sickly vapour … her flesh became a humid and spongy moss" (BO, 79). Metamorphosing into a plant, a mollusc, Hélène describes herself as "paralysed by that net of burning silk … she would never rise again to the surface of the world … she would remain for ever enclosed in that viscid darkness" (BO, 80). These metaphors of women's body and desire are unpleasant and are also found in Sartre's *Being and Nothingness.* They suggest that women's body is an impediment to transcendence. But there is a difference between Beauvoir and Sartre. Hélène's response to her sexuality in the novel is a symptom of her fear of/distance from her male partners and her inability to allow herself to experience sexual pleasure. So it is not the norm of female sexuality, as it is for Sartre, but a sign of her psychological history.

For centuries, woman's biological vulnerability, as expressed in childbirth, lactation, and menopause, served as the grounds for excluding her from political life. However, the biological and emotional effects of these processes have been rarely acknowledged and even more rarely philosophically explored. Phenomenology seeks to explore woman's lived bodily experiences, refusing objective meanings and focusing on intersubjective ones. Beauvoir draws attention to the physiological sources of pain and discomfort, as well as the social and emotional meanings attributed to them – anxiety, shame, and public embarrassment. These are not private experiences, but ones characteristic of a patriarchal and rationalist society where reason ideally prevails over the body and the women's body is assumed to be the source of disorder. Menstruation, cramps, and uncontrollable bleeding, which might be visible at any moment, are often a source of both pain and shame. The bloated body of a pregnant woman, a sign of sexual intercourse, has usually been kept out of the public sphere. Childbirth – the unbearable pain and horror of the splitting body – is an event that is rarely culturally represented. Aging and bodily deterioration leads to long bouts of sadness and even depression.

Not only modernist philosophers but also people (feminist and non-feminist) more generally have a hard time coming to terms with female bodily processes. Far from being culpable of somatophobia, Beauvoir's strategy of highlighting these processes addresses those who want to ignore or sanitize them. For Beauvoir, resignification requires radical social transformation, changes in women's attitudes and institutional practices. It is not simply an individual experiment in self-making nor a change in one's attitude. One has only to think about how important the midwifery movement has been to change attitudes and practices around the birth in order to appreciate the importance of collective struggle.

A collective struggle over women's domination by scientists and technicians, as well as social and political thinking, is required. Different attitudes to women's bodies must be instantiated. Although one welcomes technological advances that perfect techniques of body rebuilding, such as organ replacement and cosmetic surgery, such procedures are not without pain and anxiety. Furthermore, it is rational to fear the splitting, bleeding, broken, or aging body, to grieve the loss of the vital youthful body in old age. In fact, anxiety, fear, alienation, and grief are comprehensible feelings. To believe that bodily meanings are wholly socially and culturally determined tempts us to believe in the malleability of feelings and the cultural specificity of them. Such interpretations underplay the significance of the competent body and the loss and grief associated with the aged, ill, and dying body. Conceiving of the body as a social construction or cultural product moves in this direction. While one can surgically defer aging, bodily decline and death are still inevitable. Our inability to deal with the existential fact of our mortality, our finitude, causes emotional problems.

Beauvoir believes that menopause, pregnancy, and menstruation are experienced differently in different societies, for they are culturally and historically mediated. However, admitting this doesn't mean that she denies the importance of biological and sexual facts or their various patterned effects. Nature is not a blank surface written upon by society – there is an immanent order of bodily being. Ontologically the body is oriented towards competency and vitality; hence, coming to terms with aging or bodily disablement is a challenge. Also, in drawing out social patterns of persistent pain, physiological restrictions, and recurrent emotions of shame and fear – common features of bodily being – Beauvoir stresses the sedimented fields within which agency arises.

In stressing the historical variability of bodily meanings, social constructivists tempt us into believing that our sexualized and gendered experiences can be infinitely rewritten and resignified. While constructivists like Butler recognize this as a difficult social process, not a matter of choice, they do not explore the social/historical and bodily/material preconditions of such reinscriptions, whereas Beauvoir does. The sick, aging, and broken body is no longer vital or engaged in the world as the formerly competent body was. In seeing the body as culturally mediated, as the body of discourse subject to the effects of disciplinary regimes, Butler fails to adequately accommodate the transhistorical aspects of embodied experience, whether it be the reproductive body or the ill and aging body. Although she insists that the body does matter, she does not go far enough in acknowledging this. In her desire to refuse essentialism, Butler dismisses biological or physiological truths and sidesteps persistent patterns and structures of gender oppression.[24] The ill, aging, and dying body may be variously expressed and represented, but is most often the source of grief and sadness. In looking at the biophysical body and the structures of bodily experience (sensory-motor, perceptual, cognitive), Beauvoir avoids the flat docile body that is indifferent to the discourses in which it is inscribed. She valorizes vital behaviour and free and engaged action in the world with others. Furthermore, in recognizing the diversity and complexity of the social world within which subjectivity emerges, Beauvoir avoids the collapsing of sex and gender, nature and culture, mind and body – the logic of an overly discursivized position. Although she herself does not appreciate new forms of materiality, her theoretical problematic allows them to be appreciated.

POLITICAL ESSENTIALISM/NATURALISM

Increasingly complex theories of materialism that appreciate cultural and environmental factors in human agency may inform philosophic debates, but do not necessarily inform public debates. Particularly in the United States, LGBTQ activists, twenty years ago, were using biological theories to explain their sexuality. They used the discourse of "nature" to make an argument for the guarantee of their rights, claiming that one is born with an inherent sexuality, either gay or straight, lesbian, bisexual, or transgendered. Unlike the theoretical forays into anti-essentialism and social constructivism, these activists often relied on biologically essentialist arguments. They insisted that they could not be resocialized or reprogrammed to be heterosexual, so their "natural" differences must be protected as a legal right under the Constitution. Many feminists, Butler and Rubin (1994) in particular, are unhappy with this formulation of gay/queer identity. They see that any reliance on an essentialist identity fails to understand the crucial role that social, cultural, and political factors play in accepting or prohibiting sexual differences.

24 Toril Moi challenges Butler's treatment of the body as being overly defined by the sex/gender distinction. I would tend to agree there are many ways of theorizing a historically sensitive sexed body and Beauvoir provides one way of proceeding. Her theory of embodied agency has the advantage of allowing for structures of bodily experiences, without prescribing the centrality of sexuality. Moi's adaptation of Beauvoir seems to side with constructivists and hence bodily preconditions of existence as well as her ontological insights. As I have argued collective projects allow for reinscribing embodied agency where sexuality/gender are not the only preoccupations. She thereby confronts and avoids the logic of sexual pervasiveness.

Furthermore, arguments appealing to nature settle or close down debates rather than facilitating further discussion.

The biological arguments employed by these activists, Rubin and Butler have argued (Butler and Rubin 1994, 62), have conservative implications, for they have been used to consolidate rigid identities for women and LGBTQ individuals. While the social constructivist arguments are not without their problems, upon which the New Right has capitalized, returning to a form of social essentialism is not a progressive way to proceed. Social constructivism believes in increasing educational and employment opportunities as well as encouraging new identities. While these policies have had significant success, gender oppression has not been eliminated and sexist attitudes persist. Moreover, the funding of programs that assume essential or innate identities might push people into essential identifications that might not be appropriate. More recently, with medical advantages, sex change operations have increased dramatically. If operations to change from female to male are less hazardous, more successful, and even supported on health insurance plans, they are likely to be pursued.

The tendency to essentialize, or even naturalize sex, is found amongst social conservatives. Barbara Marshall's book *Configuring Gender* calls attention to the Canadian conservatives who identify "'gender feminists' as stalking the social and political life of this nation" (Marshall 2000, 99). Gender feminism is the code word for social constructivists. They have a "hidden agenda" – "a covert means of promoting homosexuality, abortion, and even the existence of more than two sexes" (104). It is believed that they are "not advancing the real interests of women ... in fact are denying 'their nature'" (104). These feminists involve a "stark rejection of what it means to be human ... women no longer defined by their sex, but by culturally imposed norms" (Da Casco in ibid.).

The term "gender feminism" has become a tool of abuse that feminists have to confront. Éric Fassin (2011) looks at France and Vatican's efforts to erase the term gender. The French State's Committee on the Change of Terminology as well as the Vatican's Council for Family reflect that tendency. Although gender had become increasingly used in France since 2000s, to identify university programs and courses in France, as well as identify forms of discrimination, the committee insisted the term gender was not part of the French vocabulary, but rather an American neologism that should not be used. They argued that the terms sex, sexual, sexist were perfectly adaptable to meet these new meanings. However in the context of same-sex marriage in France, where opposition to marriage of transsexual and transgendered couples has arisen, the language of the older law that marriage is a contract between man and a woman has been transformed into a contract between people who act like a man and woman. They believe by eliminating the idea of gender choices one protects the norms of heterosexuality. Theologians of the Vatican also called for the erasure of the term gender: the denaturalization of sex, they believed, opened the door to the same-sex marriage. The Lexicon proposed a redefinition of gender "that must conform to the natural order that is already given in the body" (Fassin 2011, 6). In this context gender remains a useful category, an important tool with a critical edge, which traditionalists want to erase in order to renaturalize sexuality and constitute difference as pathological. Fassin also points to how the concept of sexual democracy is being used in France in a highly racialized way. In 2004 Nicholas Sarkozy, then minister of the interior, advocated "chosen immigration" from "imposed immigration," thereby hindering bi-national, bi-racial marriages and limiting family reunification (Fassin 2011, 9). Immigrants are presumed to assimilate French values of laïcité, sexual equality, and liberty, which obviously discriminates against Islamic immigrants. This policy has also underpinned the 2004 law banning the Islamic veil in schools. So again the concept of sex, and the naturalness associated with it, has been used obscure the political/constructed side of the sexuality that the term gender captures. To simplify and support intolerant practices the term sex is invoked, and the term gender denotes personal choices in social contexts.

3

Beauvoir Reconfigures Social Subjectivity in the Wake of Psychoanalysis

POLITICAL ACTORS AND THINKERS are often wary of psychoanalysis. In stressing the importance of the unconscious and the imaginary, psychoanalysis has a way of dematerializing the world and unleashing the irrational. Liberal individualists are leery of psychoanalysis's identification of the split subject, which problematizes intentional rational behaviour, the latter being a foundational principle of liberal thinking. Many contemporary communitarians (Sandel, Etzioni, and Taylor) contest the assumptions of robust individualism and endorse a relational subject: recognizing that healthy subjects require that one has been sufficiently embedded in relations in the family and community. They, too, spurn a divided self and assert the need for a stable subject that emerges from strong families and communities. Many radical thinkers – feminist and non-feminist – find psychoanalysis a useful supplement to their theories of historical transformation and social justice, but some see psychoanalysis as a restriction on historical agency. Foucault, a case in point, scoffs at theories of interiority, assuming that subjectivity is an effect of the political. Even though Deleuze believed in the unconscious, he too had no interest in exploring interiority. This is not true of Beauvoir who, as we have seen, relies upon a notion of the will, but acknowledges its cultural/historical/material embeddedness, thereby qualifying its potential voluntarism.

Conventional historical materialists also see the psyche as an effect of socio-economic forces; for them, problems with the psyche can only be resolved by changes in social structures. While competitive and narcissistic impulses are privileged today and the self-determining and property-enhancing self are hallmarks of capitalist society, it is not clear that these qualities can be eliminated by a change in the social structure. While the psyche is affected by the political and socio-economic relations, most psychoanalytic thinkers would distinguish the inner psychic and exterior socio-economic realms. The unsavoury motives and suffering psychoanalysis dredges up, combined with our inability to be conscious of them and the difficulty of dislodging them, are challenges to meaningful social change and democratic politics. If people are trapped in psychological realities of domination and submission, hate and envy, how are equitable social relations and a deeper democracy best achieved?

In this chapter, we will examine Simone de Beauvoir's ambivalent relationship with psychoanalysis. Although she uses it to understand how women have become subjects, she is wary of its theoretical assumptions and political implications. This leads her to "reconfigure" a theory of embodied subjectivity that has some affinity to psychoanalysis but gives much more space to social and political worlds in reconfiguring the self. She thereby distinguishes the psychic and political, without reducing either. Her theory of the subject is very different from the French feminists of difference discussed in the previous chapter, who see the social as mediated by a psycho-symbolic order: the social world and its institutions as derivative of the psychosocial world. As such, the social world is seen in an overly sexual register. Beauvoir's theorizations also take some distance from theories that assume the subject is an effect of discursive practices (see Butler 1993; Mouffe 1996; and Haraway 1991) and those who spurn the will and the singularity of the psychic sphere (Deleuze and Guattari and the new materialists). As we have seen from the last chapter, bodily agency is not defined by a sexual or psychological register; anatomical facts structure bodily agency and that predisposes one to act in particular ways. These facts are not stable or fixed, but inflected by cultural and social circumstances.

Following Merleau-Ponty's praxiological body subject, Beauvoir's agency exceeds the psychic and engages a complex structured world. One's ability to navigate that world depends upon one's personal psychic history as well as the specifics of one's situation. My interpretation of Beauvoir and her indebtedness to psychoanalysis is novel, since most theorists have repudiated Beauvoir for being a foe of psychoanalysis. While she assumed such a stance, especially vis-à-vis the psychoanalytically informed French feminists of difference, I think she is much more appreciative of the significance of psychoanalysis in exploring subject formation.

THE LACANIAN AND OBJECT RELATIONS THEORIES OF PSYCHOANALYSIS

In contemporary social and cultural theory (i.e., gender studies, postcolonial studies, etc.), Lacanian psychoanalytic work has been dominant since the '90s. Although Beauvoir was influenced by Lacan in his early years and was especially indebted to his work on the mirror phase, philosophically she has more affinity to the less visible or well-known tradition of object relations or attachment theory derived from Melanie Klein (1988a, 1988b) and Donald Winnicott (1965). Beauvoir, like these theorists, insists on the importance of primary attachment to (M)other and reliable detachment. The goal of psychic development is to unmake present sexual hierarchies and make women more able to engage in their own projects. She fictionalizes the lives of many women who were incapable of standing or acting on their own. She wants to minimize destructive conduct (sadomasochistic, obsessive, hysterical, and neurotic behaviour). She points to the need for rich and embedded social relations. To be able to successfully assert oneself apart from one's parents or others, one must have overcome one's primary fears/desires around (M)other that may be disabling. To be more or less integrated, however tenuous one feels within oneself and however processual one is, presumes deep attachments to others and commitment to the world.

Lacanian theory focuses on the organization of the self; the symbolic and imaginary are carriers of ideological structures and meanings. The subject is produced by these meanings (codes) and structures rather than being responsive to them. Unlike Freud, Lacan wrote in the wake of Saussure's linguistic research. *Parole* (speech) is defined by *langue*, an unconscious structure that informs speech. It is in the gesture of refusal, in splitting, that Lacan (1977) believes the generative or creative power of the unconscious can be unleashed. The split subject fractures the identities that sustain instrumental, masterful, and homogenizing forces in modern society. This symbolic self precedes the social self. Thus, Lacan challenges the meta-narratives of modernity, rationality, and liberation that feed off the symbolic power of the phallus. The self is a fiction that misrecognizes itself as unified; it is an imagined identity. He describes the infant as an *hommelette* – in a state of being scrambled and disintegrated. Through language the child enters the symbolic – the cultural place of received meanings, taboos, and sexual identities. The self gradually organizes itself through linguistic codes and symbolic structures. Kristeva (1984) believes this organization also presumes a preverbal rhythm, theorized as the semiotic, as the grounds for subject formation. Freud and Lacan argue that the castration complex is the pivot on which the whole Oedipus complex turns. Freud argues that these two complexes are articulated differently in boys and girls; Lacan argues otherwise. The castration complex only denotes the final moment of the Oedipus complex in both sexes. Where the real father intervenes by showing he really possesses the phallus and the child must abandon his/her attempts to become the phallus for the mother. In renouncing his/her attempt to be the object of mother's desire, the child gives up a certain pleasure.

The Lacanian approach to subjectivity is axiomatic: Lacan focused on taking up positions within the symbolic/imaginary and real. One's relations to the world and others is derivative of one's positioning. Beauvoir tries to bring psychic development and social relations into communication, producing a very different theory of subjectivity. Even though mothers provide reliable care and a healthy body image for their girl children, their identities are produced in part by the larger culture and society in which they are valued or demeaned. Thus, in sexist societies, girls internalize self-hatred, shame, and terror of their bodies. Beauvoir also was aware of how racist societies objectified and demeaned black bodies. White values and racist practices abject various sexually and racially identified subjects (Frantz Fanon [1967, 1968] famously makes this point).

The object relations school, often referred to as the British school, takes a different approach to the symbolic order and how the subject develops. They believe we are object-seeking rather than pleasure-seeking (Elliott 2002, 69). They focus upon mother/infant relations rather than Oedipal relations (68, 75). Security of care allows one to achieve emotional connection to others; the quality of our interpersonal relations affects the transformation of unconscious desire and passion into action and speech. A more integrated and authentic self emerges from what Winnicott calls "primary maternal preoccupation" (73), allowing the child to experience itself as omnipotent and self-identical and enabling a distinction between a true self capable of creative living and a false self incapable of stable relations. Furthermore, security and trust in the world allows one to engage in risky and creative behaviour. If early relations with parents are minimal and uneasy, the child will overcome pain and frustration through ego-splitting and internal fantasy substitutes. Fantasy is not generative or creative but a substitute for failures in the environment. The primal anger towards (M)other, which is so difficult to direct at unreliable/unreachable mothers, is often directed inwards in self-destructive behaviour, or externalized in forms of hurtful aggression. For Klein, due to the death drive and maternal deprivation, the world is divided between the idealized "good" and denigrated "bad" object (85). The bad object predominates and the child is beset by fears of persecutory powers: swamped by destructive feelings and in a state of paranoid anxiety (84). In this context splitting allows the containment of destructive emotions, and is hence a defence against primitive anxieties. If the child realizes others are not simply a repository for destructive fantasies, the child will develop positive social relations, connect to others, accept the guilt of its prior state. In this depressive position the child can accept loss, reparation, and ultimately the other as separate (87). Social and political theorists have applied these understandings of psychic development to political and cultural life. Popular narratives on television, literature, and nationalism rely upon the processes of splitting, and the energy derived from it creates unity (83).

Object relations theorists presume that the unconscious passions get released, worked on, and integrated into the self, in the process of development or subsequently in therapy. The mother is optimally recognized as whole: the source of both good and bad feelings. The self becomes enlarged and flexible, rather than retaining a narrow, anxious, and rigid attitude towards the others. This allows one to reconfigure one's relations to oneself and others to establish good, stable, and connected relations, and to attempt to further one's autonomy. Hence, strong attachment allows for healthy separation and good judgment. Political theorist C. Fred Alford uses Klein to supplement the Frankfurt School theorists. Their reliance upon Freud, he argues, leads to a limiting theory of individual lives and group behaviour (91). Klein provides further insights in individual and group processes: "a society in the thrall of schizoid processes and a paranoid individualizing consumer logic" (Elliot 2002, 92). The idea of instrumental reason is linked to primary anxiety and greed, but communicative reason – Habermas's term – has affinity to Klein's notion of "reparative reason," which can deal with this primary anxiety and put it to constructive use. The group can be a source of love, affection, and concern – thereby mitigating this anxiety. He rejects the Freudian notion of the group as simply replicating authoritarian patterns of the family. However Alford writes in our society the potential of the group is not under-used. "We purchase harmony in private relations by investing our aggression in the group" (Alford 1989, 19, 20).

Lacanians believe subjects can work on themselves, live the split subject, assume the unconscious as creative, and refuse the phallus. Object relations thinkers believe that one must diminish the rigid boundaries of self and other, identify one's anger, and accommodate differences. As one becomes conscious of unconscious forces, one integrates those nasty excluded or abject bits into the self, rather than being driven by them. The possibility and desirability of mitigating the negative effects of the split are desired. In other words, where these theorists follow Freud's dictum – where "it" (id) was there, "I" (ego) will be – the Lacanians pursue the opposite tactic – where "I" was, there "it" will be (Elliott 2002, 100). If the subject accepts its lack, takes up the stance of castration and vulnerability rather than a stance of masterfulness and control, one is better off. Since minority cultures and women have been positioned socially and politically as an "it" and not an "I" – as objects not subjects – a different relationship to their subjectivity is required. They can hardly jettison a masterfulness that has been momentary at best. Decisive plans for a postcolonial society can hardly be sabotaged. Many feminists have made this point in light of the postmodern theoretical turn, which urged women to reject their agency. Since woman has not been a subject in the full sense, but more often seen as object or Other, jettisoning their agency will not contribute to their authentic subjectivity (Bordo 1990, 145). We must remember Beauvoir's refrain. "Man can think of himself without woman. She cannot think of herself without man … He is the Subject, he is the Absolute – she is the Other" (*SS*, 6). While Beauvoir does not encourage women to become stable or fixed subjects, in fact that is a source of bad faith (*désir d'être*), she does encourage women to assert themselves rather than lose themselves in the lives of their spouses and children. A life lived as socially inferior, a life lived through others (where one sacrifices one's projects, conscious choices to one's husband or children's well-being), is a life not worth living. For this reason, active engagement in the world as well as transformative identities and projects are important to political mobilization of women.

There are stumbling blocks to my interpretation that associates Beauvoir and object relations and attachment theory. First, Beauvoir spurns the unconscious and Klein relies heavily on it. Second, in sharp contrast to Beauvoir's revolutionary position, object relations theory has been used to shore up conservative social and political forces and, in fact, was taken to task by the British feminists in the 1970s (see Barrett and MacIntosh 1982) for emphasizing the exclusive bonding with mother in early childhood as essential to security and well-being. In doing so, object relations theorists imply that women should stay at home and in the kitchen. The infant's need for maternal devotion and consistency conflicts with the idea that working for a living is important to the well-being of the mother. Second-wave feminists denounced the ideas of Winnicott, Klein, and others, claiming that their ideas were being used to justify the return of working women to the home in the post-war years.[1]

So, in some sense one can hardly imagine a set of ideas more foreign to Beauvoir's disposition than those of object relations theory, since it purportedly supports the idea of a devoted mother and hence shores up

1 The ideas of the school of object relations have again returned to the political arena in the UK. The theoretical guru of New Labour (elected to govern in 1997), Tony Giddens, used the language of belonging and theories of attachment to focus on social issues and address the problem of wayward youth.

a traditional feminine role. However, object relations theory doesn't necessarily have to be seen in a conservative light. It emphasizes the significance of connections and attachments in transforming subjects. In spite of its rather conservative political guise, the theory can be converted to radical political ends, as it thinks about the preconditions of healthy subjectivity and political agency for both minorities and women. One doesn't have to have strong relations with mother, but strong relations with father, or another carer, to avoid frustrated attachment. Object relations theory turns away from the centrality of the Oedipal drama and the sexual identification that follows, by focusing on the significance of primary loving care (or lack thereof) that breeds trust. We can see how this has some affinity with Beauvoir's theory of subject formation, where the infant has a lingering and sustaining relationship with M(other). Her philosophic discourse of erotic generosity (*SS*, 289) and her belief that transcendence always has to be embedded in immanence – that subjectivity requires being open and responsive – both have strong affinities to object relations theory. Her push for a connected and engaged embodied subject articulates the need for attachment as a precondition for creativity and social participation.

There is no doubt that the Lacanian tradition has been more influential amongst contemporary social and political theorists, and has made more contributions in analyzing colonial, racist, and sexist discourses than any other school of psychoanalysis. The school of object relations, however, and in particular the works of Klein, has been of interest to both Butler (*The Psychic Life of Power*, 1997) and Kristeva (1986; Melanie Klein, 1988a, 1988b) in their works on subject formation. Insofar as Beauvoir strives for a more integrated relational self, albeit incomplete and nonidentical, a woman capable of overcoming blockages (the split subject and neuroses in psychoanalytic terms), a healthy embodied being capable of being open to others and responding to changing circumstances, she has more affinity to the object relationists than to the Lacanians. Interestingly enough, Jessica Benjamin, a psychotherapist (who interviewed Beauvoir in the company of Marg Simons), also believed in the importance of social relations in catalyzing change. Both Beauvoir and Benjamin were optimistic that through social engagement and collective projects, women could begin to transform their psyche. In Benjamin's *Bonds of Love*, she suggests that househusbands, men being actively involved in childcare, would begin to break down gender stereotypes and loosen the Oedipal drama. In *Undoing Gender* (2004) Judith Butler used Benjamin to decentre the effects of the Oedipalization of subjects and its implicit heteronormativity. As we will see, Beauvoir's critique of the nuclear family, and the Oedipalized relations, is worth noting.

Many psychoanalytically inclined feminists, in particular Anglo-American ones, were interested in Beauvoir: Juliet Mitchell and Jessica Benjamin, to name two. However, one should not forget that Beauvoir denied the unconscious, making her less than a full-fledged convert. Like Merleau-Ponty and Sartre, she assumes that our psychic processes are pre-reflective rather than unconscious – hence less deeply rooted and capable of being brought to consciousness and worked on, and less destructive in their effects.

Beauvoir's theory of the erotic resonates with the concerns of psychoanalysis, although she articulates it in philosophic language: "The erotic experience most poignantly reveals to human beings their ambiguous condition; they experience it as flesh and as spirit, as the other and as the subject" (*SS*, 414). She assumes herself first as an object; she has to reconquer her dignity as transcendent and a free subject while assuming her carnal condition; this is risky and often fails. It is a paradigm of a moral relationship insofar as it accommodates ambiguity. Interestingly one of Beauvoir's critiques of de Sade is that he failed to respect the connections of flesh: he remained a Cartesian trapped in his mind.

Beauvoir's attention to the social processes of "Othering" – how women, Blacks, and Muslims are seen as Other (or Object) by the dominant European patriarchy – resonates with contemporary psychoanalytic theories of abjection and critical race theory. When she introduces "He is the Subject: he is the Absolute, and she is Other," she recognizes how dependent woman is to man's identity. However, the process of Othering goes further, showing how man requires subordinate others – women, Blacks, Jews – to shore up his dominance. While Beauvoir is particularly astute in fictionalizing women's psychological dependence upon men, she is less good at philosophically exploring how/why men demean or diminish women to bolster their egos. On a social level, inferiority is cemented through discourses of alterity – the privileged men require demeaned and abject groups to shore up their privilege. Beauvoir's commitment to political change assumes these relations can be undone, or at least be made less destructive in their effects. Social "in" groups constitute their identity through articulating their differences from other social "out" groups. This phenomenon is not necessarily negative, though it can be if their interdependence is not acknowledged or the behaviour of the out group is deemed abject. In order to respect difference, the loosening of stable identities is required. Both attention to and organization around one's past experience – without essentializing it – is necessary in order to empower members of minority groups and move beyond their demeaned identities. The positive need for transformative identities is important; this will allow one to reconfigure one's relations with others, connecting the past/present and future. This need for transformative identities is not present in the theories of Lacanians and post-Lacanians.

BEAUVOIR AND HER INTERLOCUTORS: RETHINKING THE PSYCHIC, AVOIDING PSYCHIC AND SOCIAL REDUCTIONISM

Beauvoir's appropriation of psychoanalysis was selective. She was explicitly critical of some psychoanalytic assumptions, yet she employed some insights to further radical change at a micropolitical level. Her theory of embodied intersubjectivity has some affinity to psychoanalysis, though this is rarely acknowledged, given her well-known disdain for psychoanalytic theory and practice. In *The Second Sex*, she attributes to psychoanalytic theory a form of psychic determinism. As I show here this is based in part upon a rather narrow and doctrinaire reading of Freud and selective use of contemporary psychoanalysts. In her later years, in the 1960s and 1970s, when many French feminists found themselves attracted to psychoanalysis, Beauvoir was openly hostile. In spite of psychoanalysis's radical rhetoric, she was convinced that it had conservative implications; it sought to make women content with their roles as mother and wife. Dissatisfaction, she believed, had much to do with their subordinate and demeaned social roles, rather than being a product of their inner psychic conflicts and fears.

Politically, Beauvoir was in direct conflict with the psychoanalytically inclined feminists of her day, followers of Antoinette Fouque and the Psych and Po Collective (see previous chapter). Beauvoir's opponents – Irigaray, Kristeva, and Cixous – were more or less allied with this feminist collective and spurned Beauvoir's humanist feminism as universalist (Kristeva 1986, 193) and rationalist (Kristeva 1984, 194). Beauvoir responded in kind, vilifying these women as essentialists, as their focus on women's bodies, and distinctive female libidinal energy as a source of radical change, was restrictive. In *The Second Sex* she demonstrated that "discourses of 'sexual difference' had been exploited by patriarchy to oppress women" (Tidd 2004, 76).

Sarah Kofman, a renowned French philosopher of the 1960s, summed up the conflicts between Beauvoir's philosophy and psychoanalysis. On the eve of the fiftieth anniversary of *The Second Sex*'s publication, Kofman was interviewed about its significance in her life. Kofman believed it raised her consciousness of her subordinate status. She later claimed that psychoanalysis had had an equally radical effect on her. With psychoanalysis, she retreated from revolutionary politics (that believed changing political structures and personal attitudes could transform the world) to a position of pessimism. With an acknowledgement of an increasingly complex social life and inner unsavoury motives that are not resolvable, psychoanalysis challenges the viability of radical political change.

Although Beauvoir's fear of psychoanalysis is well known, her attention to psychoanalysis as offering insights into the production of the self is less familiar. We must bear in mind that the psychoanalysis that she was familiar with was more psychically reductionist, as it theorized the self as an effect of internal drives seeking specific objects of gratification and thereby saw the social world as secondary. Further, Jungian theories, which believe in collective unconscious and pre-given symbols, were popular (*ss*, 166). Beauvoir took some distance from these approaches by emphasizing the significance of social relations and political engagement in the construction of the psyche. She did not explore their work in any detail; instead she focused on Freud and Stekel, as well as Alfred Adler and Karen Horney.

Both Beauvoirian and Lacanian psychoanalytic models of subjectivity respect the effect that external social forces can have on one's internal life and thereby avoid seeing the psyche as produced by intra-psychic forces alone. However, Beauvoir weighs the impact of the outside on the inside heavier than the reverse. For her, the subject is relational and historically situated; although one's psychic predisposition is important in becoming a self, that becoming is more an effect of one's particular culture's social and political processes, within which the self is constituted. The feedback loop between the social and political to the psychic world must be respected.

As we have seen, Beauvoir's embodied subject presumes the entwining of the biological, physiological, psychological, social, and political fields; thus, it appreciates the effects of social engagement or alienation on women's psyches. Dire social experiences such as exile, long-term unemployment, alienation, and war will have negative effects even upon the most "healthy" self. Women who are similarly situated in terms of their class may act very differently in dire situations given their personal psychological history. Beauvoir's novels represent how women's ability to fulfil their desires and engage in political action depends upon many factors, apart from class. Anne, in *The Mandarins*, is a psychotherapist although she is married and has a life outside her family. Paula, on the other hand, has given up her career (as a singer) and tethered her life to her male partner, Henry. Though they are of the same class, they have different relations to the world and others. These relations have developed over the years, through long-standing habits/conduct so they cannot be changed easily. Given Paula's financial and emotional dependence upon Henry she is portrayed as devastated by the loss of his love and threatens suicide. Anne, on the other hand, had a long career; her financial independence and social competence allow her to navigate adverse historical circumstances as well as personal crises more easily. Anne, who has had to give up her lover, is depressed but not destroyed by her loss of this vital and loving relationship.

Beauvoir respects the importance of financial independence: a career outside the family provides women with emotional strength. Lived experiences – past memories, habits, and conduct – weigh upon the present. Beauvoir is optimistic that the past does not preclude change. One can rework one's relations to one's self and world through commitment, persistent efforts, and collective actions. It is not structural processes or social locations alone that direct change, but rather one's will, emotions (empathy, despair, or hate), that underpin such reconfigurations. Furthermore, the context provides facilitating or restrictive conditions for change.[2]

Seeing the self as determined by the unconscious, stable childhood narratives, or compulsive repetitive behaviours that are carried into adulthood, psychoanalysis is overly deterministic for Beauvoir's liking. She believes that one can overcome neurotic or destructive habits through responsiveness, action, and participating in collective projects. Thereby, she denies unconscious structures that trap people in destructive and painful conduct, rather than seeing them as pre-conscious. She recognizes the negative effect of social subordination – experiences associated with colonialism and sexism significantly affect one's psychical energy. She sees minorities – racial, gender, sexual, or ethnic – as being defined as Other and subjected to the powers of the majority. Through awareness and political mobilizing, these minorities can begin to transform their demeaned self and their subordinate relation to the world.

Today, many psychoanalytically inclined poststructuralists believe that psychological categories must be thoroughly socialized (Oliver, Irigaray, and Kristeva are cases in point). However, the greater problem is how to avoid the formalism of the Lacanian model of subject formation or a belief in a psychically structured subject that doesn't sufficiently appreciate the effects of the social on the psyche. There is the abiding difficulty in navigating between two spheres: the symbolic, which is positional and linguistic in character, and social relations, which are economic, political, and historical in nature. By rejecting the unconscious, Beauvoir does not respect the axiomatic tripartite structure of the symbolic, imaginary,

2 I will return to this issue more systematically in the next few chapters.

and real of Lacan. For her, women's inferiority is culturally and socially produced, so the phallus may be significant in current social relations, but will not necessarily carry weight in post-patriarchal relations. She allows for the crossing over between the symbolic and the social in a way that gives added effect to the social world and its institutions, thereby avoiding positioning the psycho-social life or symbolic as determinant of one's subjectivity. Again her novels establish insights: Hélène in *The Blood of Others* is able to shift her impetuous and narcissistic behaviour into empathy and responsiveness without analysis. Beauvoir believes engaged action may break down psychic neuroses; however, psychoanalytic thinkers assume that conduct is structured by stable narratives, Oedipal processes, unconscious drives, social codes, and social taboos that cannot be so easily dislodged. So until and unless a successful psychoanalysis has been performed, neurotic conduct will persist. Beauvoir, in contrast, believes social engagement might dislodge fear and narcissism and allow the self to develop.

The Lacanian world of the socio-symbolic where the phallic function is central to subject formation has debilitating effects on female/feminine agency. Lacan insists that the phallus not be confused with the penis, so although men have a better opportunity to embrace the power associated with the phallus, women must take up a position around the phallus. However, both women and men must accept that they cannot be the imaginary phallus for another; in doing so, they assume a castrated position. Nevertheless, both men and women still try to fulfil others' desires, refuse the position of castration, and thereby remain hostage to obsessive, hysterical, and neurotic relations.

While the Lacanians and post-Lacanians are not biological essentialists, for the penis is not a phallus, the tripartite structure of subject formation is the cornerstone of the social life. Social institutions, social relations, cultural practices, and historical relations are seen as epiphenomenal to one's psychosocial origins. This, Beauvoir contests, gives too much power to these processes structuring the symbolic world and speech. The effects of political and social hierarchies, exclusions, and anomie that come from being in socially subordinate relations are not fully appreciated by focusing on the micropolitical and their psycho-symbolic origins. Beauvoir believes that the psychic structure of the self is influenced by primary relations and identification with mother, father, and the patriarchal stories that animate Western society, but equally important are the subordinate social roles, economic marginality, and experiences of social anomie that characterize capitalist societies. Changes at the macroinstitutional level can effect changes at the microlevel. Institutional and social marginality can be mitigated with changes in social and economic practices and political institutions. Forging democratic practices and participation will, Beauvoir believes, significantly reduce the feelings of alienation. Furthermore, women can mitigate feelings of deficiency and inferiority by being gainfully employed. Thus Beauvoir avoids the shortcomings of an overly psychically determined subject, a problem that afflicts some of her psychoanalytically inclined opponents. Toril Moi (2000), in a position sympathetic to Beauvoir, identifies another shortcoming of the Lacanians and post-Lacanians. In focusing upon destabilizing individual identity and renewing desire, they tend to ignore the effects that collective action might have in transforming human conduct.

Beauvoir has no theory of human nature, or human essence, that dictates or prescribes human conduct; however she does presume specific human capacities, achievements, and activities as essentially human or authentic. As a being in the world, vitality, sensitivity, the will, and intelligence are privileged human experiences, not "ready made qualities, but a way of casting oneself into the world and disclosing being" (*EA*, 41). This avoids treating human conduct (as psychoanalysts do) as driven by unconscious processes: a "site of compulsions and prohibitions" (*SS*, 50). Beauvoir privileges meaning-making, freedom, and engagement with others as authentic human behaviour. This constitutes her as a weak ontologist.

Beauvoir proposes a synthesis of Freud and Adler; to correct the significance of desire. "For Freud all behavior is driven by desire, that is by seeking pleasure ... Adler replaces drives with motives, finality and plans" (53). She seeks to integrate Adler's theory of the original "will to power" or "purposiveness" (53) with Freud's theory of desire. Alongside the will to power, Adler posits an inferiority complex that leads "humans to use countless ruses rather than confront real-life obstacles that he fears may be insurmountable ... thus [he] develops neuroses" (53). Beauvoir also attends to the role of internalized inferiority in stymying women's agency. She moves away from a psychic explanation to a social explanation: "It is not the absence of a penis that unleashes this complex but the total situation: the girl envies the phallus only as a symbol of the privileges granted to boys: the father's place in the family, the universal predominance of males, and the upbringing all confirm her idea of masculine superiority" (53).

If the subject's everyday experiences are influenced by unconscious processes and internal narratives, as psychoanalysts assume, then we must accept that the world is as we experience it. Internal fears influence "how we cast ourselves into the world" (*EA*, 41). Since the body "expresses our relationship to the world" (41) then the persistence of feelings of inferiority and inner fears are significant. Beauvoir is more optimistic than the psychoanalysts about the capacity of the subject to be transformed through social experiences and collective action. Exogenous forces have effect on the personal, but she also believes that personal development and destabilizing identity can disrupt capitalism and patriarchy (Beauvoir's theory of institutions and socio-economic forces will be dealt with in the following chapter). In *The Ethics of Ambiguity* she says that "the body is not a brute fact," but nor is it an effect of social or cultural forces alone. She notes there are "physiological possibilities" yet these facts do not "determine behavior" (41).

Our capacity to act in the world, for Beauvoir, has as much to do with our embodied psyche, our social location (our class, race, gender, and age) as well as the sedimented historical patterns. Presumably, political and economic relations are structured by the logic of capitalist accumulation, and institutions are structured by hierarchal patriarchal organizational structures and the values of liberal democracy, yet none of these can be deduced from a psychoanalytic understanding of the subject.

Beauvoir recognizes the role of the imaginary on our psyches and our social lives and the dematerializing process that entails. Ideas can contribute to building radical political projects, though they can also shore up ideas that contribute to inferiority. Woman's everyday existence is mediated but not determined by social forms of inferiority. The individual must engage with the world in order to act. One takes one's bearing in history. This position allows for the combination of both psychoanalytic and historical materialist insights; the responsive individual is an engaged individual. Beauvoir does not believe that the psychic is the primary source or single site of the imagination, for she thinks social/cultural practices and political regimes have effects on the psyche of a child. One's own personal narratives and collective social practices go into producing parenting practices and growing identities. In *The Second Sex*, she looks at how women have been represented in fiction and literature in different cultures and how these depictions have contributed to woman's subjective experience (SS, 214–61). In the section on historical materialism and history, she examines how the material conditions of women's situation and the historical and political contexts produce specific fields and topographies, impediments that have to be assumed and navigated. The "body as situation" is a shorthand way of treating the overlapping of complex fields within which the embodied subject acts and is acted upon. It appreciates the body as the point of intersection of the inside/outside, subjective/objective, and material/cultural. However, the personal history of embodied subjects cannot be denied, as some are more responsive to others and open to the world, and others are not.

Beauvoir believes that woman's role in the economy and her exclusion from public life have had effects on her psyche – contributing to her sense of inferiority. One's psyche is not fixed in early childhood, for there is always the possibility of it being reconfigured in response to changing events. Beauvoir identifies woman as "a becoming" whose situation articulates both exogenous factors, such as socio-economic processes, political institutions, history, as well as endogenous features, such as one's desire and the psychic energy to creatively engage in the world and stick with one's projects. She is optimistic that the qualities of trust and capacity for action can be produced later in life, if women reconfigure their relation to themselves and the world. This requires change on both the micro and macro level. In *The Blood of Others*, Beauvoir traces how Hélène manages to become empathetic. At the outset of the Second World War she is self-centred and impetuous; she sees this shiny new bicycle and she decides she has to have it. She deceives Jean into stealing it for her. She has no remorse that she risked another's freedom to satisfy her desire. When her boyfriend mulls over whether or not he will enlist and fight the Nazis (troubled by the Soviet/Nazi alliance at the time) Hélène shows no interest in his dilemma. Her response suggests she is not communicating. She says: "The war is stupid, why would you want to go and get bumped off" (*BO*, 158). Over the course of a few years, she begins to be responsive to others, and communicate. She gives a mother and child her seat, enabling them to escape to the Free Zone, while she returns to Paris. These generous acts are portrayed as responses to the transmission of bodily affects – the eyes of a plaintive child and the perceived weightiness of a suffering child on the mother's hip prompted empathy. This act of generosity triggered other acts of responsiveness that began a transformation in her relations to others. She also visits her Jewish friend and is harassed by German soldiers who are trying to track her down. At one point it looks as if she may be arrested. In the end Hélène joins the Resistance, the ultimate act of concern and political commitment. Hélène does not make a conscious decision, a deliberative choice, to be empathetic; but rather it happens over time. One could argue that the Nazi Occupation at least in part triggered her responsiveness and openness to others' suffering. There is no reason given by Beauvoir; it just happens, then continues to happen. Hélène is not wholly transformed into a thoughtful and caring person. In fact, just before she makes the commitment to join the Resistance, she is offered a job in Germany, which she considers taking, much to the disdain of her family and friends; however, in the end, she reconsiders.

Since, for Beauvoir, the self is not self-contained but an opening onto others, one is primed for sensorial and human relations. However, this depends upon one's personal psychic history and the social circumstances one finds oneself in. The above example illustrates this process is not directed by reason, but commitment driven by emotion. Hélène moves from being impetuous and narcissistic to being able to seize present possibilities and commit to a project of change. Woman's capacity to act is often identified as thwarted in a male-dominated society; her limited horizons have as much to do with existing economic and political forces as well as her internalized inferiority complex (*SS*, 53). Hélène managed to overcome her limitations. This is also true of minority races; their capacity is an effect of the institutions and political power relations within which they operate, as well as attitudes and opinions that foster social inferiority. Their subordinate relation is both socio-structural as well as socio-psychological. However they are not equally determined. Beauvoir learned from her dear friends Frantz Fanon and Richard Wright that racism is not simply a personal attitude, but is socially structured and must be tackled with collective political and social projects.

This is where Beauvoir and psychoanalysis part company; for the latter, destabilizing existing identities and desires are key, whereas for Beauvoir this is only one ingredient. In addition to reworking one's desires, new embodied relations triggered by events and radical projects are ingredients to change. Microprocessual change requires macroprocessual change. Most psychoanalytic thinkers – even Lacan, who has done the most to acknowledge the power of the social – believe that the Oedipal struggle, obsessional behaviour, and narcissism will continue.[3] This is not true for Beauvoir: male superiority has persisted over time and is present in most cultures; however it is not a permanent structure of human existence. Female desire will destabilize present identities and even challenge existing patriarchal social structures; however, this is not sufficient for women's liberation.

At the time Beauvoir was writing, there were more conservative psychoanalysts who believed that lesbian women were denying their natural femininity. These women were defined as "viriloid," and psychoanalysts envisioned their role as helping women to adapt to their social roles as

3 Deleuze and Guattari are an exception; they believe that de-Oedipalization is possible and desirable: they imagine our desire can unleash powers to challenge the Oedipal triangle and subvert capitalism. While they equally envision a world without such narratives, Deleuze and Guattari – in contrast to Beauvoir – believe that change comes from desire, from the micropolitical. There is no belief that macro change will be beneficial. For institutions like the state, political parties, institutions are trapped into a logic of the same, a logic of capitalism, which is regressive. For Beauvoir these institutions can be reworked and again she focuses upon will and commitment – concepts absent in Deleuze and Guattari.

mother and wife. Beauvoir clearly parts company with these sorts of psychoanalysts. Moreover although Beauvoir has some affinity to Kleinian thinking, she does not theorize an infant's murderous desires to kill its mother and the fantasies and paralysis that such feelings spawn. For psychoanalytic thinkers, if inner psychic fears/fantasies are not uncovered, if one's neurosis and anxiety persist, engagement in the world will not be possible, or only of limited effect. Given that Beauvoir sees fears and anxieties happening on a pre-conscious level, they can be brought to consciousness or possibly even transformed through personal engagement and collective action. So psychoanalytic practice is not necessary. For Beauvoir, these fears, wild fantasies, and drives are less intransigent and less destructive.

We are not self-contained or sovereign subjects, but interdependent (intersubjective) beings. We do not become subjects by taking a position in differentiating moves that are linguistic in character, nor are we simply produced by our class relations or discursive practices. So breaking from the Oedipal logic or rebelling against the power of the phallus is only part of the solution. As we have seen, Beauvoir prioritizes human purposiveness, initiative, and responsiveness in a way that psychoanalysts who focus upon sexual drives do not. In being more open to events and struggles of the day, more generous to others, one can mitigate the destructive effects of capitalism. Her fictionalized character Hélène, in *The Blood of Others*, illustrates the capacity of a subject to change over time, in response to significant events like the Nazi occupation of France during the Second World War.

Beauvoir does not rely upon abstract theories of agency, but presumes we are able to change by engaging in collective projects. She says: "every concrete human being is uniquely situated" (*SS*, 4). We must take into account the dense textures of everyday social life – how we respond to events and others. These must be reconfigured. Hélène had to become less narcissistic to feel solidarity with her French friends. Beauvoir's dialectical way of thinking goes some way to appreciate the way macro processes affect our lived and shared experiences and how changes in the later can percolate up and begin to have larger effect. Making individual choices and commitments are both possible and called for. One must assume one's past and the concrete present in order to move forward. This produces a different version of materialist agency, where the subject has both less and more of a role to play, than the liberal rationalist and materialists (new and old) believe. Departing from theories of negative freedom, freedom as absolute transcendence, Beauvoir believes women's freedom is limited by their past, but also the conditions under which they act. Hence the social and political circumstances, and one's class position, will factor into what is possible.

Here, again, we see Beauvoir situated between modernism and postmodernism. Her vision of woman as a becoming – as processual – respects an historically sensitive and discursive body subject. However, her notion of the relational subject and her ontology of freedom posits a subject who struggles to be more self-realizing: someone for whom knowledge is able to facilitate "autonomous" decisions and collective projects. In so doing, she values certain normative choices and practices over others. Instead of seeing norms as simply normalizing/disciplining, as Foucault does, Beauvoir appreciates those norms and practices that further women's self-development and emancipation. Since she exists is in a context of social inferiority, woman must reconfigure her relations to others: this involves engaging in collective projects that deepen her horizons and extend her projects. However, we should not confuse her with rationalist or interest-driven thinkers, for she believes that sensory experiences, as well as rich affective/emotional relations, are important. Disclosing ideology, uncovering liberal falsehoods is not going to liberate us or direct our actions. As a "subject-in-process," woman becomes an agent as much through emotion and deepening her affective relations to others as through the pursuit of interest or truth. Beauvoir departs from many contemporary discursive theorists (like Butler, Foucault, and Lyotard) who call for the refusal of identities and the fragmentation of the self. Although Beauvoir believes one must destabilize old identities to forge new ones, fragmentation is not necessarily productive; rather she believes women must tie their past and present towards a project facilitating an open future. Further, her ontological presuppositions privilege certain behaviour – responsive, engaged, and reciprocal relations – over others. In endorsing some conduct over others, she departs from deconstructive strategies and the sufficiency of destabilizing the existent. She does not subscribe to the concept of the stable, masterful, male modernist subject that is often attributed to her as a disciple of Sartre or an existentialist thinker. In accepting one's bodily agency, ambiguity, and responsive relations to others, she does not jettison plans, intentions, or purposive action but does believe they must be supplemented by affective experiences. She attends to attuned and aesthetic conduct consistent with Merleau-Ponty's non-dualist ontology. Refusing socially sanctioned roles of mother, lover, carer as forms of oppression, she equally refuses to simply negate them. She endorses committed situated action that harnesses one's energy to others – that persists over time – rather than spontaneous revolutionary outbursts. As we will see in the chapter on Marxism, she does not subscribe to structural contradictions or historical immanence to make the revolution, but rather believes in collective struggles that harness existing historical/social forces to further revolutionary ends. Her focus on incremental change, engaging persistent and encumbered thrusts towards freedom, distinguishes her approach from the purity of communist outbursts that Slavoj Žižek and Alain Badiou subscribe to.

For Beauvoir, one's future is open, yet also patterned, sustained by one's personal psychological history and existing sedimented cultural practices, socio-economic relations, and political institutions. She approaches psychoanalysis and Marxism in a non-deterministic manner to explore how psychological patterns and the historical past structure what is possible. While there are persistent patterns and structures, there is always some space for women to reconfigure their past and overcome their absolute Otherness. One's identity factors into freedom; some docile and passive women simply accept the prevailing cultural representations and social roles, whereas others struggle against them (*SS*, 271). Those who engage in projects, whether they are in a political, economic, athletic, or aesthetic field, inject new values and new visions into their world, thus potentially transforming their demeaned identities and social hierarchies.

There are aspects of woman's psyche, her inner emotional world, that Beauvoir believes must be changed: passive attitudes are impediments to active engagement in the world. She is also concerned with woman's complicity with her oppressors. She does not believe that woman consciously wills her subordination, or her freedom for that matter. The concept of will is used to mark woman's aspirations, goals, or projects as distinct from her desires or pleasures, which she has less control over. As I have said, Beauvoir suggests that Freud's theory of desire must be made compatible with Adler's theory of purposes and projects. However, in addition to looking at the subject and its motives, projects, and plans, Beauvoir wants to take into account the specific situation in which these occur. In doing so, she relies on historical research as well as fiction.[4] In her novels, she explores concrete and complex intertwinings of cultural and material registers of experience, one's particular history as well as historical structures within which one acts. Thereby she counters voluntarist, individualist thinking – without denying human agency.

4 In *Must We Burn Sade*, Beauvoir explores de Sade's life appreciating his concrete situation, his personal history, as well as the structural situation in which he acts.

Liberal voluntarists fail to account for the self as relational and commitment as coming from both "external" processes as well as "inner resources." In fact, given Beauvoir's theory of intersubjectivity, such distinctions between inner and outer, self and other, are always tenuous, for humans are never either completely distinct nor wholly blurred. Since structuralists and poststructuralists see the self as a discursive effect and refuse the term "will" altogether, there is little space for individual initiative, or only within a particular discourse. Beauvoir employs the term in a cautious and qualified manner. In prompting women and men to will their freedom, she distinguishes spontaneous, unwilled acts from intentional projects. The revolution cannot rely on unconscious desire, nor structural contradictions, alone – it requires humans making commitments. However, the process of willing one's freedom is not so easy nor simply a matter of choice, for there must be forces of change and projects to commit to. Beauvoir mentions one of the problems of Marxism as its failure to fully acknowledge the need for commitment; while the working classes are situated as agents of change, until and unless they commit to the revolution, there will be no revolution. She makes room for complicity or resistance to power as well as the possibility of change. Women who are emotionally invested in their family – devoted to their children, and identified with the accomplishments of their husbands and children – will be unlikely to struggle for the emancipation of women. While they cannot change their lives overnight, they can change their lives over time. Their passive relationship to the world causes serious problems.

This is clearly illustrated in *The Woman Destroyed.* Monique is forty-four, happy in her long marriage to Maurice; when she finds out that he is having an affair, her friends suggest that she let the affair run its course, but she cannot. She is filled with rage and jealously. The problem Beauvoir identifies is that Monique is totally dependent upon Maurice. In her diary Monique writes, "I've lost my own image. I did not look at it often; but it was there, in the background, just as Maurice had drawn it for me. A straightforward, genuine, 'authentic' woman, without mean-mindedness, uncompromising, but at the same time understanding, indulgent, sensitive, deeply feeling, intensely aware of things and of people, passionately devoted to those she loved and creating happiness for them" (*WD*, 28).

Beauvoir spurns this selfless devotion of a woman to her family and children: Monique had let Maurice "draw her image." Although Beauvoir does not use the psychoanalytic terms "introjection" or "projection" to identify these pathologies, she recognizes the problems that ensue when women "lose themselves" in others and fail to respect the boundaries between self and other. She equally is apprised of the powers of projection, that our inner fears inform the world we see around us. Insecurity can lead a woman to project her aspirations, wishes onto her husband and children, instead of furthering her own projects. Furthermore, Beauvoir points to men's fear of powerful women, which can lead men to demean and dominate them. Both of these processes can be debilitating and undermine the potential of women to contribute to their self-development.

BEAUVOIR'S USE AND ABUSE OF PSYCHOANALYSIS

Beauvoir's relationship to psychoanalysis is more complex than most scholars admit. As Irigaray rightly points out, Beauvoir uses psychoanalysis in spite of her public disdain for it (Irigaray 1993, 10–11). Like many feminists, her attitude is characterized by ambivalence, both an aversion to and interest in psychoanalysis. On the one hand, she is highly critical of psychoanalysis's determinist and reductionist assumptions, yet she relies on psychoanalysis to help her understand how women become woman – that is, "take on their feminine identities" and "assume" their gendered roles in the present world. While Beauvoir herself does not directly reflect on this ambivalence, her approach to psychoanalysis is consistent with her spurning of systemic thinking and her desire to use whatever theory works. Psychoanalysis helps her understand the personal blockages that women experience.

In Book I, chapter 2 of *The Second Sex*, Beauvoir compares psychoanalysis to religion. "Like all religions – Christianity or Marxism – there are always 'heretics'" (*SS*, 49). She defines psychoanalysis as displaying "an unsettling flexibility against a background of rigid concepts" (49). "Sometimes concepts are defined narrowly, the phallus for example designating very precisely a fleshy growth which is the male sex organ: at other times infinitely broadened, they take on a symbolic value" (49).[5]

Beauvoir uses Freud to illustrate the significance of the body as an agent. "Freudianism's value derives from the fact that the existent is a body: the way he experiences himself as a body in the presence of other bodies concretely translates his existential situation" (68). The experience of my body in communication with other bodies expresses my existential situation. The body is not just a container for the self, but an

5 Here she recognizes the symbolic function of the phallus versus the biological function, but she gets it wrong, by identifying the latter as phallus rather than penis.

expression of the self, a stylistic mediation on the world that cannot be bracketed, even in thinking.

Beauvoir praises psychoanalysis's advance over psychophysiology: "it is not the body-object described by scientists that exists concretely but the body lived by the subject" (49). So the existence of the penis as an organ that penetrates the hole does not necessitate women's subordinate role. She contests a biological argument. The structure of the ovum might be noteworthy to scientists, but it usually doesn't figure in woman's lived experience. Hence "nature does not define woman: it is she who defines herself by reclaiming nature for herself in her affectivity" (49).

While Freud and his followers believe they are not writing philosophy and hence their work "eludes any attack of a metaphysical sort" (50), Beauvoir claims there are "metaphysical postulates behind all his affirmations" (50) that must be explored critically. She finds unacceptable "the interiorizing of the unconscious and all psychic life, as a drama that unfolds within the individual" (58). Female consciousness is the product of society; "she chooses herself through the world, finds a way of answering the questions she asks" (58). So the terms "complex," "tendencies," "determinism," "unconscious drives" (58), and inner mechanisms are inappropriate; this language fails to appreciate the role of human agency – how she chooses herself through the world. While psychoanalysis sees humans inscribed in symbolic processes (i.e., "a collective unconscious") over which they have no control, Beauvoir admits the role of the social subject in assuming these processes (56). There may be prefabricated imagery and universal symbols, which exist outside the particular contexts or sets of relations that humans find themselves in, but ultimately how these are taken up has to do with the individual.

Juliet Mitchell (1974) convincingly challenges Beauvoir's reading of Freud. The theory of universal symbolism and collective unconscious that Beauvoir attributes to Freud is closer to the ideas of Carl Jung. Although there is some evidence of the concept of the collective mind in Freud's *Totem and Taboo* (1913, 1950), for the most part Freud returns to the specific individual in his or her concrete situation to explore the meanings of dreams. In *Totem and Taboo*, he believes guilt from the act of parricide has persisted for many thousands of years and has remained operative in generations that can have no real knowledge of actually killing their father, or of the ill treatment of sons by their father. Every separate individual cannot start this process of human history anew; he possibly acquires it as a collective unconscious memory. However, doesn't this mean that meaning or symbols are given without the individual having some role in signification?

Freud does not believe in formalist analysis of dreams as Beauvoir suggests he does. In fact, when the Surrealists asked him to contribute to an anthology of dreams, Freud wrote that "without associations, and without knowledge of the circumstances in which the dream was dreamt, an analysis and an anthology do not make sense" (Roudinesco 1990, 33). Here Freud seems to depart from Lacan who believes in axiomatic formulae, where such abstract thinking is possible.

At times Beauvoir treats Alfred Adler and Wilhelm Stekel as psychoanalysts, and at other times she acknowledges their departures from Freud's thinking. She suffers from a lack of detailed and complex understanding of the permutations of psychoanalysis. She attributes to Freud "the Electra complex" and the "masculine protest," both of which are Adler's concepts. She summarizes Freud's theory of transition from polymorphous oral and anal sexuality to genital sexuality as a necessary and rigid development, whereas Freud himself represents this movement much less systematically, recognizing the overlapping of these stages. One doesn't fully transcend each phase, as Beauvoir implies.

Further, Beauvoir criticizes Freud for androcentrism, or masculine bias, and ignores his more subtle treatment of female sexuality. She insists that Freud prioritizes the masculine, for he posits the male libido as the norm and the Oedipal complex as the normal principle of subject formation; thus, the young female's desire and her identifications are deviations from this norm. Since the male libido is taken as the norm, the standard, psychoanalytic descriptions of the feminine libido are impoverished (*SS*, 58). Moreover Freud "barely studies it in itself" (50).[6] In fact Beauvoir quotes Freud: "the libido is constantly and regularly male in essence, whether in man or woman" (50). She quotes the sexologist Maranon, who declared that women who experience orgasm are viriloid (50), imagining she is quoting a Freudian. The masculinist perspective, she believes, is further confirmed in the Freudian view that clitoral

6 In Book II, Beauvoir cites insights of Karen Horney (1923–24) and Helene Deutsch (1944, 319ff.) who studied female sexuality as distinct from male sexuality. They both qualify Freud's theory of penis envy. Horney "acknowledges that fantasies of omnipotence, especially those of a sadistic character are frequently associated with the male urinary system" (*SS*, 309). Some girls desire a penis, fascinated by its visibility and its powers of exhibiting, but are not traumatized by it upon sight. Deutsch also admits that the penis can be significant for the little girl, but believes penis envy is derivative, produced "when her parents repress her autoeroticism, if she is less loved, less admired than her brothers, then she will project her dissatisfaction upon the male organ" (*SS*, 312–13). Neither psychoanalyst supports the idea that the little girl is traumatized at the sight of the penis, feeling that she has been wounded, castrated, and hence spontaneously feels inferior and desires a penis.

pleasure is deemed immature and must be transcended and that vaginal orgasm is more mature. Freud acknowledges various sites of desire that are not simply dictated by passages between erotic zones of pleasure. So the idea that women must pass from clitoral to vaginal pleasure to fulfil their societal function of reproduction is more consistent with conservative psychoanalysts than with Freud, or other more socially progressive analysts. Moreover, Beauvoir ignores his theory of original bisexuality and assumes Freud's distinctions between male and female are much more distinctly drawn than they in fact are.

Beauvoir stresses human directedness towards the world and the purposiveness of human existence and distinguishes the pleasure derived from this goal-directed behaviour from a sexual relation to the world. She uses Adler as a corrective to Freud; Adler's "will to power" (*ss*, 53) is intrinsic to human existence and challenges the focus upon unconscious motivations. More importantly, Beauvoir refuses to understand that the pleasure one derives from one's engagement with the world, one's labour, or projects are necessarily associated with sexual or genital experiences. Furthermore, Beauvoir challenges those psychoanalysts (Adler for one) who see active engagement in the world – little girls climbing trees – as a distinctively masculine pleasure.

Beauvoir claims indebtedness to Sartre and Merleau-Ponty who reconceived psychoanalysis. Instead of sexuality determining human existence, they understand "sexuality as co-extensive with existence" (50) allowing for a fundamental ambiguity. She says, "it could mean that every avatar of the existent has a sexual signification, or that every sexual phenomenon has an existential meaning" (50). Psychoanalysis sees art, work, and action as having a sexual meaning. From an existential perspective, pleasure is derived from painting, labour, or active engagement in the world; it is not simply a symptom of repressed sexual desire. The pleasure derived from sexuality and affection (aim-inhibited love) is primary: art, work, and action are not simply seen as forms of sublimation or substitution. For Beauvoir, *eros* is a pleasurable existential life force that is life affirming, that infuses both one's sexual and social activities.

If Beauvoir extends the concept of *eros*, one could make the case that she also extends *thanatos*, the psychoanalytic term for the death wish, associated with existential acts of bad faith. Those who flee their freedom, who fail to assume the facts of their past, may lapse into conventional social roles and live inauthentically. This inauthenticity takes many forms. Neurotics are trapped in self-sabotaging behaviour; instead of engaging in creative and self-affirming acts, they engage in self-defeating ones. Those suffering from melancholia – the failure to grieve the loss of a love object – have lost the capacity to act and are equally trapped in self-destructive conduct.[7] For Beauvoir, the positive force towards openness (a will to power) is privileged on an existential level. As a consequence, while she understands deep-seated and intractable psychological sources of suffering and explores how they manifest themselves in violence and conflict, she is optimistic that they can be undone through action, and not simply psychotherapy.[8]

Beauvoir's theory of subject formation is not only broadened to appreciate more socially fulfilling and creative actions, but she is more optimistic about the capacity to change. Since the subject is not driven by unconscious forces, the cause of repetitive and destructive behaviour, there is more potential for change. For Beauvoir, the inner impediments to autonomous conduct can be mitigated through action. Freud is not so optimistic: one's inner life and fears have to be reconfigured through the therapeutic process if some of the destructive effects of the unconscious are to be mitigated. Only then is some form of autonomy and creativity possible. Whereas Freud, in *Civilization and Its Discontents*, identifies sex and love as primary motives of human behaviour and their loss as sources of irremediable pain, Beauvoir adds to these pleasures: the satisfaction derived from creative work and action. She is well aware of the difficulties and failures women experience in breaking out of subordinate sexual and emotional relations with men, as evidenced in the lives of Françoise and Xaviere in *She Came to Stay* and Paula in *The Mandarins.* She describes them trapped in destructive fantasies and severely restricted by their social situations. Yet their social situations are not simply imposed from exogenous forces, but are lived uniquely given choices they have made and continue to make. Beauvoir recognizes the difficulties one has in supplanting one's behaviour; nevertheless women's lives can take on new meanings by first refusing to be complicit with their inferiority and working collectively towards change.

Beauvoir identifies the problem of sexual reductionism in psychoanalytic discourse. She contests the Oedipal complex: the idea that one's individual energy (libido) is rooted in conflicting Oedipal desires and their unsatisfactory repression or sublimation. Once Freud separates the

7 Hélène is a case in point: incapable of sustaining a sexual relation with Paul, she abjects him and the pleasure he offers; she then pursues Jean, who resists her affections, and ultimately, instead of accepting the loss, she immediately finds a lover who she is not particularly interested in, and becomes pregnant.

8 Beauvoir describes neurosis and melancholia in her novels but is optimistic that they can be mitigated through action. By stressing the purposiveness of existence and an openness towards others and the world, Beauvoir is able to offset the negative aspect of the unconscious melancholia that psychoanalysts identify in their ontological formulations of subjectivity.

sexual from the genital, she asks, what is the meaning of the sexual? It "becomes blurred" (*SS*, 50). She criticizes Freud for vagueness and for attributing too much determination to the sexual. One derives pleasure from being active and engaged and this has nothing to do with sex. Central to her argument is that Freud fails to appreciate the external social factors that contribute to woman's alienation from herself and her body. Women's inferiority complex is not the result of penis envy, but a reaction to her total situation (53). The phallocentric structures of life in patriarchal society that inform women's inner life as well as demeaned social roles make it difficult to escape feeling subordinate.

Again, this critique of Freud is not firmly established. While Beauvoir's treatment of psychoanalysis suffers from over-generalization and a failure to appreciate details and specificity, she nonetheless identifies a problem that many feminist theorists identify – the over-sexualizing of woman. Deleuzean feminists Rosi Braidotti (1991, 2002) and Elizabeth Grosz (1994) articulate a similar problem in psychoanalysis, as do Foucauldian feminists Butler (1990, 1993) and Moya Lloyd (2005). Interestingly enough, none of these theorists appreciate Beauvoir's preliminary efforts to tackle the problem of sexual pervasiveness.

Beauvoir says that psychoanalysis forgets how libido, defined "in vague terms of 'energy'" (59), is one of many ways of apprehending the object, along with touching, eating, etc.; the body is the instrument by which we comprehend the world, it is through the five senses that we apprehend it, not only through our sexual parts (*SS*, 273). But what is the relation of sexuality to other activities? And how do sensible, tactile, aural experiences contribute to human agency and pleasure? Childhood eroticism still survives in young women – "sexuality is not an isolated domain, it extends the dreams and joys of sensuality … in fact both sexes enjoy the sensual pleasures of smooth, creamy, satiny and soft" (388). These sensual pleasures are not necessarily sexual. "Man has a primordial interest in the substance of the natural world surrounding him, he tries to discover in work, in play, and in all experiences of the 'dynamic imagination' … Working with the soil, digging a hole, are activities as primal as the embrace, as coitus, it is a mistake to see them only as sexual symbols; a hole, slime, a gash, hardness, integrity are primary realities; man's interest is not dictated by the libido, but rather the libido will be influenced by the way these realities are revealed to him" (56). Work, play, and art signify ways of being concretely engaged in the world, being purposive. Pleasure from these actions and accomplishments cannot be reduced to sexual desire. This also provides an alternative to seeing the pervasiveness of sexuality desire as a determining factor in women's lives.

Interestingly, object relations theorists (Winnicott, Klein) believe that our relation to things, our trust in the world, is an effect of early relations to our primary caretaker; this is not a sexual relation but rather reflects the devotion and caring attention of (M)other. If this care is insufficient, object relations theorists believe, the infant will lapse into fantasy. This attention to the significance of pre-Oedipal life, the world of oral and anal pleasures and impulses, challenges the focus upon the Oedipal struggle as defining human agency. Giving up on expectations and desires for mother's love allows boys to identify with their fathers and move on. Object relations theory, which presumes a primary attachment to (M)other, and subsequent separation from (M)other, is less culpable of prioritizing the male over the female – male agency over female agency – for the significant Other can be male. The failure to trust others, to feel safe in the world and act, is set in motion in the early years of life. In the past this was concerned with mother/infant relations; however, today primary caretakers are not necessarily mothers or women substitutes. Benjamin believes changes in parenting practices will have psychological effects (1988, 217–18). If men are more active participants in care, the identification of women with caring practices will be challenged. Girls and boys will not necessarily see attributes of care associated with femininity and paid labour/work associated with masculinity. Perhaps, too, the fantasies associated with the all-powerful and punitive mother (as per Klein) will be mitigated if males are more involved in primary care. Object relations theory, which decentres sexual pleasures as a motor of development and appreciates more generally our capacity to engage in creative, playful relations with objects, has some affinity to Beauvoir, though there is little evidence that she was familiar with the work. While Beauvoir identified murderous fantasies, which contribute to a fear of engaging in the world, she does not attribute them to the unconscious, since she doesn't have a theory of the unconscious.

Finally, earlier versions of psychoanalysis, those Beauvoir would be familiar with, are certainly culpable of phallocentrism, not a term Beauvoir herself uses, but a concept that is apt in the present context to define her concern. Beauvoir believes the phallus and penis are highly valued in our culture and have been in most past cultures. Since most societies have been patriarchal, symbols that support masculinity – such as the phallus – are important. Beauvoir explains it as a contingent marker of privilege rather than as essential to subject formation, as Freud and even Lacan seem to suggest. Psychoanalysis takes for granted that the phallus and the father have authority and power without explaining why. The father breaks/ruptures the dyadic relation of mother and infant, but presumably so could another woman. In object relations theory, the capacity to develop a trusting and creative relation to the world is a function of the infant's relation to its mother or primary carer. Beauvoir believes the power of the phallus is a truth of existing patriarchal society, but she does not think this symbol is universal or necessary: as times have changed and approaches to parenting infants have changed, the persistence of the Oedipal dynamic will also change.[9]

In spite of Beauvoir's rather damning criticisms of psychoanalysis, she does appeal to Freud, Adler, and Stekel, as well as Havelock Ellis, Jean Piaget, and Helene Deutsch for their insights into feminine identity in Book II of *The Second Sex.* They help her portray the complexity of meanings, emotions, and symptoms associated with traditional femininity and give her own assessment of the destructiveness of femininity more substance. Like these psychoanalysts, Beauvoir focuses on the body as a threshold, an interface or medium between internal and external factors. Yet, when she applauds psychoanalysis, she does so in a way that dilutes its conventional truths. De-emphasizing the effects of unconscious sources of anger and illness and the role of the feminine psycho-symbolic order, and stressing the importance of unequal power relations between men and women and women's marginal existence, Beauvoir corrects an overly sexualized explanation of human behaviour. Introducing more reciprocal relations and new symbolic forms of femininity that help constitute woman as an agent in the world will not alleviate all forms of alienation or suffering but will, Beauvoir believes, provide a chance for significantly changing the gendered nature of our world.

Changes to the outside world (instituting reciprocal relations between men and women) would change the psyche. One of the truths of human existence is that the future is open and undetermined; it is not rooted in nature, but it is influenced by past patterns of conduct. Our sexuality is not determined by biological facts or anatomical organs, although these figure in our social lives. Our sexual identity is not static but dynamic, and must be performed. Although certain patterns reoccur (informed by the incest taboo, the Oedipal and Electra drama, and women's primary responsibility for childcare), embodied human experience is open-ended. Present forms of feminine identity are wholly unsatisfactory and have persisted throughout human history, but we are not condemned to sustain them. Contemporary psychologists

9 Jessica Benjamin makes this point in *Bonds of Love*; getting fathers to take an active role in parenting will involve less gender stereotyping.

discovered that young girls came to accept their femininity as a form of inferiority, as "mutilation" (the blood and pain of menstruation), and symptoms of sickness and guilt follow from that. Beauvoir identifies women having rejected their femininity, its shame and inferior status. But she believes that this will change as more and more women participate in the paid economy and in political life, and gain the symbolic power to reimagine themselves and reconfigure their sexual desire. She describes what it means to accept one's sex within existing patriarchal definitions but claims that in a world where women were treated as equals, femininity would not entail accepting inferiority, passivity, and docility. She sees women's desire as radiating through the body, more undulating and dispersed than male pleasure which focuses on unitary ejaculation. In a patriarchal society, Beauvoir recognizes how women are alienated from their bodies and their distinctive structure of desire, which are defined by male social privilege and male desire. Connecting with their distinctive female desire will be part of the emancipatory process.

SOCIAL FORMS OF ALIENATION

While psychoanalysis focuses on relations that are the product of one's intra-psychic life, having to do with internal psychic struggles around how desires and needs are experienced, Beauvoir dilutes their significance by denying the unconscious and working to socialize psychic phenomena. As well as being an object of male desire, woman's exclusion from public life and her subordinate social roles coincide and confer upon her an inferior status. This has obvious effects on the self. Women feel less capable of engaging in creative worldly projects than men and more often lose themselves in their maternal and domestic roles. Not only one's psyche or embodied subjectivity, but social, cultural, and economic relations all form the situation in which the individual embodied subject exists. Since Beauvoir believes we are intersubjectively constituted, our social relations have an effect on who we are and what we become; our psyche is very much affected by our identification with significant others (be they mother or father). Moreover, these Oedipal dramas could be a thing of the past. Whereas psychoanalysts tend to support the view that our self is structured by how one manages primary psychic forces of fear or desire through which the social is then mediated, for Beauvoir social relations produce inner psychic life. While Lacan has increased the effectivity of the social, he strongly believes in the power of the phallus to structure subjectivity. Beauvoir, as I have said, does not believe these processes alone structure subject formation.

In fact, women who manage to be effective participants in public life, who create and sustain projects, will diminish their primary fears. So structural changes – putting women in situations of reciprocal respect and agency – could disturb the patterns of social passivity and inferiority that women experience.

Beauvoir's study of female narcissism provides an example of the intertwining of the psychic and the social in subject formation. She explains female narcissism not simply intra-psychically as a self-defeating relation to desire (neurosis) or a problem with inner conflicts about satisfying one's desire. Instead, it has two sources: one social (macropolitical processes) and one psychological (micropolitical processes). Lacking recognition in her own right, relegated to the private domestic sphere and activities that occupy her rather than ones that are self-fulfilling, woman is self-obsessed. Worrying about her bodily form, her image, rather than engaging in projects that would be fulfilling, she ruminates over her body and that contributes to her passivity. Her sexual desires remain ungratified, given the passive social role she is supposed to assume via male lovers and the dominance of the economy of male desire.

Whereas feminine desire radiates throughout her body, male desire is localized in the penis. Beauvoir sees the body as a natural/cultural continuum. She sees the penis as something graspable, external. This helps men develop their alter ego. Since woman has no such organ and her sex is a hole, the absence of a "double" makes an alter ego more difficult. Instead of externalizing her anger and libidinal energy, she turns against herself leading to self-destructive behaviour or uses her children as substitutes for doubling.

The subject's openness to others and the world has social and psychological preconditions. In capitalist society, where the commodity form diminishes people's expressive character and sensuous labour, responsive relations are less likely. When the economy of masculine sexuality dominates woman's relation to her body, the possibility of her experiencing her own erotic feelings worsens. She becomes increasingly estranged, especially if she is compelled to fulfil a reproductive role without choosing it. In a world where women are politically and socially active and treated with reciprocity, rather than as sexual objects, they will actively participate in public life and the economy and have more control over their lives. They will be encouraged to explore and travel and spend less time ruminating over their bodies. Thus, some of the causes of female narcissism and depression will be removed. For Beauvoir, social and political changes are necessary to overcome female narcissism, but these changes alone will not eliminate the psychic causes of depression.

CRITIQUE OF DETERMINISM

In light of psychoanalytic truths, Beauvoir's understanding of the psyche appears unsophisticated: her dismissal of the unconscious and her emphasis on choice is rather crude. While this may be true, her theoretical approach to subjectivity avoids the pitfalls of both liberal voluntarism and psychoanalytic determinism. Her theory of embodied agency gives more space to the social and articulates connections between the symbolic and the social, between self and others, in ways that the Lacanians and post-Lacanians fail to do.[10] Furthermore, her work on the subject is explored within philosophic discourses. She explores power relations under the matrix of Hegel's master/slave dialectic as well as a logic of embodied generosity inspired by Merleau-Ponty. In this way, she potentially can appreciate a distinctive feminine libidinal economy. In Lacanian logic, the power of the father or phallus is important in subject formation; even in a post-emancipatory situation, women must accept their lack and assume a relationship to the phallus. Beauvoir doesn't envision these relations as necessary to subjectivity, but she does believe in responsiveness, engagement, and reciprocity, which emerge from attachment and relations of care and trust.

Beauvoir's theory of embodiment allows for the appreciation of sensual pleasures as well as the appreciation of attachment. However in emphasizing sensual bodily pleasures that are immanent in art, play, and creative sensuous labour, how do we make sense of Beauvoir's theory of choice, which has been the cornerstone of her anti-humanist critics? Beauvoir says that woman has "the role of object or Other that is proposed to her and a claim to freedom" (*ss*, 61). She relies on notions of will and choice; however, I have cast doubts on presuming them to come from sovereign subjects. One must not forget that choice for Beauvoir is intersubjective; it is a choice that arises within embodied subjects, structured social relations, and patterns of situations, which were not chosen. Further, in recognizing the role of sensuality, the transmission of affects and historical synchronization, the body and the whole situation have roles to play in agency. In her use of the term "choice" to make sense of women's agency, Beauvoir has been misunderstood. I will return to the example of the lesbian identity. Beauvoir emphasizes that one is not a victim of exogenous (patriarchal, capitalist) forces, although they clearly

10 While the Lacanians attend to the socio-symbolic or socio-psychic domain, their subject centred approach to agency is narrow, since it does little to respect the macro structures of the social.

are a factor in her oppression. Lesbianism is a subjective (personal) adaptation to a lived situation in a masculinized society. This presumes a realistic response to an adverse situation (hence, this is out of step with some psychoanalytic thinkers who presume it is the product of inner fantasies). Lesbianism involves a rejection of predominant masculine (aggressive) forms of loving and a desire for more feminine (tender) relations. Beauvoir's understanding of lesbianism as a transitional identity helps us appreciate a theory of subjectivity that accommodates choice within a situation defined by pre-existing social relations. Some women, she says, in reaction to the roughness of male sexuality, opt for a lesbian alternative, which is more sensual and less aggressive. Women choose and give themselves "a dimension of liberty," something psychoanalysts deny as they are too busy explaining identity formation in terms of "contradictory drives" (56). The behaviour of girls and women is structured by their contradictory orientations to be passive like mum or active like dad. Conflict in desire leads to dissatisfaction in one's sexual and social life. In identifying with one's femininity, which in its present form is manifest in docile, passive, and other-directed action, one's pleasurable satisfaction is insecure; it is likewise difficult to identify with a man and virility and sustain one's sexual identity as a woman.

In this way, Beauvoir is close to Stekel, a contemporary psychoanalyst, who believes that woman's frigidity or sexual anxiety is in part a rational, meaningful response to the violence women experience. Childbirth, pregnancy, and the first sex acts (55) are all painful, so it is not surprising that women seek other options. Frigidity and other pathologies are seen by Stekel and Beauvoir to be a reasonable response to fear of violence and pain in sexual experiences. Contra Freud, they both diminish the role of fantasy as underpinning the refusal of the feminine position.

When Beauvoir uses the term "choice" to explore the lesbian identity she wants to highlight a "decision" taken; however, it is not rational or deliberative in nature, but a choice within an embodied habit. Beauvoir does not dispense with the role of critical reflection; yet she acknowledges that habits and personal history are not the product of deliberation. "Women must create space within themselves that allow for distancing from the present and commitment to new projects. This counters the hyperbole of the psychoanalysts, whose theories of drive and sublimation play a role in therapeutics and in theories of individual deviance. Their usage has so dominated discussions of normal human behaviour that it renders choice and willed action problematic and undermines responsible human action. Psychoanalysis finds it difficult to support ethical behaviour because all behaviour is driven by unconscious processes; how can one assume responsibility for such acts?[11] "Replacing value with authority, choice with drives, psychoanalysis proposes an ersatz morality – the idea of normality" (*ss*, 59).

For Beauvoir, one's life choices are not determined by unconscious motivations over which one has little control but by conscious or preconscious motives that arise in contexts one has not chosen. She learned from Sartre that repressed decisions and existential choices can be brought to light with startling transformatory effects. Sartre explores the decision Jean Genet made at the age of eight: surrounded by people obsessed with private property, he became a thief and later a writer. This existential decision to revolt against conventional capitalist values of property ownership is central to understanding Genet's life choices (Sartre, 1963). But Beauvoir also learned from Merleau-Ponty about the significance of rich affective relations in working towards more reciprocal and respectful relations with others. Merleau-Ponty identifies the pre-conscious and pre-reflective attachment to the world that underpins domineering human behaviour. These relations of *Mitsein*, being with, must not only be revealed, but worked on to foster responsive and generous relations. Here Beauvoir has more in common with Merleau-Ponty than with Sartre, who fails to appreciate the role of embodied habits in agency. Merleau-Ponty identifies "perceptual rigidity" (Merleau-Ponty 1967, 103). In "The Child's Relations with Others," he focuses on rigid children who fail to respond to changes in images shown them; they cling to the first image and refuse to accept any other. Rigid subject formation has social consequences (103). Merleau-Ponty points to how men refuse to accept their ambiguity and vulnerability and project these abject feelings outwards towards others. European men often project their strong sexual urges onto Black men. He writes: "the same mechanism is called into play with the Jew … the Anti-Semite throws off onto the Jew the part of himself he does not want and is most ashamed of" (103). This mechanism contributes to hateful and intolerant feelings towards minorities. Merleau-Ponty also cites Beauvoir's "battle of the sexes" (103) as a manifestation of this phenomenon. "Men who do not want to be weak and sensitive and want to be self-sufficient, decisive, energetic, project onto woman, exactly those personality traits they do not want themselves to have" (103). Women project onto men the personality traits they wish to be rid of, or cannot

11 There were other schools of psychoanalysis that Beauvoir would not have been familiar with (i.e. object relations theory). In the psychoanalytic process, it is assumed the subject would work on the forces and narratives that keep one tied to self-destructive behaviour, and thereby facilitate agency.

assume. Merleau-Ponty describes this as a mutual disparagement; however for the most part throughout his work he ignores the structural differences between men and women. Interestingly, in exploring abjection, Merleau-Ponty relies upon Melanie Klein's distinction between ambivalence and ambiguity. "Ambiguity is an adult phenomenon" (Merleau-Ponty 1967, 103): instead of dividing the world into good and evil people, "it admits that those who can be good and generous can also be annoying and imperfect." What is lacking in rigid subjects is this capacity to confront squarely the contradictions that exist in their attitudes towards others (103). Ambivalent and rigid people cannot allow ambiguity. Their behaviour leads to social prejudices. Acknowledging one's precarious and contingent self-identity, the ambiguities of human existence allow one to be more tolerant of otherness. Defensive and hateful relations – the result of overly flexible, inconsistent, frustrating, or authoritarian parenting or the relic of upwardly or downwardly mobile families – are directed outwards to those different from oneself (106). Merleau-Ponty's contribution to a sociological understanding of pathology presents this behaviour in philosophical language, as does Beauvoir. Being closed in on oneself, untrusting, and fearful, rather than embracing one's ambiguity, produces rigidity. The rigid person – the sexist and racist – are not open to novelty or difference, but strictly uphold their identities and opinions. Merleau-Ponty believes that it is possible to move beyond this state of abjection and projection, but this cannot be achieved merely by acts of the will (1967, 96–152).

Beauvoir recognizes the processes of Othering in *The Second Sex*, how men and masculinity are privileged and women become Other. Nonetheless unlike Merleau-Ponty she relies upon her novels to chart the shift from rigid behaviour to responsive beings. Ontogenetically, humans are beings-in-the-world; however, they are not always open to others. Beauvoir's protagonists Xaviere and Hélène are impetuous narcissists, whereas Paula and Françoise sacrifice their talents for their male artistic partners. Superficially, they appear quite different. The first two are unable to be open and responsive, whereas the latter two possess a selflessness that is equally problematic. Being so open to the influence of others is as problematic as being impervious to others. Both attest to a lack of autonomy.

Beauvoir appreciates the role of the pre-rational and bodily aspects of existence as well as the desire for freedom and autonomy. While these have been deemed masculine activities, Beauvoir contests this. She believes that all humans have the potential for liberty, and a purposive and engaged existence; however, these capacities are underdeveloped in women in patriarchal societies. Many humans flee their freedom and don't own up to their responsibility in willing their values. Women do not abstractly and arbitrarily choose passivity, and the status of an object; rather, this is associated with their social existence. It is also naive of women to assume that their social existence is not affected by gender. "No woman can claim without bad faith to be situated beyond their sex" (*SS*, 4). While free actions have ontological support, they must be secured by social relations and institutions. These are not readily available to all in patriarchal societies.

Beauvoir is critical of Adler when he attributes to little girls climbing trees a "viriloid" quality, a desire to demonstrate equality with boys. For Beauvoir, this interpretation is absurd; a little girl's desires to climb trees, to write, to engage in politics are not only "good sublimations," they are ends desired in themselves (60). Adler's position is a consequence of his masculine worldview, identifying any female project involving transcendence as a "masculine protest" (60). Beauvoir believes it is an essentially human feature to creatively and purposively act in the world, not the reserve of men. Although women's social existence, has, for the most part, severely restricted women's creative and purposeful actions, it has not eliminated them. Nor does she believe all societies equally restrictive. Further, she is critical of the tendency of both "male and female psychoanalysts" (60) to describe female expressions of creativity, acts of engagement with the world, as masculine.

Psychoanalysis replaces expressions of a girl's liberty with a complex explanation of how she identifies with femininity or masculinity. It implies that the little girl will have a problem with her sexual identity if she continually identifies with father rather than mother by acting in a masculine (active) manner. And if she is driven by unconscious drives and cannot choose, then she cannot be responsible for the outcome. Beauvoir believes this determinist logic cannot explain ethical action. How can one be responsible if one does not, in effect, choose one's course of action? Beauvoir rejects both Freudian and Adlerian interpretations of femininity. To study women from an existential point of view, she says, "one must see woman as a human being in search of values within a world of values, a world where it is indispensable to understand the social and economic structure" (61).

Beauvoir emphasizes that symbols are human elaborations – they don't come down from heaven nor rise from subterranean depths, but rather are elaborated by human speaking subjects (*la parole*) utilizing language (*la langue*) in hierarchical societies. As such, she refuses the Lacanian, or formalist, approach to language, which sees its meaning as given before the subject emerges. For example, the traffic lights – green, red, and amber – determine when we can walk across the street. The symbolic meaning precedes the historically existing subject; this binary ascribes meaning that the historical subject will assume. Beauvoir admits the significance of structured meanings, but also recognizes that a historical subject must somehow assume those given meanings or not, and therefore has some role in making particular meaning?

UNDERSTANDING SUBJECT FORMATION: AN ECLECTIC USE OF PSYCHOANALYSIS

Beauvoir does not fully subscribe to psychoanalysis, as we have seen, but she does affirm some psychoanalytic truths. She provides, for example, a "theory" of subject formation that borrows from psychoanalysis, but in a diluted form, since she denies the unconscious. Her account of the significance of infant attachment to the mother and the inauguration of the separation process is quite consistent with psychoanalysis, but in a form (i.e., object relations theory) that was not prevalent in France at the time she was writing. She describes the infant being put to the breast or the nursing bottle and surrounded by maternal flesh. The infant gradually learns to perceive objects as distinct from the self – the separation process has begun. The infant is separated more or less brutally from the nourishing body and thus lives directly the basic drama of every existent, that is, their relation to the Other. He/she experiences anguish in weaning, in being torn loose from the maternal flesh (*SS*, 284–7). Much in the spirit of the psychoanalytic narrative, Beauvoir states that the process of separation of infant from mother is essential to subjectivity.

In the spirit of attachment theory, she assumes the detachment process is important. Like Kleinians and object relations and attachment theorists, Beauvoir acknowledges the need for healthy attachment to establish trust and emotional well-being; frustrated or unreliable care leads to insecurity and anxiety. Again, without theorizing the unconscious, Beauvoir treats feelings of anxiety and shame as social in nature. Furthermore she does not speculate on the horrific fantasies that inform frustrated infants, as the Kleinians do.

She also endorses the psychoanalytic narrative of sexual identification; she rejects a biological theory according to which the possession of a particular sexual organ dictates one's desire and sexuality, as well as a macrotheory of patriarchy that assumes that girls and women are socialized and programmed into accepting their social inferiority to men.

Following Freud, Beauvoir acknowledges the uniqueness of an embodied subject and the plasticity of desire. Freud's theory of polymorphous perversity presumes that desire can attach to any thing (fetish) or organ, yet there are privileged sites of desire. Beauvoir describes the young girl separating from her mother and identifying with her father and his virility; however, as she becomes aware of their anatomical differences and imagines having been mutilated, she renounces her virile pretensions and identifies with her mother. This desire to be like "father" is translated into desire for him and rivalry with her mother. Little girls "seek to break their ties with mother" to monopolize their father's love (51). Her inferiority is compensated by the affection the young girl elicits from her father or, later in life, by bearing a child who symbolically represents her power to create, and hence circulates as her substitute penis. To be able to establish a loving relationship with another, she must realize that her father is not within her grasp. If she reacts by refusing to identify with her mother, retaining virile aspirations and continuing to identify with her father, she will become frigid, male-identified, and clitoral, hence unable to lead a fulfilling sexual life as a woman.

For the most part, Beauvoir agrees with this narrative of self-formation that one finds in Freud but recognizes the complexity and contradictoriness of sexual desire; some little girls do not transfer their identity from their father to their mother, but continue to emulate masculinity. Even though she recognizes the importance of women being able to be successful in the economy or actively participate in public life, this is not sufficient for women to be liberated. Such women may not be sexually fulfilled, for their desire can be defined by masculine desire and their sexual fantasies often reiterate submissive and domineering relations.

In Book I of *The Second Sex*, Beauvoir disparages the psychoanalyst's account of penis envy, whereas in Book II, she adopts it in a diluted form, as a way of exploring women's social inferiority. She accepts Piaget's, Saussure's, and Deutsch's theories that the absence of a penis will not in itself bring trauma to a little girl, but it will have significance, especially in certain social situations. Beauvoir speculates that if the little girl's parents repress her desires for masturbation or exhibitionism, the little girl may feel less admired than her brothers, less loved. In this case, she may project her dissatisfaction onto the male organ (287, 292). Here, Beauvoir takes her cue from Adler (53), who attributes the little boy's pride in his penis to the valuation of his parents and his associates, and the little girl's failure to be admired as a consequence of her parents' failure to celebrate her.

Beauvoir qualifies Freud's theory of penis envy by again giving much more space to the social inferiority, thereby diluting the effectiveness of the psychic register. Penis envy, she believes, must be supported by a masculine culture where the penis is a sign of male privilege (54). If a society does not value the masculine, then it is unlikely that the penis would have much value. Thus, she rejects a formalist interpretation of the phallus. In a patriarchal society, woman may regret not having a penis, but it does not follow that she believes herself to be mutilated by man. Nor is she haunted by fears that her penis has been removed. The little boy takes pride in his penis and sees it as an alter ego, a corporeal expression of his value: "It is easy to see that the length of the penis, the force of the urinary jet, the strength of erection and ejaculation becomes for him the measure of his worth" (57). However, "a little boy's pride does not imply a corresponding humiliation for his sisters" since they only know this organ in its exteriority, hence "this delicate stalk of skin, can only inspire their indifference or disgust" (52). Little girls' covetousness of a penis is neither a universal nor a spontaneous experience. Such experience presumes the internalization of a culture of masculinity and a high degree of association between the penis and virility. In societies where men are not necessarily dominant, there would be no heightened value symbolized by the penis and there would be no penis envy.

Beauvoir accepts the symbolic role the penis plays in human agency, but sees it from an existential perspective. It is impossible to account for this power without starting from an existential fact: the tendency of the subject towards alienation (57). Beauvoir approaches "lack" from a philosophic register: "The anxiety of his freedom leads the subject to search for himself in things which is a way to flee from himself" (57). The infant endeavours to grasp his alienated existence in the mirror (a simplified reading of Lacan); this same need to externalize oneself in things is found in primitive peoples' use of mana or totem and civilized people's use of their egos, names, property. Such is the temptation of inauthenticity (57).

Following Hegel and Sartre, she assumes that all subjects are unhappy consciousnesses; we are never gratified or complete, nor are we fully integrated with oneself or others (*EA*, 12). In fact we are always engaged with things outside ourselves. This ecstatic relation, being forever outside oneself, is a source of action, creativity, anxiety, and sadness. The psychic lack or incompleteness – deferral, in the language of Derrida (1967) – cannot be denied; it must be accepted, which involves reconciling ourselves with our vulnerability, our mortality, our melancholia. In addition, our psychic suffering is exacerbated in a capitalist economy and in patriarchal social relations, but resolving these social structures will not eliminate alienation, which is a precondition of human existence. Insofar as one is living, one is incomplete – there is always a lack in one's being, until death (12). One can never be transparent to oneself or others, nor can one be perfectly reconciled with one's self or others; the concrete thickness of the world that one must engage makes transparence impossible.

Beauvoir identifies "the subject's tendency towards alienation; the anxiety of his freedom leads the subject to search for himself in things, which is a way to flee from himself" (*SS*, 57). The original attachment to being is not the relationship "wanting to be," but rather "wanting to disclose being" (*EA*, 12). Hence, there is a fundamental instability of being, yet an urge to stabilize oneself. However, men and women experience this instability differently. Beauvoir believes that a man has more resources than a woman to navigate fundamental alienation and anxiety. In a patriarchal society where men take up dominant social roles and where forms of masculine sexuality define sexuality, maleness is privileged and women are disadvantaged. Beauvoir mentions how male anatomy (the penis) favours active engagement. The penis is particularly well suited to serve as an alter ego encouraging self-affirmation and self expression, since it is external: it can be seen and grasped, it satisfies the desires for masturbation and exhibition. The penis "is outside himself; the very object into which he projects himself becomes a symbol of autonomy, of transcendence of power; he measures the length of his penis, he compares his urinary stream with that of his friends; later, erection and ejaculation will become grounds for satisfaction and challenge" (*SS*, 313). While this "little rod" facilitates the doubling of the self and its body, "the hole" of the vagina, in contrast, compares rather badly for the little girl. She cannot easily see it; nor can others. Therefore it does not easily satisfy her desire for exhibition or masturbation. "A little girl cannot incarnate herself in any part of her body" (293).

To compensate for this "physiological deficiency" and to serve as the basis for her alter ego, the little girl is given a foreign object, a doll: "The doll represents the whole body and it is a passive object … While the boy seeks himself in the penis as an autonomous subject, a partial substitute for the unreliability of parental approbation, the little girl pampers her dolls and dresses her as she dreams of being dressed and pampered; inversely she thinks herself as a marvelous doll" (293). She plays at being mother and learns to be dolled up (293). The little girl not only lacks a penis, but the desire to alienate herself in something other than the gaze of Others. Instead of instantiating values of creativity and autonomy, values of objectified beauty are instilled in childhood play.

To compensate for the separation inflicted through weaning, "children engage in seductive and attention seeking behaviour; the boy is forced to go beyond this stage, he is saved by narcissism by turning his attention to his penis, whereas the girl is reinforced in this tendency to make herself object" (294). While his mode of existence leads him to assert his subjective freedom, his body is a means for dominating nature, a weapon for fighting. "He engages in sport, he invents, he dares, he experiences himself as if for others" (294). But "there is no conflict between his objective figure that he is and his will for self-affirmation in concrete projects" (294). In contrast, the little girl is taught to please, to make herself a doll. Thus, conflict is manufactured between her autonomous existence and the societal norms that value her "being other) her other-directedness" (295). Not only anatomical differences but also social taboos and cultural values have a role to play in gendered agency.

The stories Beauvoir tells of how women have internalized phallic values and culture suggest that "passivity is a trait that develops in her earliest years." A boy develops a way of existing that leads him "to posit himself for himself, thereby carrying out an apprenticeship as free movement toward the world" (294). The recognition that bodies have been inscribed in masculine ideologies and practices brings Beauvoir closer to the writings of her psychoanalytic opponents.

Beauvoir uses psychoanalytic accounts of sexed identities to help her understand subject formation in patriarchal societies, in spite of her disdain for psychoanalysis. It serves as a resource to help her understand how femininity (social inferiority) is constructed and assumed by girls and women in her times. In emphasizing the importance of the social on the psychic, she respects psychoanalysis's prescriptions but not its descriptions. While the penis and phallus dominate in these patriarchal societies, their power depends upon the particular individual. The self is open to be reconfigured as male and so masculine dominance recedes. Her work, inspired by psychoanalytic research, helps her flesh out (no pun intended) her philosophy of embodied subjectivity, which tries to avoid a psychological (interior) as separate from (exterior) social existence.

PHENOMENOLOGICAL DESCRIPTIONS: RETHINKING THE IMPACT OF THE SOCIAL

In *The Second Sex,* Beauvoir sets herself the task of understanding how and why women have been construed as absolute Other. Although psychoanalysis has been useful when thinking about the nature of early childhood development, as the girl/woman grows and changes, Beauvoir is more reliant upon phenomenology. Psychoanalysis doesn't sufficiently understand the gendered nature of existence; she says that "psychoanalysis fails to explain why woman is the Other. Even Freud accepts the privilege of the penis is explained by the father's sovereignty, and he admits that he does not know the source of male supremacy" (58). In Book I, in addition to exploring psychoanalytic discourses, she explores biological and historical materialist discourses. None of these explanations prove sufficient, but all offer grist for her phenomenological descriptive method.

She shows how the implicit value systems of today's and yesterday's societies sustain women's subordination. It is clear that she uses the term Woman in a historically and culturally specific way. She defines her phenomenological method as a way of understanding the term: "Thus admitting no a priori doctrine, no dubious theory, we are confronted by a fact for which we can offer no basis in the nature of things, nor any explanation through observed data, and the significance of which we cannot comprehend a priori. We can hope to grasp the significance of sexuality only by studying it in its concrete manifestations; and then perhaps the meaning of the word female will stand revealed" (10).

Having explored various theories that explain women's subordination in Book I, we will return to look at these in subsequent chapters. Beauvoir proceeds in Book II to focus on the lived experiences of women at different stages of their development and in different contexts. In spite of the admission of a high degree of cultural and historical specificity, she makes some general statements regarding women's gendered identity. Given the dominance of the male and the masculine and the subordinate status of the female and the feminine, she says that girls and women are more alienated from their bodily agency than are boys and men (55–9).

There is some affinity between Beauvoir and the psychoanalytic treatment of the body as a threshold, an interface between the biological, social, and psychological registers of experience. Nevertheless her phenomenological descriptions of women's embodied existence allow her to appreciate inner experience and concrete freedom and avoid the timeless and deterministic patterns of psychoanalysis. Furthermore, "to regard behavior as possibly motivated by purposes freely envisaged" is important. She writes: "Painting, writing, and engaging in politics are not only good sublimations: they are ends desired in themselves" (60).

Phenomenological experiences of creativity are not dependent on psychoanalytic explanations. In exploring the sexual imaginary, she appreciates how our patriarchal society has kept women at home and symbolized femininity as inferior and subordinate. In this context, "the adolescent girl finds comfort in fields and woods … she is herself in this limitless land … In the paternal house reign mother, laws, custom, routine, she wants to become sovereign, but socially she accedes to her adult life by becoming woman, she pays for her liberation with abdication" (376). Although she struggles to escape the rigidity and patriarchy of the household, she finds herself submitting to it. Paired with social expectations of domesticity, women begin to experience their bodies as shameful. The adolescent girl approaches her developing body with uneasiness and disgrace. Disgusted and fearful of blood, she experiences her menses with anxiety. Some girls are ashamed and want to retreat to childhood; they stop eating to avoid the fleshy body and their periods, while others yearn to become maternal. Both stances involve a retreat from active engagement in the world. What is significant here is Beauvoir's portrayal of women's living bodies as the entwinement of biological, emotional, sexual, and cultural experiences. She thereby avoids essentialism and determinism. Recognizing the significance of past social meanings associated with menses, Beauvoir writes "in a sexually egalitarian society she would envisage menstruation only as her unique way of acceding to an adult life" (*SS*, 329). The menses "inspire horror in the adolescent because they thrust them into an inferior and damaged category … She would retain the pride of her bleeding body if she did not lose her pride in being human … she would feel the humiliation of the flesh much less vividly: the girl who opens up paths of transcendence in sports, social, intellectual, and mystical activities will not see a mutilation in her specificity" (330).

Young girls are active and boisterous, but as they enter puberty the social pressures of family and school try to contain and discipline their spontaneous action to fulfil the purposes of marriage and maternity. The young woman's sexuality does not affirm her subjectivity, but rather makes her into an instrument of the species (385). Insofar as women's desires are connected with reproduction, a woman can feel alienated from her body, as if her body served the social good above her pleasure. This antagonism between self and social good is manifested in the opposition of two organs: the vagina and the clitoris. The clitoris gives pleasure as it is rubbed, but the pursuit of this pleasure, psychoanalysts claim, must be demoted, as pleasure from the vagina and the reproduction of the species assume cultural priority.

Beauvoir draws attention to the mixed messages of patriarchal culture. Women are condemned to premarital chastity, though "the right of man to relieve his sexual desires is more or less openly recognized" (386). "For her the act of the flesh, is a fault, a fall, a defeat; she is obliged to defend her virtue" (386). "If she gives in she invites disdain, whereas even the blame inflicted on her vanquisher brings him admiration" (386). Sexual mores are very different for men and women. In addition, she notes that the sexual act is different. These sorts of statements have been glossed over by the French feminists of difference who suggest Beauvoir believes liberated women should emulate men and assume a male body. "Man's 'anatomical destiny' is profoundly different from woman's" (386). "Coitus cannot take place without male consent, and male satisfaction is its natural end result. Fertilization can occur without the woman deriving any pleasure" (385). Beauvoir uses the term "anatomical destiny" in scare quotes, because she believes that reciprocal sexual relations are possible in spite of anatomical differences. Sexual hierarchies are not based upon biology but are sustained by moral and social practices, and hence can be undone.

Beauvoir recognizes differences between male and female eroticism. Coitus for men has a precise biological end: ejaculation; certainly other complex intentions are involved in aiming at this end, but, once obtained, it is seen as accomplishment. She admits at the time she was writing: "it is not known exactly if vaginal pleasure ever results in a definite orgasm: feminine confidences on this point are rare, and even when they try to be precise they are extremely vague: reactions seem to vary according to the subject" (409). There is no clear conclusion of the love act. "Male pleasure soars: when it reaches a certain threshold, it fulfills itself and dies abruptly in the orgasm: the structure of the sexual act is finite and discontinuous" (409). "Feminine pleasure radiates through the whole body; it is not always centred in the genital system ... Because no fixed goal is assigned to it, pleasure aims at infinity" (*SS*, 409–10). Beauvoir relies upon the research of Alfred Kinsey and Wardell Pomeray to confirm that the clitoris is a site of pleasure for women. However, she differs from these two: "it is beyond doubt that vaginal pleasure exists; and even vaginal masturbation – for adult women – seems to be more widespread than Kinsey says" (385).

While these erotic and sexual experiences have very different libidinal economies, they can be reconciled. Bergoffen (1997, 3, 5, 56, 186, 205) has carefully teased out the logic of erotic generosity in Beauvoir's work. Beauvoir believes men are deceived by their orgasm; they fail to recognize themselves fully as flesh (*SS*, 416). Women recognize their carnal experiences and hence have a more authentic embodied experience: "The asymmetry of male and female eroticism creates insoluble problems as long as there is a battle of the sexes; they can be easily settled when a woman feels both desire and respect in a man; if he covets her in her flesh while recognizing her freedom, she recovers her essentialness at the moment she becomes object, she remains free in the submission to which she consents" (415). Nonetheless males and females are equally capable of reciprocal and interdependent relations, however in a patriarchal society women more willingly accept "the risks of finitude, vulnerability and the bond" (Bergoffen 1997, 3).

Beauvoir believes "lovers can experience shared pleasure in their own way; each partner feels pleasure as being his own while at the same time having its source in the other" (415). She says, "In a concrete and sexual form, reciprocal recognition of self and other is accomplished" (415). In the erotic situation, the ambiguity of subjectivity is achieved: women can experience themselves as both spirit and flesh, a free/transcendent being as well as passive.

Beauvoir has positive things to say about female sexuality, which for the most part have been overlooked, since her critics focus on her misogyny, or somatophobia. The body of a loving woman is valorized. It is not given to her as a tool, it is not directed towards a determinate end, a specific state; it lingers in a state of non-settlement (Heinämaa 2003, 81). As such it is open to the otherness of an-Other, assuming the risk of our vulnerabilities while avoiding the aggression of the ego of the master/slave logic.

EXPLORING BEAUVOIR'S WORK FROM A PSYCHOANALYTIC PERSPECTIVE

While Beauvoir herself rejected formalist approaches to literature as narrow, her fiction, autobiographies, and interviews provide grist for the psychoanalytic mill of textual interpretation. Having refused the unconscious, she was more optimistic that negative emotions, neuroses, and passivity could be remedied through social practices and political reform. However, as I have shown, her non-rational humanism, her understanding of contingency, ambiguity, and embodiment limits the extent to which human conflict, domination, and suffering can be eliminated from history. This is another sign of the richness of her novels: however interested she was in mobilizing radical political movements and exploring ethical and political dilemmas that humans faced, her novels cannot easily be distilled into lessons learned.

Beauvoir's concern about the conservative effects of psychoanalysis seems to be borne out by psychoanalytic readings of her own texts. Elaine Marks (1986, 187), Alice Jardine (1986),[12] and Toril Moi have subjected Beauvoir's texts – especially *Adieux* and *Une mort très douce* – to psychoanalytic readings. Surveying scholars, Marks was struck by the word *too* in Beauvoir's descriptions: "too much writing," "too many books," "too many repugnant details of Sartre's incontinence and spilling" (Marks 1986, 187). Marks interprets the extent to which Beauvoir repeatedly points out the incontinence of Sartre and of her mother as they are dying as a sign of her final triumph over these maternal figures in their state of decay. Jardine sees Beauvoir's relation with her mother in terms of a pre-Oedipal struggle; she manages to release herself from clinging

12 In "Death Sentences: Writing Couples and Ideology" (1986), Alice Jardine suggests that Beauvoir's *Une mort très douce* and her *La Cérémonie des adieux* emblematize "the poetics of an ideology that insists upon killing the mother."

to a frustrating maternal body upon her mother's death. For Moi, Sartre represents the phallic – the all-powerful and angry – mother, from whom Beauvoir also separates. Both Marks and Moi confirm this interpretation that Sartre plays a maternal role in Beauvoir's imaginary. Sartre was not a mother per se, but one who fulfilled a nurturing and most often sparing role. Beauvoir's attacks on Sartre also reflect her aggression towards one who ambivalently nurtured her philosophic development. Moi interprets Beauvoir's development as presupposing the suffocation of the maternal, her actual mother, so that she can survive.

Mary Evans (1985) reads Beauvoir's fear of maternity, as well as her negative statements about the female body, in terms of a fear of her own body. Beauvoir is often interpreted as being overly emotional and insufficiently adult and rational. This passion also informs what some feminists (for example, Christine Delphy 2000) believe was a "perverse" attachment to Sartre, and is another reason to dismiss her theoretical work.

Psychoanalytic or psychological readings of Beauvoir's life and writing are often used for politically conservative purposes to show how she was neurotically attached to Sartre and how she used young women in her need for affection. However, there are scholars, such as Karen Vintges (1996) and Debra Bergoffen (1997) who see Beauvoir's passion, emotion (Vintges 1996, 52), and desire in a positive light. In focusing on her personal flaws and outrageous behaviour, some scholars (e.g., Bair, Okely, Crosland) lose sight of her many achievements. She had the audacity to challenge the sacred institutions of motherhood and marriage, and, in *Adieux*, the status of the famous male intellectual. Of course, even when Sartre was alive, Beauvoir interrogated him, asking difficult questions about money, men, women, and sex. This is particularly true in the film *Sartre par lui-même* (1976), and is an aspect of Beauvoir's relations to Sartre that many feminists have chosen to ignore in their wish to see her as totally devoted to him.

In her memoirs and her autobiographical work, Beauvoir doesn't say much about her personal sexuality, but Marks, in "Transgressing the (In)cont(in)ent Boundaries: The Body in Decline" (1986, 181–200), argues that the theme of incontinence is too recurrent to be ignored. She interprets Beauvoir's leaking, dripping bodies as a signifier of female sexuality. Many writers were horrified by Beauvoir's insistence on describing the spills on Sartre's shirts, the wet chairs, and her mother's declining and leaking body. This, Marks feels, is Beauvoir's way of signalling female sexuality as a body out of control. Marks seems to have ignored or is not apprised of the positive comments Beauvoir makes about female sexuality, which I explored previously in this chapter. Marks's comments also seem to ignore Beauvoir's generalized fear of aging. After turning fifty, Beauvoir describes herself as having become obsessed with aging and her physical decline. Her attention to the deterioration of others' aging bodies, I speculate, is a projection of her own anxiety. As such, it tells us more about Beauvoir's preoccupation than would a simple description of fact. In *Old Age* or *Coming of Age*, Beauvoir dealt with the aging body more philosophically. Interestingly enough, she focused mostly on the male aging body rather than the female one.

Although Beauvoir doesn't believe in the unconscious per se, she does identify unmanaged emotions and dark motives that drive her characters' conscious lives, and, as a consequence, she has some affinity to a psychoanalytic approach, as we have seen in this chapter. Her fiction has provided a resource for literary theorists interested in issues of identity and the critique of essentialism. Her notion of "becoming woman" is very suggestive, especially for those who critique a stable or static subject. Postmodernists go even further than she did and call for refusing coherence and dispersing the subject. Beauvoir would have had little sympathy for such a position, which she believed would not contribute to the making of committed decisions and actions and the furtherance of one's own and others' freedom. Her literary texts provide clear evidence of how women's psychic lives – their internalization of domesticity, devotion to others (their partners and children), and passivity – impede their personal development. Though she appreciates some of the insights of psychoanalysis, she believes action, engagement in projects and movements, can prompt changes in one's psychic life. Furthermore, she believes transforming the social and political institutions and cultural practices of liberal capitalism must change if women are to be freed.

There have been concerted attacks on Beauvoir for her realism, her eschewing of psychoanalysis, her failure to appreciate the affects of fantasy and the unconscious in human behaviour, and, consequently, her overplaying the possibility and significance of commitment and rational choice in agency. And yet her approach is not without its defenders. Beauvoir's embodied problematic that links cultural representation and the situation is worthwhile, for it avoids the voluntarism (hyperconstructivism) and determinism of which much theorizing of the body is culpable. Her attention to the embodied and situated subject respects the narratives that affect subjectivity as well as historical/institutional context and economic and social structures (*SS*, 61). She respects deep non-rational connections between subjects, be they sensory or emotive, but without theorizing these as unconscious sublimations. In this way she anticipates Deleuzean affect theorists who attend to sensorial subjects, however in contrast to them, Beauvoir is not an anti-humanist – she believes humans have a central role to play in agency.

Authenticity works on the level of the ontological, as well as on the level of the political. Presumably admitting there are psychological, social, and political preconditions of freedom, she does not undermine the significance of ethical categories of authenticity and bad faith. Even if we admit, following Beauvoir, that not all situations are equal vis-à-vis freedom, this is not an argument against ethical behaviour. While Beauvoir says the most oppressed women are not as guilty as men, she also urges women to engage in political action and assume responsibility for their actions. The decisions people make depend upon their socialization as well as their psychic life, though their choices are not determined. They make or fail to make authentic choices: they end up losing themselves in men or living their lives fully. Though there may be social practices and political institutions that impede their freedom, struggling for authenticity and "personal" freedom is still a relevant concern. If we assume "lack" at the centre of our being, we cannot presume a positive and harmonious future as our goal, but there is still the possibly of embracing individual and collective freedom.

4

Beauvoir's Political Thinking: The Entwining of Existentialism and Marxism

BEAUVOIR TAKING HER BEARING IN HISTORY: THE NONCOMMUNIST LEFT IN POST-WAR FRANCE

FRENCH INTELLECTUALS AT THE END of the Second World War were optimistic about social and political change; however, they were tormented by its horrors (the extermination of the Jews, the devastation of Hiroshima, the occupation of France) (*EA*, 9). Contributing to peace and furthering the welfare of the many were amongst their goals. Given the role of communism in the Resistance forces in France and of the Soviet Union in defeating the Nazis, the moral capital of communists was high. In the first post-war national election the PCF (Parti communiste français) managed to win 5 million votes. In addition to the tremendous support for the party, the non-communist left and radical reformers were pushing for a democratic socialist future within France. The Soviet Union's heroic defence stood in sharp contrast to France's humiliating defeat and collaboration with the Nazis. This catalyzed serious soul-searching into the ills of French society. Many on the left were sympathetic to Soviet communism, although given its increasingly undemocratic and authoritarian practices it did not win unqualified support. Nor were progressive thinkers content to support the status quo politics of liberal constitutionalism since representative democracy contributed to the installation of the Vichy government and French collaboration.

As we have seen, Beauvoir is supportive of revolutionary change, but she had some reservations. Her criticisms were less vocal than they might have been given her desire to gain the confidence of revolutionary movements and counter the effects of anti-communism. She opposed dogmatic and doctrinaire Marxism to concrete struggles and furthering the participation and self-governance of oppressed minorities. She also recognized the complications of the present; during the Nazi occupation there was a single enemy, so the opposition was unified. In the post-war context, this is no longer true. In this context, her support of the Rassemblement démocratique révolutionnaire (RDR), a third party between existing Marxists and status quo politics, was important.

RDR, a radical democratic movement, emerged in 1946. It neither supported communism nor sided with liberal anti-communism, although it was sympathetic to the Soviet Union. Sartre and Beauvoir were founding members. At the outset, they collaborated with David Rousset, George Altmann, Albert Camus, Raymond Aron, and Gerard Rosenthal to constitute an anti-Stalinist non-communist left. They were against the American triumphalism that believed liberal democracy was "the way forward" but were equally cautious about committing themselves to communism. RDR pledged itself to the discovery of the "great democratic tradition of revolutionary socialism" to rally support from reformers of the middle classes who were disillusioned with liberalism and members of the working classes who were wary "of the limitations of communism in its Stalinian form" (Sartre 1949, 135).

The RDR theoretically fit the bill; however, they proved to be politically untenable and survived little more than a year. The Marshall Plan, introduced in 1947 to promote political and economic stability, provoked a dualistic Cold War mentality of "either you are with us or against us." This made in-between positions difficult to sustain. The Marshall Plan offered financial support to countries that excluded communists from their governments. Belgium, Luxembourg, France, and Italy toed the line, pressuring the unallied centre to move to the right. In reaction, the Cominform, the international organization of the communist party, followed suit, establishing economic support for members of the communist bloc. The Soviet Union urgently demanded unqualified support from its comrades, whether they were communists or right-wing socialists. In the early post-war years, the French public was less prone to adopt a Cold War attitude and spoke of the third way between East and West. However, food shortages and looming poverty seduced them to accept aid from the Marshall Plan and, with it, allegiance to American hegemony.

As the PCF became increasingly Stalinist, it considered the RDR a threat and so vilified it. The socialist party was also hostile, believing the RDR was controlled by the Americans. Both parties threatened anyone who joined the RDR with expulsion. The RDR was also subject to an internal division: the domination of its right-wing forces caused a huge split and ultimately its demise. Rousset, a concentration camp survivor and critic of the Soviet gulag, received funds from the CIA and pushed the movement towards supporting the United States. Sartre had anticipated Rousset's lean to the right and refused to attend the International Day for Resistance to Dictatorship and War, an event Rousset organized. Its pro-American bias marked the unravelling of the third way of the RDR as an irreparable division between the left and right set in.

The democratic "space in between" that the RDR hoped to occupy and the collaboration they had hoped to forge was increasingly encroached upon by pro-American and anti-communist forces, which polarized the debates and popular opinion. *Les Temps modernes* supported the RDR. Committed to vigilant thinking and refusing to choose between East and West, the journal neither exonerated authoritarian Soviet practices nor embraced anti-communism. In fact, it was one of the first journals in France to publish articles on Stalin's labour camps and the show trials of Bukharin in 1949, and was equally critical of the agenda of the Marshall Plan. The journal's editors wanted to support revolutionary change but did not want to remain silent about Soviet abuses of power. In speaking out against them, they endangered popular support, but remaining silent would mean covering up Soviet injustices and thus would derail the revolutionary vision of a humane and equitable world. They believed that non-allied revolutionary forces or democratic socialism could possibly reinvigorate communism and return it to its humanist inspiration. However, such political forces failed to emerge in Europe in sufficient strength.

Intellectual historians have represented Beauvoir's generation of post-war Marxists as utopian and dogmatic dupes of the PCF and the Soviet Union, clinging to their faith that the revolution was imminent. When they finally did speak out against communism's authoritarian practices, it was too little too late. Given their feeble critique, these post-war Marxists compromised their credibility as critical intellectuals (see, for example, Furet, Judt, Khilnani).

This portrayal of the Marxist intellectuals best fits Sartre and is less convincing when applied to Beauvoir and Merleau-Ponty. None of the three were dogmatic or utopian as charged, nor were they true believers who suffered loss of faith. None of them were inclined at any time to join the PCF, given their commitment to "vigilant thinking" and their refusal to "toe the party line." In fact, far from applying Marxist theory to contemporary events, they all made efforts to rethink Marxism, to work through the problems of violence and proletarian agency that beset communist practice. Their positions could hardly be defined as dogmatic. Of the three, Sartre was most reluctant to openly express his concerns regarding the Soviet Union because he was concerned that it would fuel anti-communist sentiments. And his justification of party power in *The Communists and Peace* (1952) was not strongly supported by those who were wary of the parties' authoritarian practices. However reluctant

Beauvoir was about contributing to anti-communism, she had a stronger commitment to exposing abuses in power. From *The Ethics of Ambiguity* onwards, she openly criticized Soviet communism. As she drew closer to Marxism in the early 1950s, she became more circumspect about her critique of Soviet practices but never remained silent. She approached her criticism via the novel form, and thus did not openly condemn Marxist projects.

There was little evidence that the Soviet Union was instantiating the humanist goals of freedom and equality it aspired to; instead, it was using internment and labour camps, authoritarian political practices, and ruthless secret police forces to shore up the revolution. State socialism had nationalized the means of production and the communist party determined the directions the proletarian state would take. So the proletarians had not assumed their role as universal agents of change. There were few signs of the freedom and equality that the revolution promised, and even fewer signs that the use of coercive state violence was diminishing and democratic socialist governance was proceeding apace. Given the opposition the Soviet Union faced, both within and outside its borders from the White Russians and NATO, as well as the Marxists' failure to prepare themselves for this "detour" through violence (as Merleau-Ponty called it in *Humanism and Terror*) Marxist intellectuals were in a difficult position: they could either lose faith, reserve judgment, or wait. Beauvoir, Sartre, and Merleau-Ponty were faced with a difficult dilemma that they tried to tackle in the most authentic way possible. Their political stances were not dogmatic, deducted from Marxist predictions, but rather evolved from their appreciation of the limits of the situation.

CONFRONTING DILEMMAS POSED BY COMMUNIST PRACTICE AND MARXIST THEORY: BEAUVOIR'S AFFINITIES AND DIFFERENCES WITH SARTRE AND MERLEAU-PONTY

To justify the "wait-and-see-policy," Merleau-Ponty provided a non-dogmatic reading of Marx and Marxism in his *Humanism and Terror* ([1947] 1969), which has often been misconstrued as an apology for Stalin. He wrote it in part to counter the criticisms of Arthur Koestler's *Darkness at Noon* (1940), which had triggered widespread dismissals of the Soviet Union by condemning its abuse of its revolutionary power. Following Marx, Merleau-Ponty argued that a non-violent stance would only sustain existing power relations and privileges (1967), for a revolutionary state in a capitalist world would be unable to defend itself from armed opposition both within and outside its borders. However, communist violence is justifiable only insofar as it bears the evidence of its humanist and egalitarian politics and refuses to justify sacrificing human lives today for some distant political goal. Since there were no visible signs of humanist values in present acts of Soviet violence, Merleau-Ponty was unwilling to endorse them, although neither was he ready to repudiate communism prematurely. This changed in 1952, when the imperialist aspirations of the Soviet Union were made clear by its support of North Korea's invasion of South Korea. When the Chinese stepped in to aid the communists and the Americans entered the conflict in support of the South, the Soviet Union committed itself to defend China if it was bombed.[1]

After the onset of Korean War, it became much clearer to Merleau-Ponty that the Soviet detour through violence was not just a detour: it had sabotaged its humanist and egalitarian goal and was becoming just another imperialist power. As political editor of *Les Temps modernes* and in a conciliatory gesture towards Sartre, who was wary of growing anti-communism in the United States and Europe and felt the need to vocally oppose it, Merleau-Ponty suggested that the journal remain silent about the Korean War, rather than strongly protest it. This disagreement provoked a serious rupture between Sartre and Merleau-Ponty, prompting the latter's departure from the editorial board of the journal and marking the end of their friendship and collaboration.

Ironically, just as Merleau-Ponty was turning away from Marxism in the early 1950s, Sartre was drawing closer to it. As Merleau-Ponty was beginning to write a critique of the Soviet Union and Marxism, which would ultimately appear as *The Adventures of the Dialectic* (1956), Sartre wrote *The Communists and Peace* (1952, 1969), justifying the role of the communist party. Beauvoir's position was quite different; she was more critical and cautious about the party, spurning its hierarchical and authoritarian practices, and concerned about its attempts to centrally direct radical politics. In this regard she had some sympathy with Merleau-Ponty, though she did not admit it. In trying to appreciate the plurality and decentralized nature of concrete political movements and their potential for democracy, Beauvoir challenged the authoritarian and narrow character of class politics as envisioned within the PCF and joined Sartre in parting with Merleau-Ponty because of his dismissal of Marxism. While she was aware of some of the shortcomings of Marxism and revolutionary socialism, she was unwilling to withdraw support from all revolutionary projects, as Merleau-Ponty had done. She describes

1 Beauvoir recounts the palpable fear of impending war the French experienced at this time when they believed that the Soviet Union might invade and occupy their country.

Merleau-Ponty as retreating to metaphysical concerns and the "inner life." They – she and Sartre – felt it was better to be supportive of a less-than-perfect revolutionary force than to retreat to social democracy as Merleau-Ponty had done.

Sartre and Beauvoir were reluctant to give up their critical sympathy towards the Soviet Union not because they were optimistic that Soviet communism was going to deliver a humane polity in the near future but because they were concerned that their withdrawal of support would only fuel anti-communist forces and hinder future revolutionary movements. When Sartre visited the Soviet Union in the 1960s, he felt that the Soviets had richer social bonds and a more collectivist spirit than were manifest in Western liberal democratic countries dominated by commodity capitalism. Beauvoir was less hopeful about the Soviet Union and more concerned about the growing forces of anti-communism and American hegemony in the West. She too assumed a wait-and-see policy longer than one might believe justifiable. All political forces are impure, Beauvoir argued; rarely is one able to support a political movement or regime that fully embodies the unambiguous values and practices for which it aims. Given the Soviet Union's behaviour during the post-war years, it was difficult to remain hopeful and uphold a position of critical sympathy. In fact, it was unconscionable to withhold judging its record of violence and authoritarian practices. Beauvoir was more outspoken in her criticisms, for Sartre believed that anti-communism was more dangerous to world peace than communism. Both, however, believed that it was better to support the revolutionary project, given the boldness of the project and its popular support. So even if it failed, which they thought likely, it might legitimize revolutionary projects and voice discontent with Western liberal democracy.

While Beauvoir and Sartre did not embrace the PCF, they were careful not to offend them. This carefulness was not reciprocated. During the late 1940s, almost every volume of *La Nouvelle Critique* (the communist party journal) attacked Sartre's work. The communist newspaper *L'Humanité* also attacked existentialists who were portrayed as lackeys of Gaullism or American imperialism (Soper and Thomas 2006, 81). The renowned communist Roger Garaudy condemned Sartre as "a gravedigger of literature" and an idealist who was turning people away from Marxism (*PL*, 140). Another leading PCF leader, Jean Kanapa, accused Sartre and Beauvoir of being enemies of mankind and went so far as to call them fascists (140). Sartre was sensitive to these opinions; when the communists criticized his play *Dirty Hands* (1955) as anti-communist, he defended the play but nevertheless terminated its run. This play (much like *Humanism and Terror*, and Beauvoir's concerns about purity of means and ends) recognizes that the leaders of the communist party could not remain absolutely faithful to ideals; they would have to dirty their hands, but that in itself would not necessarily subvert the revolution. Throughout the decade, the PCF directly attacked both Sartre and Beauvoir as exponents of "decadent philosophy."[2]

The year 1952 marked a turning point for Sartre. The head of the PCF, Jacques Duclos, was arrested during a protest of the visit of the American General Matthew Ridgeway to Paris. Both Beauvoir and Sartre believed that they had to assert their commitment to Marxism and stand up against the growing wave of anti-communism and the Cold War mentality that was spreading across Europe, especially in France. Although Sartre questioned some of the practices of the PCF, from 1951 to 1955 he wrote nothing negative about the party or the Soviet Union that might be construed as repudiation. Yet, even though he justified the importance of the PCF, saying in *The Communists and Peace* (1952, 1969)[3] that it was essential to proletarian agency, the PCF scoffed at his work. They insisted that existentialism was incompatible with Marxism without systematically establishing that incompatibility.

Beauvoir was more vocal than Sartre in identifying problems with Soviet practice and Marxist theory. In *The Ethics of Ambiguity*, as we have seen, she recognized the failure of Marxism to acknowledge that the proletariat have a free will, and have to make decisions to stand behind the revolution; their agency cannot be presumed. Further she was critical of the "chiefs" of the communist party, departing from Sartre in *The Communists and Peace* and his justification of the party in furthering proletarian power. Beauvoir was less convinced. In *The Second Sex*, she points to the subordination of women, which is not reducible to class, so she imagines other agents of change; Sartre at this time was focused upon the working classes. I believe Beauvoir had more distance from Marxist philosophy than Sartre, specifically in theoretically considering other agents of change beyond the proletariat.

In speculating on her feelings towards communism, she says, "I wonder what my position would have been like if I had not been associated with Sartre in the way I was. Close to communists because of my horror

2 Identifying Sartre's early philosophy, especially *Being and Nothingness*, as individualist is more appropriate than so labelling his post-1950 works *The Communists and Peace* and *Critique of Dialectical Reason*, which were very much influenced by Marxism.

3 In *The Communists and Peace* (1952, 1969) Sartre argued that the French working class had achieved awareness of itself as a class only through the communist party. If the working class refused to follow the direction of the party, it lapsed into what he later called "seriality" – a dispersed and goal-less existence.

of all that they were fighting against; but I loved truth too much not to demand the freedom to seek it as I wished; I would never have become a party member" (*PL*, 53). With irony she describes her and Sartre as having become fellow travellers "without anyone having invited them on the trip" (*FC*, 176). Both believed that they could influence communism without belonging to the party, but their actual capacity to do so proved rather limited. Formal communist parties, in particular the PCF, did not heed their advice. Nevertheless, their international profile as Marxist intellectuals was huge, and they contributed to keeping a revolutionary voice alive in popular journalism, though their reputation amongst "card-carrying communists" was weak.

Even though Beauvoir's comments on communism, in *The Long March* and *America Day after Day*, were on the whole positive, she was severely criticized by the PCF, which also vehemently denounced *The Second Sex.* The party had originally invited Dominique Desanti to review the book, but when she praised it for its bold contribution to revolutionary theory and its openness to rethinking sexual politics within the parameters of Marxism, the review was not accepted. Since Desanti insisted on defending its Marxist elements, the PCF found a second reviewer, who was much more in line with the pro-family policy of the PCF, was designated. The second reviewer denounced Beauvoir as a sexual libertine and decadent philosopher. Her work was seen as a threat to the nuclear family.

In spite of the PCF's hostility to Beauvoir, and her failure to stand behind the party's platform, she remained sympathetic to them until 1956. Like Sartre, she refused to denounce communism because of the growing anti-communist forces in the West and the emergence of McCarthyism in the United States. They believed the imperialist policy of the United States was a far greater threat to world peace than that of the Soviet Union. This place between positive support and repudiation – "critical sympathy" – was difficult to sustain. Their failure to join the PCF alienated them from the intelligentsia of the communist party, and their refusal to denounce the Soviet Union lost them many friends, including Raymond Aron, Albert Camus, and, after 1951, Merleau-Ponty.

After the Soviets invaded Hungary in 1956, Sartre and Beauvoir repudiated the Soviet Union as under the ghost of Stalin. During the Prague Spring uprising in 1968 and the Soviet Union's brutal suppression of its leader Alexander Dubček, Sartre and Beauvoir reiterated their support for local initiatives and popular democracy and withdrew their sympathy from Soviet communism. However, this did not mean they gave up on Marxist movements or Marxist theory. They had turned their attention to the proletariat of the south many years earlier, and this sustained their optimism and openness to accommodate diverse revolutionary movements and political struggles for justice and equality. Beauvoir drew attention to the narrowness and inflexibility of the PCF, which took its directives from the Soviet communist party and was reluctant to think about gender and race politics. Whereas Sartre remained committed to Marxism as an indispensable philosophy of the twentieth century (his *Critique of Dialectical Reason* attests to this), Beauvoir had more of a pragmatic approach. Given the fact that Marxism inspires revolutionary movements, it remains important, but to appreciate the vitality of these democratic movements (*EA*, 106) one had to move outside of Marxism.[4]

The PCF's hierarchal (anti-democratic) attitudes were evident in their poor relations to the Third World and their timidity in the face of anti-colonial struggles. It earned a reputation for failing to address claims of racism, charges still plaguing the party today.[5] Its practice of democratic centralism – that is, receiving central directives from the communist party of the Soviet Union and sending them to their underlings – was consistent with Lenin's theory of the vanguard party but difficult to square with Marx's insistence that the proletariat would have to win the battle of democracy. The Soviet Union refused to tolerate independent forms of socialism and communism in Eastern Europe and China, since, given the significance of peasantry in the "Third World" populations and the virtual non-existence of an industrial working class, the theories of proletarian agency were not specifically relevant there. It had a hard time navigating the independence of revolutionary regimes that emerged in Tanzania, Cuba, and Algeria. In fact, it tried to centrally direct these movements.

Issues of race, sexual orientation, the role of the peasantry, and the non-existence of the proletariat had not been addressed by Marx. As a consequence, Third World countries had difficulty accepting Marxism and the Soviet Union as the sole political and theoretical authority, since neither fully understood their situation. Both Beauvoir and Sartre recognized the diverse needs and struggles of developing countries long before it became fashionable to do so. While Sartre used Lenin to explain the forces of imperialism, neither he nor Beauvoir had much sympathy or use for Lenin's theory of the party and democratic centralism. They argued for creating new, non-hierarchal relations between communist

4 The PCF's reputation for narrowness and orthodoxy was well known in the 1960s. See ch. 6, for example, for Michel Foucault's complaints that the PCF completely ignored his book *Madness and Civilization*.

5 The riots of those of North African descent in October 2005 and the conditions of exclusion and poverty that led to them were not simply the product of right-wing regimes but something that the socialists and communists contributed to as well.

countries and within a revolutionary movement. Admittedly, this was difficult to sustain in a situation of class war, but it was desirable.

In the '60s, she had little faith in existing socialist societies, not because she dismissed the importance of social structural change, but because she recognized their failure to take on board forces that contributed to personal development and ultimately revolutionary change. In addition, the authoritarian and oppressive party practices of communism had become more widespread and more entrenched. In fact, the PCF's strategies glossed over the significance of individual and grassroots action. This eschewing of individual agency and bottom up action is visible in at least two debates that figured centrally in France in the 1960s: challenges to the base/superstructure model of society and the dialogue between humanists and anti-humanists. Examining these debates will not only enrich our understanding of Beauvoir's political position but will provide the basis for a more complex appreciation of debates that informed the structuralist and poststructuralist turn and the post-Marxism of Michel Foucault, Ernesto Laclau, and Chantal Mouffe.

INTELLECTUAL CONTEXT: THE BASE/SUPERSTRUCTURE MODEL OF SOCIETY

In this section I look at some of the significant debates within Marxism that provided the intellectual and political context of Beauvoir's work. Although she did not explicitly address these debates, given that she was not an academic, they did frame her praxis. As I have said previously, although one does not need to understand post-war France to understand her political insights, it does deepen our understanding of her praxis.

In *The Economic and Philosophic Manuscripts* (EPM), Marx states that the production process involves ideas and a reflective capacity and hence is never crudely mechanical. Without ideas, there is no production and no integration and stability of values. The dominant culture thesis holds that culture is a mechanism for achieving capitalist stability, society being held together by values produced by institutional power from above (e.g., the church and the education and legal systems) rather than from below. Even for Marx, class does not rule by force alone but by a combination of consent and domination; therefore, sheer force and hierarchal power is insufficient. Culture, defined as ideology, has both a role to play in disguising force and in positively challenging naked class rule.

The first generation of Marxists ignored this more subtle and revolutionary approach to culture. In particular, Karl Kautsky (1854–1938) and Georgi Plekhanov (1857–1918) define Marxism as a deterministic science of inevitable historical development. Analyzing the inner workings of the capitalist mode of production reveals the structures and laws of the development of history: that is, "the iron laws of history." This idea of culture as producing and cementing core values of capitalism or reflecting the society within which it is produced ignores the critical and subversive capacity of art. Subsequent generations of Marxists see culture as potentially transgressive, challenging the utilitarian and market-driven values of capitalism.

There were many efforts within Marxism to challenge or tinker with Marx's base/superstructure distinction to avoid mechanical determinism. Gramsci, for one, believes that the key to change hinges on the creative role of historical agents engaged in political praxis. He focuses on the political formation of the collective will of the people rather than the objective "iron laws of history" to understand change. Domination flows from above, but since humans are not simple ciphers of external forces, consensual agency must be catalyzed through interactive politics. Gramsci reminds us that the ruling classes do not externally impose their will on others but rather rule by a combination of consent, domination, and manipulation. He contrasts rule from above which may use force from hegemony, an internalized form of social control, which makes certain things appear natural, where in fact they are not. Culture and politics have a role to play in organizing meanings, values, and beliefs into a capitalist worldview. This worldview is always collective and intersubjective in nature; it is neither the product of individual agents nor simply the effect of capitalist institutions. Thus, Gramsci conceives of culture and politics in broader terms than one finds in the base/superstructure model.

Given the role Gramsci attributes to human agency and the capacity to engage in collective action, Beauvoir has much affinity to him. Following Marx's insight that politics is "an ideological form in which men become conscious of this conflict and fight it out" (Marx and Engels 1978, 5), Gramsci admits the significance of politics in revolutionary struggle. In this passage, it doesn't appear that the political can be generative but simply is the place where class struggles take place. Gramsci works on how the struggle to constitute the general will is a project not only of the ruling classes (to ensure that people internalize liberal/capitalist values) but also of the organic intellectuals, members of the working classes, or peasants, who can constitute a counter-hegemonic will to catalyze change. Culture has a role to play in this political transformation as it transcends narrow class interests and spawns new agents and forms of agency. It is a medium of change for the rising classes and challenges the old, thus fuelling a new society and social relations. Beauvoir too recognizes the role of organizations as having a potentially transformatory role. In the case of women, she banked on the idea that women participate in their liberation; suffrage and self-representation are important, but not sufficient (*ss*, 764). She also acknowledged the power of minority men to engage in political struggles that would challenge the status quo and contribute to counter-hegemonic projects. We have also seen, in the previous chapter, how the Marquis de Sade was able to transport himself beyond his class. These coalitions of minorities or those who identify with minorities contribute to emancipatory struggle; Gramsci calls these counter-hegemonic powers.

Beauvoir takes some distance from the base/superstructure logic of Marxism. Her treatment of gender is not reducible to the perspective of political economy. She stresses the importance of gainful labour in furthering women's freedom, but women's gendered relations are not reducible to the mode of production. Hence, being a full participant in the work place, having equal legal and political rights, may be necessary to women's liberation, but not sufficient to constitute woman as an agent. For women's participation in the economy and public life has to do with the gendered identity and their sense of their personal and collective power. Here I disagree with Eva Lundgren-Gothlin, who assumes that Beauvoir reverts to historical materialism, believing equality in the work place is primary (1996, 248). Lundgren-Gothlin seems to gloss over Beauvoir's insistence that socio-economic changes are insufficient. In Books II and III of *The Second Sex*, Beauvoir demonstrates how social roles, myths, symbols, and culture have important roles to play in creating women as an inferior Other. There is little reference to capitalism here – except acknowledging that the material conditions of life affect the distinctive nature of women's Othering. The development of femininity cannot be read off of socio-economic relations (capitalism) for her status as an inferior Other is informed by androcentric cultural and social forces as well capitalist property relations.

Departing from the base/superstructural model of society, Beauvoir criticized Marxist theorists as well the Soviets who instantiated it. As we have seen, socio-economic factors are important, but not determinant. She is aware of the performative dimension of politics and the play of emotions, desires, and affects in everyday life. Politics is not reducible to existing class relations or struggles. Beauvoir narrativized the problems with Marxist functionalism. Jean, a committed communist, was not accepted as one due to his class origin. Yet his commitment to emancipation was evident in the sacrifices he made for the Resistance movement in the Second World War. Furthermore Beauvoir's commitment to literature and culture also challenges a base/superstructure model. Ideas and cultural products are not simply "ruling-class ideas" (German ideology) or defined as capitalist commodities, produced to shore up existing class relations, but rather stimulate the imagination and creativity and contribute to forces of resistance. Nor are forms of consciousness simply epiphenomenal. As Marx puts it in the preface to the critique: "The totality of these relations of production constitutes the economic structure of society, the real foundation, on which arises a legal and political superstructure and to which correspond definite forms of social consciousness" (Marx and Engels 1978, 4).

Louis Althusser (1918–1990), a renowned structuralist Marxist, also rejected the base/superstructure distinction and its implicit economism, blaming it on the humanist Marxists (aka Beauvoir, Sartre, and Merleau-Ponty). Their belief in the dialectic, he believed, presumed an economistic teleology. Challenging the assertion that the economic system (the means by which goods are produced) determines the organization of society and therefore a society's political and intellectual history, he calls for the relative autonomy of the political: it is possible to study politics, law, and philosophy as activities independent of economic production. Only in the last moment on the eve of revolution will these forces cohere around the economic.

In his seminal article "Ideological State Apparatuses" (1970), Althusser distinguishes repressive state structures like the law courts, police force, and army who punish disobedience, from ideological structures that maintain power through the internal consent of its citizens. Political parties, the schools, the media, the family, and art can foster ideas and attitudes that are sympathetic to the status quo. He identifies the processes by which the church, state, and school turn people into law-abiding, productive, and devout citizen workers. These processes are not to be read from a logic of capitalist development but have some autonomy from it. The result is the introduction of a more complex model of everyday social life and change. However, this model of subjectivity is functional – serving the needs/interests of capitalism. This is very different in tone and orientation from Beauvoir's human-centred phenomenological/existential approach, which concentrates on embodied and committed praxis emerging out of intersubjectivity. Humans are never simply the effects of repressive and ideological apparatuses of capitalism, but have some capacity to challenge capitalism and liberal democracy.

While Althusser deems the mechanistic logic of the base/superstructure model problematic, he also condemns the humanist belief in dialectical and ethical praxis as naive. Rather than a subject potentially able to individually and collectively pursue humanist outcomes and disrupt the pursuit of maximum profit and the logic of capital accumulation, Althusser stresses "history as a process without a subject" (Althusser 1976, 51). Ideological discourses and practices produce the subject's relations to the real as imaginary. So identities exist prior to the subject's birth. Just as parents might plan a newborn's education and grandparents might impute character traits to the newborn, the baby gets interpellated in these various expectations and narratives before it speaks. So there is no choice, not even within circumscribed spheres, as Beauvoir admits. Butler also recognizes Althusser's shortcoming: how is it that the subject accepts being hailed? How and why does he/she internalize these norms and conventional practices? The subject must have some role to play in the process, but Althusser avoids that altogether.

Althusser rejects those Marxists who believe that relations (private property) are fetters on the forces of production. He insists that the distinction between the forces and relations of production is neither stable nor discrete. Nor can one distinguish between the economic material forces and the social immaterial relations. In considering the forces (i.e., labour power), one does not measure just the work done or the degree of exploitation of the working-class experience. Labour power is an embodiment of both productive forces and the social aspects of the labour process.

A worker's wage is defined by capital as that which is necessary to reproduce a worker and his family. This calculation includes social and cultural considerations, such as providing beer for British and wine for French workers (ISA). Furthermore, the worker's knowledge, as part of his productive capacity, involves not simply the acquisition of techniques or skills appropriate to his work but how to be a worker and how to relate to the upper classes. Thus, material productive forces always involve immaterial social and cultural concerns.

Power is not simply in the hands of the ruling classes but is more general and complex. Althusser sees the subject as a target for power whether as a member of the working or ruling classes. He includes a third consideration, the structures of power, which interpellate both classes through discourse. For instance, when a policeman hails a passerby, the passerby turns and recognizes herself as the one who is hailed; insofar as she does so, an identity is assumed. She is not a subject in herself, nor can she choose to navigate the forces and situations in which she finds herself – her subjectivity is produced by discourses in which she is named. Hence, individual choice or social relations are not the source of identity. The "identity" relation is not between people, a system, or a class, but between discursive practices, law, and the subject.

This assumption that identity is produced from exogenous factors (ideological state apparatuses) clearly departs from Beauvoir, who believes the individual has more of a role in assuming their identity as dominated, as well as a role in acting, judging, and thinking, however limited it may be due to one's class and gender position. Rejecting determinism, even if it is more fluid and less economistic – as it is in the works of Althusser – is important. Beauvoir presumes that liberal capitalist forces will limit the freedom of situated and incarnate subjects, but not eliminate it. Beauvoir begins with the embodied and situated subject who casts themself into the world and wills their own freedom. This relationship to the world reflects social/historical/cultural facts, as well as the sensory/emotional and affective registers of the subject. So, instead of seeing the subject produced by exogenous forces alone (be they material or discursive), Beauvoir theorizes the intersubjectively produced subject as having a role (in their social formations). For history is not a process without a subject, but rather history is a process of embodied and embedded subjects whose distinctive style and formations express their complex relation to material conditions.

Althusser also repudiates the thesis of alienation and false consciousness. Althusser rejects the normative theorizing of the young Marx, who assumes our nature as creative "sensuous beings" (Marx and Engels 1978, 92) is repressed under capitalism; Althusser's legal, educational, and religious institutions and discourses produce good, law-abiding, hardworking, and devout citizens, and do not simply repress or alienate free "sensuous beings" (92). Power works through the production of subjectivity itself, so subjects are constituted by these discourses, not simply repressed. Althusser's account gives performative power to the authoritative voice of the law, the voice of sanction. In the process of hailing or interpellating, the subject is simultaneously subjugated from the outside as it assumes its subject position. This ensures that some subjects are productive, law-abiding, and self-regulating, while others are not. Some refuse to submit or accept the norms imposed upon them. These diverse reactions to power serve capitalism, though they are not determined by one's relation to the economy, nor do they express the narrow interest of capitalism. Because it is impossible to determine which structure dominates at any particular moment, a more varied relation to the economy is possible. And, rather than assuming that political reforms will necessarily co-opt revolutionary forces, given the logic of immiseration, Althusser asserts that political reforms can effect changes in politics that will spill over into other domains. This more open-ended approach challenges the simplicity of the Hegelian Marxist thesis that the subject is produced as a class subject and that in negating its negative position it will create a new revolutionary identity. So while Althusser avoids a mechanistic determinism, more importantly he evacuates the subject and thereby problematizes collective agencies of change.

As we have seen, Beauvoir also rejects the "immiseration" thesis evident in *The Communist Manifesto* (1978) – the idea that over time the middle classes will decay, become miserable, and be relegated to working-class status while the working classes will become increasingly destitute and exploited until, in the end, all they have to lose are their chains and they will rise up in revolt. The negation of the worker's empty destitute existence necessitates a reversal, a new positive agent: the proletariat whose mission is the universal liberation of all from capitalist oppression. Althusser rejects not only the idea that history is teleological, moving towards an end, but also the idea that the revolution results from a single simple contradiction between the forces and relations of production – and so does Beauvoir. She rejects the idea that the proletariat is the universal agent of change, as well as the idea of history as reducible to class struggle. For Althusser and Beauvoir the revolution is overdetermined, so there are many contradictions that manifest themselves in different formations. And these formations are discrete and separate from each other, further they do not lead necessarily to revolutionary solutions.

Thus, although Beauvoir did not squarely address debates within Marxism, structuralists like Althusser placed her within the Marxist humanist camp, though as I have said, her critique of the Hegelian dialectic and historical materialism distinguishes her from many socialist humanists of her day. Beauvoir believed in the capacity of aesthetic, sensory, and social movements to catalyze revolutionary forces, thus taking a cue from the young Marx. Nevertheless, the young Marx fails to appreciate the generative powers of culture. In fact, in the *EPM* Marx describes "the worker's need to the barest and most miserable level of physical subsistence, by reducing his activity to the most abstract mechanical movement" (1978, 95). Thus capitalism "changes the worker into an insensible being lacking all needs … an ascetic, a productive slave" (1978, 95). While Beauvoir finds the notion of alienation useful to express the non-economic aspect of suffering under capitalism, Althusser considered this concept unscientific, a relic of Hegelian philosophy that Marx himself got rid of in later life.

Ultimately, Beauvoir has little affinity to Althusser, since he and the structuralists generally developed their paradigm as a polemic against existential humanism. But as I have argued the structuralists and post-structuralists like Foucault and Derrida have caricatured the position of Beauvoir and Merleau-Ponty, since they do not see consciousness of the subject as constituting. Furthermore Beauvoir's extension of revolutionary agency presumes a critique of the base/superstructure model of society, and a theory of the quasi-autonomy that bears some similarity to Althusser. Nevertheless her attention to the ethical and historical subject is very much at odds with Althusser. Like Gramsci, she appreciates the role of solidarity and collective historical subjects and refuses to see them as simple effects of social structures or discursive/linguistic practices.

However, Beauvoir's attention to the role of the individual distinguishes her from Gramsci. For Beauvoir, the self arises within intersubjective forces of the interworld; its powers are sensorially/affectively mediated as well as historically structured. Since she starts with specific embodied subjects' situation, class has a role to play in one's situation, but so do other social forces (like race, ethnicity, gender, and age). All of these forces contribute to Othering: to treating some social groups as inferior. She moves towards multiplying agents of change and is interested in forms of social control as well as practices that would transgress them. Under the present social circumstances, she identifies how micropolitical life (incarnate choice, empathy, and love) all contribute to emancipatory forces.

While the young Marx recognized the power of sensory experiences, he did not fully conceptualize their role in triggering change and resisting capitalism. Since focusing upon the structural contradictions of capitalism as catalyzing the revolution, he doesn't attend to the role of social groups or sensory experiences. Beauvoir does: she believes affective attachments and rich sensory experiences disrupt routine and hence potentially catalyze change. Hence the micropolitical realm, often captured as an aesthetic one, contributes to expanding the imagination and mobilizing commitment. Freedom is neither simply the product of intentional willing subjects, collective historical subjects, nor is it guaranteed by structures or the contradictions of capitalism. As I will show, in *The Ethics of Ambiguity* and *The Second Sex* Beauvoir believes that minority individuals (be they women, proletarian men, Jews, and/or Blacks) must commit to the revolution or counter-hegemonic struggles – one cannot rely upon the structural contradictions of capitalism alone. As we will see in the final chapter, affect transmission and emotions like empathy will have a role in commitment. They help catalyze solidarity and commitment.

THE HUMANIST AND ANTI-HUMANIST DEBATES

The debate between humanists and anti-humanists in France was sparked by arguments around the translation of Marx's *Economic and Philosophic Manuscripts of 1844* (*EPM*) and *The German Ideology* (*GI*). The translations of the *EPM* (1937) and the *GI* (1938) into French by Jules Molitor stimulated interest in Hegel amongst the Marxists, and led to a very different reading of Marxism than the PCF supported; the PCF supported Stalin's essay on "Dialectical and Historical Materialism" (1938) which saw the base directly determining the superstructure (Lundgren-Gothlin 1996, 87).

The Marx of *EPM* departed from this deterministic reading of historical materialism, emphasizing the human ability to labour imaginatively and sensuously. Marx insisted that capitalism was despicable not only because of exploitation (i.e., the extraction of surplus value) but because humans were alienated from themselves, others, nature, and the product of their labour. Under capitalism, humans were treated like things and their relations commodified; communism would change the process of commodification, in which relations and the use object's value were determined by maximizing profits. Thus, communism would materially benefit all by overcoming (both theoretical and material) exploitation. More importantly, new social relations between people and new relations between people and things would emerge. In socialist and communist society, people would have more say in the productive process – what is produced and how. As a result, alienation would be mitigated. Human labour would integrate mental and manual activities, enhance worker's control over what was produced and how it was produced, and provide an important check on overly material and economic concerns. Socialism would foster a more engaged, creative, affectively rich, and participatory life that would challenge the alienation and the priority of exchange value. Given the emphasis on reciprocal and participatory values, the *EPM* envisioned democracy as essential to socialism.

The *EPM* thus challenged the mechanical materialism of the Soviet Union that many thought was the source of socialist woes. By the 1960s, not only dissidents in the Soviet Union, but intellectuals within the communist party were mounting critiques of the economic determinism associated with its Stalinist and mechanical materialist past, especially after the Soviet invasion of Hungary. However, not all communists were appreciative of the *EPM*. The Chinese, especially, believed that its aestheticism was bourgeois (i.e., advocated elitist practice) and instigated the Cultural Revolution (in 1966) to challenge this orientation. Moreover, they tried to bring together all the communists of the Third World, especially from Indonesia and Indochina, thus separating themselves from the leadership of the Soviet Union.

Disillusioned with the hierarchies, cults of leadership, and decadence of traditional socialist aesthetics and communist party practices, many non-communist leftists in France turned to China. Semiologist and structuralist theorists embraced Chinese communism, and found its anti-humanism especially attractive.[6] Although critical of the authoritarian tendencies of Chinese communists and their inability to grasp the

6 Even the more humanist inclined (e.g., Sartre and Beauvoir) embraced Chinese communism. Despite their theoretical differences, which are many, both the humanists and anti-humanists struggled against economism and top-down politics of the USSR and

revolutionary aspects of a new aesthetic form, they felt this new outburst of energy was strategically important.

Most often, sympathies for the Chinese have been identified with the anti-humanists. Althusser is a case in point. Unhappy with the elements of Soviet communism and the embrace of Marx's humanism, Althusser produced a symptomatic reading of Marx that emphasized the scientist in Marx, not the woolly philosopher and spiritual thinker of the *EPM*. The *EPM* was deemed characteristic of his early Hegelian philosophic phase, which was transitional to the formation of his truly distinctive scientific work – *Capital*.

Within the academy, the followers of phenomenological Marxists (in particular Sartre, Merleau-Ponty, and Beauvoir) were vilified by the Althusserians, who dominated the *École Normale*. The anti-humanists challenged the central planks of Marxist humanism, namely, that the revolution is catalyzed by rational, ethical, and interest-driven subjects whose collective historical actions further revolutionary forces. For the anti-humanists, the revolution was structurally determined. While the humanists supported the ontological speculations of the young Marx, Althusser thought this work naive and unscientific.

Althusser identifies two stages of Marxist humanism, the first (1840–42) that is close to Fichte and Kant, where "the essence of man is freedom and reason" (1969, 224). "Freedom is autonomy, obedience to the inner law of reason" (224). This liberal rationalist humanism is distinct from the second form, which is closer to Hegel – a communalist humanism (1842–45). Althusser calls this "the politics of practical reappropriation" (226). "At the end of history, man has become inhuman objectivity, he merely has to grasp his essence, which is alienated in property, religion and the state to become total man, true man" (226). Althusser rejects as ideological Marxist humanism, where the essence of Man (freedom, reason, community) is the basis for history and commitment (223).

Althusser rejects the humanist focus on reflective, creative, and ethical agency – the belief that working-class consciousness will catalyze rational revolutionary action; for him, discursive structures constitute agency. As I have shown, Beauvoir expanded revolutionary agency to include minority groups as well as non-rational forces: affective, sensory, and emotional registers of experience. Furthermore, radical humanist agency is not, in fact, the product of coherent reflective agents, but rather embodied sensory actors. They are not transcendental to forces, nor is their

---

the PCF. This led them to support the more adventurous political experiments that were exemplified in Chinese communism. The Cultural Revolution, which believed intellectuals were put into the fields, challenged the elitism that seemed to plague Western Marxism.

consciousness constitutive of their action, for they are entangled, imbricated in the world and their action presumes synchronizing with material and social conditions of life. However, even if we admit the importance Beauvoir attributes to the performative aspect of politics that engages the material conditions of life (which her critics have not sufficiently acknowledged) this does not address Althusser's complaint that the humanists give too much power to reflective free subjects and their experience, even if they are decentred. Therefore, for Althusser, new forms of subjectivity cannot be relied upon to generate counter-hegemonic movements and subvert capitalism, for they are produced all the time by ideological state apparatuses. He displaces the humanist ideal of humans as "makers" of their collective history with the idea that dynamic structures produce human subjectivity. This is exemplified in the structuralist's refrain: "history as a process without a subject" (1976, 51). Rejecting the significance of human praxis, and the single simple contradiction of wage labour and capital as the motor of the revolution, the structuralists value the depth of structures and the specific synchronic moment rather than diachronic or historical development. However in relying upon structures they ignore the revolutionary role of collective and individual agency.

Structuralists assume there are deep structures that human sciences represent; anti-humanists who reject deep structures have come to be known as poststructuralists. For them, the "real" is constituted within a system of signs and codes, and human actions are effects produced within linguistic meanings and discursive practices. There are no underlying socio-economic or political structures that delimit what is possible. Individuals and groups are not in control of meaning but are subject to, or positioned by, linguistic meanings. The Althusserians labelled naive the humanist faith that history portends some immanent development – a progressive fulfillment of human purpose and meaning is challenged. In *The Ethics of Ambiguity*, Beauvoir spurned historical teleology. Far from science and history moving increasingly towards individual self-realization, self-determination, and civilization, she insists, the Second World War revealed the opposite – its perverse forms of domination and human destructiveness prove that change is not historically immanent. Instead of focusing on how knowledge leads to enlightenment and good decision-making, she calls upon passions, sensations, and reflection. Far from assuming that man was a maker of history, a sovereign conscious subject, Beauvoir explicitly contests these statements by endorsing an embodied and situated subject, never sovereign, always imbricated in forces and relations. She writes that one must reconquer freedom "on the contingent facticity of existence" (EA, 156). Hence one's birth, class position, gender, race – all parts of one's facticity have roles to play in one's freedom. Beauvoir's thorough critique of the conscious and autonomous subject puts her humanism into question, as we will see in the following sections.

BEAUVOIR AND THE ANTI-HUMANISTS

Anti-humanists and some Marxists tend to see Beauvoir's existentialism as having more affinity to liberalism (because of her voluntarist and rationalist assumptions and her attention to the individual). They presume she is an abstract humanist, where in fact, as I have shown, her corporeal and situated theory of agency (embeddedness in history and facticity) makes her a concrete or situated humanist. Even when her distinctiveness from free universal humanism is noted, her departures from socialist humanism rarely are. Rosi Braidotti is a case in point. Braidotti believes Beauvoir is a Hegelian Marxist, presuming the revolution is historically secure and driven by dialectical opposition (Braidotti 2013, 35). However, in *The Ethics of Ambiguity,* Beauvoir rejects the linear development of history and the idea that the individual can be fully realized in a collective. Since there is always "lack" at the centre of being, one is never complete, one cannot be fully integrated into the social. Beginning with the abject condition of man, she, like Marx, refuses to posit an absolute goal or principles to guide change. Instead she believes that action should emerge from engaging and negating one's abject condition. Again she distinguishes this form of radical humanism from those who believe in "complete man and complete history" (*EA*, 41).

Unlike the structuralists, functionalists, and more conventional Marxists, who focus on class relations and see subjects as instrumental to society or capitalism and produced by formations, structures, discourses, systems, and modes of production, Beauvoir believes that one is able to challenge the instrumental and interest-driven subject of capitalism through collective action and aesthetic activity. She would have had little sympathy for "the death of the subject" formulation of Foucault. Revolutionaries must make choices to commit themselves to a party, a movement, or not to commit (20). Many Marxists, she claims, have lost sight of this power. She appreciates individuality in a non-individualist form, the capacity of subjects to make choices both individually and collectively within fields of possibilities and limitations. We have an ability to reconfigure our action amongst these various fields, but we are not able to choose the situations in which we choose. In acknowledging the forces that constrain and structure our actions, she does not deny the possibility of making political and ethical choices, but sees them as circumscribed acts. However that does not mean that these interventions can't be creative or innovative. Even though we are not the source of our actions, given the role of the body subject as situation, we still must accept responsibility for our actions.

While acknowledging that social structures, sedimented cultural patterns, and historical forces constrain and structure our actions, they do not determine action. One is neither a master of one's destiny, nor a discursive effect, neither a *Träger* nor a *trace*, as Althusser or Derrida suggests. Beauvoir encourages people to reconquer their freedom on the grounds of facticity (the context in which we live, or the societal, historical, and cultural influences that comprise our possibilities of our situation), refusing oppression as well as producing new projects. Disruptive, destabilizing acts are important, but not sufficient. One must commit and persist with one's projects, but be prepared for failures and adventures, for there are no systemic or historical guarantees that radical change is imminent.

Beauvoir's understanding of embodied subjectivity is not easily overwhelmed by the anti-humanist assault. She recognizes the significance of linguistic codes and immaterial forces on action, but she does not marginalize the human capacity to creatively intervene, as the anti-humanists do. Communication for Beauvoir is driven as much by affect and feeling as by reason. This will become clearer in the final chapter of this book, where I explore more thoroughly the process by which women develop solidarity through the transmission of bodily affects and emotions. Further, since erotic relations are the prototype of resonance, reciprocity, and ambiguity, bodily communication is as important as, if not more important than, verbal communication. Remember Beauvoir describes female sexuality as radiating rather than goal driven (*SS*, 189), as responsive to others rather than treating them as a means to satisfy one's desire.

I agree with Karen Vintges, who acknowledges the significance of lack in Beauvoir's ontology, humans cannot coincide with each other – they always remain at a distance; however, through emotion (1996, 46–66) they can establish connections that fuel their solidarity and collective projects. Nevertheless they are neither self-sufficient nor sovereign. Interestingly insofar as "the will thrusts itself toward the future" (*EA*, 14), humans are always outside of themselves.[7] Without jettisoning the role of reason and rational argument in political struggles, Beauvoir admits

7 In Butler's more recent work *Undoing Gender* (2006) she presumes a minimal ontology, we are ecstatic, always outside oneself and yet linked to recognition.

the importance of emotions like empathy in overcoming solipsism, motivating commitments to struggles for justice, equality, and freedom.

Furthermore, for Beauvoir, communication is open-ended and meaning is produced within contexts in which speaking and action occurs, but what is communicated is undefined (*LIT*, 199). Beauvoir does not subscribe to the individual reflective subject as the source of meaning but presumes that each singular situation envelops the entire world (198). "This does not mean that one knows it, but that one reflects it, typifies it, or expresses the world" (199): "there is a world that is the same for us all, but on the other hand, we are all in situation in relation to it. This situation involves our past, our class, our condition, our projects, basically the entire world ensemble of what makes up our individuality" (198–9). "The singularity of our situation is an irreducible fact," she says, "but at the same time there is communication in this very separation" (199). "I am speaking to you, but you are not in the same situation, did not come here with the same past, the same intentions or the same culture." Everything is different, and though these situations open onto one another, something cannot be communicated (199). We see how Beauvoir accounts for singularity and universality: from our specific embodied position we approach others and communicate, although we have different pasts, different intentions. Yet we presume we can communicate and that the world is shared.

Much can be communicated through bodily gestures and emotions. Beauvoir argues that we accord much more importance to language than we sometimes admit: "There is no literature if there is no voice. There must be a language that carries the mark of someone" (200). A style, a tome, a technique, the author imposes his presence, his world upon me (200).

Although this means we can communicate across our irreducible singularity, there are cultural and historical conditions of life that must be accommodated. The symbolic field, influenced as it is by patriarchal and capitalist assumptions, has some impact on historical forces and existing social relations, but agency is not simply derived from reading its codes and discourses; the individual navigates these fields in a way that gives some distinctive style to his or her actions. However, many fail to take up these patterns and creatively refashion the self amongst them; they are then determined by existing social roles and patriarchal structures. It is not sufficient to theorize action as an effect of discourses, codes, or structures, for, as Beauvoir says, "language carries the mark of someone, a style, a technique" (*LIT*, 200). Beauvoir attributes our singularity to our situation – "our past, our intentions, our culture" (199). Thus, our actions are not the effect of intentions or choices alone, for action emerges from our situation (our culture and language) and presumes our capacity to synchronize with others. Thereby she avoids the charge of rationalism and voluntarism.

Beauvoir not only contests a unified theory of history (like historical materialism) but also the unitary and rational subject that is presumed to underlie the theory of historical development. Instead of being in the world like an object in a box; the embodied subject is intentional, creative, and free; consequently, ontologically distinct from things. She sees humans as beings in the world that are attached/enmeshed in the world and yet also separate. As beings of the world, we should aim to synchronize with others and the world, while acknowledging our singularity. One does not become freer and less oppressed by simply negating others or escaping the existing world, rather one must engage in collective projects that involve seeing others as a form of enrichment. Paradoxically Beauvoir urges one to disclose being: "by uprooting himself from the world, man makes himself present in the world and makes the world present in him" (*EA*, 12). This reversible relation of the body subject to the world goes some way to decentre the cognitive, potentially masterful, subject, given the significance of sensory experiences and pre-reflective embodied relations; certainty is not a goal, nor is reason ultimate register. It also challenges the idea of the totally destitute or erased subject of Marxism.

Marx (of the *EPM*) banks on the idea that the working class will be mobilized by the revelation of truth, and ideological critique will disclose how ideas are produced to legitimate the existing relations of production. This cognitive disclosure will mobilize the working classes to act in their interest and revolt. As producers of wealth, they should benefit from the value created. While Beauvoir sees the sensory and aesthetic experiences enriching one's lives and prompting political commitment, she does not deny the role of reason. The existentialist presumption that one is what one does allows for rational and intentional behaviour. One sets goals and tries to realize them, but does so in the context of pre-reflective embodied relations to the world; transparent knowledge is not a goal. Nor is the subject theorized as standing over and manipulating others or the world. Beauvoir expresses the importance of disclosing being, which involves an original attachment and presumes taking up a responsive relation to the world rather than desiring to be complete and full.

The importance of the aesthetic, the perceptual, and playfulness on the labour process posited in the *EPM* cannot be underestimated; these experiences are not surpassed by reason, nor reduced to the instrumental logic of capitalism, but rather must be given their place in human action. However in *EPM* they are tied to dialectical negations, so their truly creative and innovative capacities are under-explored. In contrast to psychoanalysts who focus upon sublimated desire, Beauvoir believes in the enhancing power of playful conduct and rich sensory experiences: "Man has a primordial interest in the substance of the natural world which surrounds him and which he tries to discover in work, in play, and in all the experiences of the dynamic imagination" (*SS*, 51). "To work the earth, to dig a hole, are activities as original as the embrace, as coition, and they deceive themselves who see here no more than sexual symbols. The hole, the ooze, the gash, hardness, integrity are primary realities; and the interest they have for man is not dictated by the libido, but rather the libido will be colored by the manner in which he becomes aware of them" (51). What links these experiences together is the capacity to initiate and engage in bodily activities. Engagement is furthered by the energy one derives from initiating and executing one's projects: the feelings of pleasure associated with creative action. Ontologically, Beauvoir privileges aesthetic play, creative sensuous labour, and freedom-enhancing projects. Unlike Arendt, who disparages work as associated with a predetermined end, and hence uncreative (1998), both Beauvoir and Marx appreciate the potential for creative labour that is separated neither from rich sensory experiences nor from artistic ones. Like Marx, Beauvoir believes in the uniquely human capacity of "the projective consciousness," the ability "to raise a structure in one's imagination" and "then to erect it in reality" (McMurtry 1978, 23). While the powers of intentional behaviour and transcendental reason (151) are limited, they nonetheless exist. While both Marx and Beauvoir understand the shortcomings of labour under capitalism, Beauvoir is more apprised of the creative potential of play and creative/aesthetic work within capitalism. However, all three – Marx, Arendt, and Beauvoir – underestimate the creative side of childcare.

Respecting a playful and aesthetic sensibility qualifies the place of reason. As human subjects thrown into the world that is not of our choosing, we must engage others and the world we find ourselves in. Ontologically this privileges interdependent and engaged actions over solitary and autonomous action, and challenges the idea of historical agents moving towards the ultimate object of freedom and revolution. Non-cognitive and sensory processes are important. Nevertheless, Beauvoir does not give up the importance of critical reflection – revealing falsehoods, mystifications, and abuses of power will further ethical stances and political action that moves towards freedom. We do not simply choose our course of action. Beauvoir believes one must respect our facticity and be responsive to others. Thus, our actions are not the effect of intentions or choices alone, for our actions must synchronize with the patterns we find ourselves within to unsettle and change them. This way of thinking challenges the charge of rationalism and voluntarism.

BEAUVOIR'S EXISTENTIAL MARXISM

In this section I further explore the distinctiveness of Beauvoir's affiliation with Marxism. Her novel interweaving of existential phenomenology and Marxism offers an ontological supplement that is appreciative of the human potential to initiate, to begin anew, in spite of restrictive social circumstances of capitalism. Bringing her ontological insights into conversation with Marxist theory helps us appreciate her distinctive contribution to emancipatory thinking. Instead of being helpless victims to structures beyond our control, or being circumscribed by the mode of production, Beauvoir believes engagement with others and the world is ontologically privileged: humans have the potential to fulfil themselves through participatory action, aesthetic practices, and political projects. Her theory of embodied and situated agency avoids the liberal Kantian approach to freedom, and corrects the teleological and functionalist versions of Marxism. Spurning the voluntarist and liberal assumptions that the individual is always free to refuse the authority of others and act autonomously, she equally rejects a determinist thesis, that we are an effect of the situation. Yet our actions are structured by our situations. Our ability to will/act is influenced by our affective and emotional life, our incarnate life, as well as by the historical/material conditions of our existence. Here we see Beauvoir's humanism: while denying that the subject is a sovereign and complete subject, she believes in the capacity of individuals and collective subjects to initiate, commit to projects, and collaborate to further collective freedom.

As I have said previously, Beauvoir avoids the rationalist and interest-driven logic associated with liberal and Marxist theories of action. Though many theorists presume that existentialist freedom is negative, entailing absolute transcendence and novelty,[8] I have been making the case that, in respecting one's embodiment and situatedness, Beauvoir sees freedom as always impure and encumbered. Most of her contemporaries on the left ignored embodied everyday life and instead focused on the macropolitical forces of capital/state and society. This concern brings her in line with ideas of Deleuze, Foucault, and Jacques Rancière. However restrictive/oppressive capitalism may be, Beauvoir always believes there is a limited capacity for self-development and collective political action to counter its corrosive forces. Beauvoir's existentialism does not "suppress [one's] instincts, desires, plans, and passions"

8 Robyn Marasco makes such an assumption: "The existentialist image of freedom is a distorted image: it feeds on the fantasy of heroic escape from unfreedom, as if the experience of freedom is uncorrupted by prevailing inequality and oppression" (2015, 19–20).

(*EA*, 14) but rather integrates them into collective action. Beauvoir envisions how affects, emotions, and reason can be harnessed in engaged action. In so doing she appeals to incarnate subjects freely engaged in the world, so she contests the Marxist immiseration thesis. In the *Communist Manifesto,* Marx presumes the working classes are destitute: they have "nothing to lose but their chains" (Marx and Engels 1978, 500). Their culture, their sensibility, and their reflective capacities are reduced to the cash nexus (475). While admitting that the working classes and other minorities are oppressed, Beauvoir believes their activities exceed their labour, hence their cultural practices and social relations have a transgressive capacity.

Insofar as Marxists assume the working classes are impoverished and their negative existence must be negated to transcend their present condition, they devise strategies that will facilitate proletarian rule. Hence, elitist practices of the intellectual and vanguard policies were justified to mobilize the workers. Again, insofar as Beauvoir contests historical determinism she denies the automatic revolutionary agency of the oppressed. Furthermore, she does not bank on the powers of the communist party to transform the working classes, for she has more faith in the capacity of oppressed minorities to act collectively without top-down directives.[9]

All too often scholars have ignored Beauvoir's thinking about democratic socialist politics, and focused instead on her struggle for sexual equality. And even when her Marxism is addressed, she is frequently identified alongside Sartre as an apologist for the Soviet Union and fellow traveller of the communist party. As a consequence, the distinctiveness of her political thinking and political strategies has been largely ignored. By returning to her work on Marxism, over the course of her life, I hope to correct this oversight. In the *Ethics of Ambiguity* Beauvoir begins to rethink revolutionary agency by challenging existing communist practices and Marxist theory. While readers are familiar with Beauvoir's critique in *The Second Sex* that Engels effaced gender, they often ignore the implications of her focus upon how women are socialized in different patriarchal societies; she does not simply read women in terms of their class relations, but attends to multiple factors of their oppression that are associated with their physiology, sexuality, and social circumstances (i.e., race, ethnicity, and class). This broadened treatment of their subjectivity exceeds class relations and material forces. As such, she offers a more complicated picture of political agency. Finally, in *Old Age,* challenging the idea that she was primarily a gender theorist;

9 Her affinity to the case made by Rancière in *Nights of Labor* is worth noting.

again, her attention to emotional/psychological structures of embodiment in addition to political economy broaden the Marxist focus upon class relations.

Even though many scholars (Bauer, Le Doeuff, Lundgren-Gothlin) believe *The Ethics of Ambiguity* is a transitional text supplanted by her theory of materially mediated freedom found in *The Second Sex*, I have shown that on the contrary *The Ethics of Ambiguity* is worthy of careful consideration. Beauvoir develops concepts of ambiguity, contingency, human lack, and incarnate will that frame her thoughts on freedom. Here she also identifies problems in historical materialism (its inclination towards determinist and dogmatic thinking, its erasure of individual commitment and responsibility) that make it less suited to revolutionary change. She also points to how these theoretical problems contributed to authoritarian actions and excessive violence – problems of the USSR.

Similarly, all too frequently Beauvoir has been identified as a Marxist humanist surpassed by the anti-humanist critiques of the 1960s, but by challenging the idea that the revolution is immanent in the movement of history, a negation of the negation that resolves histories contradictions, she takes her distance from Hegelian Marxism. In *The Ethics of Ambiguity*, she distinguishes her humanism from Kantian humanism. In the spirit of radical humanism, she says, she works within the philosophic tradition of Hegel, and Marx, who are interested in the concrete human capacity to collectively work towards freedom, but she distinguishes her thinking from Kantians who subscribe to a "complete men" and "complete history" (*EA*, 41). For Beauvoir, there are no pure subjects, abstract principles, nor absolute goals that inform emancipation. In fact, such abstract and dialectical thinking, she believes, ends up supporting politically ineffective and unethical actions. She urges revolutionaries to support existing concrete struggles, in whatever form they take. So instead of assuming that all action must be directed by the party or by the proletariat, she believes one must engage in the plurality of struggles for justice, equality, and liberty as they materialize themselves. Her practical efforts to do so will be concretized in the next chapter.

Without repudiating Marxism, she found a way of challenging its determinist and reductionist adherents. Beauvoir's existentialism provides not only an ontological supplement but also an ethical and political one, thereby both enlarging the scope and delimiting the substance of revolutionary action. In *The Ethics of Ambiguity*, she engages problems that arose in actually existing Marxist practice – specifically the problem of violence, the persistence of authoritarian and hierarchal party practices, and the absence of ethical concerns. Beauvoir's insights are less well known than those of Merleau-Ponty (whose volume *Humanism and Terror* was published in instalments in *Les Temps modernes* in the post-war years). Both believed the communist party's tactic of justifying violence and undemocratic means out of necessity, to save the revolution, could very well end up sabotaging it. Both imagined ways of reconfiguring revolutionary action that would limit excessive violence and further the equality and liberty of all. While there has been much discussion of the differing positions of Merleau-Ponty and Sartre vis-à-vis the communist party and Marxist politics, there is almost no attention to Beauvoir's thinking on Marxist revolutionary politics, which I hope to rectify.

THE ETHICS OF AMBIGUITY

In the book's first chapter, Beauvoir establishes existentialism's affinities to and differences from Marxism. The determinism and/or functionalism of Marxism fails to grasp the role of incarnate choice in revolutionary action. Dialectical materialism, Beauvoir argues, presumes the "meaning of the situation imposes itself on the consciousness of a passive subject" (20), whereas existentialist ontology believes "meaning surges up only by the disclosure which a free subject effects in his project" (20). Giving up the desire to ground freedom on an absolute value or objective reality, she says "one establishes a genuine freedom on the original upsurge of our existence" (25). Hence freedom is always situated and embodied, and never complete.

Beauvoir spurns historical materialism for its certainty and determinism: while the working classes are oppressed, structurally situated as subordinate, their revolutionary agency is not guaranteed. In subscribing to "objective history" and "necessity," Marxists avoid thinking about the revolutionary process. Even oppressed subjects must make choices. She writes: "autonomy is not the privilege or defect of the bourgeois, but the proletariat must want the revolution to be brought around by one party or another. It can be lured on, as happened to the German proletariat or can sleep in the dull comfort which capitalism grants it" (20). She makes the case for personal commitment. She identifies Marxist revolutionaries as holding contradictory assumptions: they rely on humans making commitments and yet condemn a philosophy of human freedom. They assume the proletariat must "adhere to Marxism," "enroll in a party," and "be actively attached to the revolution" (20). It is as if "to admit to the ontological possibility of choice is to betray the cause." Freedom, they believe, would make concerted action impossible (22). But, for Beauvoir, without willing their freedom the revolution would be impossible: "History would lose all meaning if history were a mechanical unrolling on which man appears only as a passive conductor of outside forces" (20).

Pejoratively, she talks about the party leaders as "chefs" (109) who presumably direct all action from the top. They too, must make political choices. Their actions are not determined by "objective necessity" but are based upon their interpretation of the situation (109). Further, Beauvoir says, a "political choice is an ethical choice: it is a wager as well as a decision: one bets on the chances and risks of the measure under consideration and in doing so one sets up values" (149). The revolutionary "does not set up absolute ends towards which my transcendence thrusts itself" (14). But in acting to maximize his/her effectiveness, he/she must synchronize with existing concrete forces of change.

Beauvoir compares Christianity and Marxism: the idea of redemption is promised at the end of life, whereas the anti-Christian humanism of the eighteenth century brought the myth down to earth, as a finished socialist State (51). Both believe in "supernatural imperatives" (8) and hence believe their actions are justified by an absolute end, be it communism or the afterlife. As Beauvoir insists, there is no absolute political end. In fact, the assumption that there is a "complete history" (41) has dire social implications: encouraging instrumentalism. "Morality is whatever serves the party," Lenin says: "I call any action useful to the party moral action, I call it immoral if it is harmful to the party" (22). This instrumental approach to action is wrongheaded and dangerous. It misunderstands the constitutive capacity of action in the revolutionary process. Action is not simply a means to an end, but it is the means by which the goals of the revolution are progressively instantiated. Without prescribing what is to be done, ethical practices have a role in setting parameters on political action. Agents exude values even though they might not be aware that they do; Beauvoir suggests that actors need be conscious of their choices. Agents are impure. They must be encouraged to act strategically as well as ethically: they must take their bearing in history as well as bear others in mind. Choice is not abstract, but grounded in sedimented patterns of the past. "Moral choice is free," she says, "yet it is always on the basis of what one has been that a man decides upon what one wants to be" (40). Here she pays attention to the embodied and situated nature of the self – the incarnate self in situation structures what is possible. One's moral choice/action does not arise out of nothing, *ex nihilo*, nor does one act, *de novo*, without a past.[10] In fact, she describes action as "a sort of predestination issuing not from external tyranny but from the operation of the subject itself" (41). Here we see how

10 Interestingly Hannah Arendt also makes this point in "Lying in Politics" in *Crises of the Republic.*

important the situated subject's past is in the revolutionary process. It is not the wilful individual, but an embodied and historically situated will that acts with others.

The instrumental position of Lenin (that the means are justified by the end) does not acknowledge that some actions, while apparently protecting the revolution from its enemies, may in fact, end up subverting the goals of the revolution. Given the absence of a working class in the USSR, Lenin introduced the notion of the vanguard party to help forge proletarian power; however, this was not necessarily appropriate for France. Beauvoir did not support the existing practices of the PCF, nor the idea of a vanguard party that informed its practices.

Beauvoir challenges not only instrumental thinking within revolutionary practice, but also the assumption that the revolution will be non-violent. Since the oppressors are unlikely to be converted to the revolution (97) they will not give up their privileges willingly; hence, violence is probable. Violence will not only affect the ruling classes; it will also, she adds, "have negative effects on the perpetrators of violence" (97). Revolutionaries were aware of this problem and spoke of the sacrifice of a generation for the collective good, but Beauvoir rejects this logic, attributing it to Hegel and teleological or developmental theories of freedom. Since the revolutionary future is not guaranteed, the suffering of the present generation may not be redeemed.

Beauvoir is well aware of the tensions between ethics and politics. Since one can never "convert oppressors" (96) revolutionary "action will not be moral." Unlike those Marxists who have skirted the effects of violence on the revolutionaries, Beauvoir is candid: "those who treat men like instruments" will "become murderers and executioners" (100). Admitting this, Beauvoir did not mean repudiate the revolution; however, nor would she necessarily justify violence as constructive in the transformation of the oppressed as Frantz Fanon did in *The Wretched of the Earth.*

For Beauvoir, the alternatives are not terrific: there is not going to be a bloodless revolution, nor are the oppressors going to give up their power, hence there will be pain and suffering in the transition. Every lost life is a tragedy, however death is unavoidable. Much in the spirit of Merleau-Ponty's thoughtful comments on Machiavelli and the revolution (1969, 102, 104), Beauvoir alludes to a distinction (without clearly making it) between violence that is progressive, instantiating the values of the revolution, and violence that is regressive, sustaining hierarchal power. In either case, violence should be kept to a minimum: not only should violent practices be used economically and not become established, but the revolutionaries ought to be careful to ensure that violent acts contribute to progressive revolutionary forces (bringing the proletariat to power). Beauvoir criticizes the communist party's execution of Bukharin on these grounds: there was little evidence that his death furthered the power of the proletariat and shored up the positive goals of the revolution. In fact, it contributed to totalitarian practices. Beauvoir suggests, much like Merleau-Ponty did in *Humanism and Terror*, that if violence is deemed necessary to protect and/or further revolutionary gains, it ought to bear evidence of its humanist inspiration in its acts; that is to say, it must manifest elements of its democratic future. If it fails in this regard, then the acts of violence are not deemed justifiable.

Those who are unaware of the historical context of post-war France will be unaware of how Beauvoir intervenes in debates with Koestler and Merleau-Ponty. Koestler fictionalized the trials of Bukharin in his novel *Darkness at Noon*, portraying the revolutionaries' dilemmas: Rubashov, the fictionalized Bukharin, vacillated between being political and being moral. Either he affirmed the party's condemnation of him as a counter-revolutionary, and therefore acknowledged that his death was justifiable, or he withdrew from politics to assume a pure ethical stance where he was blameless. Koestler portrays this stark opposition between ethics and politics; or the position of the Yogi and the Commissar (Merleau-Ponty 1969, 101–49) as intrinsic in revolutionary politics, and condemns the revolution on these grounds. The party ends up executing loyal party members over differences in strategy. In *The Ethics of Ambiguity*, and previously in "Moral Idealism and Political Realism," Beauvoir works through this dilemma differently. She rejects the universal and timeless imperatives of Kant, or the stance of the Yogi, as well as the instrumentalist (objective realism) of the Commissar or the philosophy of the party. She concludes the article on a note of optimism, believing that politics and morality can be reconciled. She recognizes that political actors always make choices that involve others hence politics has ethical implications. But she rejects acting on principle. Action is based upon judgment and calculation; so understanding is also a component of action. Holding an ethical or ideal revolutionary position is not sufficient to guarantee success. There is always the risk that one will end up on the losing side. Such was the fate of Bukharin. Merleau-Ponty calls this the tragedy of politics (Merleau-Ponty 1969, xxxiii). The revolutionary is not driven by universal moral principles as liberal Kantians are, nor do they have absolute ends to direct what is to be done; they must take their bearings in history and act with others in mind. Beauvoir challenges those who believe that revolutionary acts are necessarily instrumental and expedient. Since actions instantiate the revolution, they ought to exude its values. Also, political actors must accept responsibility for the consequences of their acts, even if they are unintended.

Beauvoir challenged the contemporary practices of the PCF that justified violence out of necessity and believed that the present generation had to be sacrificed in the name of the future social good (*EA*, 99). Here again she shares an affinity with Merleau-Ponty's argument in *Humanism and Terror.* Though violence is necessary to forge the revolution it must be used sparingly. Beauvoir, like Merleau-Ponty, challenges the Machiavellian conclusion that the means justify the end. Rather, the end must be present in the means (Merleau-Ponty 1969, 120, 126) so the goals of liberty and equality or the governance of the proletariat must be manifest in the means, even if the party is pursuing violent acts.

During the post-war years, Beauvoir, like other Marxist existentialists, was confronted with the PCF as well as the USSR, who were justifying their detours through terror as a consequence of their aggressive opponents – virulent anti-communists. While their enemies were not in doubt, Beauvoir's response to their practices was less forgiving; she writes that every regime has opponents, and even though the opponents may be in the wrong "error brings to light the truth, namely that there is a place in this world for error and subjectivity" (*EA*, 109). While the communist parties justified their violent actions and authoritarian conduct in the name of "necessity" to defend the revolution from their enemies, she finds this argument unacceptable. There will always be opponents and enemies, so their presence cannot be used to curtail debate, for thoughtful debate is essential to the revolution. "Thought, doubt, and hesitation," Beauvoir argues, "are the most radical, they undermine the world of objectivity much more than does an act of capricious act of disobedience" (*EA*, 110). She distinguishes a radical movement from an "authoritarian party which regards thought as a danger" (109). The PCF, who took their "orders" from the Soviet communist party, claimed critique (questioning authority) and tolerating difference would give their enemies the upper hand. For Beauvoir, revolutionary violence ought to endorse non-hierarchal, deliberative, and critical practices to instantiate the democratic values of the revolution: cultivating authoritarian practice would sabotage the revolutionary ends.

She locates her philosophy in the tradition of humanism, but specifically radical humanism. She sees herself as part of the tradition of theorists of freedom, yet she distinguishes her humanism from humanist philosophies that assume there is complete man and complete history (43). "Existentialism carries on the tradition of Kant, Fichte and Hegel, that assumes the world is not given, foreign to man, one to which he is forced to yield from without, but a world willed by man, insofar as his will expresses his genuine reality" (17). Hence the radical humanist refuses "to set up absolute ends towards which my transcendence thrusts itself"

(14). By refusing pre-given ends and goals, the radical humanist appreciates the complexity and open-endedness of existing struggles for justice.

Beauvoir's attention to the importance of affective/aesthetic modes of being also distinguishes her from the socialist humanists of her day. In addition to plans and projects, she insists on the role of passions and dreams in political action. If one carefully reads what Beauvoir says about adhering to the disclosure of being, it is not primarily a reflective or rational act, but presumes a communication between bodies, or between a body and the world; this responsiveness is not a cognitive act, but involves the synchronization of bodies and world that promotes freedom. Her attention to everyday corporeal action distinguishes her from other socialist humanists who were often Hegelian who privileged reason and believed alienation could be surmounted.

Radical humanism rejects objectivity and historical necessity respecting contingency. History "does not consider certain situations absolutely preferable to another. It is from a rejected situation, in the light of this rejection, that a new state appears as desirable" (18–19). "Only the will of men decides; and it is on a basis of a certain individual act of rooting itself in the historical and economic world that this will thrusts itself toward the future and then chooses the perspective where such words as goal, progress, efficacy, success, action ... have a meaning" (18). Here, Beauvoir recognizes that embedded and embodied individuals must take their bearing in history. There is no abstract or objectively true position to assume. Nor are we determined by our interiority or exteriority.

She warns us not to forget "the concrete bond between freedom and existence: to will man free is to will there to be being, it is to will the disclosure of being in the joy of existence: in order for the idea of liberation to have concrete meaning, the joy of existence must be inserted to the movement toward freedom" (135). Beauvoir contests the Marxists who treat the individual as a mere member of a class (135); the systematic politician who only cares about collective destinies (135); and the revolutionaries who scorn the "concrete benevolence which occupies itself in satisfying desires which have no morrow" (135). She says: "if the satisfaction of an old man drinking wine, a child with a balloon or a Neapolitan lazzarone loafing in the sun count for nothing, then production and wealth are only hollow myths" (135). She distinguishes herself from Marxist materialists who ignore human pleasures and human desires. But, unlike Deleuze and the post-'68 thinkers who focus on desire, Beauvoir is also interested in the social situation in which freedom and desire arise: "The movement toward freedom, assumes its real, flesh and blood figure in the world by thickening into pleasure, into happiness" (135). Worldly pleasures, human joys must be part of the fabric of freedom. This takes us some way from those Marxists who believe suffering was reducible to a mode of production and in changing our economic relations, freedom, happiness, and equality would be secure.

Beauvoir criticizes historical materialism for ignoring the importance of human agency, contingency, and the affective/emotional register of existence. If "the unrolling of history is fatal, there is no longer any place for the anguish of choice, or for regret, or for outrage; revolt can no longer surge up in any heart" (109). Such a theory ignores the role of the individual and human emotion in commitment. Not only are committed individuals necessary in the process, but they must engage their emotions as well as their interest.

Furthermore, since she envisions the individual as lack, "both within and between subjects" (Zakin 2006, 38), it is impossible to surmount alterity. She writes that "the other is recognized as identical with me, which means that in myself it is the universal truth of my self which alone is recognized … moral salvation will lie in my surpassing toward that other who is equal to myself" (*EA*, 104). However, indefinitely sacrificing each generation to the following one, this endless succession of negations is fruitless unless we produce a positive existence; but then the individuals turn out to be the substance of the real and not subjects. This is an unsatisfactory state: "if the individual is nothing, society cannot be something" (106). Instead of sacrificing the individual to the greater good, Beauvoir says, "we must affirm the concrete and particular thickness of this world and the individual reality of our projects and ourselves if the individual is set up as a unique and irreducible value, the world sacrifice regains its meaning" (106). In doing so, she upholds the ideals of democratic society confirming citizens in their individual value: their rites of justice as well their particular rituals of baptism, marriage, and burial (106–7).

Further, since one is not self-sufficient, or sovereign, but always outside and in process, "it prevents the subject from realizing itself as complete, whole, or present to itself … There is no utopian community in which the separation between subjects might be dissolved or resolved; community entails conflict, division and negotiation" (Zakin 2006, 38).

BEAUVOIR'S CRITIQUE OF SOVIET COMMUNISM AND MARXIST THEORY IN *THE SECOND SEX*

In *The Second Sex,* Beauvoir's relationship to Marxism takes a different tack. Again she criticizes Marxist theory and practice without repudiating it. She acknowledges the importance of Marx's philosophy of history, yet challenges teleological theories of history. She also speaks out against the hierarchical, rationalistic, and state-centred policies of actually existing communism. Castigating the Soviet Union's efforts to regulate the personal and sexual aspects of life (which she believed were fundamental to human vitality and social change), she calls for the state to respect individuality and privacy. She encourages embodied and situated subjects to further their autonomy. I use the term autonomy advisedly to describe Beauvoir's understanding of freedom; as we have seen, the self is an intersubjective self arising in the interworld, an embodied self who is enriched in its relations, not a self struggling to escape others. So free choice is incarnate, it is embodied and limited. We must negate or destabilize existing patriarchal relations and values, but Beauvoir implores us to embed ourselves in history and enrich our relations with others to do so. Revolutionary action requires work on the self as well commitment to collective forces of change. So freedom is not akin to the liberal notion of freedom as freedom from others.

The Soviet Union wrongly prohibited the practice of psychology and psychoanalysis because it believed that psychosexual and emotional problems were the consequence of private property, and associated with capitalist social relations. Once private property was abolished and class conflict eliminated, these problems would wither away. So, too, would the family unit. Thinking the family would perish and loyalties and emotions previously directed towards one's sexual partner and one's children would be redirected to the state and the community was a serious mistake, says Beauvoir; the individual cannot be fully synthesized or realized in community. The individual's erotic and sexual life resists integration into the socialist community; in fact, it resists socialization altogether (67). Beauvoir urges communism to limit state intervention in sexual matters and ensure privacy.

Sexuality cannot be successfully regulated as the Soviets attempted to do: a regime can try to encourage births by lightening the load of pregnancy, assisting families in childcare arrangements, or criminalizing or decriminalizing abortion, but it is impossible to reduce gestation to a job or service (67). Since the Soviets assumed all problems could be solved with socio-economic changes (i.e., abolishing private property) they reintroduced paternalistic forms of marriage and sexual practices to counter a decline in births. This crisis led them to revalorize traditional female sexual roles and the family as the basic social unit in a retrogressive move (as the nuclear family could and should be challenged). Instead of trying to foster a sexual politics based upon equality, they retreated to pre-revolutionary values and institutions. Reforging traditional gender roles in the family, rather than trying to change them, marks a lost opportunity for women. These rationalistic state-directed approaches, to sexuality, maternity, and marriage, Beauvoir finds problematic. She believes eroticism is an experience where individuality prevails over generality (67). So she condemns efforts on behalf of the party to regulate aspects of sexual life. Individual freedom, choice, responsibility must be respected. Democratic socialism will abolish classes but not individuals (67). "A true socialist ethic," she says, is "one that seeks justice without restraining liberty, one that imposes responsibilities on individuals but without abolishing individual freedom" (67).

Another shortcoming of Soviet Marxism was its failure to deal with the depths and potential of human sociality: reducing the social to socioeconomic forces reduces it to the logic of capitalism. This is too narrow. As we have seen in the second volume of *The Second Sex*, Beauvoir explores the social/psychological processes by which Western girls become women. This gendered analysis has little to do with the mode of production, or only insofar as capitalism requires women to reproduce the next generation of workers.

Because communists treated marriage and the family as an arrangement and an institution to protect private property and reproduce future generations of capitalists, it was no longer necessary in socialist society. Beauvoir finds the connections between monogamy and private property compelling but inadequate, ignoring the sexual and emotional dynamic between the couple, the intimacy that they share, and the erotic desire and domestic lives that bind them. While Beauvoir was critical of the institution of marriage, she was hopeful that reciprocal relations between loving individuals were possible. For Beauvoir, the couple is a *Mitsein*: a connected unit, a community of sorts. Human existence in capitalist society is not wholly alienated; there are intimate bonds that further human sociality.

In addition to addressing problems with existing socialist/communist practice, Beauvoir attends to problems in Marxist theory. In *The Second Sex*, her disagreement is focused on Engels, but, again, in no way is this an argument to refute Marxist theory. She believes that Engels's idea that primitive societies were matriarchal is culpable of economism. Where he states that women in primitive societies were both active participants in the economy and had symbolic powers, Beauvoir argues that they were not treated as reciprocal subjects, as moral agents, but as Other, as non-agents. Even though they had symbolic, religious, and economic powers, "they never were contenders for political power, since they lacked social standing" (80). Despite some matrilineal practices – for example, property handed down through women – these were insufficient to constitute a matriarchy. Although women had a central role to play in birth – bringing mysterious gifts to the world – their bodies were not deemed to be the source of creativity but rather mediated the creativity of god.

Beauvoir relies upon Claude Lévi-Strauss's studies of primitive societies in *The Elementary Structure of Kinship* to challenge Engels's position in *The Origin of the Family:* that primitive societies were matriarchal. Instead of the mode of production defining labour relations in primitive society, Lévi-Strauss argues kinship relations do: "The relationship of reciprocity which is the basis of marriage is not established between men and women, but between men by means of women, who are merely the occasion of this relationship" (SS, 81). Women are constituted as part of the property of men, a medium of exchange between men and groups of men. In spite of woman's economic role and her magical powers, Beauvoir argues, woman is regarded as inessential. She was not a subject in primitive societies. In fact "she is always under men's guardianship" (81). Quoting Lévi-Strauss, she says "public or simply social authority always belongs to men ... Women have never constituted a separate group that posited itself as a *for itself* before a male group: they have never had a direct or autonomous relationships with men" (80). Beauvoir does not deny that women are oppressed in capitalist societies, but Engels overstates the link between women's oppression and the emergence of private property. He provides no interpretation or awareness of the historical details to establish his case. While "the sexual division of labor and the oppression that results from it bring to mind class divisions," she says, "they must not be confused with class relations" (66). Engels's interpretation does not acknowledge the importance of biological or psychological factors that are factors in the sexual division of labour and gendered relations. These are influenced by class, but not determined by it. Beauvoir criticizes Engels in *The Second Sex* for identifying women as workers and ignoring their role in reproduction, thereby ignoring a distinctive feature of their subordination.

Beauvoir analytically distinguishes economic forms from cultural and sexual aspects of women's oppression. In doing so, she avoids the totalizing thinking of some forms of Marxism – the logic of the base-superstructure. Beauvoir does not believe that political economy determines society. While changes in the economy, political institutions, and the public sphere are necessary, these changes are not sufficient to "liberate women." "In the economic arena," Beauvoir says, "women's conquests were stunning ... For a long time, means were sought to free her from her domestic constraints ... [however] today the demands of repopulation has given rise to a different family policy" (147). Beauvoir notes that "sexual morality is at its strictest. Abortion has been banned and divorce almost suppressed: adultery is condemned by moral standards" (148). Even though women have abstract rights and are treated as equals in the economy and public sphere, she presumes the situation of Russian women has changed.

Quantitative changes (the value of one's labour), institutional changes, and qualitative changes (in the kind of relations one has with others and oneself) are necessary. A socialist economy is therefore a necessary but not a sufficient condition for women's liberation. Though there was economic equality, the USSR had to ensure that women were freed from domestic responsibilities. Also their sexual and interpersonal relations have to change. While they began to work towards sexual equality, Beauvoir regrets that they reasserted traditional patriarchal practices.

Beauvoir stresses the ethical side of politics – securing reciprocal treatment between subjects is necessary to achieve equal and free behaviour. This was not fleshed out in Marxist theory and is notably absent from communist practice. Women, unlike men, are frustrated: they are more alienated from their bodies and less engaged in the world. Whereas men's sexual vitality complements their agency, women's sexuality, in patriarchal societies, does not. Even if some women are active in the world, their lived form of femininity leaves them feeling inferior. This of course was exacerbated as the Soviet Union faced with the need to repopulate after the Second World War. So women's liberation requires not only participating in the economy and public life, but also reconfiguring her domestic and sexual relations.

In the final chapter of *The Second Sex*, Beauvoir endorses democratic socialism as the way forward, for women as well as men. By tackling the socio-economic sources of suffering and empowering people to participate, she assumes, one's life will dramatically improve. But it will not resolve our existential dilemmas. Beauvoir said repeatedly that failure is to be expected, not only of one's individual projects, but also from broad revolutionary forces. While capitalism and the socio-economic marginality produced by capitalism produced all sorts of violence (i.e., poverty, exploitation, alienation), Beauvoir does not believe that capitalism is the sole source of human suffering. Nor will the revolution put an end to human pain. Soviet strategies, which assume the individual will be fulfilled and realized in the collective, are not without problems. Beauvoir sees that our freedom and groundless existence cause us anxiety that we struggle to quell: believing in God, the state, or the Other (EA, 14, 50) provides stability to our identities and foundations for our actions. So an unconditional commitment to the Church, the communist party, or socialist movement are antidotes to anxiety, but are not recommended. Beauvoir describes how difficult it is to be satisfied with disclosing being, with respecting ambiguity. She describes a strong temptation to stabilize our being, our wanting to be. The realization of the existential tentativeness of our existence does not undermine her commitment to socialism but does qualify how one can support the revolution. This approach to the revolution distinguishes her from more traditional Marxists.

OLD AGE: BEAUVOIR'S ARTICULATION OF THE SOCIO-ECONOMIC AND CULTURAL

In Beauvoir's last nonfictional work *Old Age*, she confronts the relationship between action and structure, very much influenced by debates within Marxism. Retrospectively she felt that *The Second Sex* could have been more materialist, basing women's otherness on the facts of supply and demand (*FC*, 202), but this wouldn't have changed her argument. However in *Old Age* she added a Marxist dimension. She sees the oppression of the elderly as a result of the economic law of the capitalist market economy (Vintges 1996, 143). "Exploited, alienated individuals become throw outs, rejects, once their strength has failed them" (*OA*, 602). I confirm Vintges's interpretation that Beauvoir "introduced Marxist notions as a supplement to her phenomenological analysis, not a replacement" (Vintges 1996, 143). In exploring the social world, she accommodates social structures as well as choice, material factors as well as cultural ones. She looks specifically at men, not women. Again there is no universal experience of old age, just as there is no universal experience of being woman in *The Second Sex*. Beauvoir does not see old people as simple effects of a system, class subjects, but rather as embodied and embedded in their specific social/political/historical situation. In *Old Age* Beauvoir recognizes the role of ageism, but this experience is influenced by one's class as well as one's relation to one's body. She says all men decline physically as they age, but how they age depends on their class and other social and cultural factors. In capitalist society, where men's value is determined by work, it is difficult to make the transition from work to retirement (*OA*, 300). There are no initiations that mark the entrance into old age (9), nor prestige associated with old age, as was the case in pre-modern societies. Insofar as work is privileged, economically non-active men are deemed inferior.

Even middle-class men, who are financially secure, are likely to feel alienated upon retirement. Beauvoir uses this term to refer to one's relation to one's body as well as the commodity form. Alienation is not simply an effect of one's relation to the labouring process, but a more general relation to one's embodied being. Middle-class men (also) feel the effects of aging: not only do they experience a loss of social status due to their retirement, but they experience a loss of physical vitality due to the decline of their body. Factors like one's health, psychological history, and relations with one's family also have a role to play in one's experience. Like gendered experiences, Beauvoir says, "old age is not simply a biological fact, but a cultural one" (20). Notably, she separates "physiological facts" from "social circumstances," hence, unlike the social constructivists, for her, biology is not explicable in cultural/social terms alone. One's experience of old age is influenced by biological, psychological, and social/cultural relations. Even though experience varies across time and place, and the particular intersection of the above factors, Beauvoir makes some general comments. In Scandinavian countries where they have more material provisions for the elderly, they are better off (Tidd 2004, 105). Old people have a greater chance of survival in wealthy rather than poor societies, in settled societies rather than nomadic ones (*OA*, 90). In patriarchal societies, where old men comprise the ruling class and are deemed valuable, women are relegated to subordinate status. Old men in these societies generally fare better than old women.

Beauvoir appreciates the effects of social circumstances as well as individual differences in personal history. Our culture believes old people's lives are determined, without a sense of the future; however, our situations are singular, so how we live our old age is specific. Again the concept of inauthenticity is important. She, like Sartre in *Critique of Dialectical Reason*, believes reciprocity demands mutual respect/recognition of each other's transcendence, but this is not forthcoming: old people are defined by *exis*, being, not praxis, doing (1976, 244). They find themselves passive and alienated (though differently than exploited capitalist workers) and diminished. The old person is Other like Woman, socially and physically deemed inferior. Although biologically women's sexuality is less affected than is men's sexuality in old age, Beauvoir claims, this has to do as much with social factors as physical ones. Since men are socially active throughout their lives, they are more affected by the loss of social status; since women have had less status and have been treated as objects, they experience less loss (*OA*, 387). She says women are more likely to experience old age as liberating, since they don't have to take care of their children (543). Since women's sense of self is less dependent on paid labour, they are less diminished upon retirement.

Beauvoir urges old people to pursue ends and actions that give their lives meaning; however, this is not possible for all equally. Those who have spent their lives in arduous labour are less likely to have hobbies to occupy themselves. Not only do socio-economic circumstances affect one's capacity to engage in new activities, but one's psychological security, physical well-being, and attitude towards death all have a role to play. Structural (or socio-economic) relations contribute to the well-being of the elderly. However, this is only one factor that affects the agency of the old. She writes the situation of old people as only marginally better in socialist societies (617).

Beauvoir organized *Old Age* as she did *The Second Sex*. She begins with exogenous processes (social forces/knowledges) and then looks at lived experiences (interiorized social identities and emotions). These spheres are analytically separate, but not experientially separate. For Beauvoir, biological decline is a physiological fact, but it alone does not determine how the declining body is lived. Social, political, and personal history affect one's embodied experiences, but one's style is a distinctive expression of these forces. Beauvoir acknowledges organic bodily decline: a loss of strength, a wrinkling of the skin, a loss of teeth, diminished vitality. But these do not dictate how this "weakening" body will be lived. These facts have some effect on the individual, but the social and cultural factors have a role to play as well. The aging body, like the pregnant body, may be an impediment to action but, in a society where aging is associated with wisdom and pregnancy highly valued, these factors mitigate their anatomical impediments.

Beauvoir says there are different sorts of memory: sensory, bodily, and cognitive. In old age, memory is fragmented: it is more difficult to project oneself into an open horizon, for the past tends to weigh more heavily on the present/future as one ages. Beauvoir uses Sartre's notion of the practico-inert to inform her insights. She provides the example of her work as a writer, her writing has an existence outside her wishes; in old age, one's past, one's memories, one's history is of the realm of the practico-inert. While we feel free to do as we wish, the past weighs upon the present/future and makes change more difficult.

THEORETICAL AND POLITICAL CONTEXT: DEBATES WITHIN MARXISM

In the previous section, I explored how Beauvoir variously engaged Marxist theory and practice over her lifetime. In the *Ethics*, she criticizes historical materialism and communist practices and also provides an ontological supplement to Marxism, which provides ethical support. In *The Second Sex*, she engages problems with existing practices in the USSR and the reductionism of Engels, which she believes fails to understand the gendered aspects of existence, and hence fetters the revolutionary project. In the third section, in *Old Age*, Beauvoir understands the oppression of the aged in terms of capitalist market relations; again, however, this is a supplement to her phenomenological analysis.

As I have argued, Beauvoir doesn't presume structural changes or historical processes alone sufficed. Revolutionary action is not simply the result of external forces. She claims "the essential point on which existentialist ontology is opposed to dialectical materialism [is that] we think that the meaning of the situation does not impose itself on the consciousness of a passive subject … to adhere to Marxism, to enroll in a party, and in one rather than another" (*EA*, 20) needs a decision and that difference should not be transcended as it is in the notion of a homogenous class subject. Nor does she believe that collective agency is identitarian, or that coming to understand one's oppression will spontaneously catalyze revolution. However, understanding historical forces and synchronizing existing counter-hegemonic projects is important for her. Her intention is not only to uncover the structures, truths, or facts that impede the revolution but also to generate ethical and politically engaged action that has a chance of furthering political change and producing new forms of power that ultimately will have progressive effects. She neither explains history (in terms of a Marxist philosophy of history) nor offers the truth of history, but she insists upon collective work, pushing forward and reiterating projects of freedom and equality, whether through practical politics or cultural politics. Beauvoir pursues struggles for freedom and equality via her ethical stance, her literary work, and her support of resistance movements as well as existing revolutionary regimes.

To conclude, I return to differences between Althusser, Foucault, and Beauvoir. In proceeding to understand the workings of capitalism, Althusser did not look at collective actors but studied structural processes that defined subjectivity. Ideology or "a system of representations at the heart of a particular society" (Althusser 1970, 231ff) offers the subject an imaginary, compelling sense of reality in which crucial contradictions of self and social order appear resolved. Ideology, in this sense, is less a set of explicit political ideas than what Althusser calls a "lived … relation to the real" (Althusser 1970, 231ff). Subjectivity pre-exists one's birth and establishes an imaginary relation to the real. However he believes that science can capture the processes of structures. Avoiding Marxists' mechanical materialism and rationalist humanism, Foucault, following Althusser, was able to appreciate how discourses produce subjectivity. Rejecting the notion of ideology (Foucault 1984, 60) and its loose connection to the economic, Foucault describes the discourses and discursive practices within which subjects are constituted. The subject is not uniformly produced, and neither are the discourses agents consciously choose. One must internalize discourses to become a speaking/acting subject; these discourses make sense of the structures and context that one is inscribed in. But the relation of ideology to the real, for Althusser, is imaginary. For Foucault, discourses are constitutive of the "real."

What is left is the problem of passivity: if the subject is a discursive effect, what role does it have, if any, in who and what one becomes? If one is the effect of multiple discourses and their interaction, what role does the individual play in configuring his/her identity? Foucault appreciated that the subject is caught in relations of constraint and objectification; his striking examples are mental patients and political prisoners who are subject to scientific classification and social/spatial dividing practices. In addition, he introduces the notion of subjectivation, which posits "how the human being turns himself into a subject" (Foucault 1994, 130). In the presence of moral codes, laws, and authorities, the self works on the body and mind: performing operations on the self, techniques of the self to become an ethical subject.

Beauvoir too tackles the problem of determinism, or the passive subject, assuming both that the subject is formed within a world not of one's doing (i.e., that discourses and structures as well as transcultural phenomena inform one's stock of resources) and yet is able to act and initiate change. The world in which one acts and one's social relations delimit what is possible, but choice is not totally ruled out. This was evident in her treatment of the Marquis de Sade, Jean Blombart, and the trial of Brasillach that follows.

ETHICS AND CLASS SUBJECTS – A CRITIQUE OF FUNCTIONALISM

Marxism had done well exploring the macroprocesses of power that block equality and liberty, but not so well in accommodating pleasure, joy, or worldliness in the liberating process. Not only have they insufficiently dealt with sensations and passions, but, in treating class as the fundamental unit of analysis, most Marxists fail to take into account the microprocesses of life. Ethics is not a strong point. Since Marxists assume that the revolution is necessary to bring about a moral order, and revolutionary agency is structurally determined, there is little attention to ethical concerns. Beauvoir challenges Marxist functionalism and its indifference to ethics. In Beauvoir's fiction, she attends to how personal conduct contributes to, or mitigates one's ability to make a commitment (or will one's freedom) and stay the course of one's projects. In chapter 2, I explored some of the social and cultural processes that other(ed) women, making freedom difficult. In chapter 3, I explored some of the psychosocial obstructions to women's agency. In this chapter, I have explored how class informs "the situation" without determining outcomes. Looking at the conduct of two male characters, I suggest Beauvoir demonstrates how individuals are influenced by their class position but not determined by it. Beauvoir's fictional treatment of Jean in *The Blood of Others* and her biographical reconstruction of Marquis de Sade in *Must We Burn Sade* provide concrete examples of how material conditions interact with personal history to produce or impede ethical action and collective freedom. As embodied wilful individuals, the context of choice (be it personal and macroprocessual) is important: the Second World War provides an opportunity for Jean to be the founder of the Resistance, and the decline of the French aristocracy in the eighteenth century enables de Sade to look for vitality outside of the usual social venues of the upper classes. However, they were not simply effects of their social location. There were other courses open to Jean as a member of the bourgeoisie during the Second World War and de Sade as an aristocrat during the French Revolution.

Beauvoir expands the scope of radical politics by considering how sensory, aesthetic, cultural, and ethical experiences destabilize existing social relations and further revolutionary agency. In doing so, she explores the micropolitical processes of every day life – how desires, emotions, and human conduct can block or facilitate change. For Beauvoir, ethics do not abstractly prescribe behaviour, nor establish universal procedures that one must follow. Action involves taking others into account, treating them with respect. As we have seen earlier in this chapter, there is a tension between living an ethical and politically committed life that is not easily reconciled.

Beauvoir's treatment of the Marquis de Sade is informative. She attends to the significance of the "objective" conditions of his existence – the reality of his class's demise. He did not resign himself to his social decline; living out his sexual fantasies restored a vitality to his life. He was able to make something of the world he found himself within. She describes de Sade as the "offspring of a declining class which once held concrete power which no longer possessed any real hold on the world, he tried to symbolically resuscitate in the secret of the bed chamber his lingering nostalgia: that of a feudal despot, solidary and sovereign" (*POL*, 48). Nonetheless to read de Sade's conduct in terms of class position fails to acknowledge his distinctive transgressive actions. Not all members of his class lived their situation as he did – creatively. Beauvoir commends the Marquis for spurning aristocratic values and lifestyle: his commitment to his desires and art was admirable, though his political and ethical deficiencies are noted. Even though he had enthusiasm for the revolution, he did not act as a revolutionary. Beauvoir chides him for his failure to act as a revolutionary juror when called upon (55). He could not judge anyone, even his former mother in law, who was responsible for his years of imprisonment (55). De Sade made some effort to support the revolution; however, his identification was symbolic and did not get translated into action. Though he identified with the French Revolution, Beauvoir says, he never sided with the people; in fact, he never gave up his estate and clung to the privileges of his class. "This aristocrat haunted by dreams of despotism could not sincerely ally himself with the rising bourgeoisie" (57).

Beauvoir returned to de Sade for exploring the intersection of the erotic and the ethical. As Ursula Tidd notes, "it may seem odd to some readers that Beauvoir as a feminist and a keen analyst of women's situation of oppression in patriarchal society would be interested in the writings of the Marquis de Sade, known for his sexual sadism and transgressive erotic writings" (Tidd 2004, 43). He is commended for being true to his sexual desire, yet his erotic practices are not deemed ethical. For Beauvoir ethical life did not involve upholding principles, but rather is judged in terms of how one related to others. Beauvoir describes him as "enclosed in the solitude of his consciousness ... this autism which prevents him from ever forgetting himself and from ever realizing the presence of others" (*POL*, 60). For Beauvoir, the sexual act is ontologically privileged: it allows the appreciation of ambiguity: "through emotional intoxication, existence is grasped in oneself and in the other as at once subjectivity and passivity. Through this ambiguous unity the two partners merge; each delivered from its self presence and attains an immediate communication with the other" (60). While an erotic/loving relationship (where one is both active and passive, subject and object) is possible, de Sade did not achieve it. Instead of reciprocity, Beauvoir describes de Sade's sado/masochism – a cerebral and cold lover watches very closely for the jouissance, he has to be the author of it, because he has no other means of attaining his fleshy condition (60). He was repelled by the equality that shared pleasure creates.

Since his sexuality did not allow the ambiguity of being both object and subject, and since he did not treat others with respect, his actions were not deemed to be ethical. Unlike the potential for reciprocal sexual relations that Beauvoir points to in *The Second Sex*, there is little evidence of this in de Sade's sexual relations. Beauvoir believed he exaggerated the physical violence he caused his lovers in his sadomasochistic fantasies.

So while Beauvoir praises his commitment to his desire, which disturbed conventional bourgeois lifestyles and values, his conduct is not wholeheartedly endorsed. His class privilege allowed him access to working class women: his sexual partners' poverty meant that their consent was probably not freely given (52). De Sade instantiates the logic of master/slave – acts of submission and/or domination. While Beauvoir praised his commitment to writing, his sensual/sexual experiences did not spill into a liberatory politics. She compares de Sade's stance to artists who produced sensually exciting works but do not contribute to political projects or ethical action: de Sade "makes us think of Rimbaud's demand in favor of the deregulation of all the senses" ... "Like the hedonistic sensualism of the eighteenth century, de Sade proposed no other project than to procure agreeable sensations and sentiments ... it froze him in his solitary immanence" (90). However agreeable and dissensual these artistic experiences might have been, Beauvoir did not believe their work was liberatory.

In her treatment of de Sade we see how Beauvoir entwines Marxism and existentialism to produce a more complex theory of human agency that accommodates the effects of affects, structures, while preserving individual ethical choices. De Sade managed to act with vitality in spite of his class situation; as a member of the aristocracy his class was in decline. She admires de Sade's audacity and virtuosity, but claims that his actions, which fail to bear others in mind, are "autistic" and inauthentic. Again, challenging functionalism, Beauvoir says humans' personal history is important: "Perhaps had his affective formation being different, he would have been able to counter act his destiny, but he appeared as a fanatical egocentric, his indifference, the maniacal care with which he surrounded his debauchee, the schizophrenic aspect of his dreams reveal a radically introverted character" (57). The self matters: "had his affective formation been different," she claims, he might have allied himself with revolutionary projects. De Sade's violent actions did not contribute to the freedom of others, so while his actions might have acknowledged ambiguity, lack, and indeterminacy, and moreover were sensorially transgressive, his actions did not respect others. Nor did he act collectively with the revolutionaries, even though he supported them. Beauvoir valued de Sade for his commitment to his style and art, his ability to disrupt bourgeois identities and values, yet his individual action is found lacking; it was neither ethical nor did it contribute to collective freedom. Solidarity was absent. His actions do not approach universality. "The most salient feature of his painful experience that his life is that there was never any solidarity between other men and himself ... No common enterprise linked the last scions of decadent nobility, he was indignant at the bourgeoisie for oppressing the people, but the latter they were nonetheless foreign to him" (57).

In *The Blood of Others* Jean is portrayed in a different light. Born into a bourgeois family, Jean reconfigures his relation to his class through assuming the lifestyle and job of a worker. Interestingly, Jean's commitment to radical freedom comes with the transmission of bodily affects. Instead of identifying with his father, a factory owner, Jean adopts his mother's uneasiness regarding their class privilege – he ends up empathizing with the family's maid as well as his father's workers (*BO*, 8, 11, 12). He picks up their bodily affects and empathizes with (their) suffering. Unlike de Sade who was unable to forgo his aristocratic lifestyle and his father's authority, Jean dispenses with socio-economic privileges and bourgeois values. He refuses to become the boss in the family business, and ultimately separates from his family. De Sade acted like one of Beauvoir's deficit archetypes – the adventurer (*EA*, 58–62) – whose vitality of life does not produce ethical actions, nor contribute to freedom; Jean's acts, on the other hand, are exemplary. He treats others with care and concern; he witnesses Hélène's gruesome abortion, even though he was not her lover. He not only identifies with the workers, but becomes one. He joins the communist party, but leaves after the police kill his younger friend in their efforts to disrupt a meeting. He then decides to join the trade union movement, which has no political ties. He is comfortable with their neutrality regarding the Spanish civil war and finds the political commitment of the communist party paralyzing. His friend Marcel says: "you can't rid your self of your past," "your well-fed bourgeois past" (*BO*, 28–9). Hence Jean exemplifies Beauvoir's theory of freedom, which is situated and embodied. Jean is not an autonomous, free chooser – his freedom is situated by his past, his embodied practices, and the "objective events of the day." This doesn't mean that his past practices or the "objective events of the day" can't be altered, but they must be engaged, in his act of transcendence. In the context of the Nazi occupation of France, Jean learns that he cannot afford to stay on the sidelines; he must make a choice and act – if he doesn't he will be a collaborator. His previous embodied disposition informs his allegiance to the Resistance movement. He reenters politics and becomes one of its founders, committed to ousting the Nazis and struggling for the future freedom of all. Forging an ethical position is difficult, but through solidarity and collective action, he manages. For Beauvoir, treating humans as "things" is a crime against humanity; yet in the context of the Occupation, non-violence is not an option. Jean is deeply troubled by the fact that when acts of resistance (sabotage) are countered by Nazi reprisals, innocent civilians are killed; however if the Resistance movement ceased to engage in acts of sabotage, Jean would be a collaborator thereby contributing to the deaths of Jews. For Beauvoir acts of freedom, which rely upon others, are not always ethical, but acts of solidarity and working towards the freedom of all promotes an ethical life.

Supporting the Resistance involves supporting a movement that engages in violence – but that violence is more palatable since it is aimed at overcoming Nazi domination.

Through the characters of the Marquis de Sade and Jean Blomart, Beauvoir challenges the logic of determinism and functionalism that one finds in Marxism. She also provides a complex theory of freedom that accommodates personal choices as well as structural factors. Both are affected by their class position and their historical context, yet were able, through their concerted effort and commitment, to reconfigure their social relations and participate in revolutionary projects. Nevertheless as we have seen, there are differences. Although they both appear to have acted authentically, they did not equally succeed in acting ethically or contributing to the good of all. For Beauvoir, freedom is not simply a personal project, for it must engage with and for others.

My understanding of Beauvoirian freedom differs from that of Eleanore Holveck. She claims that Hélène Bertrand is the only important example of authenticity in the novel, whereas I think Jean is also an example of authenticity. Following Linda Singer's notion of Beauvoirian freedom (that realizes itself in engagement with and for others) Holveck sees Hélène as exemplifying the difficulties a "relational feminist" encounters in a masculinist world. While I agree with Holveck that as Hélène sympathizes with others she establishes reciprocal relations, and thereby surmounts her solipsistic and unsituated approach at the outset of the novel, I do not follow her reading of Jean as individualistic. "Jean considers himself and others as abstract individuals like stones in slices of space/time that replace or become obstacles to each other" (Holveck 1999, 14).

Instead I argue that Jean articulates a relational and incarnate theory of freedom: he establishes connections to others, and acts on the basis of those relations, thus accepting responsibility for others and his acts. He does not support liberal individual freedom – autonomy, law, and obligation – nor his family's bourgeois values or lifestyle. He, like Hélène, is a subject in process. Holveck rightly points to Jean "as an intellectual who does not want to act" (1999, 14) however this representation of Jean is inconsistent with Beauvoir's portrayal of Jean's development throughout the novel. His empathetic relations with the working classes, his commitment to change his life of privilege, his strong sense of responsibility for Hélène, and his commitment to the Resistance movement are all signs of what Holveck calls a "feminist (relational) ethic" and situated freedom. Furthermore Jean's situation dramatized the tension between ethics and politics for the revolutionary. The Resistance's acts of violence were endangering the lives of French citizens, since the Germans retaliated and innocent civilians were killed. Jean was faced with a dilemma and Beauvoir confirms that he made the right decision, however deeply troubling the loss of life, the Resistance movement had to persist – otherwise the Nazi occupation would not be opposed. While I disagree with Holveck's reading of Jean, I agree with her evaluation of Paul "as a pragmatic Marxist" (Holveck 1999, 14). Unlike Jean, Paul was untroubled by the sacrifice of human lives in the present in the name of future rewards. This notion of "socialist paradise" (Holveck 1999, 14) justifying violence was unacceptable.

EXISTENTIALISM AND MARXISM

For Beauvoir, existentialism is brought to bear on Marxism and existentialism is altered by the impact of Marxism. Although the tensions between her Sartrean-Hegelian and phenomenological leanings have been previously established, the political consequences of this theoretical amalgam have not been fully explored. While the former position stresses the need for revolutionary structural change and spurns reformism, Beauvoir's embodied phenomenological approach leans towards appreciating incremental change and the ability of the micropolitical to disrupt systems.

Both Marxism and existentialism stress the significance of the specific historical situation; however, existentialism's concern with individual action, human finitude, contingency, and responsibility add metaphysical, cultural, and ethical dimensions to emancipatory politics. Beauvoir's concern with ontology, aesthetics, and literature takes her in a different direction from the more conventional historical materialists or socialist feminists, whose work is mostly analytic and academic in focus. Socialist feminists tend to see how women's agency is defined by the totalizing logic of capital through the effect of interlocking axes of gender and class oppressions. Beauvoir, whose theoretical position presumes "singularity" (*PW*, 258) and attends to specific ways of living those material/cultural/social conditions, is less concerned with scholarly analysis of the forces of change and more with fostering radical political and engaged praxis, less concerned with systematic analyses and more interested in generating solidarity and coalitions, hence more concerned with joyful engagement with and for others, and less reliant on the dialectical overcoming of oppression. As a consequence, her radical project is furthered by fiction as well as investigative journalism, philosophy, and autobiography.

There is a deficiency of the imagination in capitalism: people do not understand that the world in which they live is organized to produce suffering, though it could be otherwise. Thus, exercising the imagination by thinking through others' moral choices is politically useful. While Marxists often believe ethical relations are only possible in a socialist and communist society, Beauvoir contests this. Her ethical concern does not involve a descent into liberal individualism or respect for abstract Kantian principles. Rather, as we saw in her relation to communism, she took a "wait and see" attitude. Without further evidence that communist practices were realizing humanist ideals of freedom, she was unable to join the communist party.

Existential Marxism complicates the project of freedom. While freedom is ontologically privileged, there are many obstacles to its full realization. Humans flee freedom and responsibility since they cause anguish. Time and again, Beauvoir identifies women as complicit with their male oppressors, because they choose material comfort over financial independence. Rather than losing oneself in existing social roles, or being defined by conventional morality or religious beliefs, Beauvoir insists that one should unsettle and take a stand against the status quo. Furthermore, she does not endorse losing oneself in the cause of communism, nor does she propose an unconditional belief or faith in the party. But one's commitment must be continually renewed and one's actions continually take their bearings in history.

She recognizes that although we are ontologically free, we have to "will our freedom" and commit to "the freedom of all" (EA, 13). So freedom is not guaranteed by exogenous forces, but must be cultivated by endogenous ones. While a freer existence is favoured, our emotional and passionate natures complicate the optimism of Hegelian Marxism that human history is directed towards liberation. Evidence of strong emotions like hate and the desire to destroy others, demonstrated during the war and Cold War years, incline one to authoritarian solutions. Fear inclines humans to act like "things," to live life as if it were fixed and unchanging or, alternatively, to treat other people like "things" (PW, 248). These inclinations and historical situations complicate and qualify the project of freedom, but do not altogether exclude it.

Instead of people affirming their liberty and embracing the openness of their existence, humans find themselves retreating into fixed social identities and values. Acquiring a fixed identity – assuming a pre-given moral, religion, or even political stance – is antithetical to radical change. Existentialism implores us to make ourselves; we are not given or fixed, but must continually recreate ourselves through action. Although we can be solitary, we are connected to others and the world we reside in as an "engaged freedom," as a "springing forth of the for-itself that is immediately a given for others" (291). People feel their fundamental ambiguity more acutely than ever: "of my solitude and my connection with the world, of the insignificance and sovereign importance of each man and of all men." "In no other age have they manifested their greatness more brilliantly, and in no other age has this greatness been so horribly flouted ... There was Stalingrad and Buchenwald, and neither erases the other" (290–1). As our hold on the world increases, the more we find ourselves crushed by uncontrollable forces, we are masters of the atomic bomb, yet it is created to destroy us (290). These historical events qualify how one approaches revolutionary projects today. Nevertheless, Beauvoir feels confident that our connectedness, our solidarity, helps our freedom proceed. Continuous work is necessary.

Unlike Marxists, who believe that the project of freedom is supported by historical and economic development or the contradictions of capitalism, Beauvoir complicates history by thinking of it as a collection/creation of concrete and more complicated actions. Agency is not only structurally defined by the mode of production, for there are other relations of subordination that are relevant. Furthermore the mode of production does not uniformly impose an identity, a life. Beauvoir's existentialism prompts one to engage these additional relations, stressing openness to difference, personal commitment, and collective political action. However, unlike Marxists, who feel there is certainty, or structural contradictions, that will lead to capitalism's undoing, Beauvoir acknowledges contingency and the belief that radical politics is plagued by failure (*POL*, 291). Nonetheless, Beauvoir insists that we must persist by embracing our finitude and acting within the limits of the possible. While our actions often fail to achieve what we intend, nonetheless we must stay our course. There is no salvation, nor any certainty that our projects will realize their goals; in fact, failures are inevitable. These existential insights do not rule out revolutionary change, but they do alter our expectations as to what one can expect from revolutionary movements.

Beauvoir does not posit an end to history, for she sees that interpersonal conflict will never be entirely eradicated. The eventual Marxist revolution may significantly diminish inequalities and injustices but will not put an end to human suffering that is associated with the ontological condition. There are no absolute truths, nor political doctrines, that guarantee that our actions and commitments will succeed; yet one's action benefits from improved human understanding, passionate commitment, and political knowledge. Beauvoir spurns the foundational approach to thinking as well as the messianic or utopian traditions, which she scorns for their naivety and theoreticism. Focusing on fitting history into the model of necessary development, such theories pay little heed to concrete struggles that don't fit their arguments. If one relies upon principles or theoretical models to direct one's action, one is unlikely to be effective. Importing a theoretical direction to history or presuming ethical meanings will not appreciate the concrete struggles that exist. Beauvoir addresses her concern with Marxist rationalism by encouraging people to align themselves with existing struggles and further the freedom of all; here, Beauvoir's anti-foundationalism bears strong resemblance to Arendt's, which also challenged theoreticism.[11]

As we have seen earlier, Beauvoir rejects determinism in whatever form it takes, just as she refuses foundational thinking, since they close debates and resolve issues rather than furthering conversations and enhancing collaboration. Such a position thwarts rather than engenders emancipatory politics. Beauvoir is critical of determinism that not only creeps into understanding subject formation (i.e. psychoanalysis, biology) (*SS*, 21–61) but, equally, finds its way into political theories (i.e., communism, Marxism/Leninism, liberalism). Interestingly, there are occasions when Beauvoir's political thinking is more dogmatic than her existentialism warrants. Sonia Kruks warns of this in her introduction to "Right-Wing Thought Today" (*POL*, 105–13). Kruks argues that Beauvoir jettisons ambiguity in the early '50s, presuming "one is with the communists or against them" (109). While I would agree with Kruks, in the context of ever expanding anti-communism, Beauvoir believed she had to take a stand. While the stand may have been vulgar, neither respecting contingency or ambiguity, nevertheless communism, and the potential for radical political change, needed to be supported, in light of rampant anti-communism in the Western world.

THE SECOND WORLD WAR: THE PROBLEMS OF ETHICS AND POLITICS – KANTIAN PURISTS VERSUS INSTRUMENTAL MARXISTS

During the Second World War and the German occupation, it was impossible to treat a German as Kant would, as an end in themself and not a means to an end. The Germans were responsible for the death of fellow countrymen and the virtual enslavement of the French population.

11 In "Lying in Politics" Arendt is critical of the role of the "Problem Solvers" (academics who are members of think tanks). Their strong commitment to their own ideas involves them ignoring facts that conflict with their theories. She gives the example of Walt Rostow's Domino Theory popularized during the Vietnam War. It had disastrous effects on US foreign policy, based upon falsehoods and misunderstandings. It contributed to keeping the USA in a very costly war.

Hence, the universal humanist position, that would treat a German as a human being like all other human beings, was naive and inappropriate.

Respecting the historical context, Beauvoir's ethics spurn the idea that abstract formulas or principles would determine just action. Beauvoir also rejects those Marxists who insist upon absolute ends, the ideas of "complete history" and "complete men" (*EA*, 41); rather, she encourages actors to begin with their abjected situation and struggle to change it. No action can be a priori justified in the name of the revolution; however, nor is she an ethical relativist. Since political action almost always involves others, as Beauvoir notes in *Pyrrhus and Cinéas*, one is always being treated to some extent as a means, as part of someone's larger project. The Other does not simply threaten my projects, but facilitates my acts of transcendence: "I need them [the others] because once I have gone beyond my own goals, my action will fall back upon them inert and useless, and if they are not carried by new projects towards a new Future … through other men my transcendence is always being extended further than the project I am now forming" (135). Nevertheless, she discriminates between actions whose instrumentality might be mitigated by contributing to the social good and those that do not. One must not judge the action from an abstract ethical viewpoint but one must take into account the present constraints and possibilities of the situation: is it leading to the freedom of all or not?

I use Merleau-Ponty's insights to supplement Beauvoir's notion of situated freedom and ethics. In "The War Has Taken Place" (Merleau-Ponty 1964b), he rejects the idea that Nazism was the product of a madman and the other common position that everyone was duped. Equally inappropriate is the idea that all Frenchmen and women are rational and ethical agents. The idea of the conmen and cops of history, he says, is equally problematic: the French population in 1939–40 was not conned or manipulated by their leaders, nor coerced by cops (the authorities) into accepting collaboration. It is not that people were entirely free rather than duped. No one in Occupied France was able to remain completely oblivious to what the Nazis were doing, nor could they live outside their power. Even the very affluent, who did not have to serve the Germans by providing them with fuel or food, were subject to their regulations and rules. Everyone in France was affected and in some sense complicit with the Occupation, unless they were those resisting the Nazi occupation – who ultimately formed the Resistance. The only heroes, Merleau-Ponty insists, are those who died and risked their lives in the Resistance (Merleau-Ponty 1964a). He warns against the moral highhandedness that seemed to prevail in post-war France; that divided the world into the good and evil. Furthermore, both Beauvoir and Merleau-Ponty acknowledge that most people, at some point, in small ways, were complicit. Those owners of restaurants, gas stations, and shops had to serve the German army. Perhaps writers were less complicit since they were not in contact with German soldiers as shopkeepers were, but they should not delude themselves; they were not pure. However, she does distinguish between those who chose to join the Resistance and were acting to further not only their freedom but the freedom of the many from those who collaborated and worked towards the perpetuation of their domination. "Those who collaborated claimed to be realists, but their first mistake was to assume that reality is given, but if all people resigned themselves to (objective reality) Hitler's victory, Hitler indeed would have triumphed" (*PW*, 181). They forgot that "history is made by men" (181). "To be sure the occupation of France was a reality, but it was equally true that the French remained free to give the event the meaning they chose" (181). She values the lucid political man "who truly has a hold on things [and] is also conscious of the power of freedom in him and others" (181). Freedom from domination was never pre-given, or destined, but had to be willed.

Beauvoir took her distance from both Kantians and Marxists. Whereas Kantians are ethical purists who believe abstract principles guide action, Marxists are concerned above all else with political effectiveness. Neither position helps us approach effective and ethical political action. Beauvoir makes this case in "Moral Idealism and Political Realism" (*PW*, 2006). The situations Kantians find themselves in make it difficult for them to follow absolute principles, and so, more often than not, they retreat from politics. Political actions involve dirty hands: acts that are impure and actions towards others that are not prescribed by the categorical imperative. Marso (2012a) perceptively argues that Beauvoir challenges the universal voice or authority of Kant, and yet appreciates a situated perspective inspired by universality.

Beauvoir is averse to an Archimedean perspective or what is often called theoreticism. Instead of respecting the limits and possibilities of the concrete situation, Marxists act with theoretical certainty. Some Marxists during the Second World War were pacifists since they saw it as a struggle between capitalist nations and believed they should remain outside the fray and wait for a renewed working-class movement to emerge before they engaged in the war. Pacifism became exceedingly problematic in the context of France's occupation; it was difficult to remain on the sidelines when the French citizen's life was so constrained. Endorsing commitment she notes: "It is absurd to ensure the defeat of those values that one wants to triumph, out of respect for them" (185).

Merleau-Ponty captures this sentiment: "Values remain nominal and indeed have no value without an economic and political infrastructure to make them participate in existence" (152). Within liberal society, Kantian principles or democratic values are simply a point of honour, not a realizable goal. The values of liberty and equality are upheld, but there is little effort to realize them. This was also true of some Marxists. To realize the egalitarian values of liberty and equality, one must analyze the situation and try to synchronize with forces that instantiate them in their practices. "It is no less absurd," she argues, "to renounce an idea under the pretext of ensuring its effectiveness" (*PW*, 185).

If they assumed an absolute political end (only a communist order would guarantee equality and liberty), then they further assumed that the more readily that state is achieved the better off we all will be. This betrays Marx, Beauvoir argues; he did not posit an absolute end, nor did he presume an instrumentalist approach to political action. "To assume the end is static, closed in on itself, separate from the means that is also defined as a thing" (184), is wrongheaded. Instrumentalism ignores the fact that certain expedient means may erode the end towards which violence is aimed. "It is a fallacy to believe that the end can be achieved by just any means" (184). Without explicitly saying as much, Beauvoir was of the opinion that instrumentalism plagued contemporary communist practice. Far from removing impediments to proletarian freedom – authoritarian practices of the communist party were creating new ones.

Where liberal Kantians portend a position of moral purity that has anti-political implications, the Marxists' indifference to ethics or means used to bring forth the revolution was equally a problem. Emancipatory politics must instantiate democratic practices and values or subvert revolutionary ends. Violent acts may be necessary temporarily but they must be justified and their humanist face must be evident. If authoritarian acts become established, revolutionary goals will be eschewed. The inner necessity of Kantianism is replaced by the external necessity (realism) of Marxism. Neither position is appropriate to further freedom;[12] the former has anti-political implications, Kantian principles of non-violence cannot be accommodated within the situation of war so actors inspired by Kant will retreat from the political, whereas the Marxists are Machiavellian and fail to realize that radical politics cannot use any means to achieve its end. In fact, some political means, however effective, will subvert the end towards which the revolution aims.

12 Though Beauvoir does not explicitly acknowledge Merleau-Ponty's influence in her thinking, his book *Humanism and Terror* was serialized in *Les Temps modernes*, and the final chapter on the Yogi/Commissar dialectic covers the same ground as Beauvoir does.

THE ROLE OF COGNIZANT EMOTION

Beauvoir supports a decentred and non-rational subject. Without supporting a sovereign rational subject and by acknowledging the effects of embodiment and others in one's selfhood, she is optimistic about the capacity of individuals to achieve some positive outcomes through critical reflection and engaged action. However, as we saw in the previous chapter on psychoanalysis, Beauvoir uses Adler to point to the importance of intentional agency and projects. If girls want to climb trees (*ss*, 60) it is not in order to become little boys – a feminist protest – but rather a basic desire for bodily agency.

Consciousness has a role, albeit tenuous and limited by its bodily being and symbolically mediated situation. One's affective and emotional life cannot be surpassed by rational argument, nor can one's sedimented habits and psychic disposition be ignored, but rather they must find their place in judgment. The anti-humanists question the assumption that consciousness directs or can unify the self, which is the source of meaning, for they believe that subjects are produced within discourses they do not control and are not the source of. No one discourse can be privileged over another. However, Beauvoir's discourse of authenticity and meaningful engagement in the world values such action and conduct.

While she admits a role for communication, it is always tenuous given that our situations (past, intentions, culture) differ. Emotion and experience underpin rational agency. Beauvoir explores this in her fiction and, most thoroughly, in articles she published in *Les Temps modernes* (recently collected in *Philosophical Writings*, 2004) about the post-war trial and execution of the French fascist writer Robert Brasillach. This article helps us appreciate the role of emotion in politics and judgment; again, unlike rationalists like Habermas, Beauvoir feels that emotion and embodied gestures can contribute to challenging existing power relations, but can also mobilize positive forces of change. Unlike contemporary affect theorists and/or vital materialists, who take their inspiration largely from Deleuze, Baruch Spinoza, and Friedrich Nietzsche, and who diminish the positive role of emotion in agency, Beauvoir sees visceral affects and emotions entwined in social and historical/cultural contexts as a positive resource. Kruks (2016) makes this case convincingly. In Beauvoir's article "Eye for an Eye" (based upon the trial of the collaborator Brasillach), she approaches the question as to whether or not war criminals deserve the death penalty. In doing so, I argue, she explores how emotion and affect influence judgment. This is also a place where she thinks through her plea for realistic morality. In 1945, the French wanted their enemies punished and wanted vengeance. So the formal trial, a presumably impartial emotionless space, is not necessarily going to satisfy those who have suffered harm. The call for revenge or retaliation, Beauvoir insists, cannot be totally dismissed for within it lies some sense of justice – the desire for equivalence. When Mussolini was executed, people thought he should have suffered more, given the suffering he caused? This desire for equity is expressed in the feeling that those who committed crimes *should* be subject to the same torture or suffering they inflict upon others; ideally they would be made to experience the pain they caused others. Of course, this is not possible, Mussolini could not be killed thousands of times, but that doesn't stop it from being their desire. Beauvoir is aware how hollow formal legal practices and procedures appear in comparison.

She says, "Indeed hate is not capricious. One does not hate a *hailstorm* or a plague, but one hates only men not because they are … of material damage, but they are conscious authors of genuine evil" (PW, 248). Instead of repressing these strong feelings of anger, Beauvoir condones their expression, at least insofar as they may lead to a durable/reasonable solution. Revenge is a human sentiment; however impossible it is to gratify it, is equally destructive to wholly ignore its effects. She speculated as to how emotion and affect can be accommodated and yet still deliver justice.

The publicity and staging of Brasillach's trial was a nation building exercise. Less concerned with working through the population's anger and arriving at an appropriate punishment for Brasillach, the trial was more concerned to judge him as standing in for all the treasonous acts of all the collaborators. So Brasillach's actions were not judged in themselves but for the greater political end – to demonstrate that acts of collaboration were treasonous and would be punished harshly. So how can justice be done?

Desire for revenge cannot be denied, yet nor can such feelings be unleashed, since they are ungratifiable. "One can no more avenge the dead than resurrect them," but "if one wants to restore a human community to its own idea of itself, to uphold the values that the crime has negated" (252) some punishment is necessary. "An abomination arises only at the moment that man treats his fellow men as objects, when by torture, humiliation, servitude, assassination, one denies their existence as men" (248). So Brasillach should be punished, even though he himself was not an actual murderer. As an editor of *je suis partout,* he contributed to the murder of thousands of Jews in naming and locating Jews in the community: in treating Jews as objects to be dispensed with, "degraded to things," he committed "an absolute evil" (248).

Beauvoir also warns against judging the entire person; one must judge specified acts. Brasillach may be a good father, a generous neighbour, but what is at stake is his writing that led to the location and rounding up of Jews. In fact, Beauvoir was surprised at how dignified and mild mannered he appeared in court – hardly the rabid anti-semite popularized in the press. "I know that on leaving the courtroom I did not desire his death, during the long sinister ceremony, he had deserved esteem rather than hatred" (257). In spite of her respect for Brasillach during the trial, she did not sign the petition of pardon. Even as Brasillach claims, he did not murder Jews nor did he intend to do so, however Beauvoir insists, one does not judge from intentions alone, but must take into account the consequences of one's acts. This enables one to approach prejudices or attitudes that aren't strictly intended, but nonetheless have destructive effects on others. "He had courageously assumed his life, claimed his freedom and owned up to his responsibility, but to deny the rages and desires of another times, to prefer emotion of the present moment to then, is to break human existence into worthless fragments" (257–8).

Feelings of hate, anger, and revenge were mobilized in the press and these are almost impossible to satisfy. Beauvoir was not surprised by the acts of reprisal against the collaborators and Nazis: French women who slept with Nazi officers had their heads shaven; prisoners slaughtered prison guards when concentration camps were opened. Beauvoir did not judge or morally castigate these acts of revenge; instead she was concerned that liberal legalism, which felt that it resolved the problem of revenge through a "fair" trial, was naive. "The official tribunals claim to take refuge behind an objectivity that is the worst part of the Kantian heritage ... They want to be only an expression of impersonal right and deliver verdicts that be nothing more than the subsumption of a particular case under a universal law ... But the accused exists in his singularity" (258). "We must stop seeing vengeance as a serene recovery of a reasonable and just order, but still want the punishment of authentic criminals ... for punish is to will the good" (259).

By allowing public spaces for strong emotions to be expressed (but not blindly acted upon) France allowed victims of the occupation to tell their stories and have others bear witness. This did not extinguish their suffering or loss, but in recognizing that others too suffered loss, through a shared experience, one might mitigate the pain from their loss. Furthermore, Beauvoir thought strong feelings of injustice and horror at the atrocities committed would hopefully foster future political commitments to collective freedom.

It is equally destructive to ignore the evil done and exonerate war criminals as simply following orders and obeying the law. While the circumstances of the war were constraining and coercive, they did not preclude choice or responsibility. Brasillach did not have to be a collaborator.

On the other hand, Beauvoir was aware that everyone was complicit with the occupiers in some way; no one had clean hands. A high-handed moralism was out of order.

There are aspects of the self that are not transparent; even when one's past and motivations are visible, one's culpability is never perfectly clear. One never acts alone; the social and political context is significant. This, for Beauvoir, does not mean that individuals are exonerated for obeying their superiors or the laws of the Vichy regime, but nor can we expect individuals to be wholly responsible for their acts, since social relations, events, and laws all contribute to one's actions.

One should appreciate that one acts out of situations one has not chosen, for this reason, Beauvoir urges one must listen to the character witnesses in the trial. If we find his acts are "a pure aberration in a life that contradicts the principles of the crime, one considers it with indulgence" (*PW*, 256). However this was not the case with Brasillach: his actions were numerous and evil. While Beauvoir admits Brasillach's affective demeanour was admirable, his acts constituted absolute evil: "When a man deliberately tries to degrade man by reducing him to a thing, nothing can compensate for the abomination he causes to erupt on earth … When it is accomplished no indulgences are permitted and it belongs to man to punish him" (257). If she had been a Christian and believed in an absolute judge, she might have opted for charity, but she believes in human values and human ethics (257); this does not exonerate him from punishment.

Ultimately, the idea that abstract principles can be applied to pass judgment is wrongheaded, because of the need to take into account the context and content of the specific crime judged. Beauvoir surprisingly admits that the war taught her to rethink a Kantian principled approach to politics and ethics. "Since June 1940 (the Nazi Occupation) the French have learned rage and hate" (246). In the past Beauvoir had on principle rejected the death penalty; however, given the gravity of the crimes of the collaborators, they ought to be punished. She rejects the Kantian moral imperative that people should be treated as a means and not an end. Such an abstract humanist principle was impossible to live by during France's occupation, as it was in the wake of the war and the advent of nuclear weapons.

Beauvoir has mixed feelings about the critical capacity of human actors (individual and collective) to forge a new world order and overcome the structural and affective violence and domination that one finds in the present. Ignorance is one impediment to change, but institutionalized power relations and longstanding hate that perpetuate violence are other impediments. These do not disappear through understanding.

Capitalism is not the only impediment to free agency; psychological factors – narcissism, sado/masochism, hate, the denial of human ambiguity (one's dependence upon others and the effects of situatedness) – also militate against freer relations. Apart from the structural limitations of capitalism, ontological and affective personal relations can erode optimism regarding change. Hate was an important factor in the Holocaust; however, Beauvoir does not give up on the possibility of revolutionary change, but by acknowledging the complexity of impediments, she is more aware of what is humanly possible. Reciprocity and mutual respect are not only the cornerstone of her ethical attitude but also central to her vision of democratic socialism.

Beauvoir is not uncritical of revolutionary projects, but she clearly does not assume they are essentially totalitarian, a common trope of the postmodernists and poststructuralists. Since they arise in specific contexts with specific agents and goals, their complexity cannot be ignored. Both Jean-François Lyotard and Michel Foucault used the term "totalizing" to repudiate the USSR and the French communist party. Both were members of the PCF and believed in the revolution but came to the realization that neither communist movement would deliver freedom and equality. Interestingly, Beauvoir never was a communist, since she never felt she could support their actual practices; yet like Sartre she also felt that she could not remain on the sidelines, for to do so would support anti-communism. So unlike the believers, Beauvoir never had faith in the communist party; however, she hoped that radical democratic socialist forces in Europe might propel Marxist/communist projects towards the values of freedom and equality. By the mid-'50s, with the Soviet invasion of Budapest, Beauvoir could no longer uphold a wait-and-see policy, and instead began to openly criticize the PCF and the USSR. However, communist practice did not warrant a wholesale dismissal of Marxism. Nor did Beauvoir subscribe to the common Marxist belief that May '68 failed because the historical conditions were not ripe.

5

Broadening Emancipatory Struggles: Encounters with Social Movements, Revolutionary Regimes, and the Media

BEAUVOIR'S POLITICAL THINKING IS AMBIGUOUS: accommodating the insights of emancipatory[1] and postmodern thinking. Beginning with specific embodied subjects, she urges commitment to projects of social and political change, which could achieve the freedom for all. Unsettling essential and stable identities, in the spirit of poststructuralism/postmodernism, Beauvoir challenges existing identities and social relations, but disruption and negation alone, she believes, will not get one far. Contrary to poststructuralist thinking (Foucault 1984) Beauvoir presumes engagement with others is ontologically privileged: collaborative action is one of the means by which people can engage and transform their affective and social life. Her ontological insights, theories of Othering, affiliation with Marxism, materialist feminism, and postcolonial projects produce a complex understanding of power and envisions ways of advancing liberation through ethically engaged action. As we have seen, Beauvoir recognizes the role of critique, but also believes that ethical/aesthetic and political action has a role in transforming society. Her theory of freedom avoids the liberal and Marxist notion that believes one can be liberated from material determinations through knowledge.[2] As I have previously shown, freedom for Beauvoir is not simply a *negation of our negative* relations, but a conversion requiring the reconfiguring of one's relations to one's embodied self, others, and society.

1 Her theory of minimal ontology, borrowed from Heidegger and Marx, privileges an authentic self-recovery of being, a freedom within facticity and history. Her ontological insights sit poorly with deconstruction.

2 Beauvoir supported consciousness-raising as a feminist strategy to further social equality, however in attending to the importance of human dispositions (sensibility, moods, and emotions) in her novels she intuitively challenges a rationalist approach to political mobilization.

This presumes engagement with existing relations in order to transform and transgress them: working to foster existing evidence of reciprocity as well as challenging existing power relations. Striving for freer and reciprocal relations is a relational and embodied practice; it is an intersubjective (social) achievement. It is not freedom from determination but, rather, involves differently connecting to others and the world. Interestingly, Beauvoir departs from the tradition of freedom that identifies self-realization as autonomy. In willing one's freedom, one does so on the grounds of facticity/history; in embedding one's will in concrete possibilities, one does not simply escape the past or pre-existing relations, but begins by creatively reconfiguring them. Though individual willing and creative engagement are necessary to freedom, they are not sufficient to be deemed authenticity. This is evident in Beauvoir's treatment of the Marquis de Sade, whose vitality and inventiveness she values, but whose autism she bemoans. In *The Ethics of Ambiguity*, she says the freedom won by tyranny or control of others is not freedom. Joining the fascists and contributing to the oppression of Others (if not their extermination) might be passionately willed, and involve collective action, but these acts of freely willing do not further the freedom of all. Hence they are not free in Beauvoir's stronger sense, nor do they contribute to radical humanism.

Her attention to ethics and ontology persisted throughout her life and served as a corrective to deterministic materialism, economism, and antihumanism that plagued Marxist theory and practice during her lifetime. Although Marx himself theorizes reflection, and the imagination, as being intrinsic to praxis, and claims he was not an economic determinist (Marx and Engels 1978, 760), many of Beauvoir's Marxist contemporaries were not convinced. They were receptive to neither the constructive role of the imagination nor the role of one's affective life or choice in action (EA, 20). Theorizing a subversive role for critical thinking, aesthetic engagement, and value choices, Beauvoir's thinking has some affinity to the critical theorists of the Frankfurt School, although there is no evidence that she read the works of Max Horkheimer, Theodor Adorno, or Herbert Marcuse. For them and Beauvoir, critical thinking is inspired by the phenomenologies of the young Hegel and Marx and encourages the renewal of the dialectical tradition that identifies a vitality in human co-existence that comes out of a connectedness in a prereflective domain and an embeddedness in society; however, unlike them, she was more optimistic about the capacity of individuals and social groups to reconfigure themselves and initiate change in capitalist society. She was less involved in exploring the destructive effects of consumer capitalism and mass society; she did not predict the emergence of

One-Dimensional Man nor the *Eclipse of Enlightenment* as Horkheimer and Adorno did. In spite of the horrors of the Holocaust and the nuclear bomb, she still believed in the potential for critical engagement and change. This is not to say that Beauvoir was not disturbed by France's collaboration during the war and disillusioned with the French public's indifference to suffering around the Algerian War, yet she held onto the possibility of political change. Being "actively attached" (*EA*, 20) to a movement enables one to engage in projects and mitigates the solipsism of liberalism and the instrumentalism and rationalism of capitalism. Yet, one must not assume human conflicts or alienation can be overcome. This is quite consistent with Herbert Marcuse in *Eros and Civilization*: here he acknowledges the necessity of basic repression, required for adequate subject formation, but he believes surplus repression, a product of capitalism, can be eliminated. Beauvoir's differences from the critical theorists, I suspect, have to do with her location in a highly politicized culture in France, rather than the USA (the home of the exiled members of the Frankfurt school). Furthermore, there are theoretical differences: Beauvoir gives more space to the affective/engaged individual. Freedom is never eliminated, though it is severely restricted "by bodily, social structured dimensions of experience," as Kruks rightly points out (2010, 259). The failures of the dialectic reversals were more a problem for the critical theorists of the Frankfurt school, since they did not reconceive the dialectic as an encumbered conversion.

Moving beyond the narrow economism and hierarchal and bureaucratic tendencies of class politics as articulated by the PCF in the 1950s and 1960s, Beauvoir embraces the need for increasing the participation and improving the representation of minorities. In appreciating the capacity of the political to both initiate radical change and begin to meet the universal needs of citizens, Beauvoir admits the effectiveness of democratic practices in mobilizing minority populations and obviating alienation and domination. Departing from economism and the base/superstructure model of society, she identifies the importance of political engagement, or what in the 1980s was variously theorized as a politics of recognition or participatory democracy. This includes acknowledging the cultural/symbolic needs of the subordinate members of society, be they working-class men, women, Algerians, Blacks, students, or Jews. These groups are not only economically exploited; they are culturally and socially dominated. Since humans need to be recognized by others, economic equality would not necessarily do the trick. Hence they need to reimagine themselves and overcome their history of misrecognition or demeanment. As in *The Second Sex* Beauvoir exposed how the social inferiority of women was produced through the economy, myths, and social and cultural practices. Women must begin to speak out, but for their political voices to be heard, the public sphere has to be open to listening. Beauvoir is also aware of the material and symbolic resources necessary for their voices to be heard. Since Beauvoir's move away from the Hegelian dialectic and transcending disembodied consciousnesses, she also distances herself from the look as the basis of recognition and tries to forge intersubjectivity in a more embodied and situated way. Furthermore for Beauvoir cultural recognition or affirmation of difference is not an end in itself but a means to a transformative radical politics.

While unlinking the socio-economic from other social markers of disadvantage, she does not deny their connection. She does not end up as a Weberian who addresses social status injuries, nor as a multiculturalist who believes respect for cultural diversity is the way forward. While she focuses upon expanding the public sphere – the sites for deliberation – deliberation alone will not liberate the oppressed. Furthermore recognition involves a more embedded and embodied approach, taking into account emotion and historical context, as Brasillach's trial made clear.

Beauvoir was known to have supported cultural movements insofar as they worked towards broadening revolutionary forces. However, her critique of dogmatism meant she did not recruit for the PCF or the socialist party. Throughout the '60s, she still hoped that socialism would provide the best path for women's emancipation, but by 1975 she had changed her mind. She no longer thought feminists should work through socialist struggles. However, as I have argued, that isn't a significant shift in her political envisioning of democratic socialism, but rather a change in strategy. She remained a materialist feminist, who acknowledged the significance of class and poverty in women's oppression. Even as early as the '50s she supported struggles for family planning and social justice that were not mediated by socialist organizations, whether they be those of incarcerated young unwed mothers in Paris (ASD, 482) trying to undo the effects of their authoritarian treatment, critical voices of students and trade unionists who opposed the PCF, as well as victims of industrial accidents (474). In addition to publicizing and publically supporting these movements, she participated in international tribunals for peace (367–76). Beauvoir's openness to the plurality and complexity of struggles took her beyond working-class interests to address more extensive claims for injustice as well as demands for cultural and political recognition. This involves a more open-ended and anti-statist approach to revolutionary politics, a respect for social movements, as well as recognition of the limits of consciousness and interest in harnessing agents of change. While socialists today often condemn social movements as fragmenting a unified left and argue that the turn to cultural politics has disabled the left, Beauvoir sees the plurality of social and protest movements and cultural politics as potentially contributing to democratic socialism rather than undermining it. Beginning with the specificity of embodied and situated subjects she moves towards mobilizing their engagement in struggle that would further democratic socialism. Her turn to culture and to the symbolic world is not a turn away from the significance of the socially structured dimension of experience. Unlike some of the post-'68 anarchists, who turn to the microprocessual and turn away from what they call the macro (molar) powers of the state and institutions, Beauvoir acknowledges both the importance of macroforces – institutional, legal, and policy changes that offer sites for furthering social equality and instantiating democracy, and microprocesses – everyday interventions that disrupt and destabilize hegemonic identities (be they class, race, or gender).

Beauvoir not only analyzes power relations to understand the macro forces of change, but she also relies upon literature as a medium of communicating micro revolutionary potential. She hopes to engage people in thinking about the everyday experiences of others as well as their own. Narrativizing her own life, she believed contributed to her own politicization, as well as acting as a mentor for others. She uses literature to think through personal impediments to freedom and happiness. To develop new political voices, she rarely provides positive role models; consistent with her empirical and analytic approach, she begins with women in abject circumstances of patriarchy and capitalism and the readers are invited to explore what impedes their agency. Through autobiography she narrativizes her own voice and her own struggles to be less defined/restricted by sexist and bourgeois socializing forces.

As I have demonstrated, Beauvoir expands the concept of agency beyond the proletarian male (class subject) to incorporate new forms of politicized subjective experiences and political resistances; in doing so, she expands political subjectivity to include oppression based upon age, ethnicity, gender, sexuality, and race. Today this may seem obvious, but in the 1940s this sensitivity to oppressed minorities was prescient. In addition, she enlarges the scope of the political by recognizing psychosocial, cultural, in addition to socio-economic impediments to change. Using theories of alterity and recognizing the complexity of forces of oppression (e.g., involving the intersections of class, gender, race, age, sexuality, etc.), Beauvoir begins to produce a more sensitive tool to understand different faces of oppression. Her belief "that every concrete human being is uniquely situated" (*SS*, 4) appreciates multiple and differentiating intersection of socio-economic and cultural forces, whilst, at the same time, she assumes we share a world in common (*LIT*, 199).

This double experience of the world: acknowledging different experiences and yet respecting the possibility of sharing experiences across difference, is noteworthy. Although her inattention to postcolonial, racialized, and queer experiences has brought criticisms, her theoretical approach can theoretically accommodate these experiences. Elizabeth Spelman may be correct in arguing that Beauvoir does not adequately explore the experiences of non-European women, yet her theoretical approach does prompt such work.[3] Furthermore Beauvoir's work contributed to and inspired the struggles of many minority women.

Beauvoir does not systematically or self-consciously write a political text to articulate her differences with Marxist theory, however evidence of the novelty of her political thinking is often glossed over. Beauvoir tries to harness contemporary political and social movements, foster democratic practices, and iron out non-hierarchal forms of political organization. This is consistent with her critiques of existing revolutionary politics, as top-down, as well as the failure to address forms of suffering not connected to capitalism. Furthermore, Marxists focus upon the party as an instrument of revolutionary change and the need to seize state power is clearly inadequate, for it tends to ignore differently situated subjects with various political and cultural harms. However she saw her interest as a supplement to socio-economic oppression, as a way of broadening Marxism, not a repudiation of it.

Within Marxist theory and specifically from the position of Lenin in the USSR, the party was envisioned as a transitional form of power that facilitates the proletariat or majority assuming their role as universal agents of change. As Marx proclaims in *The Communist Manifesto*, "the first step of the revolution is to raise the proletariat to the position of ruling class, to win the battle of democracy" (Marx and Engels 1978, 490). Not only was this not happening in the USSR, or in other communist countries, it was not happening in the French communist movement in post-war years and '50s. In fact, far from the party relinquishing their powers over the proletariat, the majority of communist parties were sustaining their powers. Instead of encouraging popular participation and democratic practices, most communist parties were engaged in top-down and anti-democratic strategies, thereby undermining the goal of rule by the proletariat. While the increasing forces of anti-communism may have

3 Elizabeth Spelman (1988, 62–5) has rightly noted that while Beauvoir in *The Second Sex* offers insightful analyses of polyvalent structures of privilege which constitute lived situations (both overarching and in particular contexts), she often falls back to discussing the sorts of privileges denied to white, middle-class (often heterosexual) women.

justified these strategies, Beauvoir was adamant that political protests and revolutionary struggle had to instantiate democratic practices.

THEORETICAL STRATEGIES TO EXPAND REVOLUTIONARY AGENCY: THE CONCEPT OF OTHER

In extending political agency beyond the proletariat and the party, Beauvoir replaces the class subject with a more complex oppressed subject. She challenges the idea of the working class as primary with a racialized, nationalized, sexualized, and gendered subject for whom power gets defined by political and cultural as well as economic forms.

Instead of using the category of the proletariat, she spoke in the less technical language of the poor and rich: since poverty not only takes the form of economic exploitation, but also cultural marginalization and social oppression, dichotomies of subject and Other have a role to play. After the war she looked at how the Nazis Othered the Jews: how the Jews were treated as objects, things, not as humans (PW, 248). In the same vein in which Beauvoir categorized Brasillach's crimes as radically objectifying the Jews, she describes the desperate situation of the Spanish and Portuguese peoples, which she witnessed on her visits after the war (between 1945 and 1947). In both countries the poor were treated as Others, less than human, with barely enough to eat; whereas the rich were subjects who had luxuries. From Madrid, she discloses "the contradictions of a capitalist country ruled by a rightwing dictatorship: excess luxury of food for the few, while the workers could not afford eggs, milk, meat, vegetables or fruit" (POL, 20). So while the poor's existence was abject, they were not wholly dehumanized, Beauvoir writes, "Children play, young girls laugh, men talk amongst themselves in cheerful voices. Poverty has not made them into resigned livestock: they remain living men, men who rebel and hope" (20). In Portugal, the differences between rich and poor are even more extreme. Beauvoir reports on the bad health resulting from a lack of vitamins, where freezing children "wander the streets half naked" (24). "In the harsh winter ... young girls root through the garbage cans of Porto" (25). Beauvoir "illustrates the division of the Portuguese people into two sorts of men; those who eat and are considered as men, and those who do not eat and are livestock" (23). Reducing humans to livestock, to the level of animal existence is another form of Othering. This invites comparison to Arendt's distinction between *zoe* and *bios*. Arendt follows the Aristotelian distinction, most notably in *The Human Condition*, where she identifies zoe with bare life and bios with political life not only with speech and action but most importantly with the condition of human plurality (Arendt 1998, 7).

The poor, zoe, who can barely meet their basic needs are hardly capable of acts of citizenship. The rich, whose needs are satisfied, go beyond bare need to the realm of bios. They are situated as political animals, capable of reason and justice. The former are demeaned and their lives do not matter, whereas the later group is privileged.

Of course, Marx makes a similar assumption, that political freedom (in Arendt's words bios) must meet the needs of zoe, and overcome scarcity. Marx believes that poverty and destitution can and must be overcome, for freedom to be possible. Capitalism has created such a wealth of goods that if there was a change in the mode of production (elimination of wage labour, radical redistribution according to need) then poverty and power differentials could be eliminated. Beauvoir too presumes that humans must overcome scarcity to be able to be free, but they must also be active participants in democratic life. However, given Beauvoir's appreciation of the complexities of power (that speaks to racist, colonial, and sexist dynamics) her revolution is more complex than the struggle between the proletariat and the bourgeoisie. Also, she is less convinced of the success of the revolution since she does not believe the revolution is guaranteed on structural grounds or as a teleological/linear development.

Again, in the spirit of Marx's theory of ideology, Beauvoir explores the processes of mystification that keep the poor downtrodden. In her report from the United States, further developed in her book, Beauvoir explores American fictions. She punctures one of most fundamental cultural myths of America: the legend that even "the little man" can become rich. This capitalist myth, she emphasizes, is pacifying to the poorer citizens who believe their freedom is unlimited, while they individually bear all fault for their failures. This myth, prevalent also today, masks social structures and prevents collective actions. Beauvoir also points to another contradiction in American democracy: race. While the "respect for the human being and for the principles that guarantee him his rights is deeply anchored in the heart of American citizens" (*ADD*, 293), racialized oppression is evident. Racism puts those Americans who believe in the Declaration of Independence and the Constitution's preamble in a situation of "bad faith." In addition, she was suspicious of the role of the judiciary in this caste society, which she saw as "allowing for the persistence of social, political and economic discrimination" (245) rather than addressing it. Beauvoir recounts evidence of racial segregation in the border crossing between New Mexico into San Antonio, Texas. Travelling in the Greyhound bus she noticed the restrooms were segregated and ranked: "White Ladies" and "White Gentlemen" and "Colored Women" and "Colored Men." The "White" waiting room and lunchroom accommodations are roomy, while the "Colored" waiting area is a "miserable alcove" (202). Beauvoir describes the heaviness of the racist world of the South: its effects are visceral. She describes her skin becoming heavy and stifling. "This is the first time we're seeing with our own eyes the segregation we've heard so much about. And although we'd been warned, something fell onto our shoulders that would not lift all through the South; it was our own skin that became heavy and stifling, its color making us burn" (202–3).

In exposing not only how the poor have been dehumanized, but also Jews and Blacks Americans, Beauvoir draws attention to other faces of oppression. Her radical universal humanism presumes economic oppression (poverty and inequality) will be addressed in addition to social harms that demean and objectify humans. In this section, I have illustrated how Beauvoir expanded Marx's ideas of the oppressed to consider multiple agents, as well as think about the process of political mobilization. By using categories of human/animal, rich/poor, privileged/demeaned, I believe she overcame the problem of economism associated with the categories of the bourgeoisie and the proletariat. The Jews were oppressed, yet not members of the proletariat; young unwed mothers were demeaned however their demeanment was not specifically associated with their class. While Beauvoir seeks to broaden Marx's thoughts on domination to include non-economic factors, she does not explicitly state this as her intention. Yet it is clear that in theory and practice she sees herself expanding the scope and strategies of revolutionary agency.

ACTIVISM AS A THEORETICAL INTERVENTION: FOSTERING COUNTER-HEGEMONIC PUBLICS

To summarize, most scholars have ignored the link between Beauvoir's activism and her philosophy. In addition to having concrete political goals, her activism provided an opportunity for her to think about how radical political agency could be enlarged to include struggles that privileged race, nation, gender, or sexuality. For Beauvoir, philosophy is not concerned with abstract models, principles, or truth claims; as an existentialist phenomenologist, she attends to her own experience – and the concrete experience of events – as she apprehends them. In other words, she believes this philosophy, inspired by existentialism, ought to help one live a fuller and freer life. In doing so one must not live a reflective life, but engage in existing struggles. She relies on fiction, biography, and autobiography, in addition to her political essays and theoretical work, to further this end. Her reflections on life in her autobiographies, as collected in *All Said and Done* and *Force of Circumstance*, are not simply her private thoughts but bear witness to how one can approach the dilemmas and difficulties of her times. In addition to looking at her autobiographies, I will examine her articles, collected in the series *Philosophical Writings* and *Political Writings*, where she reflects upon concrete historical events, as well as political and social phenomena. In doing so, she opens up an oppositional public space in order to engender an appreciation of an alternative lifestyle, and counter-hegemonic politics.

In tracing Beauvoir's activism from the post-war years to the '80s, continuities in her practice emerge. Beauvoir saw herself as a critical intellectual whose job was to disclose abuses of power and bring to light counter-hegemonic struggles that the mainstream press ignores.[4] Revealing deceptions, lies, and abuses of power, as well as representing revolutionary movements often invisible to the population at large, she hoped to contribute to radicalizing the population through informed and inclusive debate. Revealing new "facts" and destabilizing "common sense" would provide new information with which to make decisions. Publicizing injustice and new movements for change, would broaden support. However, in addition to recognizing the power of strong arguments and reason to counter hegemonic "common sense," Beauvoir saw the potential of harnessing affects and emotion to combat social injustice and material inequality.

Beauvoir's attention to the public sphere as a place where meaningful debate and conversation unfold bears some resemblance to Habermas, but, unlike Habermas, who has no time for bodily gestures and affects, Beauvoir attends to the significance of dispositions and sensibilities. She not only looks at emotion but also tracks how the transmission of bodily affects fuels political commitment. For Habermas, ideal illocutionary speech must be without passions and interests. He explicitly excludes from communicative "action" proper what he calls the bodily "movements" that may accompany it. Intentions involve bodily movements to help execute them but Habermas believes "these are elements of action

4 As problems with Marxist theory and practice manifested themselves – the lack of proletarian consciousness and agency, the party's authoritarian and dogmatic practices – radicals turned away from revolutionary force to foster radical consciousness by encouraging rich debate in civil society. In the 1980s some radical theorists began to emphasize the role of civil society in fostering radical consciousnesses and generating new forms of engagement in democratic politics. Civil society theorists (David Held and John Keane) believed that Marxists paid insufficient attention to the political. Since communism involves the withering away of the state, post-revolutionary politics in the future will simply amount to administrative tasks. This underestimates the trenchant social, cultural, and ethnic differences that are not likely to disappear with the revolution but will require political representation. Further struggles over resources (both material and immaterial) will never end, nor will they be reducible to an administrative solution.

not action itself" (1984, 97). His strong mind/body dualism fails to attend to how judgments and commitments are arrived at. Deliberation and choice are not matters of reason alone. Rather, our styles of judgment are of a piece with how we more generally engage with the world as embodied and affective beings.

Beauvoir recognizes the importance of a vibrant civil society engaged in meaningful political debate. As Arendt suggests, this is a place where people can be persuaded. Beauvoir is less concerned with the aesthetic potential of the argument to woo consent or the posture of its interlocutors, and more concerned with promoting revolutionary loyalty. Here she departs from Arendt's Republican politics. The public sphere is not simply a place to inform and rationally persuade the public, but has the potential for generating strong affective attachment and fostering strong opposition and counter-hegemonic forces (whether they be social movements, protest groups, or revolutionary struggles). Responding to social injustices and systemic suffering with empathy, Beauvoir hoped to transform this into solidarity and commitment to radical politics. Beauvoir would find some affinity with the present position of Susan Krause: while motivation requires emotional involvement, once people get motivated, they need good rational arguments to sustain their commitment.[5] Beauvoir's work on the public sphere hoped to produce strong affects to motivate as well as good reasons to sustain radical commitment.[6]

In departing from the ideal of Habermas's bourgeois public sphere, Beauvoir has some affinity to Nancy Fraser's (1996) critique of the concept.[7] Challenging the ideal of a homogenous public sphere Fraser calls for subaltern alternative publics, Habermas responded acknowledging the sites for critical publicity. The need for publicizing radical social and political movements was always at the core of Beauvoir's activism. Committed to disturbing common sense through publicity, Beauvoir is aware of how difficult it was to know what was really happening: "until 1954 I knew nothing of the true situation in Algeria, nor did I know what

5 Susan Krause makes this argument (Krause 2008).

6 Writing in the post-war years, she could not have anticipated the impact of neuroscience, or the effects of affect on political judgment agency, as is current today, however she does show some respect for the way aesthetics and emotion can muster support for injustice and can motivate a struggle. But she would challenge the idea that judgment is a post hoc rationalization of an neural event.

7 Nancy Fraser argues that Habermas's exclusion of women from the public space was not contingent but is "constitutively exclusionary … we cannot assume the liberal model of the bourgeois public space is an unrealized utopian ideal, it was also an ideological notion that served to rationalize an historically emergent form of class, race and gender domination" (1996, 76).

was really happening in the USSR and the people's democracies" (*ASD*, 36). Nevertheless her attitude towards capitalism, imperialism, and colonialism were clear: "they were to be fought against in our writing and if possible by our acts" (36). "Even if one does not know a great deal, one must take a stand; and that does not happen without hesitations and mistakes" (36). She talked about her and Sartre's fluctuations with the communist party and socialist countries. "From time to time it was shatteringly clear that we were bound to reject certain grossly discredited things – the Soviet Camps, the Rajk and Slansky trials, Budapest" (*ASD*, 36). But these atrocities did not undermine her commitment to social equality and liberty.

In "Right-Wing Thought Today," collected in *Political Writings*, Beauvoir identifies other mystifying myths/logic of right-wing thought. Very much inspired by Marx's *German Ideology*, Beauvoir considers how ideas justify, legitimate, and disguise power. She says "each new class has to give its ideas the form of universality, and represent them as the only rational universally valid ones" (*POL*, 119). But how, Beauvoir asks, "is it indeed possible to provide a universal justification for specific advantageous claims?" (119). One way, she points out, is to appeal to nature: "Nature is on the right" and it is "used as an authority for those" who will defend inequality (176). "By subordinating men to a hierarchal form and subjugating them to a pre established order, the ideology of the right … denies individuals their autonomy and their ability to achieve immediate solidarities among themselves" (177). Hierarchy and universality are removed from the realm of argument by the mystical powers of a generative and opaque nature.

Partly through this mystification, Beauvoir suggests, the privileged are not only alienated from others, but are "radically cut off from reality" (131). Far from truly being openings onto the world, capable of appreciating rich sensory experiences, she presumes the privileged treat others as subhuman. Beauvoir describes them as resisting the weight of the world, and thus cut off from worldly experiences, including the destitution, suffering, and injustice of others. She continues: "separated from the world, the individual is *a fortiori* separated from his fellow man. His sole motive is self-interest which is expressed either by empty ambition or, if this ambition remains unfulfilled, by resentment" (131). As we have seen previously, this interest driven and individualist approach to living is not supported. Beauvoir describes the life of the Marquis de Sade as "systematically [assuming] particularity, separation, and egoism" (95). Beauvoir argues the bourgeoisie refuse the reality of injustice in order to ensure that the "justice" (i.e., their justice and privilege) is protected ("Right-Wing Thought Today").

"Nature" is also used to defend inequality. It is not human arrangements, but – the right argues – natural differences that dictate social success. Beauvoir writes that right-wing thinkers "are not interested in arriving at the truth but only obscuring it" (109): "They prefer the anecdote whispers from ear to ear, because stories represent the experience of their privilege and they want no other warranty of its truth but the quality of the elite who are spreading it" (146). Only the elite are granted true humanity and taste. Right-wing writers and readers often distinguish themselves from the common, the herd, and reaffirm "natural" hierarchies to support cozy common sense.

While I make the case that Beauvoir's writing, specifically in "Right-Wing Thought Today," interjects a critical perception in the media, some Beauvoirians see this article as particularly dogmatic. Kruks is a case in point; in her introduction to the article she argues that the piece "may be of historic value, but is not very interesting outside the Cold War situation" (109). It is "marked by a striking Manichaeism; either one is with the Communists, or one is against them" (109). As Beauvoir sides with communism, in this article, she acts dogmatically, descending to the depths of the "serious man" whom she criticizes in *The Ethics of Ambiguity*. I read Beauvoir's intervention rather differently: in the context of rabid anti-communism of the early '50s, she felt it necessary to take a strong stance, even without knowing all the facts. Granted her position was bold and unambiguous, but taking a strong stance against common sense involves bracketing the ambiguity and complexity of the situation. At times, such resolve and commitment are necessary. In thinking, complexity can be appreciated; in acting, it cannot. Embedded in Cold-War Europe in the height of the McCarthy trials, Beauvoir believed she had to chose between communism and anti-communism: she chose to support the former despite all its shortcomings; it contributed to the future freedom of all, as an ideal, if not in practice, whereas anti-communism wanted to destroy this ideal and legitimate existing inequality and oppression. Her position is not dogmatic since, I would argue, it is not theoretically determined but flexible, responding to the material/historical context in which she finds herself. One is tempted to call it pragmatic – but since Beauvoir's political interventions were also informed by her philosophical foundations and strong political values, I hesitate to call it such. Engaged action that contributes to "the freedom of all" is ontologically privileged, thus supporting her radical humanism.

Beauvoir's commitment to guaranteeing a rich public sphere fostering counter hegemonic ideas was evident in her agreement to write a preface to *Treblinka* by Steiner, 1966. Without knowing the author, and without having seen the book (trusting a reviewer of *Les Temps modernes*), she was convinced of its significance and timeliness. Its reliance upon little-known documents, survivor's evidence, was destined to be criticized for anti-semitism. For this reason she felt it had to be given a fair reading. Steiner documents how Jewish people willingly went into the camps and submitted to authorities. He points to how the Nazis used Jews – the Judenrat – to manage the ghettos and prison camps. The SS attempted to divide the population into the privileged ones, those Jews who were "chosen" to assist the Nazis in running the camps, and those others, the pariah. These Othering practices made enemies of each other and therefore enemies within. In spite of the Nazis' efforts trying to divide the prisoners, the prisoners were able to form a group and became a powerful force, and rebellion broke out (*ASD*, 145). Rather than explaining resistance in individualistic terms (the selfish Judenrat versus the heroic resistors), relying upon Sartre's insights in *Critique of Dialectical Reason*, Beauvoir draws attention to how social forces and sedimented social group practices impede agency. "The Nazis serialized their victims with Machiavellian ingenuity, so they turned against one another and were reduced to impotence" (145). However through their shared experiences they generated solidarity, and ultimately collective action emerged from their serialized existence. Susan Rubin Suleiman, who wrote the introduction to Beauvoir's preface to this article in *Political Writings* (2009), was deeply offended by the parallel Beauvoir drew between the Jewish organizers of the Treblinka uprising and workers organizing to make collective demands to their employers. According to Suleiman, Beauvoir's parallel is "odd": she dismisses it as a symptom "of Beauvoir's leftist leaning and of the ongoing influence of Marxism in France during the 1960s more than anything else" (*POL*, 298). While it might appear "odd" to Suleiman, Beauvoir's interest in the social conditions of agency in oppressive situations is not at all odd. Both Beauvoir and Sartre were working on how social groups and social solidarity could be catalyzed. Reliant upon Sartre's work on the formation of social groups in *Critique of Dialectical Reason* and his categories of seriality and the practico-inert, he theorized how the products of human praxis become sedimented and produce their own demands that constrain our freedom (Sartre 1960, 124–5).

Beauvoir identified the Jews in the prison camp as serialized: unified and passively participating as a consequence of their location in practico-inert structures of the camp. This material and social fact conditioned these inmates' lives – it was a reality that individuals had to deal with. Though they were constituted passively from the "outside" by their social location and the exigencies of the camp, some were able to create internal and intentional bonds. Out of shared common conditions they were able to form a group, establish a common goal (escape), and foster strong bonds of solidarity to achieve that goal. In the end, three hundred escaped. The situation of exploited workers was different, though there are parallels: how do workers who are serialized and atomized by the capitalist mode of production form social groups and act collectively? How do workers who are externally related and defined by the practices of their workplace (the practico-inert) transform themselves into a social group? Beauvoir felt the ideas raised in *Treblinka* were timely and of public interest.

She encouraged vigilant thinking that challenged the truths of the status quo, as evidenced in her numerous editorial and authorial roles: in *Les Temps modernes* and in the *Questions féministes* collective and other radical journals. Additionally, intent upon revealing cover-ups as well as giving voice to minorities without unqualified endorsement of their struggles, she helped Sartre in founding the popular radical daily *Libération*. Occasionally Beauvoir wrote for mainstream newspapers, such as *Le Monde*, trying to inject a radical perspective in their pages, but more frequently she wrote for small radical papers such as *J'accuse*. In 1979 her commitment to ensure the representation and popularization of radical ideas extended to her taking editorship of a banned newspaper, *L'Idiot international*, which documented the struggles of working people.

Beauvoir was aware of the need to challenge ideology, reveal suppressed information, and cultivate strong attachments to radical political causes. Grounded in the events of the times, she made injustices visible, hoping to dislodge support and confidence in ruling powers and promote change. Her political praxis as well as her political thinking is manifest in her autobiographies and popular journalism. The autobiographies (published in 1958, 1960, 1963, and 1972) disclose in great detail the facts of her active political life as well as her reflections on the political events of the day. The final volume – *All Said and Done* – covers her political activism throughout the 1960s and is particularly useful in outlining her mature political praxis. Her support of what have most recently been deemed social movements is not simply a pragmatic response to the situation, but is consistent with her belief that radical agency must be expanded. Because non-material needs – for political participation and cultural expression – are preconditions for self-development as well as collective freedom, cultural politics are important. Since cultural politics do not require organized parties, and yet loosen the grip of the capitalist economy, they are embraced.

During the post-war years, she believed her political journalism would contribute to broader revolutionary and class struggles. As the Soviet Union was becoming increasingly authoritarian in the '50s, she became more openly critical of its shortcomings. She never appears to have subscribed to a unified struggle like the class struggle, or only so as it involves the coherence and collaboration of multiple forces. In *The Ethics of Ambiguity*, she notes that the Second World War provided a rare occasion when opposition to the Nazis appeared unified. But even then she sympathized with Blacks like Richard Wright, who refused to give up his anti-racist struggle and support anti-fascism, and with the anti-imperialist movements in India that refused to throw their support behind the allies who were trying to defeat fascism, for they too were their oppressors. By recognizing the plural and complex nature of resistance and revolution, she challenged the more conventional Marxist treatment of struggle as primarily class struggle between two opposing classes: the bourgeoisie and the proletariat.

Local struggles and social protests, she believes, contribute to class politics, but she insists they not be under the directives of communist or socialist parties. Operating outside traditional institutional frameworks, she encourages grassroots struggle for democracy. Her affinity to social movements' theory is clear and her connection to contemporary anarchists is clear as well. Like Alain Badiou, Michael Hardt, Antonio Negri, Gilles Deleuze, and Michel Foucault, she wanted to expand non-state action and did so by appealing to aesthetic, non-instrumental forces and specific struggles. However, unlike Foucault and Deleuze she believed in the need to struggle for changes in public policy, to utilize social and political institutions (*ASD*, 278) when necessary, and to assume state power and collectively challenge it.

In tracking Beauvoir's actions and reflections, we can see how she encouraged new agents of change and multiple sources of resistance. These outbursts of democracy were not necessarily articulated by nor harnessed to left-wing parties; rather, she supported social movements and anti-state action. However, she did not believe that "jamming the works of capitalism" or destabilizing identities alone was sufficient. Remember how she saw de Sade and Rimbaud in the same light. She was averse to assuming state power or directly engaging the state to improve the well being of the exploited. Her efforts to improve the state pension of poor industrial workers in Méru is a case in point.

BEAUVOIR'S ACTIVISM FROM '47 TO '68

In tracing Beauvoir's work as an activist – her efforts to shore up counter-hegemonic struggles (through publicizing their claims, disclosing falsehoods, promoting strong attachments, and approaching state officials)

– I will show how she contributes to the formation of a radical public sphere. In so doing, she hoped to mobilize the public to get involved in and contribute to the development of popular democratic movements.

In 1947, Beauvoir went on a lecture tour in the United States; here she spoke of the writer's responsibility to further critical debate and support emerging anti-war sentiments. In *America Day by Day* (1948), a monograph based upon her visit, she expressed her concern over American racism and hypocrisy, and emerging "Cold Warrior" attitudes. She saw the Marshall Plan[8] as a thinly veiled act of American imperialism: "in the eyes of the average American, imperialism takes the guise of charity. Their arrogance lies not in their love of power. It is the love of imposing on others, that which is good. The miracle is that the key to paradise should be in their hands" (*POL*, 75).[9] Beauvoir drew attention to the micro or personal side of American imperialism, it was not just about violent military intervention, but the American people were convinced of their exceptionalism. American ideals, values, and systems were being imposed upon the Europeans by the Marshall Plan. Consistent with her politics of ambiguity, Beauvoir expressed her ambivalence about American society: she was horrified by its systemic inequality, its culture of racism and exceptionalism; however, she enjoyed its social and cultural dynamism.

Even though Beauvoir and Sartre were not members of communist or socialist parties, revolutionary leaders around the world were keen to be interviewed by them. They provided a more sympathetic picture than the mainstream press and thus gained the reputation for being ambassadors for revolutionary regimes. Given their intellectual and public profiles, they brought media attention to these struggling regimes, often important to their survival. Beauvoir spoke on behalf of revolutionary movements that were being suppressed in the mainstream media in the post-war years, for example the revolutions in China, Algeria, and Cuba. Her sympathetic treatments were important to prompt affective support and solidarity with counter-hegemonic struggles.

She visited China with Sartre in 1955 and published *The Long March* in which she praised the Chinese Communist Party's (CCP) ability to deal with vermin, infant mortality, and poverty. She was as interested in political and cultural transformations a well as economic changes, and how

8 Marshall Plan funds were first sent to Greece and Turkey in January 1947 to deter Soviet influence in the region. In the end, all Europeans outside fascist Spain were financially supported by the Americans.

9 The theme of self-emancipation – her criticism of charity and freedom from party directives – is to be found in her early article "Moral Idealism and Political Realism" (1944).

they variously affected women and peasants. She approved of the CCP's efforts to facilitate women's entry into the labour force by introducing abortion and contraception and validating their decreased role in the domestic sphere. She was struck by the cultural differences between pre-revolutionary and post-revolutionary Chinese society. The women portrayed in Pearl Buck's *The Good Earth* in 1931, with their bound feet and subservience to men, were no longer evident. By the 1950s, women's role in Chinese society was been transformed by the communists. Yet Beauvoir's support was not unqualified. Even in the early '50s she was disturbed by the revolutionaries' zealous behaviour: they seemed to deny that they had lives or desires beyond the state. She found their decision to forgo holidays for the revolution very troubling.

Beauvoir's desire to make radical alternatives visible and to give voice to a radical perspective informed her participation in international peace conferences and war tribunals (*ASD*, 368–71). Some contemporary Marxists ridiculed her participation as sign of a reformist collaborating with the enemy. For Beauvoir, participation in peace conferences allowed critical revolutionary voices like hers and Sartre's to be represented in the mainstream. For example, in the Helsinki Peace Conference in 1955, she took up a familiar position by challenging anti-communism (which was having corrosive effects upon world peace) without backing communism. She encouraged a critical sympathy for revolutionary regimes without blindly endorsing them.

Beauvoir's support of new democratic forms of power is evident in her stance on Czechoslovakia and Yugoslavia (266). She backed these self-governing socialist countries, which were working on more cooperative forms of labour and strengthening mechanisms for popular decision-making. Because they refused Soviet directives and pursued an independent and locally informed socialist strategy they were repudiated by the Soviet Union and the PCF. Tito was deemed an enemy of the Soviet Union, and Czechoslovakia's local democracy was punished with violent aggression. Beauvoir's efforts to support democratic outbursts, grass-roots power, brought her into further conflict with the PCF.

However, Beauvoir and Sartre believed their roles in publicizing new revolutionary movements stood them in good stead with communists. Both believed they were able to exert some positive influence on the Soviet Union and on communist parties more generally. However, some argue that their influence was modest or negligible, particularly post-1956 when they openly criticized the USSR and the PCF.

From 1960 to 1966, they spent several weeks per year in the USSR. Pleased by Khrushchev's thaw in 1962 (306), she was increasingly aware that the liberalization in Soviet culture was shortlived (312). In 1966, she and Sartre unsuccessfully pressured the Soviet government to release the Jewish poet Joseph Brodsky from a Soviet prison. The following year, intent upon protesting the incarceration of dissident writers, they refused an invitation from the Soviet Writer's Union (Appignanesi 2005, 149). Their criticism of Soviet anti-semitism was not without effect – if not on the government itself, then within the broader international community.

As the Cold War thawed, writers and intellectuals joined together to speak about the role of politics and literature. Beauvoir participated in many popular public forums on culture (*ASD*, 312). Again, we witness her non-aligned approach. She refused the characteristically liberal notion of "art for art's sake," where writers felt they were totally free from social and political forces to capture the transhistorical truths of good literature. Yet she also repudiated the communist parties and Marxist theorists who thought literature and culture played a didactic role in molding new proletarian citizens. She spurned the *proletkultur* movement (socialist realism) that muzzled artists and writers by insisting their work be defined by the party or act in the service of the revolutionary state. Sartre was also critical of the communists' approach to culture, which gave precedence to science and degraded literature to the level of propaganda, and their silencing of dissidents. Beauvoir challenged those Marxists who believed art and aesthetics were to be seen in terms of the logic of capitalism. Like Western Marxists, Beauvoir believed that art, literature, and film could lay siege to capitalism. The production and appreciation of art resisted the commodification of capitalism and challenged a market mentality. While art is commodifiable, it exceeds commodification.

Fiction, too, may be produced within a specific historical context, but it is more than ideology. Beauvoir says she distrusts a humanism that is too indifferent to the aesthetic and historical efforts of former times (*EA*, 92). "If the world behind us were bare, we would hardly be able to see anything before us but a gloomy desert" (93).

Beauvoir, Sartre, and Merleau-Ponty were all involved in International Cultural conferences, in particular East/West Encounter (1956). Speculating on how literature was being used in the construction of new societies, Merleau-Ponty and Sartre believed that writers could have a productive role in educating illiterate people and young children, as long as they weren't told what to write. "If I were asked to suppress myself in my writing, that is, to write books wherein I would not say what I know to be true, I would refuse" (Merleau-Ponty 1992, 56). Sartre anticipated Western writers would deplore this restraint on their intellectual life, but argued for engaged writing, which was not subject to external discipline (51). Fiction contributed to the politicization of subjective experience, for it brought to visibility the voices and perspectives of others, thereby allowing people to temporarily empathize and understand the dilemmas others encountered. Her ethical position that manifests an openness towards others and their mutual respect had political implications – democratic socialism.

While Beauvoir and Sartre have a reputation for being dogmatic Marxists (see Sunil Kilhani and Tony Judt), this is a glib treatment of their activism and one that accords much more with Sartre's writings of the early '50s than Beauvoir's. Sartre was committed to challenging anticommunism, and therefore approached Soviet shortcomings cautiously (before 1956 and the invasion of Hungary). This involved exploring the situation of the USSR – providing an understanding rather than a critique (Merleau-Ponty 1992, 52). However, neither simply supported worldwide revolution: their support was more qualified. Beauvoir, in particular, is more discerning, challenging hierarchies in power and prejudicial behaviours wherever they appear. Communist regimes that tried to regulate people's private lives and deny personal liberty where appraised. They visited Cuba, where they interviewed Castro and Che Guevara, and left-leaning regimes in Brazil and Algeria; although they communicated the achievements of these governments, they were not uncritical of their sexual politics and discrimination against gay men. She praised Tito's efforts on the economic front (*ASD*, 266) but was critical of his policy towards dissident writers. While these regimes were making some progress on the economic front, moving towards providing goods and services to the poor, Beauvoir was concerned that they did not support democracy nor respect the individuality of their citizens. She publicly criticized Cuba's repression of homosexuals and failure to tolerate criticism, opposition, and sexual differences. In the early 1960s, she was optimistic about the prospects of meaningful radical change in China, Cuba, and Algeria, but her optimism turned to disappointment as their repressive and undemocratic practices were revealed. Even before Algerian independence in 1962, Beauvoir was skeptical about women's status dramatically improving in a politically independent Algeria under their authority. Her involvement in the Algerian struggle for independence highlighted her specific interest in Muslim women as well as the more general struggle against colonialism. She did not see Algerian independence as part of a universal working-class movement, for it addressed the specific needs and goals of a postcolonial society struggling for self-governance in a predominantly Muslim milieu. This posed particular problems for Muslim women and men.

Beauvoir supported popular political struggles for self-governance amongst formerly colonized countries as well as struggles for social justice on behalf of repressed minority groups within societies. For a short time it was possible to hope that "the emancipation of the underdeveloped countries in Africa would bring fresh life to civilization," "but the gloomy forecasts of Dumont have been confirmed" (*ASD*, 448). Her support of postcolonial societies was prescient, yet she was not naive: "growing population out paces economic growth, progressive regimes were overthrown and poverty and exploitation persist" (448). She found "no great comfort in Latin America either"; her revolutionary contacts in Venezuela, Bolivia, and Colombia apprised her that the chances of success were almost non-existent (450). Acknowledging Allende's victory in Chile, she was perceptive: "in all likelihood there is no future in it, alas" (450). Fully aware of the political, economic, and demographic difficulties these countries faced, she was not utopian.

Firmly committed to democratic socialism, she criticized existing institutionalized power, and supported socialist projects as outbursts of democracy, but nevertheless drew attention to socialism's failure to meet its democratic goals. What distinguished her activism from more conventional Marxists was her ability to appreciate the specific, local, and social character of struggles without directly linking them to the class struggle. In addition, she did not assume these struggles should be directed by an institutionalized communist or socialist party. Without endorsing all those who claimed to be revolutionary (i.e. she did not endorse the feminists of difference), she nevertheless was optimistic that many struggles were ultimately connected to further the demands of the revolutionary left – the demands of liberty and equality.

An example of her engagement with local and concrete protests and her effort to build democratic citizenry from the bottom up is evident in her work exposing an industrial accident in the small town of Méru (11 May 1967). The radical paper *J'accuse* approached Beauvoir to write an article to publicize this exceptionally horrible industrial accident (*ASD*, 474). This short article has been translated and reprinted in *Political Writings* (287–91) as "In France Today, Killing Goes Unpunished." A factory packed with gaseous substances, for the manufacture of insecticides and beauty products, blew up. Witnesses saw young girls rushing out, in flames from head to foot, half naked, screaming. Of eighty-seven workers that day, fifty-seven were taken to hospital; three died. The hospitalized were subject to painful treatment that went on for at least a year and a half. The manager had quit several months earlier as a consequence of his disgust with the shoddy running of the factory. The current director was charged with negligence and sentenced to manslaughter by negligence. His penalty was limited to one year and a fine of 20,000 francs, and within a few months he was working elsewhere.

Beauvoir found the director and company seriously negligent, allowing health and safety violations: stockpiling too many potentially lethal gases, using faulty equipment, not carrying out safety measures. Also the inspectorate did not provide adequate safety checks. A fifteen-year-old boy was responsible for monitoring the plant safety and his protests of leaking gases were ignored. The accident could have been avoided had the factory been inspected by a health and safety inspector. This tragedy was exacerbated by the legal system that did not adequately punish the director and a social security system that did not fully cover those injured workers who were not fully incapacitated. Beauvoir not only publicized this industrial disaster but helped women who were severely burned to receive compensation from the state. This particular case reveals how concrete and specific Beauvoir's activism could be and how she focused on reform within the system rather than simply dismissing these complaints as an inevitable outcome of capitalism. She believed that reform would deepen and extend democratic forces. This would fuel future counter-hegemonic forces.

Beauvoir's action was not taken under the auspices of the PCF, nor the socialist party, nor was it part of the non-communist left. Although she linked the exploitation these women workers suffered and the failure of the liberal democratic state to ensure workplace safety to the power of capital to maximize profits, she did not seek to mobilize these women to the PCF or recruit them to join (other) existing left-wing parties, nor did she speak in a universal revolutionary voice. Her work did not involve general theoretical or grand ethical statements, but she used her skills as a writer and critical thinker to make sense of and publicize this particular tragedy in everyday language. She visited Méru many times in 1971 to cover the horrific industrial accident that occurred four years earlier (*ASD*, 474). The behaviour of the Inspection Service, the law that pardoned the plant director and the social security were "scandalous" (475). Beauvoir was called upon after four years to assist "the victims who were trying to combine to try to get a better deal on their pensions" (477). She became familiar with these girls who were mostly daughters of peasants, and "realized how necessary it was that the left-wing press, persecuted by those in power, should exist." She urges "The gauchiste papers … to tell the workers about what is happening within their own class – a subject that the bourgeois press either ignores or misrepresents" (478). While she hoped that these women would understand how their tragedy was a result of cost cutting measures, efforts to maximize corporate profit, she refrained from directing them. Such a tactic would ultimately hinder their political mobilization and be anti-democratic. She facilitated and nurtured their participation in their own struggle for social justice and thereby encouraged what today we call "performative politics." In doing so, she fostered their self-development and local and concrete forces of democracy, and escaped the Marxist teleological thinking of her day. Through the lens of situated universality, she believed that she contributed to radicalizing the populace without directing them.

In endorsing concrete struggles against social and economic injustice, Beauvoir believed that she was extending and strengthening anti-hegemonic forces. These women and their community were emotionally bound to this injustice given the suffering and loss they incurred. In Badiou's terms, this situation of injustice demanded a response, an ethical commitment. This is precisely how Beauvoir responded: she was committed to keeping alive the event, which the local authorities and government wanted to bury. She managed to get concessions from the state that it had been unwilling to offer at the outset. Unlike Foucault, who saw this work of taking a stand against the wrongs of the state as ethical (Foucault 1984, 379), Beauvoir saw this action of publicizing industrial crimes as political work: contributing to counter-hegemonic forces and enlarging the public sphere. Here she states her antipathy "to the revisionism of the USSR, the new bureaucracy set up by the Trotskyists" and the traditional left wing that "accepts the system, defining itself as a respectful opposition," sympathizing with the Maoists, "who stand for a root and branch denial of it" (*ASD*, 478). "In a country," she says, "that is resigned, half asleep, they stir things up, they arouse public opinion" (478). This is precisely what Beauvoir sought to do.

Beauvoir sustained the fidelity of the workers by popularizing the event, helping them gain compensation, and keeping alive the struggle. While these events did not explicitly further socialism, they did build counter hegemonic sentiments. These women realized how the state upheld the interests of the capitalist factory owners rather than make them accountable for their disregard for their workers' lives. Beauvoir also participated in many concrete struggles in Paris, such as the protests of unmarried mothers who were unjustly treated, women who were physically abused, and those denied contraception and abortion. These claimants were committed to rectifying miscarriages of justice. Far from contributing to the fragmentation of the left, by encouraging women to engage in protest around issues that directly affected them, Beauvoir politicized women, who might not otherwise be active participants. While these young peasant girls, or poor working-class women, might not have identified with the proletariat, in the process of their struggles, they had increasing sympathy for those who were excluded and oppressed. Nonetheless, she felt their engagement broadened and deepened support for radical structural change. However discrete and autonomous some struggles appeared on the surface, Beauvoir believed that change was best served through engaging diverse local struggles, which people were affectively bound to. In the process, forces of democratic socialism would develop.

ACTIVISM AND THE STUDENTS: MAY '68

Since I deal with Beauvoir's involvement in Algerian War in the next chapter, I will detail her activism in the '60s to May '68. May '68 marked a watershed in liberal democratic politics. Students were protesting the American war in Vietnam, authoritarian party politics that were silencing dissent and denying popular participation, as well as hierarchal educational practices. These protests spread throughout Europe and the Americas. Beauvoir was an active participant and documented her reflections on these events in her autobiography *All Said and Done.* Again, instead of assuming the role of the universal intellectual, someone "who knew the true and best for all" (Foucault 1986, 68). Beauvoir fostered grassroots power and supported the students and teachers in articulating their own needs and desires. While she recognized the strength of proletarian agency, she believed that disgruntled teachers and students should collaborate with the working classes and thereby broaden the base of their resistance. May '68 confirmed her belief that although the students and workers were differently situated, they could collaborate and work towards common goals.

In France, students and teachers in *lycées* and universities went on strike to criticize hierarchical teaching practices, mass education, and their alienation from French society. As early as February 1964, Beauvoir notes, "Kravetz, the president of the student's union, wrote an article for *Les Temps modernes,* in which he attacked the system of lectures; he called for a complete transformation of the relationship between teachers and students" (*ASD*, 454). "The students launched a campaign to reject all subordination of rank, and student's subordination to the needs of technology" (455). She saw these complaints as consistent with student action elsewhere. There were parallel movements in Germany, Japan, and the USA (notably Berkeley, California). The students wanted more of a role in determining what and how they were taught, and more say in their democratic societies. In 1965, Berkeley students protested violations of their free speech: their right to be involved in off-campus issues, the civil rights movement, and the anti-war movement.

In France as well, the student protests went beyond their specific interests to a general critique of society. When their protests were met with police violence, trade unionists joined them and the government feared not only civil unrest but revolution as well. For Beauvoir, this illustrated the capacity of minority groups (other than the proletariat) to catalyze a general strike and their potential for broadening emancipatory agency: "The Metro and buses stopped, banks closed and people had no ready cash. Citroen went out on strike. Employees of the national French radio station who were involved in the civil disturbance were fired. By May 24th 9–10 million workers were on strike" (*ASD*, 459). Student protest in May '68 met with such acts of state power that the protest escalated to an all out war against the French state. Rank and file trade unionists supported the students, though the communist party clung to its role as *chef* (*EA*, 109) of the revolution. Though Beauvoir believed the revolution required cooperation and solidarity, collaboration between the students and the proletariat, this did not happen. Both Beauvoir and Sartre were annoyed by the leadership of the PCF, and by the trade unions who refused to allow their workers to collaborate with the students. The Confédération française démocratique du travail (CFDT) and the Confédération générale du travail (CGT), two powerful French unions, joined the marches in the early days but did not allow their members to be part of the collective discussions and debates that the students organized. Beauvoir reports that when the students went to striking factories, the unions would not let them in (*ASD*, 459). Eventually de Gaulle took command, dissolved the National Assembly, and called for a new election in June, which he won. After several weeks of manned barricades and insurrectionary politics, the leaderships of the PCF and the unions called off the struggle. A deal was struck between the PCF, the trade union movement and the government to end the confrontations. The rank and file members of the unions and the PCF were terribly disappointed; they felt betrayed. The coalitional movement that was forming was hijacked. The resistance and violence ended precipitously, although the social and political effects were long-lasting. Not only did May '68 involve serious critiques of existing forms of liberal democracy, Beauvoir believed these events confirmed the authoritarian tendencies of the PCF and the hierarchies within the union movement.

Although the insurgence and discontent began with the students and teachers, Beauvoir did not see their movement as separate from that of the striking car workers or public employees. She was critical of the behaviour of the unions who, following the PCF, dismissed the role of the students and teachers in the struggle. Following from the assumption that the proletariat was the universal agent of change and the PCF their living representative, it was assumed that the students should defer to their leadership. The crisis the students faced, Beauvoir insisted, was connected to problems of late capitalist society, and consequently the students would have to cooperate with the working classes to resolve it, but their struggle was not reducible to class interests. The student movement, she argued, was not a romantic outburst but a response to problems in neo-capitalism: "The students getting more and more numerous, seeing no future ahead of them, formed the focus at which the contradictions of neo-capitalism exploded. This meant the entire system was at stake and this directly involved the proletariat" (*ASD*, 464). However, the specific forms of student alienation, larger classes, authoritarian educational practices, were not problems that could be addressed by the proletariat. Beauvoir insisted that the students should articulate their specific interests and goals and, in the process, would establish grounds for collaboration. This was beginning to happen in May '68, until the leadership of the PCF and the trade union movement squashed this.

Beauvoir's pessimism regarding the PCF was not new, as we have seen. She challenged the idea of the party's central directives and assumption that the proletariat is the universal agent of change. Like Marx, she believed that first the battle of democracy should be won, but, unlike Marx, she supported democratic reforms and promoted multiple agents of change. Even before May '68, she was critical of the PCF's and the Soviet Union's unresponsiveness to local outbursts of democracy (i.e., in Yugoslavia, Czechoslovakia) and their authoritarian practices, which did not take seriously the opinions of disgruntled people, social movements, and intellectuals. Her criticism of the PCF intensified as the party's need to orchestrate and control the direction of the revolutionary movement led them to collaborate with the French government and exclude the students and even the rank and file of the trade union movement from discussion. The government and the CGT (a communist-led union) produced a deal to end the general strike in late May, but the membership of the CGT refused to ratify it and the students were left out of the process. To protest this Sartre put his name to a pamphlet, "The Communists Are Afraid of the Revolution" (Sartre 1998, 150), in which he accused the PCF of deliberately betraying the radical coalition between the students and workers and betraying the student hope for a new revolution. For Beauvoir, May '68 confirmed how different groups can collaborate to broaden the revolutionary base, yet the events also illustrate how hierarchal practices and elite politics can destroy collaboration.

EFFORTS TO RETHINK MARXIST POLITICS AFTER MAY '68

Sartre and Beauvoir's disdain for the undemocratic communist party practices led them towards a different form of Marxism: Maoism. Interestingly enough, in spite of their theoretical differences, some structuralists and poststructuralists, as well as the humanists, found

Maoism compelling.[10] Foucault, Althusser, Badiou, Kristeva, and the *Tel Quel* group embraced Maoism. It informed the Marxist Leninist Students at the École Normale as well as the Gauche prolétarienne. Maoist revolutionary socialism, Beauvoir notes, "does not accept the system but stands for a root and branch denial of it, it [is] preferable to the revisionism of the USSR and the new bureaucracy set up by the Trotskyists" (*ASD*, 478). Unlike the PCF, which perpetuated hierarchies and top-down decision-making, Beauvoir believed the Maoists were innovative, supporting "'fresh forces' in the young, the foreigners, the unorganized workers in small provincial factories, so much less under the influence and control of the unions than those in great industrial complexes. They encouraged action of a new kind – wildcat strikes and sequestrations" (478). Beauvoir was attracted by the French Maoist appeal to new agents/agencies of change and their efforts to tackle the problems of hierarchies that beset conventional left-wing politics. Departing from narrow proletarian politics and centralized political authority, the Chinese found themselves rethinking existing Marxist political strategies.

Maoism pursued non-economic change and struggled to forge new relations between the elite and the peasants. Mao was convinced that nationalizing the means of production was not enough to ensure that power would be in the hands of the workers and peasants (446). Departing from the more traditional Marxist theory of power that focused on the industrial working classes and unions, Mao adapted Marxism to the Chinese people's specific situation, and supported peasant-led socialism. Challenging the hierarchical party tactics that characterized the Bolsheviks, Mao wanted people to have the right to speak; he wanted to empower the peasantry. The cultural revolution made efforts to ensure the Chinese peasants developed their capacity to participate in social and political life. This involved not simply producing new ideas but also creating new relations between the educated middle classes and the peasants by transferring social and political power to the masses and putting the intellectuals in the fields and the factories. Beauvoir believed this was an interesting experiment and consistent with some of the students' desire to overturn institutionalized hierarchies and get rid of elitist knowledge.[11] Rejecting the Soviets' abstract deductive logic of the

10 Richard Wolin's (2010) *The Wind from the East: French Intellectuals, the Cultural Revolution, and the Legacy of the 1960s* recounts this turn to Maoism.

11 It should be noted that the violence and suffering that the Cultural Revolution perpetrated was not known at the time. The experiments in forging new social relations between the peasants and intellectuals, however necessary, were bound to be undemocratic, given the Confucian elitist culture of the country.

proletariat and their economism, Beauvoir believed that Maoism was more responsive to the specific needs of the local population.

Beauvoir's interest in Chinese communism was qualified by strong reservations. Her position was not dogmatic, but grounded in a careful assessment of Chinese communist practice. She did not appreciate its triumphalism or its socialist realist approach to art and culture. In addition, she was concerned about its failure to protect individual liberty, its micropolitics of dogmatism, and demand for self-sacrifice (ASD, 447). When she first visited China in 1955, she was troubled by the workers' dogmatic and naive enthusiasm for the revolution. Just as the Soviets assumed the revolution would completely reconcile the individual and the community, eliminating the need for family and a private life, so too, did the Chinese communists, who gave up three weeks of holiday to work for the revolution. These workers also sacrificed their privacy for the revolution; the communist state was effective in rigorously regulating their personal lives, as well as cultivating an erotic attachment to the state. Beauvoir found this particularly troubling, for she recognized that true democratic socialism would abolish classes, not individuals (SS, 67). There would always be tensions between the individual and community; desires could not be regulated: they should never be submerged with collective interest. Personal (erotic) desires were disruptive of, or in tension with, the social order. These tensions should not be synthesized or expunged but respected (66). A politics that recognized differences and deviance was important. A revolutionary state that assumed that it could put an end to all social conflict or eliminate the individual was naive and dangerous. Instead of trying to harness concrete affective attachments for change, they tried to destroy them, thereby producing new enemies (i.e. the liberated woman). This evaluation is entirely in keeping with Beauvoir's more general insights in *The Ethics of Ambiguity*: total unconditional commitment to a political cause or movement was an act of bad faith, for it denies the reality of contingency and the need to judge revolutionary actions case by case. She was furthermore troubled by the top-down directives of the party, and the zealous followers of the Chinese revolution with their dogmatic and naive publications (ASD, 447).

Beauvoir, sympathetic to Mao for tackling the problems that the Soviet Union had failed to confront but concerned about the revolutionary zeal of his followers, was more cautious in her support of Maoism than was Sartre, for whom striving to break down both power differentials within the party and hierarchies between the workers and intellectuals was particularly important. He strongly identified with the Gauche prolétarienne, a pro-Maoist organization in France, which, Beauvoir tells us, allowed him to come to terms with his middle-class guilt. Mao's theory of the intellectual empowered him to act alongside the working classes.

Beauvoir was critical of Sartre for letting his Maoist friends persuade him "to take part in foolish ventures" (*ASD*, 14), such as the occupation of the basilica of Sacre Coeur in an attempt to gain public sympathy for a militant who had been disfigured by tear gas. The CRS (Compagnies républicaines de sécurité, the French riot police) physically brutalized the protestors. By luck, Sartre and a few friends escaped unscathed through a back exit. Given Sartre's fragile health, Beauvoir believed that he should not engage in such antics.

Street action and civil disobedience were necessary tactics, yet Beauvoir did not think it was appropriate for her, or Sartre, to pursue such actions. While writing may be deemed elitist, it was the form their activism should take, as it was appropriate to their particular skills. As writers, they were well situated to publicize revolutionary movements and local struggles for justice, as well as assume the role of the public intellectual. She used her status as a writer with an international reputation to draw public attention to radical causes and to exert pressure on public officials to be more responsive to the cries of the oppressed. Her actions encouraged minority groups to get involved politically, to take up their own causes and push for democratic social changes. To mobilize the oppressed, Beauvoir pursued her writing in the mainstream press and in novels. In later life she was involved in film production.

Consistent with her efforts to enrich the public sphere and include voices of the oppressed, she and Sartre took over the editorship of radical papers that had been banned and whose editors were imprisoned. Sartre became the official editor of *La cause du peuple*, a paper for the Maoist Gauche prolétarienne; Beauvoir took over the editorship of *L'Idiot international*, a paper that represented the daily life and struggle of the working classes and focused on, for example, exposing health and safety violations.

After May '68 and for the first time since the Second World War, left-wing papers had been confiscated by distributors. To publicize this censorship and to protest the government's heavy-handedness, Beauvoir and Sartre organized news conferences and took to the streets to sell the papers: "*Read La cause du people* – support the Freedom of the Press" (Appignanesi 2005, 154). They orchestrated other celebrities to do the same. Although they were not arrested, they were taken to the *préfecture de police* in the back of a paddy wagon to have their identities checked. This caused quite a stir. Sartre's celebrity status excluded him from the demeaning exercise of checking his identification. It is reported that de Gaulle said to the police, in reference to Sartre, "You cannot arrest Voltaire" (Crosland 1992, 407). Given the high profile of many of those involved in this struggle, and the fact that this was the first act of censorship since the war, the story caught the attention of the national and international presses – not without Beauvoir's help. She coordinated a media event through a broadcast by Radio Luxembourg, newspaper photographs, and TV coverage. The drama associated with the "arrest" of this elderly intellectual couple drew further attention to the cause. Semiotically, the image of two senior citizens being carted off to prison as serious security threats was laughable.

Some cynically condemned Beauvoir's display of media savvy. She managed to use her stature as a writer and public intellectual to influence politicians and garner media for her radical causes. As these new mediums of film, photography, and TV became increasingly significant, she learned to utilize the image and emotion as well as the printed word and argument.

THE WOMEN'S MOVEMENTS: COLLABORATING TO FURTHER SOCIAL EQUALITY

Beauvoir's pluralist and incrementalist approach to political agency is evident in her activism and specifically in support of feminism. Impressed by the energy of the women's movements and protests in the late '60s Beauvoir turned her attention to the MLF in 1971. Given the importance of class and material inequality in her thinking this was less a turn away from socialism and more a support for a lively and engaged movement for social equality. In addition to supporting women and students as new agents of change, she expressly endorsed diverse strategies to further the liberation of women. She wrote articles and novels, demonstrated in the street, lobbied politicians, and appeared in films and photographs. In order to further the politicization of women, she supported reformist as well as revolutionary tactics, putting pressure upon the state at the same time as cultivating popular resistance to state activities. There is some debate amongst feminist scholars around her feminism. When Alice Schwarzer, an MLF activist, interviewed Beauvoir for the first edition of *Ms* magazine in the US (July 1972), she made much of Beauvoir's statement "I am a feminist" announcing Beauvoir's "conversion to feminism" (*FW*, 10). However Sylvie Chaperon notes Beauvoir had announced her feminism in an interview in November 1949. Her commitment to feminism was evident as well in articles written as early as 1947. Throughout the '50s and '60s there is further evidence of her persistent commitment to feminism. Prior to her research for *The Second Sex*, Beauvoir said she hadn't attended to her identity as a woman; but the research and writing process highlighted, for her, the specific conditions of women's gendered situation.

Beauvoir was not an armchair intellectual: she answered hundreds of these letters and spent much time with anonymous women and young academics to encourage their independence. Reaching out to the population at large, in 1959 she wrote prefaces to two books authored by Lagroua Weill-Hallé (1960, 281–7), which were central to the family planning, contraception, and abortion movements. The concern with reproductive choice was in stark contrast to the PCF's pro-family position. In the same year (1959) she wrote an article for *Esquire* magazine on Brigitte Bardot and the Lolita Syndrome. In spite of the actress's role as a sex symbol, Beauvoir was sympathetic to Bardot's attitude of cultivated indifference towards men. "She speaks only faintly of getting married, she declares enthusiastically that she adores the country and dreams of taking up farming" (123). Appealing to the bourgeoisie who value farming and finance, Bardot is portrayed as always knowing the price of things; she follows the stock market closely and gives her broker well-informed instructions (124). "Bardot is bent on becoming, she does not cast spells, she is on the go" (124); she is hardly reducible to a sex icon. In fact, Beauvoir believes Bardot opened up a conflict between those who believe sexual mores are fixed, enduring, and thought she "embodied the immorality of our age" and those who believe mores should evolve. Bardot challenges certain taboos accepted by the conservatives, specifically their distaste for forward-looking notions of sexual autonomy. This article was meant to politicize uneducated women and those who read film gossip – she hoped to persuade such readers.

What was new in 1971 was not that Beauvoir became a feminist, but rather that she refused socialism's leadership of women. In spite of the insufficiencies of actually existing socialism, Beauvoir never gave up the ideals of equality and liberty for all. She had struggled since the late '40s to support social justice and structural change and extend radical political agency. Her feminism from 1949 onwards was part of that commitment. Hence her affiliation in the Mouvement des Femmes (MLF) was with the materialist/socialist feminists in the collective and not with the radical feminist current, who were concerned primarily with sexual freedom and lesbian politics. Anne Zelensky has a different reading of events: she does not believe Beauvoir converted to feminism in 1971, and she was not late in joining the MLF, which Alice Schwarzer had implied. "In fact it had just got started when Beauvoir asked to meet us" (*FW*, 182).

On 5 April 1971 Beauvoir signed the "Manifesto of 343" published in the "Nouvel Observateur." Three hundred and forty-three women admitted they had had an illegal abortion, a tactic the MLF used to push for decriminalizing abortion. She had not been marginal to this event, nor was she a late joiner; in fact, Beauvoir had proposed the original list of personalities to be recruited. She and others faced criminal prosecution since abortion was against the law. They called for free and legal access to abortion, arguing that 800,000 to 1,000,000 French women had illegal abortions per year, under unsafe conditions; women were not treated as other humans, they didn't have a right to their bodies (*ASD*, 479). "The Manifesto galvanized efforts for reform. Others mockingly dubbed it the Manifesto of 343 sluts" (Sanos 2016, 164). In June 1971, Beauvoir and Halimi formed the feminist group Choisir, aimed at legalizing abortion. In October 1972, they defended Marie-Claire Chevalier in the Bobigny trial. A seventeen-year-old unmarried daughter of a subway driver had been raped and underwent an abortion. Unable to afford the fees of a medical doctor, she went "to someone who had learned to do abortions for herself" (Sanos 2016, 165). She was tried and acquitted under the 1920 law.[12] Nevertheless from a feminist standpoint the grounds of her acquittal were less than satisfactory. "She did not freely and deliberately choose to commit the act with which she was charged … but was subject to the moral, familial and social pressures" (167). The judge's argument reproduced gender stereotypes. Much like the Boupacha trial ten years earlier, 30,000 transcripts of the case were sold within a few days. Pressure on the French government, from feminists and from members of the medical establishment (who declared that they would perform abortions), intensified. In 1975 France caved in to national and international pressure. In 1973, Roe versus Wade had overturned restrictions on abortion in the USA, in 1966 Britain had legalized abortion, in 1974 West Germany had, so France could be seen as following suit.

Throughout the '70s Beauvoir participated in protests, campaigns, and intellectual work around feminist issues. In 1974 she was named director of Les Droits des femmes, a predominantly liberal feminist social movement that lobbied the state for the rights of battered women (Tidd 2004, 80). Many Marxists saw this as a reformist and exclusively feminist venture, yet it was consistent with her efforts to politicize women. She also optimistic that commitment to gender equality would contribute to coalitions with other struggles for social equality.

She became editor of the materialist feminist journal *Questions féministes* in 1977 and insisted that *Les Temps modernes* have a women's section to explore the effects of patriarchal power in everyday situations. She became involved in local, national, and international struggles for

12 The 1920 act was passed after the Great War with the purpose of ending the neo-Malthusian movement forbidding pro-contraception propaganda and outlawing abortion.

women's rights and against violence against women: supporting struggles for free contraception, abortion rights, women's self representation, and participation in social movements. So, although theoretically she favoured a socialist/feminist position that recognized the need for social structural change, she also called for cultural change and strategically supported reformist or distinctively women's issues. In *The Second Sex* she calls for women to fight for their rights (*SS*, 75). Again, this was consistent with her belief that cultural as well as political reform would be necessary to disrupt woman's Otherness, her social inferiority and inequality. Encouraging social reforms and diverse agents of change, apart from the proletariat would not fragment or dissipate socialist politics but contributed to the proliferation of democratic subjectivities and thereby would broaden struggles for social inequality.

While many Beauvoirians see Beauvoir's feminism as a turn away from socialism, I argue that it is consistent with her earlier reflections on Marxism and socialism. Beauvoir's eclectic approach to theory meant she, too, opposed the theoretical certainty of conventional Marxism. While many theorists turned to anarchism and post-Marxism, in the wake of May '68, totally disillusioned with the communist party, Beauvoir had never been totally supportive of actually existing communism and socialism. Nevertheless she remained committed to emancipatory projects.

In the 1970s, Beauvoir shifted her interest and attention towards women's movements and away from revolutionary movements. Again, her politics were driven not by abstract ethical concerns or a feminist doctrine, but by her interest in engaging in energetic struggles that promised the freedom of all. She didn't turn away from socialism, or Marxism, but supplemented her socialist support by including plural forces of change. In fact, in 1972, when she identified herself as a feminist in *Ms* magazine, she still accommodated socialism. "Now when I speak of feminism I mean the fact of struggling for specifically feminine claims at the same time as carrying on the class war" (*ASD*, 491). Although her beliefs in freedom and equality had not fundamentally changed, the forces that she found around her had. It was no longer sufficient to call for revolutionary socialism to rectify the situation of women: women must organize and struggle for their liberation independently of Marxist revolutionaries. In 1949 she had been more optimistic that women's opportunities would evolve as society became more democratic and more socialist, gradually moving towards equality; this, however, had not happened. The status of women had scarcely changed at all in France, she notes in 1965, "in spite of some easing of matrimonial legislation and the legalization of birth control, abortion remained strictly forbidden and women exclusively performed household tasks. Their claims as workers were stifled" (*ASD*, 488). Marxists promised equality for all, but were rarely concerned with gender equality.

Although Beauvoir identified herself as a feminist, she did not generally support separatism until the '70s; earlier, she believed that men should be part of the movement and part of the solution. Here she dramatically departed from the French feminists of difference, primarily Irigaray and Cixous, "who celebrated distinctively feminine qualities, values or ways of life. [To] believe this would mean acknowledging the existence of a specifically feminine nature – that is to say agreeing with a myth invented by men to confine women to their oppressed state. For women it is not a question of asserting oneself but of becoming full-scale human beings" (494).[13] However in 1975, Beauvoir endorsed separatist political strategies. In interview with John Gerassi she rejected her former position (that a socialist revolution would achieve sexual equality) since there was no evidence that masculinist values and power had been challenged in socialist countries. Furthermore, she defended lesbian separatism as a strategy for change, noting that sexism was alive and well in left-wing organizations. Furthermore she acknowledged the modest improvement in women's situation over twenty-five years was due to feminism not socialism (in Tidd, 2004, 81).

While Beauvoir had changed her mind that socialist projects would liberate women, she argues that feminism is, by definition, left wing, because it is fighting for total equality – social equality is implied in the fight for sexual equality (79). As a materialist feminist, Beauvoir focused both on the particular struggles of women and on more general emancipatory struggles from the perspective of women. At the outset, she supported wages for housework, however by the mid-'70s she argued that housework ought to be shared between women and men. Unlike many socialist feminists, who are historical materialists and see women's oppression in terms of patriarchal and capitalist axes of oppression, Beauvoir loosened up the base/superstructure framework to admit the relative autonomy of political and cultural phenomena. Employing categories of alterity and recognizing the intersections of subjectivity based upon race, sexuality, gender, and class provided a more subtle and

13 Although the feminists of difference believed that women had distinctively feminine qualities, they did not subscribe to essentialism; in fact, as we see Beauvoir herself felt women had a distinctive sexual/erotic life that should be allowed to develop, if the masculinist libidinal economy was challenged. So there are fewer theoretical differences between Irigaray and Beauvoir than their political stances would lead us to believe. Of course the separatist strategy of the French feminists of difference was different from the socialist feminists.

complex approach to oppression than class struggle alone. Furthermore I will argue, in the next section, her attention to how women have been culturally demeaned and treated as inferior, and her struggles for instantiating rights and practices that guarantee mutual respect, treating women on par with men, resonates with the politics of recognition.

Her awareness of women's deep-seated social inferiority led her to support the extension of women's rights as a means to further women's equality (*SS*, 75). Rights are not sufficient to grant women equality, but their effects need not be circumscribed by liberal democracy. Beauvoir believed they would contribute to the politicization of women and thereby further projects of radical humanism. She recognized the importance of rights to counter sexual inequality, protesting the treatment of battered women and the unwed mothers institutionalized in a Paris residence (*ASD*, 282, 283) who were disgraced, infantilized, and even beaten by their parents and authorities for their "sinful acts." Beauvoir wanted these young women to be respected and treated as humans rather than "bad girls." "If they were children then the law affecting adults should not be applied to them" (483). Her intervention was not explicitly related to class politics but was the struggle for these women's just treatment. Again she believed that furthering their specific claims for respect and dignity would contribute not only to their own freedom but to the freedom of all.

6

Rethinking the Role of the Critical Intellectual: Liberating or Colonizing?

BEAUVOIR'S POLITICAL ACTIVITIES during the Algerian War (1954–62), in particular her defence of Djamila Boupacha, provide the backdrop on which to discuss the disputed role of the intellectual. Boupacha, a member of the FLN (the Algerian independence movement), was tortured and raped by French soldiers to garner information. In protesting her torture, Gisèle Halimi, Boupacha's lawyer, solicited Simone de Beauvoir's assistance to mount her defence. Beauvoir's intervention raises the question of whether an intellectual can represent a marginal group or it is impossible to escape appropriating minority voices and thereby contributing to their disempowerment. At the time, the reputed father of postcolonial theory – Frantz Fanon – complained that French intellectuals were narcissistic, more concerned with blemishes on their republican honour than with the suffering of the local Algerians. Their work did not contribute to the development of the Algerian independence movements, but kept the Algerians subordinate. I will use Beauvoir's activism around the defence of Boupacha to explore debates around the universal/specific intellectual, identity/post-identity politics, the use of recognitional (affirmative) versus transformatory strategies, and, finally, the role of affective/emotive experiences.

It is also worth noting again that French philosophers all too readily glossed over Beauvoir's contributions to activist theory and practice. As a Sartrean and later a feminist, she was either seen as having nothing new to add or her feminist convictions were too overly narrow to qualify her as a public intellectual. Not only did the male-stream thinkers find her ideas lacking, but also her contemporary poststructuralist critics believed that her universalist thinking was indifferent to difference. It was assumed that she upheld male norms and values for women. As I have shown, Beauvoir was much more sensitive to difference than is acknowledged by these critics and she did not cherish the sovereign rational subject (EA, 2). In fact, beginning with differently situated embodied subjects, taking into account their cultural, socio-economic, and political circumstances, she works to help them live a less restrictive life. Departing from the idea that women would be fully realized in socialist society, she also resisted positing universal goals and abstract principles that movements should abide by. As I have argued in the previous chapters, her radical humanism avoids an economistic logic and appreciates multiple agents of change and numerous struggles for justice, encouraging activists to embed themselves in existing projects of freedoms: struggles against cultural harms, sexual objectification, and colonial relations supplement concerns over economic exploitation, thereby broadening emancipatory politics.

Her appreciation of difference and plurality brings her into dialogue with identity theorists of the '80s. In fact, she has some affinity to them, as I have shown; while her ontology problematizes identity, she nonetheless appreciates the significance of identification and transformative identities in complex and decentred forms. In identifying, naming forces of oppression, she hopes to acknowledge past/present suffering and begin to catalyze strategies to overcome it. Unlike her poststructuralist critics – who refuse identity and spurn experience, believing that in naming and recognizing oppression one will unwittingly affirm and thereby sustain the forces of oppression[1] – Beauvoir believes that identity strategies can be transformative, insofar as they avoid essentialism and begin to tackle the forces that sustain oppression.

In contrast to more conventional Marxists, who identify the proletariat as the universal agent of change, the rational solution to history, or early feminists who saw educated white women as the privileged agent, Beauvoir appreciates the plurality of voices of struggle as well as the generative capacities of emotion and affect. She moves away from totalizing strategies – the aggregation of interest and the centrality of rational argument – and moves to accommodate plural struggles and different registers and valences of political agency. I draw upon her work as an activist intellectual to negotiate between identity and poststructuralist politics, as well as engage contemporary reflections on the role of emotion and affect in politics.

As discussed in the previous chapters, Beauvoir and Sartre's support of the PCF and silence over Soviet practices (before 1956) alienated poststructuralist thinkers, such as Foucault (1984) and Lyotard (1984), and revisionist historians like Furet (1981), Judt (1992), and Khilnani

1 Patchen Markell (2000) makes this argument.

(1993).[2] However, their critics have failed to acknowledge Beauvoir's efforts to address problems in communist practice, as I have shown in the chapters on Marxism. In fact, their commitment to reconciling liberty, ethics, and revolutionary socialism – by extending the scope of politics, through reconfiguring radical agency – provides more space to the situated relational subject and avoids the logic of the vanguard party. So while she did not renounce or denounce communism (until the mid-'50s), the existence of the Soviet work camps and secret police, and the intolerance of opposition and vigilant regulation of everyday life made it impossible for Beauvoir (or Sartre for that matter) to support actually existing communism.

As I have argued, Beauvoir's political ideas cannot be assumed to be Sartrean; she had a different attitude to the PCF. Furthermore, while Sartre argued that Marxism was unsurpassable, Beauvoir had more of a strategic interest in it. Insofar as it inspired contemporary struggles for freedom, it was valuable to a broader struggle for freedom. This attitude towards Marxism was not common to other French intellectuals at the time. There was strong support for communism amongst the students of Althusser (Foucault); however, May '68 catalyzed a dismissal of revolutionary socialism. The politics of the party and privileges accorded the Marxist intellectual came into disrepute. They were reiterating hierarchal and bureaucratic politics rather than eradicating them.

Lyotard believed that Marxism has lost its significance. Its grand narratives were no longer plausible (1979). Progression towards social enlightenment, emancipation, and its totalizing tendencies lost their credibility in the face of the gulag. So, he believes, one must turn to specific struggles and can do no more than offer *petits récits*. Foucault agrees that Marxism lost its salience. The Marxist intellectual who works in the modality of "universal," the "exemplary," the "just-and-true-for-all" (Foucault 1984, 68), is not only naive but also dangerous. Both were wary of revolutionary projects and the politics of universal intellectuals. They both believed contemporary intellectuals should be engaged in specific, everyday struggles. The work of the specific intellectual would be more effective than the universal intellectual. Their target was Sartre, and Beauvoir by association, who travelled around the world embracing the revolution in all its forms. Without significant local knowledge, according to Foucault, they supported local radical movements. Foucault

2 Francois Furet, Sunil Khilnani, and Tony Judt are renowned revisionist historians who claim the post-war French Marxist intellectuals, who were all more or less faithful to and uncritical of the PCF until the late '50s and '60s, diminished the credibility of the radical left by forestalling their critique of the communist policies.

charged them with acting as universal consciences/consciousnesses, inspiring and directing revolutionary change without being apprised of the work they did. Without in any way trying to direct the Algerian revolution, Beauvoir helped the movement proceed, very respectful of her position as a French intellectual. Far from believing she had truth which had to be disseminated to all, her situated perspective problematizes liberal/enlightenment notions of objective truth, "an Archimedean perspective – view from nowhere" (Marso 2012b). These criticisms attributed to Sartre and Beauvoir were exaggerated: their interventions were always based upon local activists and promoted grassroots politics while being wary of the power of the intellectual. Furthermore this ignores the qualified and critical positions that both Beauvoir and Sartre held vis-à-vis communist and socialist revolutions (*ASD*, 36). Also I show how Foucault himself was culpable of errors of the universal intellectual during the Iranian revolution.

As I have previously argued, the May-68ers' dismissal of the Marxist intellectual is glib. While communist intellectuals were subject to directives of the party, and presumed they had the "truth" that would be handed down to the people, this was not true of Beauvoir. Her pluralistic approach to radical movements was suspicious of the top-down tactics of the "chefs" (*EA*, 109). They did not possess the truth; furthermore, her critique of historical materialism as deterministic and the Hegelian dialectic as teleological avoided the logic of totality. She did not fit the specific into teleological development – but tried to trace the specific lines of struggle to see how specific struggles could enlarge revolutionary struggle (generally). Her commitment to social equality and liberty and hence a politics of democratic socialism, was both universal in scope, but specific in practice. Beauvoir immersed herself in everyday struggles as they emerged in their specificity and concreteness with these values in mind. As we saw in the previous chapter, she was involved in specific struggles: helping women workers gain compensation after a factory fire (*ASD*, 474), battles over reproductive rights, and the mistreatment of unwed mothers (482), to name a few. So while many of the student Marxists abandoned revolutionary socialism in the wake of '68 (for its totalizing and totalitarian stance), Beauvoir had never condoned this totalizing stance, so she was not theoretically troubled by the failures of communism.

Both Marxists and post-Marxists struggle over the role of the intellectual. They were unclear whether a privileged individual could contribute to the empowerment of the oppressed or was certain to colonize them. In Marxist theory, the intellectual is not *of* the working class yet works towards the victory of the working class. This makes the intellectual both useful to the struggle, but also suspect. Further, it is assumed the intellectual can further proletarian agency but cannot take-up the emancipatory mission as liberator. For the proletariat was the universal agent of the revolution. Only the oppressed can assume this role. This leads to several key questions. Since the working classes/proletariat were not assuming their emancipatory role, what could be done? Since they were so immiserated or lulled by capitalism, the party and/or the committed intellectual had a pedagogic role to help the oppressed understand their interest and mobilize them to support the revolution. Marx himself had not envisaged the need for the party, since he imagined the working classes were ready to assume their political roles. However, he did see how middle-class intellectuals could meaningfully support the revolution.

More recently, Bourdieu argues that intellectuals have more autonomy than most subjects, since they are relatively free from market forces (see Bourdieu and Duverlie 1987, 205). As we have seen in previous chapters, Beauvoir is aware that one's social location has effects on one's conduct, but she is adamant that it does not determine what one thinks or what one does. Jean, in *The Blood of Others*, supports this position, confirming Bourdieu's position: radical intellectuals are freer from their ties of class, since they are engaged in revolutionary politics. Specifically in *The Second Sex*, Beauvoir argues that more educated and committed women are more suited to explore/understand women's oppression (*SS*, 14). So, unlike the Hegelian Marxists who assume that the most oppressed or exploited women are ideally suited to understand and change the system, Beauvoir argues their experience does not necessarily equip them to translate their experiences into words. "Yet they know the feminine world more intimately than do men do because our roots are in it" (14) and that will potentially make their understanding more apt. However, she does not believe this knowledge justifies her and other middle-class intellectuals to direct the struggle, but they undoubtedly have an important role to play.

Authorities, like the party and the intellectual, came under attack in May '68. Foucault, Deleuze, and even Sartre believed the intellectual should move over and let the working classes speak and act (Ross 1990, 115). They did not need the intellectuals to analyze their situation or help them determine their interests. It was not knowledge or know-how that they lacked, but power. Beauvoir was also aware of the need for workers, students, young unwed mothers, dependent wives, colonized subjects to develop their skills and participate in public life. Although she thought the intellectual had a role in publicizing their struggles, these oppressed minorities must commit to their struggle and persist.

Since the communist party and the communist intellectuals had shown little interest in empowering the oppressed, they were condemned.

THE EXISTENTIAL SUPPLEMENT

Existential philosophy holds that everyone is "free" and has to invent their own ethical/political stance in the context of material and political restraints. There are no abstract maxims, moral rules, or absolute political truths to determine what is to be done; one is responsible for judging each case on its own. One must give up seeking the guarantee of one's existence outside oneself, as well as believing in unconditioned values or unambiguous choices (*PW*, 291). This means that revolutionary socialism or democratic socialism will be judged in terms of its specific actions, not in terms of intentions or future goals. Further, there are no pure agents of change: neither the proletariat nor the intellectual. Beauvoir does not believe that the intellectual is a universal consciousness/conscience who assists universal agents of change. She says: "Universal absolute man exists nowhere" (*EA*, 112). "Whereas for existentialism, it is not the impersonal universal man who is the source of values, but the plurality of concrete particular men projecting themselves toward their ends on the basis of situations, whose particularity is as radical and as irreducible as subjectivity itself" (17–18). Thrown into the world, a free spontaneity "adheres to the concrete and particular, by which it defines itself by thrusting towards a goal" (26). This act of "adhering to the concrete and the particular" challenges both top-down politics and universal agency.

Beauvoir presumes freedom has a material as well as an immaterial aspect. One acts on the basis of "physiological possibilities, but the body itself is not a brute fact. It expresses our relationship to the world, and that is why it is an object of sympathy or repulsion" (31). So the body is the entwining of the material and the symbolic, history and culture. The past does not determine the present, but it is not without effects. The subject is both embedded and embodied; yet moving towards a specific goal presumes emerging "into an open future" (82). So there is an indeterminacy and impersonality to the act of freedom for "freedom cannot will itself without willing itself as an indefinite movement" (31). Moral choice is free and therefore unforeseeable (40), yet she reminds us "it is always on the basis of what one has been that a man decides upon what he wants" (40). Hence assuming one's past is important as well as reconfiguring one's relations to others. As I have said, ethical and political freedom involves others. Lori Marso confirms my reading of Beauvoir, pointing to Beauvoir's commitment: "We are responsible to ourselves and others to expand the scope of freedom for all by collectively altering the political conditions in which our acts play out" (Marso 2012a, 177).

Beauvoir appreciates the importance of history: the context in which our acts play out. Actors must appreciate recurring subjective patterns (*EA*, 41) and structures that circumscribe the field of political action, yet history is contingent and indeterminate. Exterior or macroforces have effects on one's situation, as well as one's personal history: "There is a sort of predestination issuing not from external tyranny but from the operation of the subject itself" (41). Here she recognizes how one's past figures into the present and future. Politics must respect lived experience – where the past and present, the personal and public entwine. Here, the emotional and affective spheres of life are as important in cultivating or impeding revolutionary change as structural and historical forces. Accommodating the affective, pre-personal aspects of human agency as a factor in action, she challenges reasoned argument and structural forces as the stuff of politics. However unlike the Deleuzeans who focus upon the disruptive capacity of affect, in contrast to the compliant effects of feelings, Beauvoir believes emotion too can further change, and not simply further the molar powers of the state, family.

Beauvoir's ontology privileges genuine human existence. This does not prescribe a substantive or "collective end" of history, but privileges certain political values and experiences over others. In making a commitment to a specific concrete struggle, Beauvoir argues, one responds to an injustice, one is "true" to a cause.[3] Does Beauvoir believe we can be true and committed to *any* cause? No. Free projects must be universalizable: "in willing oneself free," she says, "one wills the freedom of all" (73). This does not predetermine political means or goals, but it does rule out certain freely willed actions (i.e. authoritarian and hierarchal practices) that deny another's freedom, and projects that are not addressed to all. Treating a human as if it were an object to be manipulated denies human ambiguity. Projects that instantiate those practices, such as National Socialism, or slavery, are unjustifiable. Political projects that are divisive and bellicose are also refused. To treat the other as if it were an object to be manipulated or coerced is to foreclose human ambiguity and freedom. In fact, it is to commit a crime against humanity (*PW*, 249). Furthermore, to embrace scientific, historical, or psychological models as dictating human conduct loses sight of our human capacity to

3 This ethical attitude, which Badiou also traces, cannot be applied to any event but a "true" event, an event addressed to all. So sexist, racist, xenophobic movements are ruled out, as they are for Beauvoir. See Critchley 2013, 44–9.

distinguish ourselves from the situation – act responsibly and freely within the parameters of a situation.

Beauvoir's ontological speculations provide ethical and political direction. Although human wilfulness, moving spontaneously towards others, may be a precondition for freedom, it is not identical to effective freedom. To be "truly" free, one must make freedom one's project. It is not simply sufficient to wish for the freedom of oneself and others, but one must work towards its realization. Beauvoir recognizes this process as continual and fraught with anxiety. We are tempted to avoid the continual choice "in laziness, heedlessness, cowardice ... we (regularly) refuse or flee our freedom" (*EA*, 25). Yet, it is essential to further freedom and accept responsibility for our acts. In spite of the difficulty in doing so, since I never act alone, I must assume responsibility for acts that I have willed, but also those that I collaborate with.

Not only do Beauvoir's existential assumptions involve a rethinking of the Marxist intellectual, as we have seen, but they also prompt a rethinking of identity politics. Exponents of identity politics have a different understanding of authentic action and representation. It is not about our appropriate relation to human existence, as existentialists assume, but markers of minority identity. Minority groups are concerned with identity markers that determine who is an authentic subject. From this perspective, Beauvoir's privileged status rules her out as a representative of minority women. More recent debates have problematized the delimitation of group identity: given the complexity and multiplicity of group identifications, it is difficult to delimit who is part of the community and who is not. Since everyone's social location is unique, Linda Alcoff convincingly argues, "one could imagine that one could only speak for oneself. And even when one speaks for oneself, the speaker momentarily creates a public self, just as when speaking for others producing a more unified self that any experience can support" (Alcoff 1991/1992, 10). So the problem of representation underlies all cases of speaking for, whether I am speaking for others or myself. So aspiring for authentic group representations is illusory. This isn't to say that it would not be better for members of marginal groups to "represent" themselves, to come to their own truths, insofar as it is possible. It is also important to encourage intellectuals to listen and let minority groups speak for themselves and determine their priorities and strategies as much as possible. But, admittedly, there are situations when oppressed groups can benefit from intellectuals/activists taking up their causes and speaking for them, helping them explore their needs, understand their situation, and establish their goals. Both Linda Alcoff and Gayatri Spivak are concerned that identity and poststructuralist politics have precipitated a retreat of the intellectual from the public space (Alcoff 1991/1992, 17; Spivak 1988, 275). While there were clearly problems when privileged feminists spoke on behalf of all women as if they understood their situation and knew how to proceed, the total retreat from speaking for, as well as the self-abnegating intellectual who endorses such a position, is problematic. When Foucault and Deleuze endorse the idea that workers or the oppressed know their best interest, and can articulate it unproblematically, as well as propose strategies, Spivak believes they have dismissed ideological critique, overly hastily. The case of Boupacha will provide further fodder for reflection. Consistent with Foucault's rituals of speaking, Alcoff suggests one must look at the text, the utterance, as well as the social location of the speaker and the discursive context. We will look carefully at Beauvoir's narration of Boupacha's story of torture and rape, her social location, and the discursive context, to better appreciate her speaking or representing Boupacha. Her activist intervention must be understood in the context of her inability to tell her own story and even if she managed this, it was highly unlikely that the French or international press would have picked it up. So Beauvoir's and Halimi's speaking for Boupacha were vital for her defence and a fairer trial. One could also argue – contra Fanon – that left intellectuals who exposed stories of torture and bloodshed aided the cause of Algerian independence, since telling their stories in the French popular press challenged the one-sidedness of their press. So getting another convincing account might have helped.

Beauvoir finesses a position between identity and post-identity or poststructuralist politics in an interesting way. She anticipates some of the insights we attribute to identity politics; marginalized and excluded groups (women, Blacks, the working classes) are in need of recognition and affirmation, since their oppression has been cultural as well as material in nature. However, recognitional strategies, forged under negative situations, are not simply to be celebrated. Nancy Fraser makes the case that recognitional strategies risk essentializing and reifying minority responses to their oppressive situations (2000, 108). Such strategies not only replicate stereotypes, but also the attention to cultural factors of marginality has been at the expense of recognizing the material factors that contribute to marginality (110). Hence these recognitional strategies don't confront the gravity of the problem. Beauvoir's literature provides sites where she engages women's subject formation, often identifying rather negative aspects of their lives, but in doing so she hopes to encourage women to understand their complicity and work on themselves. Obviously, there is much that cannot be changed by the individual, but there is much that can alongside others. Beauvoir believed that through the process of writing, telling their stories, oppressed minorities would develop an understanding of their situation. This could lead to self-development and contribute to the creation of new public selves, which members of their social group would benefit from. Beauvoir believed fiction as well as non-fiction could contribute to the emergence of new feminine imaginaries and identities that link one's past experiences with present transformatory projects. Recognitional strategies need not sustain their past negative relations, but could contribute to new affirmative identities that will help minority women overcome the forces that oppress them. She recognizes the positive need for identifications, past and present, in transforming oneself and others. These are not fixed, or essential, involving the discovery of an authentic group identity. But, rather, in assuming the past, trying to reconfigure it, Beauvoir believes one will loosen one's ties to the past. Promoting new identifications is a partial strategy, to mitigate past identities, but this strategy will not necessarily tackle the socio-economic and institutional underpinnings of oppression; this requires long-term commitment to collective projects of change.

Theoretically Beauvoir differs from those poststructuralists who dispense with processes of identification[4] – new and old – and revolutionary agency. But like them, Beauvoir's politics presumes concrete agents emerging out of a specific situation. One responds to a specific injustice; one commits oneself to rectifying this injustice. One's work is not based on a universal abstract self, nor the presumption of identity arising from one's social locations, but rather focuses on the "concrete work" to be done. This allows agents from various social locations (classes, races, genders) and subject positions to work/commit to a project. While poststructuralists like Butler and Brown presume that collaborative politics is the way to proceed, I believe Beauvoir's work on the defence of Boupacha is a good illustration of how collaborative work without identity of social location would proceed.

4 This is not true of Ernesto Laclau and Chantal Mouffe (1985), who refuse social (i.e. ethnic, linguistic) identification as reactionary but encourage the proliferation of radical democratic political identifications to deepen the democratic matrix. The search for an original agent and need to dispel the differences within by projecting it outward on an external enemy (Other) creates exclusionary and hateful practices. However, they, like other poststructuralists, see the subject as an effect of multiple discursive subject positions, hence agency is dynamic and able to assume diverse democratic struggles.

BEAUVOIR'S DEFENCE OF BOUPACHA: THE WORK OF A CRITICAL INTELLECTUAL

Djamila Boupacha (Beauvoir and Halimi 1962) provides evidence of Beauvoir's action as a critical intellectual. She does not assume that she is representing Algerian women or the political movement struggling for Algerian independence – the FLN – but rather is committed to defending Boupacha, who is seeking to charge and convict her rapists: French soldiers. She avoids some of the pitfalls of the two theoretical positions sketched above: she neither appeals to "genuine" identities to justify her intellectual work, nor does she presume one's social location dictates political agency. She doesn't speak in a universal voice that presumes to abstractly know what is to be done, but nor is her activism intervention totally relativist.

Beauvoir appreciates the need for identification and the importance of one's past in forging counter-hegemonic projects while recognizing that essentialized and static identities can tie people to the past in an unhealthy way. She does not simply affirm past/present identities, but does so only insofar as they further shifting old identities to support new ones. For Beauvoir, one must assume one's past to move beyond it. Recognitional strategies do not stabilize and legitimate the past, but help the process of transformation proceed.[5] This involves working on one's past experience, discarding old loyalties, dismissing hackneyed ways of thinking that contribute to one's oppression, and formulating new progressive identities that inspire new political projects. This process may be tenuous and open-ended, but identification is important in the process of personal and social change, particularly in light of the role identification plays in radical politics today. One need not assume "a collective conception" (*EA*, 108) of subjectivity, nor espouse an abstract human identity to promote collective work; Beauvoir believes one can respect difference and yet work alongside others towards a common goal (108).

5 Beauvoir does not reflect Nancy Fraser's sharp distinction between affirmative and transformative strategies, where the former sustains and legitimates the past, Fraser argues, and the latter facilitates systemic change. Many poststructuralists have assumed a similar position (Patchell Markell, Wendy Brown) arguing that recognitional (identity) politics, in the spirit of the former, affirms and sustains the past, and is an inclusive strategy, and to be spurned in the name of transformatory politics. Beauvoir sees more continuity between recognition and transformation. In being recognized one is socially validated; this positive experience does not merely affirm or reify a stable identity, but encourages one to participate in social groups and political movements thereby furthering the transformation of one's identity.

The poststructuralist tactic of strategic essentialism spurns even the minimal ontology Beauvoir asserts, assuming that one adopts an identity (e.g., Black woman) for pragmatic purposes only. This underestimates the importance of one's experience in impeding or facilitating political change. Beauvoir believes one needs to assume one's past to reconfigure one's relations with oneself and others. Yet she warns against preserving the past's hardened and mummified forms (95). In this context, the past involves "an appeal to the future, [the past] must destroyed in order to be saved" (95). A political identity must not essentialize the past, nor does it require one to lose oneself in a political cause. Commitment to a movement should not reify past identities, nor should it presume unqualified support, for one must continually affirm one's commitment based upon the judgment of the movement's success. While political alliances may be temporary and contingent, as poststructuralists believe, changes in one's relations to oneself and others are preconditions for assuming a position that is able to make such alliances, and for sustaining them.

The assumptions of strategic essentialism underestimate the kind of work necessary to catalyze social attachment and political change. It is not just a question of temporarily allying with a cause but affiliating with such causes over the long run that produces loyalty and successful collaboration. Beauvoir's long-standing commitment to radical causes was essential to her collaborative work around Algerian independence. Her support for Algerian independence was not something she slipped into temporarily, but grew out of her years of support for anti-colonial and emancipatory movements. Her work was inspired in part by her non-rationalist (radical) humanism. Although she recognized that she was privileged and, further, that her privilege was premised upon the oppression of native Algerians, she still supported their struggle for independence. Not that they shared experiences or where part of a collective, but she empathized with their sufferings and based her political commitment upon a desire to combat their injustice and inequality.

While she was outraged by France's conduct in Algeria, she refused to join some of her comrades who directly involved themselves in underground activity and violence. Although she admitted that such direct action might be the most authentic anti-colonial response, she felt that her role as a writer in disclosing the cover-ups of the French government and the abuses of military power would be significant. She explained her role as a critical intellectual: "If one wanted to remain faithful to one's anti-colonialist convictions and free oneself from complicity with this war, then underground activity remained the only possible course. I admired those who took part in such action. But to do so demanded total commitment, and it would have been cheating to pretend that I was capable of such a thing. I am not a woman of action: my reason for living is writing" (*FC*, 461).

So when Gisèle Halimi, a young activist attorney who was defending Djamila Boupacha, asked for Beauvoir's assistance, she agreed. She was not an armchair intellectual who simply wrote for the love of writing, but was actively engaged in the struggle to defend Boupacha. Her activism was a sign that she acknowledged the injustices that the colonized Algerians had experienced and supported their independence. Beauvoir's commitment to this cause came after years of feeling helpless and desperate to do something to contribute to Algerian independence.

IMPASSIONED JOURNALISM – DISCLOSING FACTS AND ENDORSING AFFECT

Boupacha, along with her father and brother, was arrested by the French army in Algiers and tortured in order to extract information about the whereabouts of two militant leaders. Her interrogators tried to force her to relinquish her belief in Algerian independence and act as a stool pigeon. Over thirty-three days, she was subject to physical battery, solitary confinement, persistent electrical shocks, bath torture, cigarette burns, and rape with a bottle. Legal reports described her as lashed to a chair, completely naked, while her captors spat mouthfuls of beer on her until she was dripping wet. Electrical terminals were twisted around her nipples, vagina, and anus, and electrical shocks were delivered to her body (*DB*, 29). In the end she falsely confessed to having planted a bomb in a café although it never detonated. Upon investigation, she insisted that her confession was false and extracted under duress. She had been warned by prison guards not to lodge any complaints of abuse to the authorities, but she refused to obey. The resulting trial, in pursuit of her attackers (1961), exposed these details to the world and horrified the French.

Beauvoir wrote several articles and co-authored a book with Halimi[6] telling Boupacha's story. She and Halimi formed the Djamila Boupacha Committee to intensify and coordinate their strategies and to ensure the publicity of her legal defence. They put pressure on various French officials to obtain a postponement of the trial to allow for the investigation of Boupacha's allegations. They also wanted to protect her witnesses and family from harassment and bring her torturers to justice. After much

6 Although this book was not published before the war's end, it garnered a worldwide audience and continues to provide testimony about the treatment of Algerians by the French.

pressure, they were successful in moving the proceedings out of Algeria to Caen in France.

The trial was highly publicized. The judge asked that photos of the prison guards responsible for the torture be submitted for identification, but the army commanders refused to comply, making it impossible for Boupacha to identify them. When the Treaty of Evian to end the war was signed in March 1962, prior to the trial's completion, her tormentors were included in the general amnesty given to all prisoners of war and French officials, and so they were never brought to justice.

Beauvoir's journalism blurred the distinctions between reason and emotion: the force of logic and the strength of passion. She based her plea for justice for Boupacha on careful arguments substantiated by facts as well as the explicit revelation of the acts of torture. By describing the "facts" in graphic detail she hoped to evoke strong emotions amongst the liberal or left-leaning public. She uncovered stories that the mainstream French media had ignored. She also challenged the government's narration of events and managed to persuade a segment of the French public of its crimes. Her description of events was harrowing: she hoped to solicit compassion, rage, and sympathy. As a critical intellectual, disclosing the "facts" that the state were covering up was not a trivial accomplishment given the powers and weight of French nationalism and the French population's "comfortable indifference" to their Algerian colony (65).

Beauvoir harnessed emotion in her work as a critical intellectual and, in so doing, parts ways with rationalists like Habermas. This was not a manipulative tactic, as we have seen, but was consistent with her recognition of the role of embodiment and emotion in political judgment. Our judgment presumes we are emotional and rational beings who are socially/historically situated. In publicizing the rape and torture of Boupacha by French soldiers in graphic detail, a story not told by the mainstream French press, Beauvoir hoped to influence the French public. She wrote an article for *Le Monde* that broke with the conventional story of the civil war, identifying the atrocities committed by the French armed forces. Departing from the norms of objective and balanced journalism, Beauvoir stood squarely behind Boupacha and the Algerians struggling for their independence. For example, François Mauriac wrote an article for *L'Express* that Halimi describes as "deceptively mild and ironic" (DB, 65) by comparison. Beauvoir's article was so inflammatory that the government ordered the seizure of all copies of the paper in Algiers and condemned her scandalous attitude. It was feared that the article would produce a public outcry. However, the French government's censorship drew attention to her article both in France and abroad.

As we have seen, Beauvoir rejects the idea of an impartial or balanced account: all stories and actions exude values and interests. The assumption of objective and balanced journalism is challenged. Facts do not speak for themselves, but must be interpreted. Beauvoir urges thinkers to be aware that the narration of a story presumes the values of the writer, yet she does not believe that relativism ensues. Since one is obliged to act ethically – in furthering the freedom of all – actions are not self-interested unless they are also in the collective interest. Thoughts and actions must take their bearings in history, work towards expanding one's own and other's horizons. In taking one's bearings with others, one also is respectful of others, and then one is more likely to be effective and moral. As situated beings, one must be apprised of one's values and how one's actions contribute to projects of collective freedom. In the case of the Algerian war of independence, 1960–62, one could not both agree with Beauvoir and support the position of the French state that wanted to keep Algeria a colony.

Beauvoir was aware of the problems associated with the assumptions of objective, dispassionate truth. Critiques of rationalism have proceeded apace since her death. Followers of Habermas endorse deliberation and dialogue in public spaces as a means to achieve popular consensus. Critics operating within or outside the deliberative model point to the role of emotion in debate. Susan Krause believes emotion, not reason, motivates one's commitment to the deliberative process. Further critics of deliberation, including Iris Young, show how disagreement rather than consensus is important to the public. In the context of Clinton welfare reform in 1996, social activists and social workers were asked to consensually come up with ways of implementing policy changes, so they would be implemented in a most humane way. Young notes that their right to refuse to cooperate with the changes in welfare reform, their failure to deliberate, was important to those whose welfare benefits and services were being cut (2001). Since they did not want to collaborate with the changes in welfare reform that reduced resources and services, challenging consensus was worthwhile. The deliberative model of democracy presumes logical argument and dialogue between interlocutors will deliver or approach consensus. Since emotion is incommunicable it is excised. This underestimates its significance. Not only do people have to be motivated to be involved in deliberative situations, but emotions sway people to support causes, whether they may appear irrational or unjustifiable. Beauvoir astutely acknowledges how important emotion and affects are in mobilizing support for radical political movements. Festivals, art, poetry, songs, theatre all are employed to mobilize feelings, furthering empathy and helping commitments. Far from being restricted to rational arguments and disclosing "facts," activists and intellectuals,

Beauvoir would argue, rely upon emotion. Beauvoir was no stranger to the use of emotion, as is evident in her description of events for Boupacha's defence.

The recent turn to affect and the vital materiality of things has involved a turn away from the significance of emotion (Bennett, Connolly). It is assumed matter is living, creating dissensual affects that disrupt usual habitual patterns and are to be distinguished from emotions that shore up well-worn paths of feeling: hate, empathy, love. Affect theorists tend to focus on autonomous affects, transmitted between humans and the environment or the human and non-human assemblages, believing these will transcend identities and connect otherwise heterogeneous beings and becomings. On the other hand, emotion and feelings help consolidate identities and contribute to compliance with the molar powers of the state and family. Beauvoir as we have seen believes emotion and feeling can be revolutionary: sympathy and compassion connect people to others, and foster collaborative work that might diminish negative emotions. This will be explored in the following chapter. Unlike the affect theorists who gloss over the role of emotion and bodily communication between humans, Beauvoir's approach is able to accommodate this domain and reveals how emotion and affects can trigger political commitment and action. Nonetheless the fruitfulness of her problematic has been glossed over.

This is unfortunate. In addition to strong negative affects and emotions (like hate and fear) that play into popular political prejudices, there are strong pleasurable experiences, of love or empathy, that also bind people to political affiliations, through processes that one is not fully aware of. I am thinking here, for example, of the way racism or sexism is affectively communicated between bodies as disgust. In her journey in the southern states Beauvoir describes: "Something fell onto our shoulders that would not lift all through the South; it was our own skin that became heavy and stifling, its color making us burn" (*ADD*, 202–3). Here affect is directly linked to Beauvoir's radical humanism, which opposes social inequalities on all fronts.

Obviously Beauvoir was not cognizant of subatomic matter or neuroscientific advances, though she was aware of the power of affects, the spontaneous powers of the physiological body. However she is more interested in human affects, and theorizes affects and emotion as more closely knit than do the affect theorists.

Affect and emotions are entwined, and mediate one's mode of being-in-the-world; these are not consciously chosen but corporeally expressed: how one casts oneself into the world is expressive of one's style. Beauvoir's phenomenological disposition takes her in a different direction than contemporary theorists of affect. For Beauvoir, one's capacity to be responsive or receptive is an effect of the particular embodied self, whereas affect theorists believe these experiences are not subjective but impersonal. Nevertheless, Beauvoir has it both ways; she says, "What is most essential in the human condition and in man's relation to the world is precisely what is defined by this unity of the world that we express and yet at the same times this singularity, this detotalization of the points of view that we take on it, or rather – since the term 'point of view' is a little idealistic – the situations in which we find ourselves in relation to it" (*LIT*, 199). So she says, "There is a world that is the same for us all, but on the other hand, we are all in situation in relation to it" (198). This allows for impersonal experiences as well as personal communication with the world.

Affect theorists focus upon impersonal reception of affects (flows of energies from things) and, as such, have strong connections to radical empiricists. Furthermore their flat ontology of immanence and their anti-humanism divert them from thinking about human emotion. Being open to the world, one imagines, allows a receptiveness to the sensible that is anatomically driven, but given subsequent lived experiences, for Beauvoir, affect gets channelled into subjective emotions. These differences will be elaborated in the next chapter, where I explore *The Blood of Others* in more detail.[7] Since Beauvoir is interested in embodied subjects, rather than humans as a part of non-human assemblages, affects are often tied to/mediated by emotion. Affects may trigger sympathetic emotions, which prompt political commitment and action. Beauvoir assumed as much. Her detailed description of Boupacha's torture presumes the power of negative affect. Visualizing French troops spitting beer upon Boupacha's naked body, knowing that electrical wires were attached to her nipples and vagina sending electrical currents through her body, hearing that a bottle was used to rape her, Beauvoir elicits visceral responses from her readers. Beauvoir wrote to incite support for her cause. Her description of the torture and rape would have been difficult for many women and men to read. However Beauvoir believes her effectivity of affect would have to do with the specificity of the embodied subjects being-in-the-world: people who were sensitive to the suffering of others, who had experienced cruelties of the war, who were inclined to popular democracy or left-wing causes, would probably be deeply moved by her account. And, alternatively, conservatives, strong nationalists, and racists

7 In the next chapter I show how the scent of rich carpets, the light of large open sparkling windows, the warmth and rich sensations from comfortable overstuffed furniture are linked to guilt rather than pleasure.

would likely have abjected the Algerians or focused upon the counter-violence of Algerians. French nationalists/conservatives treated the Algerians as Other, less than civilized, not real Frenchmen/women worthy of respect. Furthermore, those groups who wanted to preserve Algeria as a colony would no doubt have dismissed this work as a piece of a left-wing ideology.

Beauvoir is aware of the effects of affect and emotion on rational debate. Introspection is important because in bringing these pre-reflective affects to consciousness, their destructive effects can be diminished or their intensity acknowledged and this energy can be directed towards more positive political ends. She counts on harnessing the emotions of horror, empathy, and anger to garner support for the Algerian cause. This would work only if the readers were more disposed to identify with the Algerians and not the *pieds noir* (local Frenchmen who worked in Algeria) who were endangered by the FLN's acts of violence.

Affect theorists think otherwise; sensations trigger dissensual moments, irrespective of embodied subjects. Since they see humans as lively subatomic matter, and the non-human world as actants/agents that affect humans, they challenge human exceptionalism. Differences between humans and non-humans are differences in degree not kind (Coole 2010, 20–1). Humans are part of matter/energy flows/systems as are non-humans. While Beauvoir's interest in affect and emotion decentres the rational subject, she is not a monist or a flat ontologist. When she does attend to the power of immanence (things themselves), she sees them in relation to a specific sensory human subject, whereas affect theorist focus on impersonal affects, how we are viscerally affected by the deep descriptions of torture. Unlike the vital materialists, anti-humanists who deny human exceptionalism and transcendence, Beauvoir subscribes to a modest human exceptionalism: we must attend to the concrete thickness of the world (*EA*, 104) and synchronize with others' bodies in order to act, to will our freedom. Both Susan Krause and Sonia Kruks make the case for a modest exceptionalism arguing that reflective capacities and norm responsiveness distinguish human from animal life, banking on these capacities to foster progressive forces of change.

Beauvoir is aware of both positive and negative affects and emotion, and believes that both potentially serve the ends of social equality and liberty. Descriptions of Boupacha's torture will produce strong visceral affects – disgust as well as anger, triggering sympathy for the Algerian struggle for independence. She herself responded to the Algerian crisis in this way: anger at the supine French press, disgust with the colonial government's regime of oppression and terror; rage at the French public's indifference to the tortures when revealed, exasperation at the insincerity of many French intellectuals. She enters into this story of injustice to reveal an untold and shocking story. Her passionate engagement in this struggle for justice appreciates the power of affect and emotion: although they are not easily communicable in words, they have effects. Women would cringe at the descriptions of torture; many would "feel" the indignities of her nudity and feel furious at the conduct of the French army. Beauvoir did not treat emotion as an experience to be bridled or ignored, as many philosophers do, but as an integral part of human existence that can and should be engaged to actively mobilize action. Not in the service of any action, mind you, but rather as a force in promoting empathy, mitigating injustice, and fostering collective freedom.

Ironically, many of Beauvoir's own biographers find her passionate engagement in the Algerian war excessive and dismiss it on those grounds. They seem to be unaware of the positive role she attributes to emotion or sensory experiences in her philosophy. Here, again, Beauvoir was prescient; more recently, the responses of Iris Young, Judith Butler, and Susan Krause (above) suggest the positive role of emotion in the public space. Iris Young endorses emotive speech, activism, and extra-institutional action to counter the primacy of educated rational argument and to empower minorities (2001, 675). Judith Butler stresses excitable speech – the creative and disruptive capacity of cultural practices to challenge the status quo (1997, 90). Yet like many feminists, she recognizes how transformatory identities must be secured in institutional arrangements. Anne Phillips (1992), Iris Young, and Judith Butler (2006) acknowledge the role existing institutions play in protecting transgressive identities, thereby calling for the deepening of democracy, yet they also stress the significance of impassioned grassroots movements to pressure the state.

Beauvoir is aware of the potential for using emotion to further political struggles, yet she does not endorse emotion without qualification. She encourages strong feelings of empathy and injustice towards the Algerians struggling for independence. But not all strong emotions are productive. For example, as we have seen in *The Mandarins*, Paula's devotion to Henri makes her overly dependent on and vulnerable to his attention. When he leaves her, she falls into a deep depression hallucinating wild thoughts. While passionate commitment and collaborative action to combat oppression are politically productive, unbridled emotion harnessed to unreciprocal relations can be destructive. The mutual jealousy of Xaviere and Françoise in *She Came to Stay* also provide examples of the damaging effects of obsessive love and dependency.

Existentialists in general, and Beauvoir in particular, are often charged with rationalism. Because she focuses on choice and uses what appears to be a universal philosophic framework, it is assumed that she fails to respect the materiality of the body and the importance of social and economic circumstances. Yet, as I have shown, Beauvoir's thinking accommodates pre-conscious experiences and non-rational conduct of a specific embodied subject. In willing one's freedom, one should adhere to the disclosure of freedom generally and ensure that one's acts further the freedom of all.

One's pre-personal/pre-reflective relation to the world is not an instrumental one, but an affective one. The sensible thickness (*EA*, 104) of the world is not there simply for the body to use, or cognitively to understand; rather the body-subject coils over the world and expresses itself as both object and subject, active and passive, as sensible and sentient. In their preliminary attachment to the world, humans are part of life's vital upsurge. As a free spontaneity "one adheres to the concrete and particular, by which it defines itself by thrusting towards a goal" (26). Yet one experiences dehiscence, the gaping open of life, the revelation of divergence of parts, hence one's relation to the world is non-identical. However, insofar as one adheres to a concrete and particular thrusting towards an end, one is grounded in action that temporarily sutures over the gaps of existence. This preliminary relation to the world is affective and bodily, imaginary and material, captured in perceptual and aesthetic experiences. This will be explored further in the final chapter on political fictions. Given the non-cognitive and embodied nature of these links, between subjects and the world, fiction is an apt medium for communicating pre-reflective experiences.

TOWARDS A COALITIONAL POLITICS

The defence of Boupacha was the product of three women working together, none of whom shared nationality, ethnicity, or religion. It was not their identities nor their subject positions or social locations that drew them together, but their work in common:[8] Gisèle Halimi, a Tunisian Jewish activist lawyer; Djamila Boupacha, a Muslim hospital worker and

8 Interestingly enough, poststructuralist feminists such as Judith Butler and Wendy Brown believe that radical politics should be coalitional and premised upon the work done, not on identity. This collaborative approach was anticipated by Beauvoir, who acknowledges that projects, work done – and not identity – should underpin political action; however, for Beauvoir commitment to the project emerges from some experience of oppression (which can be variously defined) and presupposes a commitment to change. See Stavro 2009. One's position is not fluid, easily changeable, and strategic, but emerges out of one's particular situation and a long-standing commitment.

member of FLN; and Simone de Beauvoir, a French Catholic intellectual and novelist. Beauvoir was more privileged than Boupacha and Halimi, for she was not subjected to a subordinate position in terms of nationality, class experience, or the particular sexisms of Islamic or Jewish cultures. Nonetheless, her gender experience was a source of oppression.

Beauvoir was able to be politically effective without leading, directing, or representing the FLN. She did not present herself as the leader of Algerian women to those outside Algeria, nor did she take on the pedagogic role of mediating Algerian women's existence, making sense of their struggles in feminist or anti-colonialist terms. In fact, Beauvoir never met Boupacha (for which Halimi criticized her), nor did she join the FLN.

Far from directing any policy, she tried not to interfere in their policy. When Boupacha was released from prison and abducted by the FLN, she pressured Beauvoir and Halimi to demonstrate publicly on her behalf. Beauvoir refused to do so, citing her wish not to interfere in the policy decisions of the FLN, nor pass judgment prematurely in ways that might discredit their movement at this critical moment. By lending support to their struggle without interfering with their political decisions, she was able to resist colonizing the voice of the colonized. She did not see herself as an agent of revolutionary consciousness, nor did she assume she was the bearer of objective truth. Rather, Beauvoir's efforts were more limited and grew out of her ability to be responsive to Boupacha's concrete situation and her specific need of defence.

In the spirit of Bourdieu, one could make the case that Beauvoir's relative autonomy from market and social status gave her the "freedom" to appreciate and represent the collective good. As an independent scholar, Beauvoir was not tied to professional commitments at the university, nor was she tied to the values of the capitalist economy. However, Beauvoir herself thinks differently; her decision to work on Boupacha's defence grew out of her long-standing work as an activist and her commitment to radical causes. Her work on Boupacha's defence and its role in Algerian independence reflects her commitment to further the freedom for all. So, far from assuming a universal, objective position, above particular interests, grounding her intervention in the FLN's collective struggle for freedom furthered their collaboration. Her engagement was as emotional/affective as rational.

As I have suggested, Beauvoir did not try to represent Muslim women, or Algerians struggling for independence, though she does speak on behalf of Boupacha. Identity theorists of the 1970s and 1980s would have argued that, in speaking on behalf of Boupacha and the FLN revolutionaries, she expropriated their stories. However, if one looks at the discursive context, it is much more difficult to make this claim, since Boupacha's story and the FLN's account of the war would not have been heard if renowned French writers had not taken up their pens. As a well-known novelist and critical intellectual, Beauvoir was ideally suited to expose the illegalities and prejudices (racial and sexual) of the French in their conduct of the war. She had the cultural capital and the reputation to be listened to and heard. Because of her international profile, popular newspapers were willing to give her a platform to express her opinions.

Although Beauvoir was tormented by her privilege she did not use that as an excuse to retreat from assisting Boupacha. She did not shy away from acting in others' interests, but pressured the French government, in particular her former friend André Malraux who was then the minister of defense. Not only were Beauvoir and Halimi effective in their defence of Boupacha, but their collaborative work contributed to the independence movement and was endorsed by the FLN. Further, in Alcoff's terms, since Boupacha and the anti-colonial cause benefited from their work, their speaking for her could be justified.

To understand the basis of Beauvoir's coalitional politics, we must explore further how she negotiates identity and post-identity politics. Identity politics presumes that those of the same racial, gender, or ethnic group identity act in unison. Identity politics narrowly defines participants and representatives as those who share experiences and attributes. On these grounds, Beauvoir herself would be disqualified from speaking on behalf of the Algerians. Beauvoir equally avoids the paths of the post-structuralists who jettison experience and the role of identification in the process of change. In being discursively constructed, poststructuralists argue one is constituted by multiple discourses and one can move fluidly from one discursive position to another. They do not consider how important the experience of marginality, in whatever form it may take, is to furthering or impeding commitment. Though the poststructuralists endorse coalitional politics, they do not understand the preconditions of collaboration. One must make a choice as Jean and Hélène did in *The Blood of Others*, but that choice presumes one's embeddedness in the situation and reconfiguring of one's relations to themselves and others. Commitment is not primarily the product of deliberation, but more the result of being open to others and the world and synchronizing with projects of collective freedom. Such work demands loyalty and sustained commitment; being defined by one set or discourses or another (the logic of poststructuralism) is hardly sufficient to the task. Emotions of attachment, experiences of oppression, and communication of these experiences facilitate collaboration with other marginal groups and this provides the glue of coalitional politics.

Beauvoir's experience of sexism and her twenty-five years of commitment to radical political projects (at both theoretical and practical levels) made her a viable and reliable ally for the Algerian cause. She neither endorses substantive and essential identities that would ground agency, nor does she refuse the process of social identification as necessarily wrongheaded. Her theory of relational social being, where identities make sense in a field of differences, reminds us that identification is a complex and dynamic process, and not necessarily regressive. While identities may affirm the past and thereby stabilize it, Beauvoir's approach involves assuming past identities and reconfiguring them to promote new transformative identities. This involves what many poststructuralists would call affirmative strategies, yet, for Beauvoir, these don't keep women attached to their present wounded social location, as Wendy Brown argues, but help them take up more radical positions.

Given the popularity of Foucault and his critique of the Marxist intellectual, it might be useful to situate Beauvoir in this context. Beauvoir's work does not fit Foucault's stereotype of the universal intellectual as a free-floating consciousness that is able to adopt a transcendental position and thereby represent "the just-and-true-for-all" (1984, 68). One's concrete situation is an important factor in reflection; it has a role to play in thought and action without determining either. This also means that one cannot be a surveilling (impartial, ungrounded) consciousness that knows what is good for all; rather, the intellectual is more modest in her expectations and goals: she tries to further the struggle.

Both Beauvoir and Foucault encourage self-fashioning, that is, reconfiguring oneself to act in accordance with one's chosen ethos in the context of present cultural/social fields. However, there are differences: Foucault sees this work as work on the self, transforming himself into a work of art, whereas Beauvoir sees self-making as intersubjective – involving others. For Foucault, this self-making project is described as an ethico-political choice (343); while Beauvoir might agree that political action is also ethical, she believes that collective action can escape domination, whereas Foucault does not. Vintges astutely points out their differences: "Beauvoir distanced herself from an aesthetic attitude to life, i.e., striving to transform one's own life into an autonomous a work of art" (1996, 102). Beauvoir dismissed writers like Oscar Wilde and Anaïs Nin for this reason (*ASD*, 170). "But she never gave up her commitment to her art of living. For Beauvoir, art of living is ethics rather than aesthetics" (Vintges 1996, 102). I might add to Vintges: the art of living also involves collective and collaborative action.

Beauvoir, like Habermas and Arendt, believes that one can act in concert (presuming a realm of intersubjectivity) without denying the difficulties of consensual action; they do not dismiss it as a goal. Foucault believes that "consensuality always implies a degree of nonconsensuality" (1984, 379). While the above three would agree and, further, recognize it might not be achievable, they still struggle towards consensual action as a goal, presuming action based upon some consensus is potentially better, freer, and healthier. While Foucault admits that consensuality is a "critical idea" (379), he says: "he is not for consensuality, but he is against non-consensuality" (379). It is difficult to determine what this would mean politically. Presumably some consensus is required to work together towards a goal, yet some dissensus is admissible.

Given Beauvoir's assumptions that we are never integrated with ourselves, let alone others, that our situations are singular yet we share the world, she assumes a non-identitarian politics, yet is optimistic that communication can further consensus and contribute to building coalitions between social groups. We don't have to set common goals, in fact she is opposed to establishing a strong ontology. Here she has some affinity with Foucault, who says, "The questions that I am trying to ask are not determined by a pre-established political outlook and do not tend toward the realization of some definite political project" (375). Foucault believes Beauvoir's politics is "abstract and limiting" (375). While having political values may be limiting, they are not necessarily abstract, nor does this prescribe action. Beauvoir admits she has a clear attitude towards capitalism, imperialism, and colonialism (*ASD*, 36), yet they do not prescribe what is to be done. Further, she is committed to further freedom and social equality. Here she differs from Foucault. He fails to appreciate how she believes the philosopher ought to take his/her bearing in history, and from within this concrete situation, and given his/her values, certain courses of actions are ruled out of court, yet there are no directives. However this pre-established political outlook was not acceptable to Foucault.

Foucault challenges Arendt's distinction between power and domination, as well as Beauvoir's belief in engaged action. In fact, he uses the example of Beauvoir and Sartre's theory of engagement to illustrate "how theory does not protect philosophers against disastrous mistakes"; nor does it inform their action. "None of the philosophers of engagement – Sartre, Simone de Beauvoir and Merleau-Ponty, none of them did a thing" (1984, 374) during the Resistance. However, Foucault is ignoring the fact that their philosophy of engagement evolved after the war. He is also ignoring the role Sartre played in anti-fascist literary organizations. Further, these philosophers of engagement did not assume that ideas can be applied to a concrete situation to direct one's action, as Foucault implies. Foucault seems to be ignoring the role that ideas and knowledge have in the public sphere. Clearly they do not protect people against making disastrous choices (Beauvoir insists one always takes a risk in acting) but action informed by historical knowledge and a commitment to emancipation probably has more of a chance of success than uninformed action. Further ideas can be useful in mobilizing political action. Foucault believes a political stance like Marxism dictates goals and conduct, so he jettisons it; as a form of power/knowledge, however, Beauvoir herself criticized Marxism for these very reasons in *The Ethics of Ambiguity*. But this critique did not involve her repudiating Marxism. She had a more modest expectation from theory and more pragmatic approach to revolutionary change, allowing more flexibility and less dogmatism. Beauvoir's commitment to radical values do not dictate what is to be done, but nor is any action justifiable to save the revolution. She does not end up in a relativist position for some actions do not contribute to the freedom of all; these actions are not endorsed by Beauvoir.

Foucault believes that ethics should be upheld as a political act, for there is often no room for politics. In an interview in 1976, he talks about the situation in Poland: the French left cannot act politically; they cannot send in troops to liberate the Polish resistance movement. However, the acts of Soviet repression should be critiqued on ethical grounds. He complains that the Marxist left in France were reluctant to do so, given "the non-acceptance of what was happening" (1984, 377). Foucault calls for the turn from politics to ethics. Foucault takes as his point of reference the PCF and those of the non-communist left, like Beauvoir and Sartre, who were critical of Soviet repression. Furthermore Beauvoir and Sartre would have seen their acts of critique as both ethical and political, and entirely consistent with their revolutionary politics. Foucault uses the term political in a very restricted way, as if it involves state action, armed struggle; Beauvoir in contrast saw her protest of the PCF as political.

Foucault looks to the early Greek aesthetic in *Care of the Self* to illustrate ethics as a practice. Their acts were not derived from principles, nor from truths, but were concerned with how to live with others and how to manage their bodies. However, Foucault's work does not consider socio-economic forces: the regimes of slavery and female subordination were rife in ancient Greece. Could the care of the self be oblivious to these realities? For Beauvoir, self-making requires that one takes one's bearings in the historical material world. Insofar as she believes this, caring for the self is not unaffected by the subordination of women, slavery, and other forms of social hierarchy. One could not simply bracket the slavery that ancient Greek society relied upon. Referring back to Beauvoir's treatment of the Marquis de Sade, he could not fully escape his aristocratic past, however it could have been lived differently. Since Beauvoir believes one is optimally obliged to further the freedom of all, one's care of the self is not a self absorbed, aesthetic act, but must take others into account and contribute to their freedom. Since her politics is not abstract or derived from theory, but grounded in concrete everyday living, Beauvoir's support of Algerian independence emerges out of her embodied and historically situated experiences – leading the life of a radical intellectual in a vibrant political culture in Paris. She does not escape her experiences, her privileged social location, but she works from within it to expand revolutionary agency (Kruks 2012, 91–123). The trajectory of her life confirms the conscious and affective experiences that underpinned her transformation from an apolitical philosophy student/teacher during the Second World War to a politically committed intellectual in the post-war years and beyond. As a renowned writer and political activist on the left, she was first inspired by communist and socialist imaginaries; however, she believed actually existing socialism failed to live up to expectations. Despite changes in her philosophy and support of Marxism (as her conditions changed) she never abandoned her philosophy of engagement. She found herself involved in diverse emancipatory projects – this was reflected in her commitment to feminism, anti-colonialism, and anti-racism, as well showing solidarity for specific socialist/communist projects.

Beauvoir does not exemplify Foucault's intellectual whose expertise and interventions are specific. Her knowledge of Algeria and Islam and their relation to France was limited; she failed to fully understand their cultures or the divisions within Arab Algerians. She tended to support the FLN, whose members were younger and more Western, rather than the religiously inspired Islamic groups. Just because Beauvoir was not an expert on Algerian politics did not mean her work was ignorant of the particular, as Foucault implies. Her goal was not to provide a detailed solution to the road towards independence (here a specific intellectual might have been a help). She had sufficient knowledge of the situation to endorse the FLN and not the Islamic/Muslim groups. Further, she was trying to mobilize support within France for the Algerian cause, not trying to direct the revolution. She provided a critical voice in the French public sphere – exposing the French government's hypocrisy and abuses of power. Her success in this work illustrates the abiding importance of intellectuals whose work is to publicize struggles around the world.

Beauvoir and other intellectuals like her were hugely effective in rallying public support for the Algerian cause and extending support to multiple anti-colonial struggles that emerged within Africa and Asia in the late twentieth century. Her work is concrete, yet insofar as she embraces radical change and pushes for the freedom of all, her work is best described as situated universality. Interestingly, Foucault himself acted as a universal intellectual, on occasion; in 1977 he supported the revolutionary regime of Ayatollah Khomeini. The results were disastrous: he interviewed Khomeini and was impressed by his ability to enlist popular support. This had been lacking in the previous liberal inspired regime of the Shah. However, he had not done the work that Beauvoir and other intellectuals did on the eve of the Iranian Revolution. In fact, his ahistorical approach proved disastrous. Within a few weeks of Ayatollah achieving power, he exhumed conservative Muslim values that targeted women, homosexuals, and any group on the left. So, far from being allied to forces of popular democracy, this movement was allied to anti-democratic forces. Beauvoir's response, steeped in the work of local activists, was aware of the regime's (and broader movements') authoritarian tendencies. One should not be too harsh on Foucault for his mistakes; many intellectuals have supported revolutionary regimes that proved counter-revolutionary. My concern is the larger theoretical concern: if Foucault's ethos, or aesthetic approach, is not grounded in a concrete analysis of existing political and social forces, will it not lead to disasters? Foucault praised the Muslim religion since it captured popular affective/emotional forces and harnessed them to a political movement, hence taking a distance from current liberal forms of democracy. While this non-rationalist, anti-technocratic movement was *potentially* democratic, it proved not to be in practice. Had Foucault explored this regime beforehand, there would have been little room for optimism, since this movement itself was not inspired by democratic values and democratic practices, but by highly hierarchal ones. Further steeped in the Koran, the sexist and homophobic attitudes were not surprising.

THE HISTORICAL CONTEXT OF THE ALGERIAN WAR: VARIOUS INTELLECTUAL RESPONSES

Most of the French intellectuals on the left supported Algerian independence from France. Camus was an exception. Unlike his former intellectual friends of the resistance, Camus refused to support the idea of an Algeria liberated from France and abstained from speaking against the French colonial government. In 1957, after his award of the Nobel Prize, he spoke to students at the University of Uppsala, where in response to a heckler, he is reported to have said the French government had committed only minor errors (he later denied having said this). Here he delivered his famous line: "I believe in justice, but I would defend my mother before justice" (Le Sueur 2001, 111). These comments catalyzed angry debate amongst intellectuals and activists in North Africa and France. Camus's reputation as a member of the resistance and a critic of state power was tainted by the importance he placed on his private life. Beauvoir and Sartre reproached Camus for his abstract liberal humanism,[9] which supported passivism and condoned censorship. Former friends, subaltern poets, raised their voices: Jean Senac accused Camus of "Eurocentric paternalism" (128). Taleb, a Kabyle poet, was morally disgusted with Camus's desire to halt their rightful independence. Camus's politics of innocence denied the original oppression and violence done to the non-European Algerians by the Europeans (135). Many reminded Camus that many Algerians had watched their families and mothers being tortured and killed. Camus publically repudiated the wrongdoings of the colonial government, but felt he could not support the acts of terrorism of the revolutionary forces.[10] While Camus believed he remained neutral, his critics condemned his position for playing into the hands of the "ultras" – the right-wing terrorists.

There was no thought of power-sharing amongst most left-wing intellectuals, though they differed as to the culpability of the French soldiers. Francis Jeanson, a radical intellectual, supported the Algerian nationalist cause financially, intellectually, and morally. He was an editor at the Paris publishing house Éditions de Seuil and had written an introduction to Frantz Fanon's *Black Skin, White Masks*, a psychoanalytic exploration of black dependency in a white world published in 1952. Like Sartre, he felt that Algeria required the French to leave so that the people could reconstitute their national identity. In 1957, Jeanson went into

9 However, their differences had emerged much earlier. Beauvoir's negative response to revolt in *The Ethics of Ambiguity* was, I would argue, directed at Camus, who refused to support revolutionary movements since they would always involve the sacrifice of individuals, and hence were not justifiable. In contrast, Beauvoir is aware of the problem of revolutionary violence, both in terms of its effects on those who perpetrate it, as well as the loss of lives. Beauvoir believes each act must be justified and attention be paid if theses acts were furthering the values of the revolution or instantiating totalitarian practices. So whereas the ethical trumped the political for Camus, Beauvoir, who was more committed to emancipatory projects, saw the ethical and political as entwined.

10 Unlike others on the left who were horrified by de Gaulle's return to power, Camus had some faith that de Gaulle would be able to forge reform, but this was not to be. Camus's death in a car accident (6 January 1960) meant he would not witness France's departure from Algeria and the FLN's assumption of power.

hiding in Algeria and assembled an underground network of both French and Muslims to aid the Algerian nationalists. The network did not take orders from the FLN, but showed solidarity with it while remaining autonomous. Many of these network members were subsequently arrested and were convicted of treason (Le Sueur, 230). Their trial was described as "a political happening," "a circus"; it became the site where the radical left could voice the urgency of Algerian independence to the French public and also the context in which treason and the limits of what the French intellectuals were willing to do were explored (234).

The day of the trial, 121 of the most prestigious radical writers and artists signed a manifesto giving French soldiers the right to desert: "the right of insubordination and draft resistance." Simone de Beauvoir, Jean-Paul Sartre, Marguerite Duras, Michel Leiris, and André Breton were amongst the signatories. A more modest manifesto from the moderate left attracted over 1,000 signatures. Raymond Aron, Roland Barthes, Georges Canguilhem, Jean Maries Domenach, Claude Lefort, Maurice Merleau-Ponty, Edgar Morin, and Paul Ricoeur[11] signed it (235). Although it did not advocate the right of subordination or desertion, it expressed concern with the moral choices the French government imposed upon young French citizens.

The intellectuals were divided between those who supported the Algerian revolutionary movement and those who preferred negotiated peace and diplomacy. The former group felt that Algeria presented a decisive moment of socialist progress, although some Marxists refused to participate because they believed that the FLN was not sufficiently socialist and too strongly wedded to its Islamic identity. Merleau-Ponty's position exemplified the critical moderates: he refrained from open discussion of Algeria because he did not want to get involved in the heated debates between the conservatives and radicals. He did not support the Marxists or the non-communist left who supported immediate decolonization. In fact, he argued in *Notes on Madagascar*, written at the time of the conflict, that the colonizers were not simply exploiters and oppressors but made meaningful contributions from which the locals benefited (Merleau-Ponty 1967, 330).

Others, like Beauvoir, had a more complicated position. She supported the liberation of Algeria, but did not wholeheartedly endorse the actions of the FLN. She was concerned that the FLN did not and would not support the equal treatment of women. Also there were rather

11 Whereas those who supported the moderate manifesto consisted of academics, philosophers, and political theorists within the university.

heinous acts of torture (counter-terrorism) that other liberationist movements were engaging in that were hardly justifiable. But she refrained from openly criticizing the FLN since she did not want to destabilize or delegitimize them.

Beauvoir supported her former students and friends who engaged in acts of civil disobedience and were facing death penalties for their involvement in the war. She signed the *Manifesto of 121* and did much to publicize the colonial abuses of power (i.e. the atrocities committed by the French army and the harassment of locals who had any support for the liberation movement). Her involvement in protests, her committee work, and her journalism exemplify what Iris Young (2001) has in mind when she calls for emotively engaged public activism. She demonstrated solidarity with the independence movements, by supporting their activists as well as by marshalling popular French attitudes.

Beauvoir, amongst others, employed the universal republican discourse to promote the Algerian cause. France conceived of itself as a republic, yet the acts of violence and torture that the local Algerian population endured, the denial of their freedoms of expression and organization, and their subordinate status were sufficient to cast doubt on the French ideals of liberty, equality, and solidarity. While she employed this discourse to be persuasive, her own revolutionary position was not based upon the values of the Republic. For she was an ardent democratic socialist.

Many on the left did not fully appreciate the divisions amongst the Algerians and how that might figure into a post-liberation world. Their backing of the FLN, rather than the more Islamic faction led by Messali Hadj, who was bearded, religious, and appeared culturally very different (Le Sueur 2001, 12), earned them the charge of Eurocentrism. As nationalist violence escalated, Muslim Algerians who had been made French citizens during the war were painted less and less as Western and more and more as Muslim. The differences within the independence movement, as well as the increase in intra-Algerian violence, were glossed over by the radical French intellectuals, who saw in the FLN a democratic future. Leftist journalists came up with the phrase "Algerian Jacobinism" to describe the cutting of throats, noses, and lips, which in fact had nothing to do with the French Revolution but was connected to the premodern Muslim punishment for breaking communal obligations and expectations. The left tended to see the Algerian anti-colonial struggle as part of the worldwide proletarian revolution, not in terms of Algeria's own specific goals. While the charges of Eurocentrism may be apt, since they supported the more Western voices of the FLN, nonetheless they did believe that the FLN upheld the values and engaged in practices most in harmony with their democratic socialism.

EVALUATION OF BEAUVOIR'S ACTIVISM: THE ENTWINING OF REASON AND EMOTION

Beauvoir's political activism has been ignored by many scholars who have written on the French left; see, for example, Judt (1992), Khilnani (1993), Debray (1979), and Ross (1990). What does one make of this invisibility? Is it attributable to her feminist focus, which many scholars, especially of a particular generation, have little interest in? Is it because of the extent of her emotional attachment? Or is it the consequence of a general perception that she simply tags along after Sartre? Beauvoir's biographer, Deirdre Bair, describes her "as spending the turbulent 60s following Sartre everywhere" and "spending most of her days hanging around various groups formed by men" (1990, 159). Portraying her in this way, as a kind of "groupie," living through the achievements of men, was a common sentiment, but hardly appropriate. Sartre was not involved in Boupacha's trial. Furthermore Beauvoir's involvement in the Algerian struggle was not simply around women's issues, she also went to court to defend her male and female activists and students who were involved in anti-colonial struggles.

Margaret Crosland describes Beauvoir's autobiography, *Force of Circumstance*, written when she was distraught by France's continued presence in Algeria, as "one long moan" (1992, 388). Another Beauvoir scholar, Terry Keefe, describes her in the same period as fixated on "the idea of being party to atrocities committed on the French side" (1983, 38–9). Okely, too, is suspicious of Beauvoir's motivations, seeing her outrage at the French as reflective of her "apparent egocentrism" (1986, 121). To treat her work with Boupacha and her support for Algerian independence as obsessive and overly emotional in this way is to feminize and ultimately disqualify her activism. These biographers, who share the rationalist values of Western philosophy, have normalized the impartial (male) voice of reason as the ideal. Demeaning Beauvoir's work as emotional, partial, and feminine, they not only ignore the epistemological critique of rationalism, which casts doubt upon the possibility of impartiality and objectivity, but also they ignore the significance of passion in commitment. In fact, are not outrage and anger an appropriate response to the violence, bloodshed, and suffering that ensued?

Beauvoir's response is all too readily dismissed for its emotion, but the distinctive character of her activism has been under-explored and her courage has been underplayed. Writing a book denouncing the French armed forces and sympathizing with a potential female terrorist did not endear her to many; she received death threats after its publication. She openly engaged with high-powered intellectuals such as Albert Camus and Frantz Fanon, neither of whom were intellectual lightweights and both of whom held strong stances on the Algerian crisis. After Camus's declaration, "I love Justice; but I will fight for my mother before Justice" (Le Sueur 2001, 88), Beauvoir publicly denounced him for his liberal humanism, for prioritizing the value of the individual over the collective, the private over the political, and this undermining revolutionary movements. When Camus insisted that not a single life should be sacrificed in the name of the revolution, she replied that the loss of a single life is a tragedy, however to assume Camus's absolute non-violent position had anti-political implications – problematizing most projects of collective freedom. To take the high road, the non-violent option, as Camus had done, involved withdrawing from politics. Beauvoir was also concerned about the question of Muslim patriarchy. She was not wholly convinced that a victory of the FLN would put an end to women's oppression.[12] The participation of many female insurgents in the war was a fact, she insisted, yet the FLN routinely underestimated their numbers and involvement. Her disagreement with Fanon reflects her feminist concern, something Sartre did not share.

A distinctive feature of Beauvoir's activism is her concern with sexism, which was seen by many male intellectual historians and Marxists to be a subordinate struggle. For Beauvoir, sexism was as corrosive as capitalism on one's future freedom. As an embodied subject, one's sexuality is always entwined with one's race and class, and therefore not subordinate, but potentially present in all political struggles. She confronted sexism not only in the attitudes of the FLN but also amongst the French authorities and the editors of *Le Monde*. The issue of the army's rape of Boupacha was at the forefront of Beauvoir's struggle for a fair trial, especially because she thought it was not taken seriously. M. Patin, the president of the Committee for Public Safety (which was responsible for protecting France against external threat and internal terrorism), claimed: "I was rather afraid that she might have been violated per annum, as was done on occasion with the Vietnamese in Indochina" (*DB*, 54). The editors of *Le Monde* requested that she replace the word vagina with womb when describing the rape. Beauvoir refused, but the editors changed the word to belly when her article went to print. They also asked her to rephrase her description of Boupacha as a virgin, although her defence depended

12 Interestingly, the FLN proved itself not only sexist, but authoritarian in its political practices. The Marxist left had turned to Algeria as the next potential expression of revolutionary vitality, but the FLN did not put faith in socialism, or democracy. Nonetheless, their overthrow of their colonial past triggered sympathy amongst Marxists. Their refusal of a truce on innocent civilian casualties in 1955 may have foreshadowed their undemocratic disposition.

on establishing that she had been a virgin and was no longer one since her hymen had been perforated by a bottle. Since Boupacha admitted to hiding members of the FLN in her bedroom, Algerian papers were skeptical about her status as a virgin at the time of her arrest, and the media in general described her as "a loose woman." Beauvoir even confronted sexism in Boupacha herself; she was distressed that Boupacha shared the Muslim belief that her loss of virginity meant she was no longer a candidate for marriage.

Thus we can see that Beauvoir was not simply a dupe of Sartre, nor did she follow his lead on the Algerian War. Her interest in women distinguished her position from his, and her concern that the FLN did not support women activists was not a concern of Sartre. In the late 1950s, Sartre was preoccupied with rethinking Marxism in the *Critique of Dialectical Reason* and focusing on class struggle as the motor of change. As we saw in chapter 4, Beauvoir recognizes that class inequality is not the primary or sole source of oppression, nor is economic change alone sufficient to guarantee justice. Admittedly there is some affinity between the struggles of subordinate groups, but there is no presumed unifying agent of change (i.e., the proletariat), or the party or the intellectual. For she did not believe humans share the same project, though she was optimistic they could be choreographed. Boupacha's specific situation illustrates a complex logic of oppression in which economics, race, and religious subordination are evident. As a colonized people, the Algerians were denied their economic and political freedoms, while racist attitudes and religious intolerance intensified their oppression. Given the sexist attitudes and practices within Islam, Boupacha's domination was multiform.

In recognizing the irreducible separateness and yet interdependence of human beings, Beauvoir departs from Sartre's early individualistic assumptions that humans are autonomous actors who always find themselves in conflict. She consciously sets herself the task of challenging these assumptions. Where the gaze of the "Other" is a source of alienation for Sartre, for Beauvoir the "Other" is not simply hostile but can recognize and confirm one's project. Not only can the Other facilitate or further one's work, but the gaze of the Other can negatively judge projects. Seeing oneself from the eyes of the "Other" (i.e., the Algerians) provides an important ethical point of view: "I needed my self-esteem to go on living and I was seeing myself through the eyes of women who had been raped twenty times" (*FC*, 369). The "Other" who judges is an Algerian woman who reproaches Beauvoir for being French. It is difficult to justify her own existence as a French citizen in the eyes of the Algerian, since the actions of her government are so heinous and because she has benefited from France's colonial past. This is a much more sophisticated treatment than Sartre's understanding of the gaze.

It is important not only to see Beauvoir as distinct from Sartre, but also to recognize her approach to others and history as illustrative of her radical humanism. Since Beauvoir does not see the self as a sovereign rational subject with a comprehensive theory of history, she is not overwhelmed by poststructuralists' and structuralist Marxists' critiques of humanism. She acknowledges the structures, discourses, situations that weigh heavily on our free and responsible choices (Caputi 2006, 111), however, unlike the anti-humanists she still affirms the potential for committed action that is ethical and free.

As relational beings, we make our own decisions. Our subjectivity emerges from intersubjectivity – the individual is a thoroughly social self, not the source of itself, and as such it is not a master of its actions. Exogenous factors like class, gender, and ethnicity affect our decisions, for they produce knowledges/myths/identities that inform our actions. Our knowledge is never transparent or complete, but always affected by political and social changes. Our intersubjective existence does not prescribe what to do but recognizes that we cannot be free alone. We must act alongside others with similar desires and goals. We are not self-determining, for intersubjective existence, as well as political, legal, and social institutions, as well as our relations to the economy, limit both the fields in which we act and the facts known. We cannot be ethical alone. Beauvoir urges us to take up an attitude of care and respect towards others. We are all implicated in the acts of our governments. We have to take a stand either to support these acts or criticize them for we are responsible for what the state does and we are complicit if we do nothing to change them. Collective responsibility has progressive consequences.

Beauvoir recognized the interdependent nature of subjectivity and freedom before Sartre. In *Pyrrhus et Cinéas* (1944) she identifies others not simply as a threat to one's existence, as Sartre did at the time, but as positively confirming and extending one's projects. Freedom is not something one can achieve alone – one's freedom is connected to others. As early as 1948, she was aware of the complicated oppression in Algeria: it could not be understood simply in class or racial terms. She states: "The Arabian fellah is oppressed by both the sheiks and the French and English administration; which of the two enemies is to be combated?" (EA, 89). The French proletariat's interests are not the same as those of natives in a colony. Which tactics are adopted? It is a question of opportunity, efficiency, and virtuosity. There is no ready-made answer; it depends upon the urgency and possibilities provided by the situation. She cites the example of Richard Wright, who refused to give up his anti-racist campaign during the Second World War in the context of a general struggle against fascism. In the end, she hopes specific struggles will not fall into the "fanaticism of seriousness" (89), treating their particular goal as an absolute end. One must assess the situation to know what is possible, and not simply assume one can do as one wishes: "Here the question is political before being moral … Each one must carry on his struggle in connection with that of the other and by integrating it into the general pattern" (89).

One must be aware of the rhetoric of freedom. When one justifies the freedom of "the directing class" (90), one implicitly denies the freedom of the exploited class. One cannot be free and/or ethical and at the same time contribute to enslaving or suppressing others. Genuine freedom wills itself as "an indefinite movement through the freedom of others" (90). One cannot be a patriot supporting France's colonial policy and also believe one is acting freely and authentically. Similarly, one could not support the collaboration and a Nazi future, since "a freedom which is interested only in denying freedom must be denied" (91). The oppressor does not demand the freedom to oppress, but fights in the name of civilization, of institutions, or monuments; he defends the privileges of the past (91). Beauvoir goes still further, claiming that everyone is obliged to struggle against oppression. Although the oppressed are more engaged than those who do not experience oppression, "every man is affected by this struggle in so essential a way that he cannot himself be moral without taking parting in it" (88–9). Recognizing the freedom of all does limit one's freedom; she declares: "Freedom is not the power to do anything you like, it is to be able to surpass the given toward an open future; the existence of others as a freedom defines my situation and is even the condition of my freedom" (91). While Beauvoir wrote *The Ethics of Ambiguity* years before the Algerian crisis, one can see how her solidarity with Algeria makes sense in terms of its ethical and political perspective. Furthermore her work on women's gendered existence in *The Second Sex* also informs her work on behalf of Boupacha. Here again "she emphasizes that freedom cannot be gained through personal choice but only through a process of complex social transformation" (Marso 2006, 86).

Beauvoir's journalism exemplifies how emotion and reason, theory and practice, ethics and politics, are entwined. She does not accept that a journalist speaks from an impartial neutral stance but recognizes that a story is always told from a particular place imbued with values and interests and with a specific audience in mind. One always makes choices that are evident in the stories one tells. Challenging the ideas of the innocence and impartiality of knowledge, Beauvoir stresses the role of commitment and political struggle. She uses emotion in her journalism and her fictional writing because she saw it as having philosophical value and political currency in mobilizing support for radical politics. Yet she was also apprised of the shortcomings of relying upon sensory affects, emotion, or aesthetics alone.[13]

She was well aware of the political effectiveness of portraying the suffering of a single individual with whom readers could identify. She shared Camus's sentiment that "a dead man has no substance unless one has actually seen him dead; a hundred million corpses broadcast through history are no more than a puff of smoke in the imagination" (Camus 1948, 38).

Beauvoir's moral outrage with the war and the French indifference to it is clearly communicated in her work. Emotion is not something that should be vetoed in the name of truth and reason, but is a rich dimension of human nature that must be harnessed to causes of justice. She argues that everyone must act and no one is free from blame: "I am an accomplice of the privileged classes and compromised by this connection; that is the reason why living through the Algerian war was like experiencing a personal tragedy" (*FC*, 652). She describes living in Paris during the Algerian War as more difficult than living in Paris during the German occupation because most people ignored what was going on in Algeria as if it had nothing to do with them or their lives: "Yes, I was living in an occupied city ... I loathed the occupiers even more fiercely than I had those in the forties, because of all the ties that bound me to them" (*FC*, 384–5). She blasts French complaisance: "The most scandalous aspect of the whole scandalous affair is that people had gotten used to it" (*DB*, 65). Emotion and responsibility will help the case of justice proceed. Beauvoir does not defend her middle-class privilege, but neither is she paralyzed by it. It does not stop her from taking a stand against the government and supporting the liberation forces. She describes herself as a "profiteer" benefiting from class and educational opportunities afforded by wealth drawn from France's colonies and yet she supports the Algerians' freedom to challenge the French state. She refuses a

13 Herein lies her critique of surrealism: "The constant negation of the world, by word, of the act by the act, of art by art was realized by Dada incoherence, by following a strict injunction to commit disorder and anarchy one achieved the abolition of all behaviour, and therefore of all ends and of oneself." To avoid the nihilism of its conclusion (suicide, drugs), she says, "they are unable to avoid returning to the positive, the serious. The negation of aesthetic, spiritual, and moral values has become an ethics; unruliness has become a rule. We have been at the establishment of a new Church, with its dogmas and its martyrs, today there is nothing of the destroyer in Breton; he is a pope" (*EA*, 55).

principled moral stance that dictates what is good and bad objectively and equally denies feeling pure and vindicated in her Marxist stance. In fact, in seeing herself from the perspective of the Algerians, she realizes she is no different from the patriots who are killing them: "I'm French. The words scalded my throat like admission of hideous deformity. For millions of men and women, old men and children, I was just one of the people who were torturing them, burning them, machine-gunning them … I deserved their hatred because I could still sleep, enjoy a walk or a book" (FC, 384).

ETHICS AND POLITICS: PRINCIPLE AND VIOLENCE – THE DILEMMA OF MEANS AND ENDS

Beauvoir invokes ethical arguments to draw attention to issues of social injustice and political oppression. She does not justify any revolutionary regime or movement in abstract terms or from a theoretical lens alone. She does not let a political doctrine (like Marxism) dictate her political choices. Revolutionary movements must be judged case by case. She cannot support those that are stuck in authoritarian and undemocratic practices however relatively progressive they might be in challenging hierarchies and institutionalized power. Since the FLN had the chance of greatly improving the freedom of the many, she champions it, in spite of its sexist practices. If, however, its violence did not manifest its emancipatory goals, she would have withdrawn her support.

Debates around communist violence provide the context to think through broader problems of ethics and politics. For Beauvoir, approaching action in terms of Kantian principles or Marxist instrumentalism is deficient. Arthur Koestler's *Darkness at Noon* (1940), informed by Kantian philosophy, condemned violence outright and presumed the existence of pure subjects. On the other hand, orthodox Marxists justified any act of violence as necessary to the revolution's future, and were thereby guilty of instrumentalism. Beauvoir challenges the Kantian ideal of the categorical imperative, that is, that one should always be treated as a means to an end and not an end in itself. This was not possible during the war, when the Nazis were clearly oppressors, enemies, who were intent on denying the French their freedom. During the war, the enemy was obvious; there was a single oppressor. That is not true today: it presumes a level of distinctness of self and Other that is not possible. To realize the value of freedom and equality, she believes, on occasion, will mean that one's own projects will be threatened. Kantian ethics presumes that the moral worth of an act can be determined abstractly and formulated into principles without considering how historical context complicates this process (*PW*, 178). Justice might require compromising one's principle – that is, on occasion treating one as a means and not an end. During the war one could not respect the Germans as friends. By prioritizing the ethical and acting always on principle, Beauvoir insists, one has a hard time acknowledging evil or dealing with enemies. Such a Kantian stance has anti-political consequences.

Beauvoir is also wary of the ethical indifference of the instrumental Marxists who justify acts of violence in terms of the political goal of freedom. One cannot wait until freedom is achieved to think about ethics and morality. In fact, she argues that choices presume values and ethics. So, even if we claim to be acting in terms of political necessity, those acts have moral/ethical implications and must still be justified. Instrumental Marxists argue that one couldn't act as Marx predicted since the white Russians and enemies of the revolution must be combated with force and violence. The party was not fully apprised of the effects of these actions on the revolution. Authoritarian practices and excessive surveillance and domination will ultimately erode the end towards which the revolution proceeds. Beauvoir believes that the political goal of collective existence presumes mutually respectful and democratic relations with others. These cannot be deferred for long. While there is no morally prescribed path or action, ethical indifference cannot be tolerated until freedom and revolution are established.

Beauvoir is critical both of the Marxist's indifference to ethics and of the Kantian's purity of means and agents. Whereas the former is ethically indifferent and thus may allow atrocity and suffering, the latter's high moral standard eschews compromise, shuns violence, and involves a retreat from the political. In situations such as Algeria, war and violence are unavoidable. Beauvoir does not justify violence as necessary but believes each act of killing is a scandal and each must be considered specifically. There is no ready-made formulation – the death of one French soldier may be justified if one hundred Algerians are freed. The Marxists who believe that violence is a necessary means to a future of freedom will subvert the revolutionary end, if violence is not used expeditiously, economically, and towards the goal of freedom for all. She abhors the violence used by the OAS and the French army. On the other hand, a position of moral purity, such as that of Camus, where not a single death is justifiable, leads to shoring up the status quo. Since oppressors are not likely to be converted to the cause, violence will be necessary; however, since the revolution is not guaranteed, one cannot justify the sacrifice of this generation for the future collective good. Actors inspired by Kantianism avoid dirtying their hands. Rather than engaging in acts of violence, they retreat from politics and the possible loss of life and reaffirming the status quo. Hence this position has anti-political implications. In the end, Beauvoir's work as a critical intellectual supported the anti-colonial struggle and hastened the termination of the war and thus reduced the deaths, bloodshed, and suffering that would have occurred if the war persisted. Thus, this kind of activism can be seen as ethical. Its efforts were to minimize the violence used, rather than taking up a non-violent position that would shore up the status quo, which sustained oppression (and its structural violence).

Political relations that are oppressive and hierarchal must be transformed if democratic socialism is to be realized. Reciprocal and responsive behaviour towards others requires dismantling hierarchies and relations of domination. If collective freedom and more reciprocal relations are to be achieved, ethical purity will have to be compromised. The Kantian moral imperative will unlikely be up to the task for, in a world of institutionalized violence, individuals cannot be treated as ends in themselves. The purity of the Kantian principle would have required Beauvoir and Halimi to keep Boupacha's personal welfare and her rights uppermost in mind. After her trial, Boupacha was released, and the FLN returned her to Algeria against her will. She wanted to remain in France and was convinced that, since she had been raped, she was no longer marriageable. Halimi was willing to campaign for her return to France, but Beauvoir was not. Halimi took up a Kantian position – that the rights and welfare of the individual are primary – and so she was willing to support Boupacha against the wishes of the FLN. Beauvoir's position prioritized the political and the collective good. Cognizant of the importance of the FLN's health and legitimacy in newly independent Algeria, she was unwilling to risk the common good for the particular personal good of Boupacha. Politics in this case trumped ethics. As illustrated previously, there is often a tension between ethics and politics, which may or may not be resolved. Here Beauvoir prioritized the common good over the individual good. In this case she considered the political well-being and legitimacy of the FLN as more important than a single woman's welfare at this crucial historic juncture.

These actions were not above reproach. After Beauvoir's death, Halimi launched an attack on Beauvoir for being instrumentalist: "For her, Djamila was one victim amongst thousands, a useful case, in the battle against torture and the war ... For her, understanding the nature of the battle was more important than the person at stake" (Halimi 1990, 301). Halimi's accusation ignored Beauvoir's larger commitment to the freedom of all. She was not concerned with Boupacha per se but more engaged in the work around her defence and the revelations of the atrocity committed by the French soldiers. They had different priorities and perspectives. Halimi, as a lawyer, saw Boupacha as a case of human rights abuse, so Boupacha's rights were primary. Beauvoir saw her work in broader political terms and was more interested in collective struggles than in individual rights. However, as we have seen in the previous chapter, she does not justify acts in terms of a collective good, for it must further the freedom of individuals as well.

Some feminists argued that Beauvoir treated Boupacha like a poster girl – used her for the greater revolutionary cause.[14] After all, she persuaded Picasso to draw her picture and included it on the first page of *Djamila Boupacha*. She also approached other notables to contribute to the book. Is this not further evidence that Beauvoir "used" Boupacha to further her revolutionary reputation? Boupacha's youth and beauty were factors in the campaign, helping to gather support for her cause. Had she had been old, or middle-aged, or unattractive, Beauvoir's campaign might have been different. But since Beauvoir's media campaign was used to further justice for Boupacha and did not treat her badly in the process, was it not justifiable?

Some feminists argued that Beauvoir appropriated Boupacha's story and the narratives of the suffering Algerians. Kruks astutely cites Spelman's argument: "People enjoying being in the saddle of compassion may have disincentives to cancel the suffering that provides the ride" (in Kruks 2012, 116). Fanon made a similar case. The French intellectuals, he argued, were motivated by their own conscience and guilt, rather than the needs and suffering of the non-European Algerians. Was Beauvoir's activism driven by her guilt or genuine concern for the colonized? Even if she was genuinely concerned was this the best course of action. Again Kruks's words will be used as they capture the dilemma. "Silence and inactivity may be the best course for the privileged to follow, especially when an underprivileged group has become capable of articulating its own demands" (2012, 116). However this was not the case of Boupacha or the Algerian war.

While it may be true that Beauvoir spoke on Boupacha's behalf, her story of torture would not have been heard in France or abroad if renowned intellectuals had not taken up her case. Again I confirm Kruk's position. "When the oppressed cannot speak or cannot speak as effectively, or one is asked to be an ally, the better use of privilege, may well be to deploy it in order to speak and act for others" (116). For seven years

14 Gisèle Halimi makes this case: "I expected a sister-in-arms and discovered more and more an entomologist … For her, Djamila was … a useful case in the battle against torture and war" (in Murphy 1995, 283).

after the war began, barely a word was written in the mainstream French press to support Algerian independence. Beauvoir's privileged relationship with the media and the French public opened a space for these stories to be heard nationally as well as internationally. However ethically dubious some of her specific actions may appear, she still worked towards the greater freedom of the Algerian people.

Beauvoir's philosophic position that individual freedom must further collective freedom may make her refusal to help Boupacha return to France understandable, since helping Boupacha would end up demonizing the movement. We must remember that for Beauvoir ethical action cannot be determined abstractly, on the basis of principle, for values must be made to participate in history, so the situation is important.

While the suffering and harm done by both sides was regrettable, it was the context in which Beauvoir's activism was played out. What might have been reproachable in a time of peace and in the context of an established democracy is understandable in a time of revolution or open conflict. The Algerians saw the French as occupiers and murderers; the French saw the Algerians as ungrateful dependents and terrorists. This situation of war was not conducive to compromise, deliberation, negotiated settlement, or ethical action. Just as in the Second World War, when Beauvoir had insisted that one could not treat the German occupiers as unique individuals but as enemies, so the Algerians could not treat French forces and French authorities with respect, nor vice versa. This is not a justification for barbarism. In fact, Beauvoir reproached the French for not following proper procedures in the conduct of war and not treating the Algerians in a spirit of the republican values of equality and fraternity. Torture was unacceptable, as was the armies trying to block Boupacha's inquiry. As we have seen, Beauvoir was apprised of the effects of violence on the oppressed. Since the oppressor is unlikely to convert and thereby give up their power and privilege, violence is necessary; however, she fears that when the oppressed use violence, they themselves turn into executioners and murderers. To ignore the incidence of violence, bloodshed, and mutual suffering, and presume that an ethical principle could dictate action in a revolutionary situation, is naive and dangerous. However, if violence is to be progressive, it must be used with restraint and to further the realization of revolutionary values.

In a situation of violence and oppression, to refrain from acting or speaking out is to absent oneself from the struggle. Beauvoir claims that this is irresponsible. She does not believe absolute morality or principle should determine what is to be done, but rather one's decision is based upon the freedom of all. "Since it is true that each is bound to all … each is interested in the liberation of all" (EA, 112). Karen Shelby incisively summarizes the situation. "For Beauvoir the overall goal out of which each person must make meaning of her life is the search for the conditions that will allow all people to choose their freedom" (Shelby 2006, 94).

Employing authoritarian measures is only justifiable if it is furthering the values of an emancipatory movement. As an existentialist, who is trying to further the freedom of all, there is not really a choice between upholding the former colony or supporting independence, for the colonizers deny the freedom of the majority and, as such, are deemed opponents of freedom. In a world of oppression, the collective struggle trumps individual freedom: the future of the FLN was more important than Boupacha's wishes. Hopefully individual projects of freedom connect up to larger emancipatory forces. "We must end by abolishing all suppression: each one must carry on his struggle in connection with that of the other and by integrating it into the general pattern" (*EA*, 88–9).

Beauvoir identifies the ideas that underpin the practices of colonial rule; the "enlightened elites" believe that if the natives were given the rights of self-determination, they would live quietly in their villages without doing anything, which would be harmful to the higher interests of the economy (140). Since "women" and "indolent negroes" (140) are seen to be "eternal children who live in an infantile world" (141), and choose to live in "a state of stagnation" (141), they are not ready for freedom. Beauvoir clearly contests these Eurocentric statements: Algerians and women are oppressed – culturally, politically, and economically – but they are fighting for their freedom.

MOVING BEYOND THE UNIVERSAL INTELLECTUAL

As we saw in chapters 4 and 5, by the 1960s problems with Marxist revolutionary agency had become apparent. Skeptical that a proletarian revolution could bring forth popular power that would end exploitation and domination, wary of the undemocratic acts of the communist party and the repeated failures of the proletariat to seize power, former Marxists became increasingly disillusioned with the Revolution. The problems of proletarian agency led to a rethinking within Marxism (Deleuze, Guattari, Sartre, Beauvoir) and outside of Marxism (Foucault, Derrida, Barthes, Georges Bataille). Both groups called for more pluralistic and pluralized political movements that respect a multitude of desires and forces. While the former group remained committed to revolutionary projects, the latter did not. However, as proletarian politics offered little hope for change, the "Third World" and women's struggles became new revolutionary sites for the former. The later group focuses upon desire as an antidote to power.

The unwillingness of many Marxist intellectuals to withdraw their support from communist parties, and the canons of Marxist theory, left many critical intellectuals in a dilemma. As the prospects for changing the authoritarian practices of the communist parties in the Soviet Union and Eastern Bloc seemed bleak, many of the communist and non-communist left turned their attention to the revolutionary potential of the Third World – the "proletariat" of the south. Beauvoir and Sartre were no exception. Foucault scorned the communist and non-communist left, for their naive assumptions about power and change, that is, their assumption that the proletariat, or any unified agent for that matter, would bring forth freedom and equality. Power is not simply imposed on the outside from the top down, but is internalized and percolates up from the bottom. Domination is intrinsic in revolutionary politics, hence, for Foucault, all collective action is tainted. Most Marxists are naive, he believes, and fail to think of the diverse sources of repressive power, the social practices and institutions that help to create subjectivities in interpersonal/institutional arenas – what Foucault calls the microprocesses of power – must be acknowledged. Further, revolutionary practice involves relations of domination and authoritarian practices; collective movements and radical parties are tainted by such practices. Foucault criticizes the PCF for failing to address the problems of madness and incarceration, and their own authoritarian practices. The party did not own up to the powers of discipline they employed on academics, party members, and local populations to foster their legitimacy (Foucault 1984, 51–75).

For Foucault the "intellectual is not to establish laws or propose solutions or prophesying … [it] must not try to attain leadership, but work within [the movement]" (Foucault 1991, 160). Foucault believes that his role as an intellectual allows him to facilitate changes, but he never claims to be the one who knows how to solve problems. "I would like to facilitate this work, with its special problems, without delegating the responsibility to any specialist, much less to myself" (1991, 159–60). Derrida also supported the idea of the intellectual working alongside a social or political movement and contributing to it, rather than directing it. The intellectual must have the flexibility of mind to be open both to the unforeseeability of experience, as Foucault claims, and to the novelty of an event, as Derrida insists. Interestingly enough, the Marxist intellectual, much reviled by Foucault and Derrida, is equally attentive to temporality and contingency, as witnessed in Beauvoir's conduct. Beauvoir did not direct the FLN, but worked alongside it. She made no effort to lead or enlighten Muslim women, but simply was committed to a just trial for Boupacha. When she supported the FLN, she did not do so as if the movement was the bearer of truth and morality, but because it was the most favourable agency for change in the present.

The intellectual, or professor, Derrida notes, is not like the scientist who confines himself to describing states of affairs in objective terms but must accept responsibility for what he professes, portraying the performative aspect of theory (Derrida 2002). This is consistent with Foucault's ethos – we do not act according to principles or prescribed behaviour, rather we are guided by how we have chosen to live our life – that guides the performance. Being an intellectual requires listening to evidence, not leading a movement but taking part in it. This takes us some distance from the Marxist intellectual who is the faithful member of the party, following orders and leading insurrections, but it is not that far from the work of Beauvoir.

We are not guided by absolute truths, dogma, or blueprints; for Beauvoir, we must engage in politics and justify our actions on a case-by-case basis insofar as it is contributing to a future of freedom. Today, some argue that political commitment based upon Truth and dogma is dead. In fact, philosopher Karen Vintges believes that Beauvoir's ethics is practical – the art of living – without a foundation in Truth or God (1992, 5). Beauvoir was prescient in identifying the problem associated with truth; it leads to certainty, dogma, and even martyrs. When the "chefs" (*EA*, 109) of the party dictate what is to be done, and believe it is based upon objectivity, flexibility and responsibility are spurned. She bemoans the party's failure to admit doubt, or individual choice, in their decisions. "I regret that the non-communist left should have grown as monolithic as the party itself. A left-winger must necessarily admire China without the least reservation; take Nigeria's side against Biafra and the Palestinians against Israel. I will not bow to these conditions" (*PL*, 437).

Dogmatism leads to fanaticism. Instead of seeing struggles as concrete and specific, they are believed to have the answer to freedom. Beauvoir refuses such an approach believing that struggles may contribute to emancipatory forces, but might also fail. She sees politics as an open creative process – a committed response to an event – a miscarriage of justice, or a situation that requires support.

In acting freely, we must commit ourselves to a course of action we do not control; nonetheless, we must be responsible for our acts. Our commitment must be continually reassessed in the light of events, changes in material situation, and we have to judge each case in itself. While Beauvoir supported the FLN, she was critical of their policy towards women. She did not remain silent, but openly engaged in debate.

PROBLEMS ASSOCIATED WITH RATIONALIST POLITICS

Beauvoir's theory of embodied subjectivity addresses problems that arise in rationalist thinking. Even though many political theorists give some consideration to the non-rational preconditions for rational action, few are willing to give a wide berth to emotion. The primacy and purity of reason has been challenged not only by psychoanalysis and poststructuralism but also by phenomenologists. I have shown how Beauvoir respects the role of emotion in politics – mobilizing commitment and sustaining support.

More recently the turn to "affect" in cultural and political theory has led to the consideration of visceral affects that don't reach consciousness.[15] Whereas emotion reiterates predictable cultural responses, shoring up identity, affect theorists insist that affect is able to transcend identities and connect with otherwise heterogeneous beings. While passion can foreclose as well as open up generosity (see, for example, Connolly 1991) and thus can have negative as well as progressive political effects, affect is believed to be positive in effect. This is contestable, for it difficult to separate the affective and emotive in practice. Further openness or withness presumes an attitude that is not given, but is an achievement. Many humans may be unable to experience this. This is where a phenomenological corrective may have a place in debates. Respecting one's specific being in the world, as Beauvoir does, challenges the presumption that affect transmission is impersonal and fixed. Beauvoir challenges the sharp distinctions between affect and emotion and the pejorative thinking around emotion. As we have seen, emotion can positively enhance ethical conduct towards others; it is hardly to be spurned as mundane and predictable. Further, as my treatment of Hélène in *The Blood of Others* illustrates, responsiveness to others can be cultivated. People's behaviour is not fixed by early brain networking, nor by inner psychic life. Changes occurred in Hélène over the course of the war and the German occupation without the assistance of psychoanalysis. She was able to change her spontaneous disposition, which favoured selfish and intolerant behaviour, by changing her conduct towards herself and others

Since the effects of affect don't reach consciousness, or so affect theorists argue, it is difficult to harness and translate these pre-political rhythms or wild forms into an efficacious politics. Diana Coole makes

15 Erin Manning distinguishes "affect" – the initial visceral connections, "with-ness of the movement of the world" – from "emotion," which refers to culturally encoded and culturally variable sentiments (2006).

this point (1996); presumably such affects exist and even possibly are indifferent to the disposition of differently embodied subjects. However, employing them for democratic political purposes is a problem.

Another shortcoming of affect theory is that affects are presumed to occur at a subliminal or unconscious level, hence radical groups could employ manipulative tactics to further their cause. However, as we have seen in the previous chapter, Beauvoir disputes using any means to further the revolution. Since manipulative tactics would not further the development of the proletariat, they would likely derail a central aim of the revolution, popular power.

While the contemporary appreciation of affect is definitely beyond the bounds of Beauvoir's thinking, her appreciation of the primary pre-personal affective relation with the world that eschews instrumentality and reflection is worthy of attention. She is aware of the shortcomings of rationalism, as we have seen; she imagines commitment to group projects as shored up by our pre-personal and pre-reflective attachments to the world. We see this via Anne in *The Mandarins*: taking a risk, falling in love, reinvigorates her life. Attachment is presumed and intersubjective existence is enriched by improved social ties. Her embodied subjectivity gives space to emotion or the non-rational (bodily processes) in the construction of subjectivity, although it does so in a less systematic way than posited in the contemporary theory of affect.

Both Marxist and radical identity theorists assume that political agency flows from the experience of suffering and exploitation. So it is the experience of oppression and one's understanding of it that gives the agent the capacity to begin to change his/her conduct and consequently begin to catalyze changing the world. But this presupposes that revolutionary movements foster such knowledge. This puts intellectuals, relatively privileged members of society, on the margins, since they do have the experience of oppression. Marxists have a more complex understanding of the role of the intellectual. As the revolution approached, Marx envisioned that members of the bourgeoisie, the intellectuals, would break away from their class and identify with change. Although intellectuals are not themselves exploited, their loyalty towards the revolution and their empathy with the suffering of the working classes equip them to help the proletariat assume their liberatory role. The intellectual must not assume the role of leadership – nor should the party, for that matter – or only insofar as they facilitate the proletariat coming to power. Proletarian agency would ultimately overturn the hierarchies of leader and led, the powerful and powerless, and bring forth democratic power. Wary of the intellectual's role in the revolution, some Marxists disagreed with this scenario. The communist party, especially in the

Soviet Union, had a more troubled relationship with the intellectual; it wanted the intellectual to be under party directives. Antonio Gramsci also had concerns with middle-class intellectuals, and supported organic intellectuals, recruited from the working and peasant classes. As we shall see in the next chapter, in *The Blood of Others* committed middle-class intellectuals worked for the revolution and should not be repudiated for their class roots.

In light of the wane of revolutionary politics in the '80s, intellectuals were more likely to push reform and give primary importance to tackling prejudices and minority representation rather than revolution. Many call for the use of existing forums of democracy to counter inequalities and disadvantage. Working within public spaces and outside traditional frameworks of power to publicize and pressure governments is one set of tactics; the other is to employ existing institutions to deepen democracy. Deliberative democrats and multiculturalists assume that minorities must have space within the public sphere and within policy-making venues to articulate their interests and develop their voices. Further, they demand group rights and cultural protection from the state.

More radical intellectuals, who felt deliberation was insufficient, pressed for redistributive strategies and more inclusive public policy to counter power differentials. Rather than simply affirming one's distinctive identities or giving representative powers to minorities, they worked towards changing the system over time. Their reforms, they hoped, would prove to be non-reformable. Beauvoir had some affinity to this approach. It is important to support existing struggles for justice; over time these will contribute to the broadening of revolutionary potential. The cumulative effects of piecemeal reforms may be radical. Rather than assume or take up a "pure" revolutionary position that has little traction, she encourages people to adhere to projects of freedom that emerge out of their situations. Furthermore, she spurns abstract collective agency and urges people to commit themselves to specific struggles that capture their interests and desires. Those committed to emancipation are less convinced of the capacity of existing democratic institutions and frameworks to accommodate group interests or identities and therefore work outside the system to disrupt it or foster their minority group identity and counter-hegemonic projects. While Beauvoir believes in the importance of supporting counter-hegemonic projects, she does not believe in the purity of means and agency, so she is willing to working on existing institutions and existing political forces to transform them to enhance future freedom.

Beauvoir supported emergent anti-colonial and Marxist revolutionary struggles as they presented themselves. Sensitive to class as well as racial and sexual subordination, she did not impose Marxist theory on existing movements and forces to make sense of them, but tried to gauge their progressiveness from their actual social and political practice. Genuine freedom must will itself as "an indefinite movement through the freedom of others" (EA, 90). Her receptiveness to others' struggles and her openness to rethinking Marxist politics not only is refreshing but allows her to avoid the essentialism and theoreticism that plagues contemporary identity and Marxist politics.

Her defence of Boupacha does not rely on their shared feminine identity, nor did she share the liberal sentiment that it is possible to put oneself in the place of another, irrespective of one's subject position. Because she was neither colonized nor working class, Beauvoir's defence of Boupacha was not based upon identification. Nor did she assume that she could dip into any struggle and take up a position that was good for all. Radical politics grew out of a deep commitment and an embeddedness in concrete struggles. Although she had a commitment to the universal values of equality and liberty, her theory of situated and sexed subjectivity balks at an abstract universal perspective. Beauvoir's aspirations were inspired by her commitment to freedom, anchored by a concrete and located intersubjectivity engaged in specific struggles that she hoped would serve the "universal cause of freedom" (EA, 90).

7

Fictions of Politics: Affect, Idea, and Engagement

IN RECENT YEARS, there has been a turn to literature as a means of doing political theory and of thinking politically (see Nussbaum 1990, 1999; Stow 2007). Recognizing that emotion as much as reasoned argument contribute to our decisions and inform our judgment, means that literature and film have gained prominence in understanding human action. As the place where emotions are made visible, literature contributes to a broader understanding of human conduct.

Literature not only is able to give emotion and sensible experiences their due, but it also permits various viewpoints to be explored without offering pat solutions. Even though the world may be seen from the perspective of the main narrator or author, usually multiple perspectives are portrayed in a drama; hence, the narrative is polyphonic. Fiction explores the complexity of people's decision-making capacity and value-driven action, giving the non-rational, perceptual, aesthetic, emotional/affective new significance.

Encouraging marginalized people to tell their stories, and having others witness them, has led to an increased appreciation of the role of literature in democratic strategies. Yet since the discipline of political theory is dominated by unrepentant rationalists who believe emotion is dangerous and leads to poor judgments, there is still some resistance to using emotion and literature as political resources. Reason, these thinkers believe, should guide action, and emotion should be bracketed to achieve rational decisions. Far from encouraging emotion, it should be limited: giving a wide berth to strong emotion will have negative consequences. Some argue that being either overly empathetic or filled with hatred leads to extreme positions. While some emotions (i.e., of compassion, generosity) may contribute to democratic experiences, the inclusion of hate, contempt, revenge, and resentment shore up negative experiences that curtail democratic experiences. So while emotion is an important facet of human life that cannot be ignored, neither can it be relied upon to cultivate a democratic sensibility of openness and mutual respect.

Beauvoir, on the other hand, links affect, emotion, and reason in an interesting way. She obviously was not aware of the contemporary work on neuroscience – the way in which brain patterns established in early life produce strong affects which unconsciously determine human conduct – but she does appreciate the importance of biophysical, affective, and corporeal facts on human agency. In doing so, as I have shown in chapter 5, Beauvoir avoids social constructivist conclusions. In addition, she respects the roles of emotion and affect in fostering political conviction, as evidenced in her document on Boupacha, considered in the previous chapter. In this chapter, I will more fully and specifically consider her exploration of emotion and affect in literature, and how they contribute to a democratic sensibility of responsiveness and mutual respect. In contrast to the affect theorists, inspired by Deleuze, who are concerned with non-human autonomous affects and sharply distinguish affect and emotion – diminishing the significance of the latter in liberating subjects – Beauvoir is interested in embodied affects that are entwined with emotion and history and further human freedom.

The fictional world of literature and the aesthetic world of images and sensations provide mediums for the expression of emotion and affect. One cannot rely on analytic argument to understand emotion for it is best communicated in concrete descriptions. Often, visual figures/ strong images capture strong affects better than words. Additionally, Beauvoir was apprised of the use of images for political ends: she recruited Pablo Picasso to draw Boupacha and used this image as the cover of her manuscript, no doubt given the power of the image (Picasso's reputation was certainly also a factor).

Beauvoir also recognized the power of graphic descriptions to persuade. In her *Le Monde* article, she refuses to excise the word vagina from her text. She described Boupacha being raped with a bottle and tortured by electric currents that were attached to her breasts and vagina. She had no difficulty drawing attention to the striking images of women's shaved heads, marking them as guilty of "sexual" involvement with the Nazis occupiers. Images communicate strong negative affects and can be successfully mobilized to political ends. While rich image or thick descriptions cannot fully capture the complexity or intensity of actual sensation or memory, powerful expressions can foster empathy and lead to political commitment.

Political theorists' turn to literature and aesthetics is enhanced in a post-Kantian world where the aesthetic/affective register of experience is deemed to be as significant as reasoned argument in forging judgment or promoting consensus. Both Kant and Arendt assumed that people could agree on aesthetic judgments without offering rational arguments. One could be pleased with a novel, yet not have solid arguments to support or explain that experience. One could like a painting, but not be able to put one's feelings into words. Hence, the aesthetic turn assumes and cultivates the sensitivity of the people. It does not require that one be tutored in the philosophy of history to pass judgment. Beauvoir's appreciation of the roles of passion, desire, responsiveness, and interest in politics dovetails with this aesthetic turn.[1] But let's not attribute too much novelty to this turn.

The turn to fiction is often represented as bold and innovative where, in fact, literary devices, rhetorical concerns, and familiar tropes have informed political thinking since the time of Aristotle and the Greek rhetorical tradition. Rhetoric requires attending to the specifics of the audience and trying to persuade. In rhetoric, one is not solely concerned with the manifest content of the speech, but the concepts, frameworks, and tropes that help establish meaning. Rhetoric too has a long history in political thinking. One only has to reflect upon Thucydides's recording of Pericles's funeral oration. Pericles was acutely aware of different constituencies within the audience.

Recognizing the importance of the character of the speaker ("ethos" to the ancient Greeks), the speaker's location within the social milieu and to the audience (in the above example), and relation to the legal and political conventions all challenge the idea of abstract universal meaning (a challenge with which Beauvoir would certainly agree). Political knowledge, by its nature, dwells not in the realm of objective truths but in the realm of appearances. Arendt makes a similar point.

Many contemporary democratic thinkers believe that literature has a unique role in political thinking not only by contributing to the self-knowledge of the reader and writer but also by expanding one's knowledge of minority groups. Literature may concretely illustrate difference and heterogeneity. By putting oneself in the shoes of others, one is engaged less intellectually than emotively and affectively. This allows one to appreciate, if only temporarily, specific sufferings, as well as their motivation. Obviously reading novels, and better appreciating the situation in which others live, is not sufficient to root out prejudice. But Martha Nussbaum believes the cultivation of sympathy and compassion

1 The essays in Nikolas Kompridis's edited volume (2014) *The Aesthetic Turn in Political Thought* assume that political life involves one's corporeal or bodily existence and hence is innately artistic. To capture this domain of life political theory must embrace aesthetics.

will develop a moral understanding and thereby contribute to diminishing prejudice. Inhabiting, if only imaginatively and temporarily, the lives of others in a novel helps to combat the ignorance and unfamiliarity with an "alien" (minority, for most) culture that contribute to bigoted actions.

In cases when the telling of one's story is going to contribute to the self-development of a minority member, should it not be told by a member of that minority social group? While this is preferred, it is not always easy to determine which woman can speak for a particular minority group. As I mentioned in the previous chapter, members of oppressed minorities are not always positioned to tell their stories and get them published. Furthermore, retreating from speaking for another may have negative consequences, as Linda Alcoff has argued: if one abstains from speaking for others, it is politically irresponsible, for it allows oppressive discourses to go unchallenged and tends to make people not accountable for what they say, thereby making advocacy and coalitions impossible (Alcoff 1991/92).

Cultural Marxist Raymond Williams drew attention to the power of fiction to politicize the working classes as well as communicate their situation to others. Stories of struggle and suffering have to be told and read by members of the working class to gain awareness of the depth of their own oppression. Quoting Williams, Nussbaum notes the significance of literature in catalyzing political change: "Moreover we should not, as socialists, make the extraordinary error of believing that most people become interesting when they begin to engage with political and industrial actions of a previously recognized kind … For if we are serious about even political life we have to enter that world in which people live as they can as themselves and then necessarily live within a whole complex of work, love, illness and natural beauty. If we are serious socialists, we shall then often find within and cutting across this real substance – always in its details, so surprising and often vivid – the profound social and historical conditions and movements which enable us to speak, with fullness of voice, of a human history" (Nussbaum 1995, 72).

Beauvoir has a similar faith in the politicizing role of literature; her portrayal of the disastrous effects on women who live through their husbands and children helps raise feminist awareness. This is the intent in *The Woman Destroyed* and *The Mandarins*. The concrete details of one's daily living – how specific women subordinate themselves to their spouses, partners, and lovers, the dilemmas they confront, the decisions they make, and the pain they suffer – are most vividly communicated in fiction. These narratives are singular but not unique, for they communicate something of the lives of women who devote themselves to others. The stories can be shared and are intrinsically political.

As Raymond Williams directs political activists to read to understand the culture of the working classes, he also encourages the working classes to write and read; so does Beauvoir. While her work seems to be preoccupied with the experiences of women with whom she came in contact, mostly bourgeois, she supported working-class women to write. Her support for Violette Leduc is a case in point. Beauvoir not only acted as a mentor and literary advisor – meeting with Violette every other week to provide advice – but she financially supported her. Beauvoir arranged for a small monthly stipend (ostensibly from Gaston Gallimard) and when Violette's mental health was compromised, she paid for her psychiatric treatment (*LIT*, 5). Consistent with Beauvoir's concerns with the micropolitical, how women's dispositions and habits blocked their agency, she felt it was important to understand how women are complicit with social pressures that oppress them. Leduc's class position thwarted her life as an author; however, so did her distinctive way of living her class.

The act of writing not only contributes to the author's self-realization but also serves a broader social end of bringing women's experiences into visibility. In addition to empowering various social groups of women, the novel gives voice to different women's experiences within those social groups. For Beauvoir the novel has the power to capture complexity and difference, as well as the power to politicize its readership and thereby enrich public spaces.

Not all fiction was radical in substance; in fact, Beauvoir complains about famous writers (e.g., D.H. Lawrence) whose work served politically conservative ends (i.e., the objectification of woman). She emphasizes, however, the power of the writer and critic to draw attention to sexist behaviour as she herself does in *The Second Sex*. Recognizing the power of literature to extend the scope of women's imagination and contribute to their freedom, she also recognizes the possibility of the novel reiterating conventional social roles and thereby restricting women's horizons. However enriching and inspiring literature may be, Beauvoir does not believe that fiction is sufficient to liberate women, Blacks, Muslims, or the working classes. While literature is a form of political action, it cannot displace the need for women to work together for collective political ends (whether they be changes in policy or institutions). Literature can help us understand minority experiences, but that does not necessarily lead to changing the world. Hence, political activism, mass protest, the mobilization of dissent, or even armed rebellion may be required.

MARTHA NUSSBAUM AND SIMONE DE BEAUVOIR

Martha Nussbaum believes that literature helps democratic citizens develop inclusive and responsive conduct towards minorities; developing one's literary imagination furthers moral action. Judith Butler does not believe there is anything distinctive about literature and that insofar as texts refuse normalized/naturalized identities all fictional and non-fictional texts will further progressive ends. For Butler, those literary qualities and characteristics that Nussbaum suggests – e.g., simple resolutions, exemplary characters, and moral lessons – are problematic. Beauvoir's thoughts on literature fall somewhere between these two thinkers; like Nussbaum, she believes literature can have a pedagogical role, although she does not believe good fiction provides a moral perspective. Like Butler, Beauvoir sees the subject-in-process; for her, good fiction does not offer stable subjects, exemplary characters, clear resolutions, or pat conclusions, but allows for self-narration and the witnessing of the stories and events of others. She eschews ethical writing that is didactic, which Nussbaum seems to support. However, since Beauvoir subscribes to a narrative form and a pedagogic function, unlike the postmodernists, she believes that humans can come to understand themselves and the events of the world better in the process of writing and reading narrated events (even fictional ones). Nonetheless, good literature allows readers to enter the text and interpret in their own way – thus championing pluralism. This is thanks to the postmodern awareness that there is no stable, preconceived meaning that the author presumes. Scorning didactic literature, Beauvoir nevertheless believes literature can communicate philosophic ideas and ontological assumptions of ambiguity, contingency, non-essentialist yet historically open subjects, and the projects of human action and freedom. However, she supports a non-directive pedagogy. This creative process is also evident in the reader, who will not be pressured to follow certain ideas, but will make up their own mind in the course of reading the novel. For Beauvoir, good fiction, like good art, is non-directive and transgressive, challenging common sense, conventional meanings, and instrumental knowledge.

Both Nussbaum and Beauvoir believe that literature will enlarge one's understanding and contribute to just decisions and freer actions. For Nussbaum, literature provides a moral education – it asks us to concern ourselves with the lives of others who are distant from us. She is quite clear that emotions can work in tandem with rule-governed forms of reasoning to produce good judgments within existing political institutions and practices. Beauvoir, too, believes that emotions of compassion and empathy can lead to good political decisions. In disclosing the complexity of women's lived experiences through specific lives, Beauvoir appreciates concrete impediments to free agency as well as fictionalizing the capacity of women to reconfigure their lives. Other parallels between these two is that they both believe literature can supplement philosophy without displacing it, both believe that philosophy's effort to approach the universal is important, and both refuse the poststructuralist disposition that sees the universal as necessarily a sign of Eurocentrism. Both Nussbaum and Beauvoir believe literature has a role in political change that should not be underestimated; yet they do not believe it is sufficient to dislodge deep racial prejudice or injustices.

There are similarities between these two women and there are obvious differences. While Nussbaum believes that fiction works to counter prejudice, Beauvoir believes that fiction will contribute to counter-hegemonic projects and thereby challenge existing institutions and practices. While Nussbaum identifies the importance of moral education, Beauvoir aims at an education that radicalizes her readers. For Beauvoir, literature is not about producing better judgment within existing liberal democratic institutions. Rather, she challenges liberal justice as excluding women and minorities from power. Justice will require radical change and a moral education will reveal how one's self development should work towards the freedom of all.

Dissimilarities between Nussbaum and Beauvoir are evident in their political differences as well as their approaches to humanism. We are well aware that Beauvoir's radical humanism is associated with Hegel and Marx: she is interested in the human capacity to collectively work towards freedom. She clearly distinguishes her humanist thinking from Kant and Kantians who subscribe to "complete men" and "complete history" (EA, 41). For Beauvoir there are no pure subjects, nor absolute goals, that inform emancipation. From within a Kantian framework, Nussbaum has an idea of the ideal end and ideal means of achieving that end. In *Cultivating Humanity: A Classical Defense of Reform in Liberal Education* (1997), Nussbaum supports a liberal humanities education to cultivate humanity. In her view, this is the same as educating for world citizenship. But what does it mean to cultivate humanity? According to Nussbaum, one cultivates humanity and cosmopolitan attitudes by developing various capacities. Specifically, she identifies three capacities: the capacity for critical self-examination and critical thinking about one's own culture and traditions; the capacity to see oneself as a human being who is bound to all humans with ties of concern; and the capacity for narrative imagination – the ability to empathize with others and to put oneself in another's place.

Nussbaum believes literature plays an important role in cultivating reflexivity – and an appreciation of the classics contributes to a liberal education. Literary imagination is important for Nussbaum to cultivate humanity because, much in the spirit of Arendt, it gives access to representative thinking – "thinking in the shoes of another." Studying other cultures and reading their literature helps build bridges, furthers understanding, and cultivates empathy. Nussbaum hopes to cultivate attitudes that are respectful, tolerant, and empathetic towards non-Western peoples: literature is a resource of cosmopolitanism. However, she still upholds the privilege of Western texts, and the intellectual openness guaranteed by liberal democratic values and American institutions.

Entering into debates around culture wars in the 1990s, Nussbaum concluded that the liberal humanities curriculum is the way forward. She took a stand against those who pushed for the expanding education to include non-traditional texts and non-Eurocentric thinking. She believed the canon of literature and philosophy nourishes the development of morality and allows for enlarged political judgment. Women's literature and minority fiction must be read, she says, but the tolerant and inclusive values of liberal democracy were needed to frame such readings. Here Beauvoir and Nussbaum part ways; though Beauvoir, too, appreciates a new universalism,[2] it is not linked to liberal values or American culture. In fact, while Nussbaum believes in individualist values, and the institutions that protect them, she appears to be unconcerned about the power differentials preserved and the marginalization of non-Western cultures.

While Beauvoir saw literature as fulfilling a pedagogic role, she did not uphold the idea of a liberal education, or the idea of enjoying the literary or philosophical classics per se. She was very much aware of how women, Blacks, etc. were demeaned or erased in the canon. She was also highly skeptical of the philosophical canon that marginalized women as objects and subjects of research. So, unlike Nussbaum, who believes in a liberal arts education, Beauvoir was supportive of minorities telling their own stories, and challenging the liberal status quo. She did not revere ancient and modern classics, for she was aware of the role culture plays in sustaining power differentials. Beauvoir talks about the universal in a negative register, as embracing the idea of Mankind, as a mirage (*EA*, 157) that preserves the powers and justice of the privileged. She writes: "Mystification is one of the forms of oppression" (98).

2 Interestingly, Edward Said's most recent reflections on critical humanism are more in sync with Beauvoir. His renowned book *Orientalism* acknowledged how Western imperialists employed humanist thinking to colonize non-Western culture. Imperialists not only sought control of property and resources, but wanted Western philosophers, historians, and cultural theorists to make sense of Middle Eastern culture. This had the effect of effacing their cultural practices, by seeing them through the lens of Western liberal ideas. However, more recently, in light of the strength of Islamophobia today, he calls for a critical humanism that admits that humanism can be Eurocentric (a reassertion of Western cultural power) but is nevertheless a useful strategy to counter growing anti-Muslim sentiments.

For Beauvoir, good literature is rarely a classic, since classics have tended to exclude women and minorities and therefore have contributed to our gendered and racialized existence. Beauvoir makes an interesting comment in *The Ethics of Ambiguity* that respects the ambiguity of her own radical politics. She writes: "One can live without Greek, without Latin, without cathedrals, and without history. Yes, but there are many other things one cannot live without ... I would distrust a humanism which was too indifferent to the efforts of the men of former times ... no doubt the study of Greek and Latin does not have this living force in every age ... the fact of having a past is part of the human condition; if the world behind us were bare, we would hardly be able to see anything before us but a gloomy desert" (92). Beauvoir acknowledges the importance of past human efforts to disclose being; she believes things may act as living forces and "increase human powers" (92) and hence broaden our horizons. Yet she is fully apprised of the deficiencies of a past in which the freedom of women and minorities was structurally inhibited, so these efforts may have negligible effects. Structural changes are necessary to enhance individual freedom; however, she warns, structural changes alone will not produce freedom: "In order for the idea of liberation to have concrete meaning, the joy of existence must be asserted in each one, at every instant ... if the satisfaction of an old man drinking wine counts for nothing; then production and wealth are only hollow myths ... The movement toward freedom assumes its real, flesh and blood figure in the world by thickening into pleasure, into happiness" (135). So even if structural changes and the redistribution of wealth did occur, it would be a hollow victory if it doesn't produce joy. And joy has to do with one's authentic existence as well as with structural changes.

BEAUVOIR'S FICTION AS POLITICS

As political theorists turn to literature to provide a new model for thinking about politics, which avoids the narrow rationalist disposition of deliberative thinking, there is a growing belief that literature is a necessary part of the education of democratic citizens. People who are not familiar with philosophic arguments or political theoretical debates are often readers of fiction. Imaginatively inhabiting the lives of others brings one closer to these imagined others, thus mitigating the foreignness and stereotypes that haunt popular culture. Accepting Beauvoir's understanding of good fiction (as that which narrates the lives of minority Others), a successful story allows the reader to follow the ability or difficulty others have in confronting life and its dilemmas. Does this presume a fundamental identification with others in spite of differences? There has been much ink spilled over whether or not one must identify with the protagonist if one is to undergo this empathetic or pedagogic experience. Presumably the reader must be brought into the story and identify with the protagonist or alternatively feel sympathy for some of the characters in the novel, if not the protagonist. One can be drawn into the narrative through empathy rather than identification. In fact, over-identification with the protagonist and failure to see differences between one's own situation and that of a minority Other could become a problem.

Contemporary poststructuralist literary theorists have raised the problem of identification. Strong identities presume strong exclusions. Freud anticipated their insight. In *Civilization and Its Discontents*, he warned of how communities bound by love require a scapegoat – others to hate. This exclusionary logic symbolically annihilates the Other, and establishes a new transcendental object or subject. On a personal level, strong acts of identification serve to deny the heterogeneity of others' lives and contribute to an essentialism that privileges one's own values and subjectivities. Strong forces of identification are as problematic as the liberal humanist assumption that as humans we are more or less the same. If we are more or less the same, we can think, deliberate, and judge for the other, thereby riding roughshod over differences in experience and subject position.

However, in rejecting strong identification in social and cultural living, poststructuralists in general fail to understand the indispensability of communication: we don't have to be in the identical situation to empathize with another's suffering. Empathy presumes understanding our shared vulnerability, not necessarily presuming identification. Bucking the poststructuralist trend, William Connolly recognizes that identity claims acknowledge difference and that difference claims presume there are those that can be identified. He recognizes the indispensability of identity but disturbs its dogmatization into essential static identities. Mouffe and Laclau, too, recognize that identities are relational, hence never static. They refuse fixed social identifications – identities associated with pre-existing racial, linguistic, or ethnic groups – as politically regressive, yet they encourage the formation and proliferation of new radical democratic political identities. New identities are formed around new political demands, work to be done, rather than around past identities. Beauvoir, too, is an anti-essentialist, as we have seen, encouraging commitment to a cause or project, rather than an identity. Although she is more optimistic about collective work, and long-term commitment, she believes that commitment must be continually renewed. One does not devote oneself to a cause or movement indefinitely; one must continually reassess one's commitment.

However, there are similarities between Beauvoir and poststructuralists; she differs from them in her optimism around collective agency and the possibility of communicating across differences. She also believes that identifications can be transformative, a belief that underpins her fictional and non-fictional work. If women identify with her protagonists, or at least come to see the gendered aspect of their existence, they will gradually take stock and possibly imagine alternative identities. In addition, feminists organizing around a "we," loosely defined by their shared experiences and projects, is not a problem (as it is for poststructuralists). Feminists not only have rallied support around negative identities but have also formulated new positive transformative identities.

She is also more optimistic about the capacity to enlarge one's situation through shared understanding and communicative action. This communication is not simply linguistic but involves corporeal and emotive registers of experience.[3] Through mutually communicating experiences and sufferings, one does not inhabit the situation of the other, but approaches it. Hence, some cognitive and affective understanding of difference that does not involve colonizing the voice of the subaltern is possible. She does not presume that one can speak as the Other, but a movement towards the Other, a responsiveness, allows one to get out of one's skin and appreciate the Otherness of the Other. The ontological categories of "being in the world" and "being open to others," as expressed by Beauvoir, account for pre-reflective communication that one can build on to enhance the accommodation of minorities.

While Beauvoir appreciates the role of literature in challenging popular mystifications and furthering shared experiences, she does not believe that literature should directly serve political ends. She was highly critical of socialist realism, where aesthetics were politicized. If literature is defined by a political goal it is unlikely to be good literature. Italo Calvino makes this point in his book *The Uses of Literature*: "When politicians and politically minded people pay too much attention to literature, it is a bad sign – a bad sign mostly for literature, for it is then that literature is most in danger" (in Stow 2007, 1).

While one can learn from a novel, literature does not provide answers to specific political problems. It does allow a creative and self-directed "dialogue" to emerge between the reader and the text. Such openness is less possible in an analytic or philosophic text, where the power of logical argument prevails and a singular conclusion is presumed. This is also

3 In *The Blood of Others*, we will see how Jean entrains the negative affects of his suffering cook and his father's workers; this responsiveness leads him leave his bourgeois family and become a socialist.

unlikely in a novel defined by political ends, a concern raised by Calvino. Beauvoir challenges the idea that aesthetics should be subjected to a narrow political purpose or goal. If a novel is written to send a strong political message or has been circumscribed by political authorities, a practice prevalent under Stalin in the Soviet Union, then it is unlikely to be subversive.

At the time Beauvoir was writing, the socialist realists had a strong position on literature, believing that it reflected existing class relations and should provide role models for the rising proletariat. She found this stultifying. Like the communists, she wanted to catalyze a radical political sensitivity, but unlike them she did not want to produce a didactic text. Nor did she believe that art simply recorded social reality, or reflected the ideology of the times; this reflection theory of art denied the transgressive/creative capacity of art. She refused to abide by the communists' overly didactic or instrumental approach to culture. At the same time, she took a stand against the idea of "art for art's sake" – the idea that art was totally separate from the political and that politics tarnished or sullied art. The novel, she believed, was situated in a specific socio-historical and cultural context, yet was potentially able to illuminate some of the common mystifications of its times. To fictionalize situated universality was her aspiration. Beauvoir summarizes her comments on literature in the following passages: "Literature is not about recording the real, but establishing communication with others by starting from the singularity" (*LIT*, 199) of experience. The writer's "work must manifest his existence and bear its mark – and he imprints his mark on the work by his style, by his tone of voice and by the rhythm of his recital. No particular kind of writing is a priori privileged, none is condemned. The work – if it has succeeded – is defined, in all cases, as a universal singular which exists in the imaginary mode. By such a work, the author gives himself a fictitious constitution" (*ASD*, 130).

Maurice Blanchot attacked Beauvoir's philosophic novel as a "thesis novel" (*roman à thèse*) that illustrates ideas and teaches lessons and, consequently, is not good literature. While there is a tendency in some of her works to direct the reader towards a particular conclusion, I will argue that her texts avoid preaching or offering pat solutions and manage to respect ambiguity and contingency. She does not create predictable characters without surprises and tragedies; rather, her novels track "subjects-in-process." Nor is the end anticipated early on in the plot. For the most part, she avoids directing the audience to a particular judgment or conclusion. Recently, Simon Stow, in *Republic of Readers*, coined the term "pedagogy of indirection" to demonstrate the value of linking political theory and literature (2007). Beauvoir has something to offer in this regard. Unlike those theorists who turn to literature as a model for political theory, she uses literature and what she calls the metaphysical novel as a supplement to philosophy, without abandoning the contributions of philosophic arguments and historical analysis. Beauvoir rejected philosophic system building and systematic thought and hence appreciated the work of Søren Kierkegaard. Both rejected Hegelian philosophy that saw conflicting truth claims as moments of continuous thought that proceed towards a conclusion; they also reject the idea that the individual is realized in the social whole, and that "the individual is a moment in abstract spirit" (EA, 104). They both experimented with different ways of writing philosophic texts. Phenomenology, which offered descriptions, was one avenue she explored, but in addition her turn to literature was another way of writing philosophic texts.

LITERATURE AND METAPHYSICS

Beauvoir's interest in combining literature and philosophy began as early as 1927 (before her acquaintance with Sartre). In her student diary, she praises the philosopher Henri Bergson for recognizing that the novel is "able to disclose reality in its fundamental temporality," an "absurd reality of changing impressions that is distorted by the intellectual understanding" (in PW, 264); the novel is able to appreciate shifting perceptions across time.

In her 1946 article "Literature and Metaphysics" (PW, 2006), she picks up where she left off, twenty years earlier. Beauvoir speaks of the rapprochement of philosophy and literature. Since the search for certainty and foundational knowledge has proved untenable, contemporary philosophy has turned to subjectivity, temporality, ambiguity, and the singular. Literature has an increasingly important role to play in the exploration of these aspects of life.

Since philosophy cannot explain the world, or formulate a stable experience of the world, metaphysics is no longer concerned with a world beyond this one but with one's empirical, worldly being. The metaphysical is infused with, inseparable from, and does not transcend, one's life. Beauvoir appeals to childhood experience to give us a sense of what it means to experience the metaphysical: "The child discovers with astonishment their being-in-the-world as they experience their bodies … The child concretely discovers his presence in the world – his abandonment, his freedom, the opacity of things, and the resistance of foreign consciousnesses. Through his joys, sorrows … hopes each [man] realizes a certain metaphysical situation that defines him more essentially than any of his psychological aptitudes" (PW, 273). Elsewhere, Beauvoir describes this experience as ambiguity. "Man" experiences himself "as pure interiority," as a thinking reed as well as a thing that feels himself "crushed by the dark weight of other things" (*EA*, 7). Beauvoir, in her fiction, suggests that this ambiguity must be assumed and explores how ambiguity is assumed, or how it is fled in bad faith.

Existentialism grasps the essence at the heart of existence; it does not translate truths from philosophy into literary form but manifests an aspect of metaphysical experience that cannot be revealed other than in its subjective singular and dramatic character (*PW*, 274–5). Hence, the novel "tries to reconcile the subjective and objective, the absolute and relative, the temporal and historical aspects of reality" (100). The metaphorical and descriptive capacity of literature captures the mood and tone of lived experiences, the singular and dramatic character, that which is difficult to communicate in simple language. Hence, literature provides something that philosophy, in its struggles towards clarity and certainty, cannot.

The metaphysical novel is not intended to be a prop for philosophy. Beauvoir does not imagine that singular experiences need be distilled into philosophic concepts and then used by philosophers. If this translation were possible, she asks (*PW*, 270), why would one use a novel when it would be more expedient to use direct language? Clearly this prereflective and anonymous relation between mind and body, self and other, reason and emotion, is not accessible through direct language but requires metaphor, allegory, and indirect language: "So although philosophy and literature have drawn closer, they remain distinguishable" (Merleau-Ponty 1964a, 28). Literature helps philosophy capture prereflective and embodied experiences: the joy of enjoying a glass of wine (*EA*, 135). This reality does not nullify philosophy's contribution to knowledge but recognizes its limitations.

While philosophy gives the reader an intellectual meditation on human experience, the novelist offers mediation on an imaginary plane, presenting the experience itself prior to any elucidation (*PW*, 270). A different kind of experience, saturated with emotion and bodily sensations, is elucidated in the novel. The world prior to thought, the world as sensed and experienced, is the substance of a novel, thus allowing opaque experiences to be approached and felt, but not definitively explained, for that would saturate them with reason.

THE METAPHYSICAL NOVEL

Using a narrative form, the metaphysical novel grasps human lives, events, and the totality of existence in their temporality and their singularity (*LIT*, 199) providing a form of knowledge that is not available otherwise. The novel elucidates unique situated experiences. Yet Beauvoir is optimistic that her narratives, however expressive of concrete and particular experiences, resonate and communicate with her readers across time and place. She does not see the writer simply portraying the real (*ASD*, 130), but rather as orchestrating exchanges between characters in situations that have been fictionalized. These stories are not universal in the sense of capturing timeless truths, but, insofar as they explore the metaphysical in human existence, they approach universality.

The novel discloses what Beauvoir means when she identifies "woman as becoming." Challenging the realist novel and its assumption of stable characters, her women characters do not have a fixed or stable identity, but nor are they so fluid as to be defined by forces and people outside themselves. Here, again, Beauvoir parts company from poststructuralists who trouble identities and focus upon the fluidity of experience. Beauvoir recognizes that woman is an open-ended process, but she does not gloss over her facticity. She says, "It is clear that no woman, without bad faith, can claim to situate herself beyond her sex" (*SS*, 4). Not only does she encourage destabilizing identity, unsettling the past, but she also assumes women must engage in collective projects to transform themselves. Instead of working on disruptive experiences alone, at the level of embodied subjectivity, Beauvoir encourages women to bind and direct their energies towards projects of change. For institutional and policy changes can ameliorate the situation of women – change that transforms the micropolitical level of life.

Beauvoir urges women to engage in history, take up the struggle for equality and recognition; she knows personal conduct and sexual desire must be rewritten. She has been criticized by feminists for not offering positive heroines in her books. But since she is writing from the present, a present structured by patriarchal relations, very few women have managed to live a creative, productive, and engaged life. In the service of feminist pedagogy, it is important to portray not only the social forces but also the personal choices that impede women's autonomy rather than merely celebrate positive characters. The closest she comes to portraying a heroine is Anne in *The Mandarins*, who manages to avoid suicide in spite of a deep loss that she experiences. Beauvoir, unlike Nussbaum for example, is not interested in portraying exemplary characters, for that would gloss over the complexity, ambiguity, and lack associated with human life. Beauvoir spurns heroes, heroines, and pat solutions, appreciating the interdependence and incompleteness of subjectivity, the extent to which material/historical factors structure what is possible. However, in spite of these limitations she urges women to engage in projects.

Both of her early novels – *The Blood of Others* and *She Came To Stay* – illustrate her understanding of the self as complex and relational, displacing the notion of a fixed personality who confronts every situation in the same way. The novel form allows for the portrayal of the "subject-in-process" circumscribed by things, past relations, and structures, yet able to more or less negotiate its relation to the world and others.

THE THESIS NOVEL AND ADVENTURES IN NEW NARRATIVE FORMS

The literary critic Maurice Blanchot distinguishes the metaphysical novel from the thesis novel. The philosophic/metaphysical novel is informative but not didactic, whereas the thesis novel, he insists, is driven by ideas that teach a lesson or prompt "a moral conversion." Whereas the philosophic novel preserves ambiguity and "gives itself as a means of discovery and not as a means of exposing what has already been discovered" (PW, 264), the thesis novel concludes with clear resolutions and communicates pre-existing truths. *The Blood of Others*, he argues, is a thesis novel, whereas *She Came to Stay* is a philosophic novel. In *Force of Circumstance*, Beauvoir admits "Blanchot was right" – *The Blood of Others* is a thesis novel that fails to appreciate the ambiguity of existence and ends in a "univocal conclusion reducible to maxims and concepts" (FC, 622, 625). She attributes this to the moral period of her life and distinguishes it from *The Mandarins*, where she successfully avoids this "pitfall" (FC, 359).

I disagree with both Beauvoir's and Blanchot's assessments. The characters in *The Blood of Others* are not simply bearers of ideas, nor does Beauvoir fail to respect the fundamental ambiguity of the human situation by simply resolving the problems that appeared at the outset in a predictable way. While it is true that Hélène overcomes her egocentric behaviour and makes a political commitment, the process by which this comes about is not predictable. Nor are the personal dilemmas facing Jean clearly resolved by the end of the novel.

Further, some of the clarity of their positions is prompted by the context. Blanchot ignores the significance of the wartime setting. It presents the occupied with the stark choice of being complicit as passive collaborators or joining the Resistance. He further evades the complexity of the issue of commitment as Beauvoir draws it. She explores the class relations of the major protagonists: these determine neither their political commitment nor their behaviour towards others. Although the working classes and poor are structurally situated to experience the injustice and oppressiveness of the system, their position does not guarantee their commitment to change (EA, 20). The working classes are not always revolutionary, nor are they essentially good subjects. Nor, for that matter, are the middle classes always supporters of the status quo. This was evidenced in the commitments of Jean. He severed relations with his family due to his sympathy with the communist party, yet his pursuit of revolutionary politics was met with suspicion by his communist comrades. Nor did his eventual role in the resistance curry favour with his mother, who did not condone his spilling the blood of others. To say that the characters in this novel express pat ideas, or are simple supports for political and philosophic ideas, misses the complexity of the personal and political "becomings" that Beauvoir explores.

Blanchot is right to note that the characters of Françoise and Xaviere in *She Came to Stay* do not offer pat solutions to the dilemmas they face. They were not exemplary. Both fail to resolve their inner conflicts and unblock impediments to their freedom, but they reiterate their difficulties in a different form. In the first part of the novel, Françoise's emotions are repressed and Xaviere's are unbound; by the end their respective relationship to their emotions has dramatically reversed. It is as if they have adopted the other's behaviour. The repressed Other within Francoise's character finds affinity with Xaviere's impetuous conduct. This suggests no core stable self – neither Xaviere nor Françoise are autonomous selves as their subjectivity presumes their relations to others. Yet their conduct is more problematic since it reflects their unconscious and unmanageable vacillation between controlling and submissive desires. Here, Beauvoir offers two negative examples of women living their lives, in contrast with the more positive transformation that one finds in the character of Hélène.

Further I disagree with Blanchot who believes Beauvoir's novels fail to respect the ambiguity of time. These novels allow for temporality to be seen through the memory and development of a character through time. The future is connected to past and present behaviour, yet one's life is open to be rewritten. As humans, we grasp the world from our particular embodied situation, that is, a complex set of time/place/body syntheses. The world is not simply our perception or our experience of reality, for the real is unthinkable and always eludes us. We are an opening onto a world that is socially and relationally constituted, and therefore we can appreciate different perspectives of an event, through different narrations. And the time of these interventions is significant. In *The Blood of Others*, various women's experiences of the war are narrated, particularly how they reacted to daily fear and insecurity and the loss of their male companions or their fears of such loss. Through giving space to these different experiences, a fuller understanding of the event emerges. The war is not simply a composite of multiple private experiences, which are effects of interior psychic structures; rather, through an exploration of intersubjective lived experiences, we get a fuller, deeper, more complicated picture of life in occupied Paris. The transformation in Hélène's life from a narcissist to a committed member of the Resistance had at least in part to do with the extreme and shared experiences prompted by the Occupation.

WRITING AS A FORM OF ENGAGEMENT: BEAUVOIR AND SARTRE

So far we have explored the interplay and intersection of philosophy and literature, how the novel elucidates and deepens our understanding of human existence without employing philosophic categories. Beauvoir's novels explore the specificity of the human subject "in process," and neither is the subject assumed to be stable nor does it develop predictably in history. Individuals do not simply illustrate their class position, nor are they an effect of their historical situations. She eschews pat solutions to human dilemmas. The universal tone of Beauvoir's articles on the metaphysical novels, written in the early post-war years, may appear at odds with her subsequent interest in *littérature engagée,* a phrase she appropriated from Sartre. But I believe there is less of a rupture than one might think.

The later term coincides with a more politically active stage in her life, yet it is a specification of an engaged, embodied, and situated approach that she endorses throughout her life. In *What Is Literature?* (1948), Sartre focuses on the political power and responsibility of prose writers and speakers: "The committed writer knows that words are action. He knows that to reveal is to change and that one can reveal only by planning to change. He has given up the impossible dream of giving an impartial picture of Society and the human condition" (Sartre 1948, 37). Such a position clearly takes a stance against the nineteenth-century movement of "art for art's sake," inspired by Baudelaire and Flaubert and their commitment to pure form untarnished by political and social concerns. What is less obvious is how Sartre and Beauvoir avoid overly politicized art. They took part in several international symposiums on art and politics, expressing their sympathy with revolutionary movements, but they never endorsed the Soviet or Chinese cultural practices that they believed constrained artists and writers. They challenged reflective theories of art, which assumed art reflected a period in capitalist social development, or that it must reflect future role models for communist citizens. They envisioned art and literature as having a subversive potential – able to challenge or elude the power of capitalism. Without directly serving to educate the proletariat, or providing them their correct models as how to live, they believed the good novel would have progressive political effects on the proletariat as well as members of the bourgeoisie, women as well as minorities.

Beauvoir's understanding of literature as a form of "engagement" is not to be understood narrowly, defined by a specific political commitment or harnessed to the interest of the proletarian or emancipatory movements. Art has a transgressive role, Beauvoir believes, for it challenges popular myths, "common" sense promulgated by the powers that be. Rather than having a unitary voice, the philosophic novel stages conversations and actions between individuals with different voices and from different perspectives.

The political, for Beauvoir, is broader than politics; it is about not only actual struggles between existing political forces, but also concrete personal relations. The struggle between the characters on the left in the post-war years, as fictionalized in *The Mandarins*, reflects the micropolitical reality of embodied subjects. Communicating the complexity of the situation in post-war France and the disposition of the protagonists involves the narration of "the singularity of life" (ASD, 130). For this reason, her autobiographies, memoirs, and diaries are political. Writing, for her, is a form of self-realization that contributes not only to her personal development but also to an enriched public debate that is politically inspiring without being politically determined. Most of her writing has political implications, but it is not didactic in the sense of being driven by a specific political end or lesson. In narrating the lives of women, she brings to visibility women's experiences of subordination (in a complex and concrete form). She argues against realist theories of art, art as propaganda, and against submitting art to a political purpose or political agenda for that would undermine its transgressive side. Art and literature should not be in the service of proletarian culture, nor women's culture for that matter, but rather should critique existing values and lifestyles. If the state, or the party, restricts or produces art for its own sake, its subversive potential is undermined.

Narrating personal stories, imaginatively representing and speaking about personal experiences, furthers self-knowledge as well as worldly understanding. Paul Ricoeur says, "There is no self-understanding that is not mediated by signs, symbols, and texts; in the final analysis self-understanding coincides with the interpretation given to these mediating terms" (1992, 15). Literature allows for self-realization, but it has a further "political" function, for it brings to view experiences that were previously invisible. Beauvoir conceives the political broadly, anticipating the notion of the personal as political, the hallmark of second-wave feminism in the late 1960s. She believes that her fictional accounts of women – dying, aging, losing themselves in the lives of their husbands and children – will have a positive effect on women readers who will be awakened to the effects of patriarchal and capitalist society on their lives.

Literature becomes the place where people's existing relations with others are portrayed and one's mode of being in the world is witnessed. It thus takes on a testimonial function. Beauvoir's roman à clef, *The Mandarins*, along with the three volumes of her autobiography, her autobiographical novels that focus on her mother's death, and her *Adieux* (her reflections upon the last years of her life with Sartre) all recount the events of her life. Although she does not see the literary form as simply a way of coming to know herself, in the process of writing *The Second Sex* she does come to understand how she was made into a Woman, how she became Other. Given the significance she attributes to historical events in her writing, the role they play in her autobiographical accounts, and her acknowledgement of intersubjective or shared experiences, her writing goes beyond a private diary towards a public performance of her life. As we have previously seen, Beauvoir dismisses the pretensions and illusions of realist and objective approaches to events, and yet her account is not simply a private perspective but a meditation on the political and social world to which she bears testimony. Holveck emphasizes the testimonial function that literature plays in Beauvoir's work: "This involves the play between sedimentation as a personal obligation to bear witness to an event experienced collectively and the innovation of an individual to disrupt and refine the collective narrative" (Holveck 2002, 32).

Bearing witness to the events of the early post-war years, Beauvoir documented her visits to many countries in the throes of revolution and suffering. Making visible events that were silenced or absent from the popular press was her intention. She tells us that in this way she emulates Charles Péguy, a turn-of-the-century novelist who defended Dreyfus not because he was innocent, but because of his heroic courage. The novel allows acts of courage – such as those of the May '68 students, Algerians, and imprisoned Soviet writers – to be appreciated in a stylized form. But her narration of these events redefines the popular mainstream media and produces narratives of struggle.

Authors communicate their style of being-in-the world as they respond to the concerns of their times. During the late 1960s Beauvoir was concerned not only with the political claims of the students, feminists, and postcolonial movements but also with the micropolitical, evident in her concern about the objectification of women's bodies, the lack of mutual respect and responsiveness. Her fictionalized accounts of aging, the physical decline and ultimate death of her mother, and her everyday life experiences of writing and travelling might be considered banal and not particularly political. For this reason, many French communists called her a bourgeois thinker, and her work on sexuality libertine and dangerous. Yet in her hands the political implications of the everyday and the not-so-everyday (i.e., the actions of the Resistance and revolutionaries) are effectively conveyed.

Beauvoir writes, but also reflects on the act of writing in two short pieces, "Mon expérience d'écrivan" (1956) and "Que peut la littérature" (1965); both are reprinted in *Philosophical Writings* (2004). Again, here, she takes up her concern with metaphysical knowledge and pursues her interest in *littérature engagée.* She begins with Sartre's thoughts on fiction, specifically referring to his book on Flaubert. She uses two of Sartre's terms, the "singular universal" and the "detotalized totalities" (EA, 122). Writing manifests the "singular universal" through the examples of life that it presents. Values that are created by the proper exercise of freedom have a universal dimension in that any other human being could make sense of them in a similar situation. Universality manifests itself in the unique authentic project. Good literature will manifest or disclose this "singular universal," and, if it succeeds, it "detotalizes the totality"; that is, it subverts the totalizing processes of capitalism. Thus Beauvoir assumes that the novel expresses an act of engagement by expressing the "singular universal" (or as I have previously called it "a situated universal"). But, in doing so, the singular exceeds the presumed totality: "Man, mankind, history do not form a totality but are detotalized" (122). Their separation does not exclude relation. Their adventures are finite, yet they open onto the infinite future (122). The concrete situation it portrays is able to capture both the specificity and the generality of the epoch and of the milieu (PW, 449). In communicating and expressing one's concrete and embodied situation, literature holds open the possibility of "carrying the universal" (456).

While Beauvoir and Sartre share a political disposition towards writing, there are significant differences between them. Sartre spent more time on historical characters (e.g., Charles Baudelaire, Jean Genet, Gustave Flaubert) than Beauvoir. Her work on de Sade and Bardot is an exception. Rather than writing about renowned figures, Beauvoir more often focused on anonymous women and their ways of navigating their troubling situations. Feminist concerns frame her novels, but not his. In addition, she writes a lot about herself and the difficulties she faces day to day. Her autobiographical work is vast, documenting most periods of her life, whereas Sartre's autobiography *The Words* (1964) is a slim volume.

Although Beauvoir attends to the effects of bourgeois society on her characters, she avoids treating subjects as defined by their class position.

While she is sympathetic to Sartre's project of existential psychoanalysis, she does not subscribe to his notion of existential life choices that will give meaning to subsequent human behaviour. Sartre sees Jean Genet's life as deriving from an existential choice he made early in his life. Through her fictional work, Beauvoir explores dense connections and concrete relations that are not consciously chosen but corporeally and habitually lived. She portrays women not only painfully engaging in destructive acts but also deliberating, making choices, and acting, limited both by the opacity of their embodied habits and by their historical situation. She is inspired by the Sartrean concern for existential psychoanalysis, the need to know what decisions or non-decisions underpin human actions and life experiences, but also by Merleau-Ponty's attention to bodily habits. Like Sartre, she respects choice, but unlike him, she attends to the concrete bodily habits and sensibilities within which choice arises. One may not know or understand the complexity of one's desires/wishes or dispositions, but that does not stop us from making choices informed by them. Recognizing that these non-rational/non-deliberative factors play a role in one's decisions and judgments brings her closer to the ideas of Merleau-Ponty.

One's relations to things and to others is not cognitive, not deliberative, but rather influenced by affect, emotion, and diffuse bodily reactions that are the grounds of behaviour. Beauvoir senses that we are less trapped by the guilty and repetitive behaviour that Freud calls neurotic. As we saw in the character development of Hélène in *The Blood of Others*, it is possible to overcome destructive behaviour towards oneself and others without analysis. Hélène's change was triggered by an act of kindness that over time prompted a more responsive and open being, able to give to others. However, the context of the war was a factor in her change. She was unable to live the life she had previously lived: the conditions of Occupation called out for solidarity. Implicit in the novel is the understanding of how one becomes a woman: cultural and social processes are internalized and external (patriarchal and capitalist) social forces are taken up. From within a situation one has not chosen, one always has the opportunity to act in a way to reconfigure one's existing relations with others. There are no guarantees that one's intentions will be successful: one must accept "failures" (*POL*, 291) and disappointments and yet persist in one's projects. Beauvoir also portrays the failures to escape destructive behaviour, in particular in her portrait of Paula, whose delusions and obsessions lead to an emotional breakdown.

This draws attention to another difference between Sartre and Beauvoir. Sartre's *What Is Literature?* was written after the publication of his massive philosophical work *Being and Nothingness*, where he was at his

Cartesian best; the author in full control of his project calls for the transparency of writing. Beauvoir refuses these rationalist assumptions. This has consequences for her understanding of writing: "I set great store by nuances and ambiguities ... Existence ... cannot be reduced to ideas, it cannot be stated in words; it can only be evoked through the medium of the imaginary object; to achieve this, one must recapture the surge of backwash, and the contradictions of life itself." Insisting that life escapes and exceeds the author's intention, she adds: "We expect novelists to evoke the flesh and blood presence whose complexity, singular and rich existence exceeds any subjective interpretation" (*FC*, 319). The act of writing, expressing the complexity of emotions and experiences, is always going to exceed the author's and reader's efforts to make sense of these experiences. The role of affect is important to disrupt habits.

THE BLOOD OF OTHERS: NURTURING EMPATHY AND COMMITMENT THROUGH THE TRANSMISSION OF EMBODIED AFFECT

Contemporary affect theorists (Brian Massumi, William Connolly, Jane Bennett) are interested in disclosing the power of things – either as actants or via their ability to activate humans. Focusing on the non-human world of lively matter, they take us away from human emotions. While Beauvoir does attend to autonomic processes like blushing or heart palpitations, she is interested in how the transmission of affects between humans can contribute to change. Far from being part of the anti-humanist tradition of Deleuzean affect theorists, Beauvoir is interested in the differential capacity of subjects to entrain affects and how that responsiveness leads to change. Again, in spite of Beauvoir's use of the concept choice, she attends to how pre-reflective, sensory, and emotional aspects of being must be reworked to alter one's habits and liberate women. From egocentric, impetuous, and cruel behaviour (specifically towards her boyfriend Paul) at the outset of the war, Hélène gradually adopts a more caring and responsive relation to others, which culminates in her joining the Resistance. Her transformation is not the result of rational deliberation or conscious choice, but as a gradual shift that is initiated by her entraining bodily affects. Hélène transitions from a narcissist to a responsive and committed woman. Several events of affect transmission catalyze her change. She waits for the car to be refuelled, she eyes a mother and child. Beauvoir describes the weight of a child and the concerned look of its mother affecting Hélène. She offers up her seat to the free zone. Hélène befriends a mother and daughter, and, in a reciprocal gesture, they share their meagre supply of food. The daughter persuades a Nazi officer to take Hélène with them to Paris. It is not that Hélène decides to become less selfish, more empathetic, nor is she described as undergoing, a moral conversion, but rather the look of a child, the offer of food, trigger acts of generosity.

Beauvoir also describes how the war triggers acts of solidarity. Their shared conditions of suffering provide the possibility of forming social groups with common goals. However, there is still a role for the individual. "To adhere to Marxism, to enroll in a party … and in one rather than another, to be actively attached to it, even the Marxist needs a decision whose source is only in himself" (EA, 20). This is again evidenced in the character of Hélène; her acts of generosity do not connote that her character is transformed. In fact when she is back in Paris, she is tempted by a German businessman to take a job in Germany. Even though her parents and friends are shocked, she proceeds with a dinner invitation/interview. But it is the sheer affluence of the offerings – food that she hasn't seen for ages, readily available to all these Germans – that sticks in her throat. She refuses dessert, chocolates, cigarettes, and ultimately the job offer itself. Again her decision is driven not by deliberation, but by her ability to respond to the affects of others. At first the presence of the gorgeous food and sumptuous surroundings fill her with delight, but as dinner progresses, and she reflects on her friends who were imprisoned and her French compatriots who were starving, it becomes impossible to eat. It is not that she learns to be responsive, but she does become more empathetic, and this supplants her narcissism, which is evident at the outset of the novel. Beauvoir traces her becoming, which culminates in her taking risks to save her Jewish friend and joining the Resistance movement. Hélène is able to overcome emotional conflicts within herself, as well as with others, and ultimately become self-realizing. The novel illustrates how ethical behaviour and political commitment are achieved; previous habits and dispositions are dislodged by the transmission of affects that lead empathy and the building of social ties. In doing so, Beauvoir counters the Kantian position that people are rational subjects who make ethical choices and Habermasians who assume our actions are deliberative.

In *She Came to Stay*, Beauvoir uses Françoise and Xaviere to think through two very different forms of relational subjectivity that are equally debilitating. They did not rework their selfish habits and resentful dispositions, but remain trapped in them. Françoise acts like a Kantian and tries to live according to an abstract principle of moral reason; she exemplifies the rationalist who is driven by the "I ought." Xaviere is like a Kojèvean Hegelian, stressing the importance of desire as a motivating factor of action; she exemplifies the "I want." Although many readers will not know – and don't have to know – the philosophic backdrop, they appreciate the striking contrast in the way the two women behave towards each other and towards the world. Françoise's overly rational and managed approach to life is in sharp contrast to Xaviere's impulsive, impetuous, and unreflective reactions. Neither has a healthy response to their emotions, nor a responsive and caring relation to others. Françoise represses her feelings and Xaviere vents hers upon others. Although Françoise tries to mentor Xaviere and invites her into their home, she is more concerned with remaining attached to her partner Paul, who has fallen in love with Xaviere, than with helping Xaviere. Although their positions are portrayed as (philosophically) irreconcilable, towards the end of the novel, instead of softening their rigid approaches and accommodating the other within, they assume each other's subjective positions – at least temporarily. Beauvoir does not theorize their behaviour as a fierce form of abjection, projecting onto the Other those attributes that one consciously spurns, yet abjection is evident. The ultimate statement of their reversal is evidenced in Françoise's murder of Xaviere, a crime of passion. Unanticipated, this rational woman, who at the outset of the novel suggested that Xaviere be invited to live with her and Paul, ends up murdering her.

The Blood of Others, in contrast to *She Came to Stay*, portrays woman's capacity to change over time. Hélène develops from an impetuous women incapable of thinking of others, incapable of even regulating her desire or acting in her own interest, to someone who is responsive and caring. She benefits in the process from building social ties and meaningful relations and ultimately commits an act of bravery.

Blanchot criticized *The Blood of Others*, believing that it was driven by a pre-formulated ethical and political position and provided a simple resolution to the human condition. I disagree. Over the course of the novel, a compelling transformation of character is portrayed and various approaches to ethics are explored. Unlike the Kantian who upholds the universal law of truth-telling, Hélène's story illustrates the importance of breaking laws and lying. Given the choice of lying to protect her friend from the Nazis rather than giving her up, Hélène declares that Yvonne is her sister, and thus saves her life. Challenging principled approaches to ethics – thou shalt not lie – Beauvoir suggests one must, in these circumstances, lie to protect one's friends.

Beauvoir's novels deal not only with the complexity of ethical positions, but the complexity of political commitment. As members of the bourgeoisie, Beauvoir's and Sartre's revolutionary commitments were often objects of scorn, a problem associated with Marxist functionalism tackled in *The Blood of Others*. One's class does not determine one's revolutionary position, but rather presumes choice and commitment. Jean, born into a bourgeois family, is unable to live comfortably with his privilege; he decides to live the life of a worker. In doing so, he cuts off his ties with his family and his privileged job and tries to join the communist party. In spite of his strong commitment to the struggle Jean is not accepted by his fellow communists – much in the same way that Beauvoir and Sartre were dismissed as bourgeois intellectuals by the PCF.

In addition to approaching the problem of Marxist functionalism, that the working class are revolutionary by virtue of their social location, this novel complicates that scenario; Jean ends up being one of the founders of the Resistance movement, just as Sartre and Beauvoir proved to be committed to revolutionary projects. Beauvoir also fictionalizes how habits and dispositions are reworked to effect changes on the micropolitical level. Change in Hélène's relations to herself and others precedes her political commitment to the Resistance movement. It is not affects alone, but affects entwined with emotion (empathy) in specific embodied subjects that build social ties and further commitment to change. Unlike Hélène, who is portrayed as a narcissistic girl, Jean is shown to be empathetic to the sufferings of his family's maid and unease about his family's status; Beauvoir describes Jean's empathy to the working classes and his discomfort with his family's wealth: the scent of good food, the sensuousness of rich carpets, the light of large open sparkling windows, the warmth and rich sensations from comfortable overstuffed furniture are linked to guilt rather than pleasure. The emotion of guilt was transferred from his mother and mediates his experience of his home. Herein lies the incipience of his action; his guilt about his privilege, his responsibility for others, his desires to rectify this situation, impel Jean to leave his home, live as a worker, join a trade union. His conduct and identifications foreshadowed his radical politics and commitment to others' freedoms.

Beauvoir also uses this novel to approach the problem of revolutionary violence. Yet, instead of justifying the violence that ensued during the Resistance, Jean was rightly tormented by it. The novel begins and ends with Jean describing Hélène as his inspiration and admitting his sense of responsibility for her death. He feels directly responsible for the loss of the blood of others, the blood of his comrades. His mother reproaches him for being responsible for lives lost. He is also troubled by the Resistance movement's acts of terrorism. But there is no easy answer: either they refuse to shed the blood of others, and thereby submit to Nazi victory, or they risk the lives of others and shed their blood to defeat the Nazis.

Jean is exemplary: someone who willed their own freedom and in doing so willed the freedom of all. Yet he is not morally pure. His conscience/hands were dirty. However laudable his contribution to the freedom of all (i.e. the resistance), rather than projects of oppression (i.e. the collaboration), it did not absolve him of responsibility for its good and bad acts. Since his actions were structured by forces and circumstances outside his control, Beauvoir does not believe that Jean should be fully responsible for what happens. In personally feeling responsible for the blood of others – the death of those in the resistance and the death of Hélène – he assumes too much responsibility, presuming that violence was avoidable in the struggle against the Nazis or that he was responsible for Hélène's choice to join the Resistance. Beauvoir believes death and killing are always a scandal. They have to be justified, never a priori or before the case, for they have to be judged in terms of how successful their acts were in realizing the values of freedom and equality. In this case, Jean's acts were justifiable, since they did contribute to the defeat of the Nazis. Interestingly, Beauvoir pursues the philosophic ideas that we see in *The Ethics of Ambiguity* in *The Blood of Others*: the problems associated with violence and commitment – the difference being that she is able to develop the alternative positions more fully in the novel through the voices of Jean, Jean's mother and father, and Hélène.

LITERATURE: THE WITNESSING OF CONCRETE FREEDOM

Fictional writing expresses the author's imagination and elicits the imagination of the reader. Since writers are trying to capture that which is complex, opaque, and not easily communicated in simple language, images, metaphors, and all sorts of rhetorical devices become important. A narrative is useful since it allows something that cannot be articulated in simple words to be expressed through descriptions of the surroundings and portrayals of habits and behaviour. In *The Blood of Others*, Hélène's self-development is tracked: we see her gradually moving away from egocentric, impetuous, and destructive behaviour towards more responsive and caring relations to others. The language of self-development is overly restrictive, presuming a telos that is out of character with the false starts, failures, and open-endedness of the process of becoming. Linear development or notions of maturity do not capture Beauvoir's concepts of "subject-in-process" and a "being-in-the-world." Agency presumes relational beings who achieve coherence over time through continuous performances. This process is not linear or developmental, for there is always backsliding as witnessed above in the actions of Hélène. There are no moral or political conversions, for we must be open to reevaluate our positions case by case.[4] Since we are beings-in-the-world, we must be

4 This illustrates Beauvoir's strategic support for the PCF and the USSR. In the early '50s Beauvoir held a wait-and-see position; however by the mid-'50s she no longer could remain silent, and openly criticized their tactics.

sufficiently secure and flexible, open to synchronizing with new forces and new events. Rather than wilfully asserting oneself and trying to master outside forces, Beauvoir urges us to take our bearings in history.

Beauvoir describes how the novelist actively incarnates their experience through metaphor and narrative, the chosen medium for uncovering the singularity of the meaning of being. In disclosing the meaning of being, one discloses "the-self-in-process." Beauvoir comes to know herself and the world as disclosed in time and space through stories told. The self does not precede this act of self-making, which is at the same time an act of disclosure. Literature allows the portrayal of the self in relation to things, in interaction with others, and in the process of action, thereby eschewing a univocal perspective and the assumption of objective truth. The writer imaginatively choreographs unique interactions in a particular historical context. One of the most touching sequences is Jean's description of his luxurious house that loomed over the grimy workshop on the ground level. The description of Jean's affluence, his identification with the suffering workers, and the guilt associated with his privilege anticipate his later political affiliations. This novel discloses Beauvoir's political values and disposition, her concerns with the PCF, her support of the Resistance. But it does not dictate any specific political goals.

Literature should not be harnessed to specific political purposes or social ends – it would become didactic, and interfere with the individual process of identifying (or not identifying) with characters, of constructing meanings from amongst a plurality of perspectives. The "truths" gleaned from our intersubjective experiences mediated by aesthetics cannot simply be applied to the existing situation to guide one's decision-making or action. Yet one cannot ignore the feelings of pleasure that arise from reading a good novel. The successful novel has the power to explore a complicated situation; whether or not it moves someone to act in a compassionate way is another matter. It might contribute to knowledge and/or conviviality, inspire solidarity, or trigger a sense of shared humanity. Herein lies its richness as a medium of expression.

In contrast to many novelists who focus on form – and whose work provides the matter for semiological or psychoanalytic readings of events and actions – Beauvoir and Sartre, as we have seen, are inspired by "a realist narrative" that provides an imaginative social history. In addition, Beauvoir employs the novel as a means of exploring philosophic ideas and approaching political dilemmas that will resonate with others and gesture in some way towards improving the existing world. This approach to literature is out of tune with the semiology or the nouveau roman, which both refused narrative structure. This was also out of step with the currents in contemporary French cinema; one need only remember how Jean-Luc Godard, for example, spurned the logic of a beginning, middle, and end. So while it might be argued that Beauvoir's novels were not experimental in terms of their form, their content was innovative and forward looking. Her non-moralistic tone in the death of Xaviere, her unsentimental approach to Anne's achievements and sacrifices in *The Mandarins*, do not lend themselves to pat political choices. In fact, her novels provide a space where ambiguity, human dilemmas, and choices are played out in a complicated way. I think her ability to explore the microprocesses of power in the lives of human beings remains compelling.

Literature does not squarely expose nor contest the bourgeois world, but does both indirectly and subtly by revealing contemporary social norms and their disastrous effects. In doing so, Beauvoir's novels bear testimony to the unfulfilled universal values of bourgeois society (i.e., freedom and equality) and the individual's heroic, or not so heroic, efforts to confront their dilemmas and lead lives driven by values. In contrast to postmodern theorists of literature – for whom the universal is rejected as Eurocentric, norms are considered necessarily normalizing and oppressive, and "only the marginal, perverse and aberrant can escape this dreary regimenting" (Butler 2004b, 14) – Beauvoir recognizes the capacity of her fiction to challenge bourgeois sexist culture. She does not believe that all norms are equally negative and oppressive; struggles in the name of liberty and equality are valued ontologically: committed action, inspired by equalitarian and democratic values, is politically privileged. Hence norms and values are not deemed to be normalizing in the post-structuralist sense of the term; for Beauvoir they open up opportunities for acting and can enhance social and political change. Beauvoir manages to avoid some of the concerns that the postmodernists articulate, without retreating from collective politics, falling prey neither to static, fixed essences nor a universal narrative of Marxism that predetermines the course of events and human agency. She has a theory of action.

Beauvoir's democratic socialist purpose is to make not only economic goods but cultural ones available to all. Today cultural critics are hesitant to claim knowledge of what is good for all, since the making and assessing of learned culture, we are told, is subject to social exclusions based on ethnicity, race, etc. They consider the universal aspirations of culture that Beauvoir espouses (i.e., understandings of human existence) Eurocentric or masculinist, and her struggle for good literature both elitist and exclusionary. In the wake of May '68, the public critic, who presumably has the authority and knowledge to shape public taste, has been debunked. "The death of the author" – the renowned refrain of Roland Barthes (1968) – has heralded the era of the reader, since the author is no longer considered a resource for understanding the meaning of the text. The proliferation of meaning and the loss of standards of evaluation mean that all interpretations of a work are endorsed. This theoretical move coincides with other anti-authoritarian cultural practices that dismiss not only authors but also trained experts or critics. Our contemporary world of the blog – and the instant recording of opinion on the Internet generally – has furthered this unseating of the critic. We don't need authorities to mediate our opinions or allow us to speak, for we can immediately respond to any work.

Although being of that generation in which the cultural critic had some role, and being a critic herself, Beauvoir was aware of the problem of elitist culture. In fact, her interest in securing a large audience led her to write for newspapers and, in the last years of her life, she turned to film. She believed popular fiction allowed sensitive and thoughtful members of the public to participate imaginatively in the lives of others. They did not need to be familiar with philosophic debates to appreciate the metaphysical novel, for the novel form introduced them to contemporary philosophical concerns through emotional involvement rather than logical argument. As we saw in the introduction to this chapter, modern critics such as Martha Nussbaum share Beauvoir's belief that reading a novel may open a space for the reader to appreciate the experiences of a subordinate and oppressed member of society in a more sympathetic light. But unlike Nussbaum Beauvoir does not endorse liberal democratic values and institutions as the framework in which non-Western culture is to be assessed. Not that Beauvoir wasn't guilty of Eurocentric sentiments – but rather her emancipatory framework, which accepted difference and strove for embedded freedom for all, eschewed the values and institutions so often associated with liberal societies.

Challenging the persistence of narrow conventional norms, practices, and moralistic attitudes and exploring many unacceptable and unpopular themes, Beauvoir shocked the public not only in what she wrote, but also in how she lived her life. Her private life was very public and the stuff of popular fiction. Her refusal to marry, her unorthodox "family" of friends and intellectuals, her bohemian lifestyle, and her sexual relations with both men and women, some of them much younger than her, scandalized the bourgeois French mentality. In *The Blood of Others* she deals with abortion and sexual abuse, concerns not usually fictionalized. Her work on the Marquis de Sade is equally bold, especially in light of her feminism. She refuses to take up a moralistic or dismissive attitude towards his sadomasochistic sexual practices; in fact, she praises his resoluteness and refusal to repress his unorthodox sexual desires. Since his behaviour did not seriously harm anyone apart from himself (he paid the onerous penalty of spending thirty years in a French prison), she holds up his behaviour as praiseworthy, for he remained true to his beliefs and desires and continued to write prolifically.

Beauvoir also praised the work of actress Brigitte Bardot. Again she was not moralistic or judgmental but, as a cultural critic, engaged a figure of popular culture in order to "educate" the general public. Far from teaching women of the evils of being sexually objectified, she took Bardot's refusal to be cowed by men into accepting sexually submissive or obliging roles as evidence that the sex symbol was "liberated" from conventional restrictive feminine behaviour and refused to play "the good girl" (*BBLS*, 1962).

Beauvoir's positive affirmation of Bardot is entirely in keeping with the negative depictions and tragedies throughout Beauvoir's novels: she portrays women who "lose" themselves in their male lovers or in their children's lives, and thus repeatedly draws attention to women's failure to affirm their own existence and to engage in their own projects. Feminists have criticized Beauvoir for not producing many positive role models for women, but they have glossed over those whose lives she did endorse – herself being one example, as well as Bardot and Violette Leduc. It is not surprising, given the forces that "defined" women's being as otherness, that the times in which she lived might not have afforded many positive role models. Furthermore, the negative models of Beauvoir's fiction are dramatic and tragic, and thus enhance the political message of her work. She is not so narrowly political as to support only those women who become political militants, but instead supports writers, artists, and accomplished professionals.

Since Beauvoir struggles to attend to concrete singular experiences in their complexity, contingency, and ambiguity, her novels do not endorse individuals unqualifiedly nor do they offer pat solutions. If one has learned anything from Beauvoir, it is the inability to employ models and principles or to learn lessons in any simple sense. Her fictional writing is suggestive but it does not dictate what is to be done, nor teach one how to live one's life. Sitting again between the modern and postmodern, Beauvoir believes culture furthers self-realization and collective political agency. One is encouraged to remake oneself through one's writing, and this is not an individual act, but an intersubjective one; it is not a wilful act, or only insofar as its wilfulness is embedded in culture and history. Such a work of art must assume contemporary cultural practices and aesthetic traditions to speak to the problems/preoccupations of our times; in this way writing takes up a relation with its forebearers and takes on concerns of the situation, providing a broadly political focus. So she is more optimistic about the capacity to learn from conversations, without believing that understanding produces effective action.

Like Merleau-Ponty, Beauvoir is interested in fiction's capacity to supplement philosophy. Both believe that human existence in its pre-reflective and embodied forms is best approached obliquely in fiction. The sensory, sexual, and tactile world of experience is often ignored in philosophic arguments or scientific theories that concentrate on analytic precision and certainty. Beauvoir and Merleau-Ponty are not driven to retrieve the lived experience for its own sake, but, by grounding thoughts and action in bodily being (that is, being-in-the-world), they tap into metaphysical experiences, a collective pool of energy and memory.

Beauvoir's commitment to revolutionary theories of Marxism and feminism often makes it easy to misunderstand her approach to liberation: dramatic socio-economic changes are necessary, but one must inspire and mobilize human agents. Herein lies the significance of literature: it helps women, the working classes, and minorities to understand their oppression as political, as something changeable, and to engage in the world and act politically. Literature does not displace political action (nor does it ever pretend to since it continually presents itself as fiction) but does help it proceed by leading people to understand the specificity of how the authoritarian projects play themselves out on the self. Although Beauvoir is indebted to political doctrines (i.e., Marxism, democratic socialism, and feminism), for her they do not dictate what to do but, rather, help her understand the fields in which our acts are structured and help us stand up for radical democratic actions. Literature has a role to play in the project of self-making, for the imaginary and narrative acts are important in writing oneself beyond the present. Beauvoir insists that humans create themselves within a context that they do not choose, but still they can and should make choices as to how to live their lives. As we have seen, she explores this through many genres – literature, autobiography, plays, philosophy, and the political essay. She also anticipates the significance of emotion and affect in catalyzing change, but her human-centred approach distinguishes her from the anti-humanist position of the affect theorists.

Conclusion

IN THIS BOOK, we have witnessed how Beauvoir confronted the political problems of her day by supplementing or reconfiguring existing political discourses. Not only did her fiction, autobiographies, and eclectic approach to philosophy help her activism, as I have shown; I also believe they help radical emancipatory thinking more generally. We see how a committed philosopher manages to act in a world where it was difficult to support existing radical political parties, but also a world that continually undermined and thwarted radical movements. Without despair, Beauvoir managed to act and think in a way that fostered her personal freedom as well as the freedom of all. Focusing upon Beauvoir's gender politics and *The Second Sex* glosses over her broader emancipatory thinking to be found in *The Ethics of Ambiguity*, her novels, and her essays. Many interpreters have overplayed Beauvoir's intellectual and political debt to Sartre and therefore have not appreciated Beauvoir's distinctive embodied approach that avoided his youthful individualism as well as some of the shortcomings of his mature Marxism. Supporting grassroots movements with diverse claims as well as class politics; acknowledging that the macropolitical is as significant in generating change as the micropolitical; and fostering ethical responsibility without forgoing political effectiveness, Beauvoir manages to provide new ways of thinking about emancipation. I have inserted Beauvoir's ideas and activism to think alongside and against various discourses and debates. Although it was not her express intention to provide a more inclusive and complex theory of freedom, as I have shown, through integrating her ideas, she managed to do so. In spite of the fact that anti-humanism, posthumanism, and new materialism appear to dominate theoretical spaces today erasing or severely curtailing human powers, using Beauvoir I have made a case for a corrective. Obviously, the problems associated with a sovereign, self-sufficient, rational actor are well rehearsed; yet erasure of human agency is equally problematic, I believe. This problem has plagued structuralists and poststructuralists and continues to afflict the new materialists and the affect theorists. In denying qualitative differences between the human and non-human world, affect theorists make human agency even more problematic. As we have seen, Beauvoir had some ambivalence in seeing the body as wholly socially constructed, believing "there are [bodily] conditions without which the very fact of existence would seem impossible" (*SS*, 24). So one could imagine her supporting the anti-humanists' idea that bodily agency presumes the mineralization of bone to assume the upright position. Further she recognizes that the preservation of life is something that links the human and non-human and is not a distinguishing feature of the human. Beauvoir does go on to say, however, that unlike the non-human, humans are reflective, aware of death, and interested in surpassing their limits (*PW*, 289). Reflective choice, intention, and norm responsiveness impact their situation – marking a difference in kind from the non-human world of rocks, not simply a difference in degree. Furthermore, to tackle the pressing problems of our times – the intransigent social hierarchies and sedimented power relations – expanding human and non-human assemblages are insufficient. Human initiative and action will be necessary.

Beauvoir's appreciation of sensory and emotional experience enlarges the political; however, unlike contemporary affect theorists who focus on the power of things and severely diminish human agency, she reconceives human agency to accommodate these non-rational as well as linguistic processes. Beauvoir's turn to fiction and autobiography helps accommodate the non-rational aspect of experience; however, she stills feels it is necessary to respect human choices, conscious plans, and linguistic analysis. For Beauvoir, action also requires others – the synchronizations with the emancipatory projects of others, an embeddedness in history – in order to make a difference. Beauvoir believes that one must assume the givens of the situation and act within the limits of the possible; thereby she respects the socio-economic, political, and cultural fields within which choice emerges. "It is not a mysterious essence that compels men and women to act in good or in bad faith, it is their situation that disposes them more to seek the truth to a greater or lesser extent" (*SS*, 15). Although Beauvoir insists upon willing, one's choices and actions are affected by exogenous factors.

Returning to the subject to help structural change and Marxism proceed, she theorized the roles of affect, ethics, and commitment to further political engagement. Unlike the structuralist and poststructuralist, who tie ethics and responsibility to disciplinary practices and political strategies of control, Beauvoir sees ethics and responsibility as vital to change. Having appreciated the role of human agency, she does not lapse into voluntarism or idealism, for she recognizes the significance of the material/historical situation and bodily structures in working towards freedom. As we have seen in the course of this book, she expanded the agents of change as well as the mediums of radical politics. She fostered grassroots struggles that she believed would contribute to broader democratic socialism. As we have seen throughout this book, Beauvoir's materially and historically sensitive body subjects allowed her to intervene in events to further radical human agency, be it through her essays, her activist engagement, or her fiction. While acknowledging the complexity of power relations both at the micropolitical and macropolitical levels of life, nonetheless she believed in the possibility of emancipation from oppression. Her critiques of existing revolutionary parties and undemocratic, intolerant social practices were prescient, but unlike the thinkers of the post-'68 generation, she remained optimistic that collective political change was possible. In setting her ideas and activist practices in conversation with significant political theoretical debates that have challenged minority human agency, whether it be gender/sexed identities, psychoanalysis, socio-economic structures, or political attitudes and institutions, I have shown that she has a way of traversing these fields without being stymied. In addition, I have shown how historical/social contexts and events informed both her theoretical interventions and her practical politics. Beauvoir's activist politics were not derived from theoretical formulas or philosophies of history, but informed by existential Marxism and grounded in present realities. As such, tracing her action allows the reader to appreciate how a committed radical acts and thinks within the limits of the possible. Instead of assuming a principled or abstract position, Beauvoir embraces existing struggles to broaden revolutionary movements, thereby avoiding the dogmatism or theoreticism that afflicted many of her contemporaries. This approach to radical agency, which is philosophically and ethically inspired whilst also being grounded in the concrete, transcends her time and the confines of revolutionary politics.

References

WORKS BY BEAUVOIR

ADD: *America Day by Day* (2002)
ASD: *All Said and Done* (1993)
BBLS: *Brigitte Bardot and the Lolita Syndrome* (1962)
BO: *The Blood of Others* (1964)
DB: *Djamila Boupacha* (Beauvoir and Halimi 1962)
EA: *The Ethics of Ambiguity* (1948)
FC: *Force of Circumstance* (1987a)
FW: *Feminist Writings* (2015)
LIT: *The Useless Mouths and Other Literary Writings* (2011b)
OA: *Old Age* (1977b)
PC: *Pyrrhus et Cinéas* (1944)
PL: *The Prime of Life* (1988)
POL: *Political Writings* (2012)
PW: *Philosophical Writings* (2004)
SS: *The Second Sex* (1974, 2011a)
WD: *The Woman Destroyed* (1987b)

Beauvoir, Simone de. 1944. *Pyrrhus et Cinéas.* Paris: Gallimard.
– 1945. "La phenomenologie de la perception." *Les Temps modernes* 2 (November): 366–7.
– 1948. *The Ethics of Ambiguity.* Translated by B. Frechtman. New York: Citadel Press.
– 1954. *She Came to Stay.* Translated by R. Senhouse and Y. Moyse. New York: Norton. First published in 1943.
– 1960. Prefaces for Marie-Andrée Lagroua Weill-Hallé, *Le Planning familial* (Family planning) and *La grande peur d'aimer* (The great fear of loving). Geneva: Editions Gonthier.

– 1962. *Brigitte Bardot and the Lolita Syndrome.* First Four Square Book, New English Library Ltd.
– 1963. *Memoirs of a Dutiful Daughter.* Translated by J. Kirkup. Middlesex: Penguin Books. First published in 1958.
– 1964. *The Blood of Others.* Translated by Y. Moyse and R. Senhouse. London: Penguin. First published in 1945.
– 1974. *The Second Sex.* Translated and edited by H.M. Parshley. New York: Vintage Books.
– 1977a. *The Mandarins.* Translated by L.M. Friedman. London: Fontana Collins. First published in 1955.
– 1977b. *Old Age.* Translated by Patrick O'Brian. Harmondsworth: Penguin.
– 1987a. *Force of Circumstance.* Translated by R. Howard. London: Penguin.
– 1987b. *The Woman Destroyed.* Translated by P. O'Brian. New York: Pantheon Books.
– 1988. *The Prime of Life.* Translated by P. Green. Harmondsworth: Penguin. First published in 1960.
– 1992. *Letters to Sartre.* Translated and edited by Q. Hoare. London: Vintage. First published in 1990.
– 1993. *All Said and Done.* Translated by P. O'Brien. New York: Paragon House. First published in 1972.
– 1994. Preface to *Treblinka,* by Jean-François Steiner, xix–xxiv. Harmondsworth, Middlesex: Penguin. First published in 1966.
– 2000. *America Day by Day.* Translated by C. Cosman. California: University of California Press.
– 2004. *Philosophical Writings.* Edited by M.A. Simons and M.B. Timmermann. Urbana: University of Illinois Press.
– 2011a. *The Second Sex.* Translated by Constance Borde and Sheila Malovany-Chevallier. New York: Vintage Books.
– 2011b. *The Useless Mouths and Other Literary Writings.* Edited by M.A. Simons and M.B. Timmermann. Urbana: University of Illinois Press.
– 2012. *Political Writings.* Edited by M.A. Simons and M.B. Timmermann. Urbana: University of Illinois Press.
– 2015. *Feminist Writings.* Edited by M.A. Simons and M.B. Timmermann. Urbana: University of Illinois Press.
Beauvoir, Simone de, and Gisèle Halimi. 1962. *Djamila Boupacha: The Story of the Torture of a Young Algerian Girl That Shocked Liberal French Opinion.* Translated by Peter Green. New York: Macmillan.

OTHER WORKS CITED

Alcoff, Linda. 1991–92. "The Problem of Speaking for Others." *Cultural Critique* 20, no. 1 (Winter): 5–32.

Alford, C. Fred. 1989. *Melanie Klein and Critical Social Theory: An Account of Politics, Art, and Reason Based on Her Psychoanalytic Theory.* New Haven, CT: Yale University Press.

Althusser, Louis. 1970, 1971. "Ideological State Apparatuses." In *Lenin and Philosophy and Other Essays.* New York: Monthly Review.

– 1976. *Essays in Self-Criticism, Part 1.* London: New Left Books.

– 2006. *Philosophy of the Encounter.* London: Verso.

Andermahr, Sonya, Terry Lovell, and Carol Wolkowitz. 1997. *A Glossary of Feminist Theory and a Concise Glossary of Feminist Theory.* London: Arnold.

Appignanesi, Linda. 2005. *Simone de Beauvoir.* London: Haus Publishing.

Arendt, Hannah. 1972. "Lying in Politics." In *Crises of the Republic.* New York: Harcourt Brace Jovanovich.

– 1993. *Truth and Politics in between Past and Future.* New York: Penguin.

– 1998. *The Human Condition.* Chicago: University of Chicago Press.

Astruc, A., M. Contat, and G. Séligmann (Directors). 1976. *Sartre par lui-même.* Film. France.

Bair, Deirdre. 1990. *Simone de Beauvoir.* New York: Summit Books.

Barrett, Michelle, and Mary MacIntosh. 1982. *The Anti-Social Family.* London: Verso.

Barthes, Roland. 1968. "Death of the Author." In *Image Music Text.* Translated by S. Heath. London: Fontana.

Bauer, Nancy. 2001. *Simone de Beauvoir, Philosophy, and Feminism.* New York: Columbia University Press.

Benjamin, Jessica. 1988. *The Bonds of Love: Psychoanalysis, Feminism, and the Problem of Domination.* New York: Pantheon.

Bennett, Jane. 2001. *The Enchantment of Modern Life: Attachments, Crossings, and Ethics.* Princeton: Princeton University Press.

– 2010. *Vibrant Matter: A Political Ecology of Things.* Durham: Duke University Press.

Bergoffen, Debra. 1997. *The Philosophy of Simone de Beauvoir: Gendered Phenomenologies.* New York: SUNY Press.

Bordo, Susan. 1990. "Feminism, Postmodernism and Gender Scepticism." In *Feminism and Postmodernism,* edited by L. Nicholson. New York. Routledge.

Bourdieu, Pierre, and Claude Duverlie. 1987. "Esquisse d'un projet intellectuel: un entretien avec Pierre Bourdieu." *The French Review* 61, no. 2: 194–205.

Braidotti, Rosi. 1991. *Patterns of Dissonance.* Cambridge: Polity Press.

– 1994. *Nomadic Subjects: Embodiment and Sexual Difference in Contemporary Feminist Theory.* New York: Columbia University Press.

– 2002. *Metamorphoses towards a Materialist Theory of Becoming.* Cambridge: Polity Press.

– 2013. *The Posthuman.* Cambridge: Polity Press.

Brison, Susan. 2003. "Simone de Beauvoir: Interviews and Reflections." In *Cambridge Companion to Simone de Beauvoir*, edited by C. Card, 189–207. Cambridge: Cambridge University Press.

Brown, Wendy. 1995. *States of Injury: Power and Freedom in Late Modernity*. Princeton: Princeton University Press.

Buchanan, Ian. 2008. Introduction to *Deleuze and Guattari's "Anti-Oedipus": A Reader's Guide*. London: Continuum.

Butler, Judith. 1986. "Sex and Gender in Simone de Beauvoir's *Second Sex*." In *Simone de Beauvoir: Witness to a Century. Yale French Studies* 72: 35–49.

– 1990. *Gender Trouble: Feminism and the Subversion of Identity*. New York: Routledge.

– 1993. *Bodies That Matter*. New York: Routledge.

– 1997. *The Psychic Life of Power*. Stanford: Stanford University Press.

– 1999. "'Bad Writer' Bites Back, Response to Martha Nussbaum." *New York Times*, 20 March.

– 2004a. "Merleau-Ponty and the Touch of Malebranche." In *The Cambridge Companion to Merleau-Ponty*, edited by T. Carman and M.B.N. Hansen. Cambridge: Cambridge University Press.

– 2004b. *Undoing Gender*. New York: Routledge.

– 2004c. *Precarious Life: The Powers of Mourning and Violence*. London: Verso.

Butler, Judith, and Gayle Rubin. 1994/1995. "Sexual Traffic: An Interview with Gayle Rubin." *Differences*, Winter: 62–100.

Camus, Albert. 1948. *The Plague*. Translated by Stuart Gilbert. New York: Vintage Books.

Caputi, Mary. 2006. "Beauvoir and the Case of Djamila Boupacha." In *Simone de Beauvoir's Political Thinking*, edited by L. Marso and P. Moynagh. Urbana and Chicago: University of Illinois Press.

Carr, N. 2010. *The Shallows: What the Internet Is Doing to Our Brains*. New York: W.W. Norton.

Chanter, Tina. 1995. *The Ethics of Eros: Irigaray's Rewriting of the Philosophers*. New York: Routledge.

Chelliah, Jane. 2014. "Austerity and Gender Neutrality: The Excluding of Women and Mothers from Public Policy in the UK." In *Mothering in the Age of Neoliberalism*. Edited by Melinda Vandenbeld Giles. Waterloo: Demeter.

Connolly, William E. 1991. *Identity/Difference: Democratic Negotiations of Political Paradox*. Minneapolis: University of Minnesota Press.

– 2002. *Neuropolitics*. Minneapolis: University of Minnesota Press.

Coole, Diana. 1996. "Is Class a Difference That Makes a Difference?" *Radical Philosophy* 77 (May/June): 17–25.

– 2007. *Merleau-Ponty and Modern Politics after Anti-Humanism*. Latham: Rowman and Littlefield.

– 2013. "Agentic Capacities and Capacious Historical Materialism: Thinking with New Materialisms in the Political Sciences." *Millennium: Journal of International Studies* 41, no. 3: 451–69.

Coole, Diana, and Samantha Frost, eds. 2010. *New Materialisms: Ontology, Agency, and Politics.* Durham: Duke University Press.

Critchley, Simon. 2013. *Infinitely Demanding: Ethics of Commitment, Politics of Resistance.* London: Verso.

Crosland, Mary. 1992. *Simone de Beauvoir: The Woman and Her Work.* London: Heinemann.

Debray, Regis. 1979. *Le Pouvoir intellectuel en France* (Intellectuals of modern France). Paris: Grasset.

Deleuze, Gilles, and Félix Guattari. 1987. *A Thousand Plateaus: Capitalism and Schizophrenia.* Translated by Brian Massumi. New York: Continuum.

– 1994. *What Is Philosophy?* Translated by H. Tomlinson and G. Burchell. New York: Columbia University Press.

Delphy, Christine. 2000. "The Invention of French Feminism: An Essential Move." In *French Feminism Reader,* edited by Kelly Oliver. Oxford: Rowman and Littlefield.

Delphy, Christine, and Sylvie Chaperon, eds. 2002. *Cinquantenaire de Deuxième Sexe.* Paris: Syllepse.

Derrida, Jacques. 2002. "The University without Condition." In *Without Alibi,* edited by P. Kamuf. Stanford: Stanford University Press.

Deutsch, Helene. 1944. *The Psychology of Women.* Vol 1. New York: Grune & Stratton.

Deutscher, Penelope. 2008. *The Philosophy of Simone de Beauvoir: Ambiguity, Conversion, Resistance.* Cambridge: Cambridge University Press.

Duchen, Clare. 1986. *Feminism in France, from May '68 to Mitterrand.* London: Routledge.

– 1987. *French Connections: Voices from the Women's Movement in France.* Amherst: University of Massachusetts Press.

Elliott, Anthony. 2002. *Psychoanalytic Theory: An Introduction.* Durham: Duke University Press.

Evans, Judith. 1986. *Feminism and Political Theory.* London: Sage.

Evans, Mary. 1985. *Simone de Beauvoir: A Feminist Mandarin.* London: Tavistock.

Fallaize, Elizabeth. 1998. *Simone de Beauvoir: A Critical Reader.* London and New York: Routledge.

Fanon, Frantz. 1967. *The Wretched of the Earth.* Translated by C. Farrington. New York: Grove Press.

– 1968. *Black Skin, White Masks.* London: MacGibbon and Kee.

Fassin, Eric. 2011. "A Double-Edged Sword: Sexual Democracy, Gender Norms and Racialized Rhetoric." In *The Question of Gender: Joan W. Scott's*

Critical Feminism, edited by Judith Butler and E. Weed, 143–60. Bloomington and Indianapolis: Indiana University Press.

Ferguson, A. 1990. "The Problem of Desire: Simone de Beauvoir and the Lesbian." In *Hypatia Reborn: Essays in Feminist Philosophy*, edited by A. Al-Hibri and M. Simons. Bloomington and Indianapolis: Indiana University Press.

Foucault, Michel. 1984. *The Foucault Reader*. Edited by P. Rabinow. New York: Pantheon Books.

– 1991. *Remarks on Marx: Conversations with Duccio Trombadori*. New York: Semiotext(e).

– 1994. *The Essential Foucault*. Edited by P. Rabinow and N. Rose. New York: The New Press.

Fouque, A. 1991. "Women in Movements Yesterday, Today, and Tomorrow: An Interview." *Differences* 3, no. 3: 1–25.

Fraser, Nancy. 1995. "From Redistribution to Recognition? Dilemmas of Justice in a 'Postsocialist' Age." *New Left Review* 212 (July/August): 68–93.

– 1996. *Justice Interruptus: Critical Reflections on the "Postsocialist" Condition*. New York: Routledge.

– 2000. "Rethinking Recognition." *New Left Review*, May/June: 107–20.

– 2003. "Théorie de la société et théorie de la justice : Entretien avec Nancy Fraser." *Variations* 4 (Automne): 21.

– 2007. "Recognition: A Two-Dimensional Approach to Gender." *Studies in Social Justice* 1, no. 1 (Winter): 23–35.

– 2008. *Scales of Justice: Reimagining Political Space in a Globalising World*. Cambridge: Polity Press.

Freud, Sigmund. 1950. *Totem and Taboo*. London: Routledge and Kegan Paul.

Furet, François. 1981. *Interpreting the French Revolution*. Translated by E. Forster. Cambridge: Cambridge University Press.

Fuss, Diana. 1989. *Essentially Speaking: Feminism, Nature and Difference*. New York: Routledge.

Gatens, Moira. 1993. *Feminism and Philosophy: Perspectives on Difference and Equality*. Cambridge: Polity Press

Genz, Stéphanie, and Benjamin Brabon. 2009. *Postfeminism: Cultural Texts and Theories*. Edinburgh: Edinburgh University Press.

Gerhardt-Brunner, Susan. 2004. *Why Love Matters*. London: Routledge.

Gorz, André. 1982. *Farewell to the Working Class*. London: Pluto Press.

Grosz, Elizabeth. 1994. *Volatile Bodies: Toward a Corporeal Feminism*. Bloomington: Indiana University Press.

– 1995. *Space, Time, and Perversion*. New York, Routledge.

Halimi, Gisèle. 1990. *Milk for the Orange Tree*. Translated by D. Blair. London: Quartet Books.

Haraway, Donna. 1991. "A Cyborg Manifesto: Science, Technology, and Socialist-Feminism in the Late Twentieth Century." In *Simians, Cyborgs and Women: The Reinvention of Nature*, 149–81. New York: Routledge.

Harding, Sandra. 1986. *The Science Question in Feminism*. Ithaca: Cornell University Press.

Hardt, Michael, and Antonio Negri. 2004. *Multitude: War and Democracy in the Age of Empire*. New York: Penguin Press.

Hartsock, Nancy. 1986. *Money, Sex, and Power: Toward a Feminist Historical Materialism*. Evanston: Northeastern University Press.

Hass, Lawrence, and Dorothea Olkowski, eds. 2000. *Rereading Merleau-Ponty: Essays beyond the Continental Analytic Divide*. Amherst: Humanity Books.

Hayles, Katherine N. 1999. *How We Became Posthuman: Virtual Bodies in Cybernetics, Literature and Informatics*. Chicago: University of Chicago Press.

Heinämaa, Sara. 2003. *Toward a Phenomenology of Sexual Difference: Husserl, Merleau-Ponty, Beauvoir*. Lanham: Rowman and Littlefield.

Hekman, Susan. 1990. *Gender and Knowledge: Elements of a Postmodern Feminism*. Boston: Northeastern University Press.

Hennessy, Rosemary. 1994/1995. "Queer Visibility in Commodity Culture." *Cultural Critique* 29 (Winter): 31–76.

– 1998. "Disappearing Capital: The Queer Material of Sexual Identity." Paper presented at the Centre for Interdisciplinary Gender Studies, University of Leeds, October.

Hird, Myra J. 2002. "Feminist Theory on the Move Again: Exploration of New Materialism." Paper delivered at the Canadian Political Science Association Meetings University of Toronto, 30 May.

Holveck, Eleanore. 1999. "*The Blood of Others*: A Novel Approach to *The Ethics of Ambiguity*." *Hypatia* 14, no. 4 (November): 3–17.

– 2002. *Simone de Beauvoir's Philosophy of Lived Experience: Literature and Metaphysics*. Lanham: Rowman and Littlefield.

Honig, Bonnie. 2013. *Antigone Interrupted*. Cambridge: Cambridge University Press.

hooks, bell. 1984. *Feminist Theory: From Margin to Center*. Boston: South End Press.

– 1994. *Teaching to Transgress: Education as the Practice of Freedom*. New York: Routledge.

Irigaray, Luce. 1992. *Je, Tu, Nous: Toward a Culture of Difference*. Translated by A. Martin. New York: Routledge.

– 1993. *An Ethics of Sexual Difference*. Ithaca: Cornell University Press.

Jackson, Stevi. 1996. *Christine Delphy*. London: Sage.

Jagger, Alison. 1978. *Feminist Frameworks: Alternative Theoretical Accounts of the Relations between Women and Men*. New York: McGraw-Hill.

– 1983. *Feminist Politics and Human Nature.* Brighton, UK: Harvester Press.
Jameson, Fredric. 1991. *Postmodernism: Or, the Cultural Logic of Late Capitalism.* Durham, NC: Duke University Press.
– 1994. *The Seeds of Time.* New York: Columbia University Press.
– 1998. *Cultural Turn.* New York: Verso.
Jardine, Alice. 1986. "Death Sentences: Writing Couples and Ideology." *Poetics Today* 6, no. 1: 119–35.
Jones, Kathleen, and Anna Jónasdóttir. 1988. *The Political Interests of Gender.* London: Sage.
Judt, Tony. 1992. *Past Imperfect, French Intellectuals 1944–1956.* Berkeley: University of California.
Kant, Immanuel. 2007. *Critique of Judgment.* Oxford: Oxford University Press.
Keefe, Terry. 1983. *Simone de Beauvoir: A Study of Her Writings.* Larousse: Harrap Publishers.
Khilnani, Sunil. 1993. *Arguing Revolution: The Intellectual Left in Postwar France.* New Haven: Yale University Press.
Klein, Melanie. 1988a. *Love, Guilt and Reparation and Other Works 1921–1945.* London: Virago.
– 1988b. *Envy, Gratitude and Other Works 1946–1963.* London: Virago.
Koestler, Arthur. 1940. *Darkness at Noon.* Translated by D. Hardy. London: Mass Market Paperback.
Kompridis, Nicholas. 2014. *The Aesthetic Turn in Political Thought.* London: Bloomsbury.
Krause, Susan. 2008. *Civil Passions: Moral Sentiment and Democratic Deliberation.* Princeton: Princeton University Press.
Kristeva, Julia. 1984. *Revolution in Poetic Language.* New York: Columbia University Press.
– 1986. "Women's Time." In *The Kristeva Reader,* edited by Toril Moi. Oxford: Blackwell Press.
– 2008. "Aux risques de la liberté." *Le Magazine littéraire* (Janvier): 57–9.
Kruks, Sonia. 1990. *Situation and Human Existence: Freedom, Subjectivity, and Society.* New York: Routledge.
– 2010. "Simone de Beauvoir: Engaging Discrepant Materialisms." In *New Materialisms: Ontology, Agency, and Politics,* edited by Diana Coole and Samantha Frost, 258–80. Durham: Duke University Press.
– 2012. *Simone de Beauvoir and the Politics of Ambiguity.* New York: Oxford University Press.
– 2015. "Materiality and 'The Marxism Question' in the Work of Simone de Beauvoir," delivered at the American Political Science Association Meetings, 3 September 2015, San Francisco, CA.

Lacan, Jacques. 1977. *Écrits: A Selection.* Translated by A. Sheridan. London: W.W. Norton.

Laclau, Ernesto, and Chantal Mouffe. 1985. *Hegemony and Socialist Strategy: Towards a Radical Democratic Politics.* Translated by Winston Moore and Paul Cammack. London: Verso Press.

Latour, Bruno. 2005. *Reassembling the Social: An Introduction to Actor-Network Theory.* New York: Oxford University Press.

Le Sueur, J. 2001. *Uncivil War: Intellectuals and Identity Politics during the Decolonization of Algeria.* Philadelphia: University of Pennsylvania Press.

Lloyd, Moya. 2005. *Beyond Identity Politics: Feminism, Power and Politics.* London: Sage.

Lundgren-Gothlin, Eva. 1996. *Sex and Existence: Simone de Beauvoir's "The Second Sex."* Translated by L. Schenck. London: Athlone.

Lyotard, Jean-François. 1984. "Answering the Question: What Is Postmodernism." In *The Postmodern Condition: A Report on Knowledge.* Translated by George Bennington and Brian Massumi. Minneapolis: University of Minnesota Press.

Mahmood, Saba. 2005. *The Politics of Piety: The Islamic Revival and the Feminist Subject.* Princeton: Princeton University Press.

Manning, Erin. 2006. *Politics of Touch: Sense, Movement and Sovereignty.* Minneapolis: University of Minnesota Press.

Marasco, Robyn. 2015. *The Highway of Despair: Critical Theory after Hegel.* New York: Columbia University.

Markell, Patchen. 2000. "The Recognition of Politics: A Comment on Emcke and Tully." *Constellations* 7, no. 4 (December): 496–506.

Marks, Elaine. 1986. "Transgressing the (In)cont(in)ent Boundaries: The Body in Decline." In *Simone de Beauvoir: Witness to a Century. Yale French Studies* 72: 181–200.

Marshall, Barbara. 2000. *Configuring Gender: Explorations in Theory and Politics.* Peterborough: Broadview Press.

Marso, Lori. 2012a. "Simone de Beauvoir and Hannah Arendt: Judgments in Dark Times." *Political Theory* 40, no. 2: 165–93.

– 2012b. "Thinking Politically with Simone de Beauvoir in *The Second Sex.*" *Theory and Event* 15, no. 2, *Simone de Beauvoir Symposium,* edited by Kathy E. Ferguson and Lori J. Marso.

Marso, Lori, and Patricia Moynagh. 2006. *Simone de Beauvoir's Political Thinking.* Urbana and Chicago: University of Illinois Press.

Marx, Karl, and Friedrich Engels. 1978. *The Marx/Engels Reader.* Edited by R. Tucker. New York: W.W. Norton.

Massumi, Brian. 2002. *Parables for the Virtual: Movement, Affect and Sensation.* Durham: Duke University Press.

McMurtry, John. 1978. *Structure of Marx's World-View*. Princeton: Princeton University Press.

Merleau-Ponty, Maurice. 1962. *The Phenomenology of Perception*. Translated by Colin Smith. London: Routledge and Kegan Paul.

– 1964a. *The Primacy of Perception and Other Essays on Phenomenological Psychology, the Philosophy of Art, History and Politics*. Translated by J. Edie. Evanston: Northwestern University Press.

– 1964b. "The War Has Taken Place." In *Sense and Non-Sense*. Translated by H. Dreyfus and P. Dreyfus. Evanston: Northwestern University Press.

– 1967. "The Child's Relations with Others." In *Signs*. Translated by R. McCleary. Evanston: Northwestern University Press.

– 1968. *The Visible and the Invisible*. Translated by Alphonso Lingis. Evanston: Northwestern University Press. First published in 1964.

– 1969. *Humanism and Terror*. Translated by J. O' Neill. Boston: Beacon Press. First published in 1944.

– 1974. *Adventures of the Dialectic*. Translated by J. Bien. Heinemann: London. First published in 1955.

– 1992. *Texts and Dialogues*. Edited by Hugh Silverman and J. Barry. Translated by M.B. Smith. New Jersey: Humanities Press.

Mitchell, Juliet. 1974. *Psychoanalysis and Feminism*. London: Penguin.

Mohanty, Chandra Talpade. 1991. "Under Western Eyes: Feminist Scholarship and Colonial Discourses." In *Third World Women and the Politics of Feminism*, edited by C. Talpade Mohanty, A. Rosso, and L. Torres. Indianapolis: Indiana University Press.

Moi, Toril. 1990. *Feminist Theory and Simone de Beauvoir*. Cambridge: Basil Blackwell.

– 1999. *What Is a Woman? And Other Essays*. Oxford: Oxford University Press.

Mouffe, Chantal. 1996. "Democracy, Power and the 'Political.'" In *Democracy and Difference: Contesting the Boundaries of the Political*, edited by Seyla Benhabib, 245–57. Princeton: Princeton University Press.

Murphy, Julien. 1995. "Beauvoir and the Algerian War: Toward a Postcolonial Ethics." In *Feminist Interpretations of Simone de Beauvoir*, edited M. Simons, 59–65. University Park: Pennsylvania State University Press.

Nussbaum, Martha. 1990. *Love's Knowledge: Essays on Philosophy and Literature*. New York: Oxford University Press.

– 1995. *Poetic Justice: The Literary Imagination and Public Life*. Boston: Beacon Press.

– 1999. "The Professor of Parody." *New Republic* 220, no. 8 (22 February): 1–13.

Okely, Joan. 1986. *Simone de Beauvoir*. New York: Pantheon.

Oklowski, Dorothea. 1999. *Gilles Deleuze and the Ruin of Representation*. Berkeley: University of California Press.

Panagia, Davide. 2009. *The Political Life of Sensation*. Durham: Duke University Press.

– 2013. *Impressions of Hume: Cinematic Thinking and the Politics of Discontinuity.* Lanham: Roman and Littlefield.

Pateman, Carole. 1988. *The Sexual Contract.* Stanford: Stanford University Press.

Phillips, Anne. 1999. *Which Equalities Matter.* Cambridge: Polity Press.

– 2013. *Our Bodies, Whose Property.* Princeton: Princeton University Press.

Phillips, Anne, and Michelle Barrett. 1992. *Destabilizing Theory: Contemporary Feminist Debates,* edited by A. Phillips and M. Barrett. Stanford: Stanford University Press.

Rahman, Momin, and Anne Witz. 2002. "What Really Matters? The Concept of the Material in Feminism." Paper delivered at the Canadian Political Science Association Meetings, University of Toronto, 27 May.

Ricoeur, Paul. 1992. *Oneself as Another.* Chicago: University of Chicago.

Ringart, N. 1977. *Liberation* (1 June).

Rodgers, C. 1998. *Le Deuxième Sexe de Simone de Beauvoir, un heritage admire et conteste.* Paris: L'Harmattan.

Rosenthal, I. 2016. "Aggression and Play in the Face of Adversity: A Psychoanalytic Reading of Democratic Resilience." *Political Theory* 44, no. 3 (June): 337–62.

Ross, George. 1990. *Intellectuals against the Left: The Case of France.* Socialist Register 26.

Roudinesco, Elizabeth. 1990. *Jacques Lacan and Company.* Chicago: University of Chicago.

Rubenstein, Diane. 2012. "'I hope I am not fated to live in Rochester': America in the Work of Beauvoir." In *Theory and Event* 15, no. 2, *Simone de Beauvoir Symposium,* edited by Kathy E. Ferguson and Lori J. Marso.

Sanos, Sandrine. 2017. *Simone de Beauvoir: Creating a Feminist Existence in the World.* New York: Oxford University Press.

Sartre, Jean-Paul. 1948. *What Is Literature?* Translated by B. Frechtman. New York: Philosophical Library.

– 1952. *The Communists and Peace.* London: Hamilton.

– 1955. *No Exit and Three Other Plays.* Translated by S. Gilbert. New York: Vintage.

– 1960. *Critique of Dialectical Reason Volume I.* Translated by A. Sheridan-Smith, edited by J. Ree. London: Verso.

– 1964. *The Words.* Translated by I. Crephane. London: Penguin.

Scott, Joan. 1992. "The Evidence of Experience." In *Feminists Theorize the Political,* edited by Judith Butler and Joan Scott. New York: Routledge.

Shelby, Karen. 2006. "Beauvoir and Ethical Responsibility." In *Simone de Beauvoir's Political Thinking,* edited by L. Marso and T. Moynagh. Urbana and Chicago: University of Illinois Press.

Short, Jase. 2014. "Thinking Utopia: Fredric Jameson's Critical Theory of the Postmodern." Paper presented at 15th Southern Appalachian

Undergraduate Philosophy Conference, 22 February. http://www.academia.edu/6593474/Thinking_Utopia_Fredric_Jamesons_Critical_Theory_of_the_Postmodern. Accessed 7 January 2017.

Simons, Margaret. 1999. "Beauvoir Interview (1979)." In *Beauvoir and the Second Sex: Feminism, Race, and the Origins of Existentialism.* Lanham: Rowman and Littlefield.

Smith, Dorothy. 1987. *The Everyday World as Problematic: A Feminist Sociology.* Boston: Northwestern University Press.

– 1990. *The Conceptual Practices of Power: A Feminist Sociology of Knowledge.* London: Routledge.

Soper, Kate, and L. Thomas. 2006. "'Alternative Hedonism' and the Critique of 'Consumerism.'" Working paper. Institute for the Study of European Transformations.

Spelman, Elizabeth. 1988. *Inessential Woman: Problems of Exclusion in Feminist Thought.* New York: Beacon Press.

Spivak, Gayatri. 1988. "Can the Subaltern Speak?" In *Marxism and the Interpretation of Culture,* edited by C. Nelson and L. Grossberg, 271–313. Basingstoke: Macmillan Education.

Stavro, Elaine. 2009. "Rethinking Identity and Coalitional Politics; Insights from Simone de Beauvoir." *Canadian Journal of Political Science* 40, no. 2 (June): 439–64.

– 2000. "Re-reading *The Second Sex*; Theorizing the Situation." *Feminist Theory* 1, no. 2: 131–50.

Stow, Simon. 2007. *Republic of Readers? The Literary Turn in Political Thought and Analysis.* Albany: State University of New York Press.

Tidd, Ursula. 1999. *Simone de Beauvoir, Gender and Testimony.* Cambridge: Cambridge University Press.

– 2004. *Simone de Beauvoir.* Routledge: London.

Townson, Mark. 2009. "Canadian Women on Their Own Are the Poorest of the Poor." *CCPA Monitor,* October.

Vintges, Karen. 1996. *Philosophy as Passion: The Thinking of Simone de Beauvoir.* Bloomington: Indiana University Press.

White, Steven K. 2000. *Sustaining Affirmation: The Strengths of Weak Ontology in Political Theory.* Princeton: Princeton University.

– 1999. "As the World Turns: Ontology and Politics in Judith Butler." *Polity* 32, no. 2 (Winter): 155–77.

Wilson, Elizabeth A. 1998. *Neural Geographics.* London: Routledge.

Winnicott, Donald. 1965. *The Maturational Process and the Facilitating Environment.* London: Hogarth.

Wolin, Richard. 2010. *The Wind from the East: French Intellectuals, the Cultural Revolution, and the Legacy of the 1960s.* Princeton: Princeton University Press.

Young, Iris Marion. 1985. "Humanism, Gynocentrism and Feminist Politics." *Women's Studies International Forum* 8, no. 3: 173–83.

– 1989. "Throwing Like a Girl: A Phenomenology of Feminine Body Comportment, Motility and Spatiality." In *The Thinking Muse: Feminism and Modern French Philosophy*, 51–70. Bloomington: Indiana University Press.

– 1990. *Justice and the Politics of Difference.* Princeton: Princeton University Press.

– 1997. "Unruly Categories: A Critique of Nancy Fraser's Dual Systems Theory." *New Left Review* 222 (March–April): 147–60.

– 2001. "Activist Challenges to Deliberative Democracy." *Political Theory* 29, no. 5 (October): 670–90.

Zakin, Emily. 2006. "Unsettling of the Universal." In *Simone de Beauvoir's Political Thinking*, edited by L.J. Marso and P. Moynagh. Chicago: Illinois University Press.

Zerilli, Linda. 1992. "A Process without a Subject: Simone de Beauvoir and Julia Kristeva on Maternity." *Signs* 18, no. 1 (Autumn): 111–35.

Index